MW00773952

Andrew Low
and the Sign of the Buck

Andrew Low
and the Sign of the Buck
Trade, Triumph, Tragedy at the House of Low

Jennifer Guthrie Ryan
Hugh Stiles Golson

Frederic C. Beil
Savannah
2011

Published in the United States of America by
Frederic C. Beil, Publisher
609 Whitaker Street
Savannah, Georgia 31401
www.beil.com

LIBRARY OF CONGRESS CATALOGING-IN-PUBLICATION DATA
Ryan, Jennifer Guthrie
Andrew Low and the sign of the buck:
trade, triumph, tragedy at the House of Low /
Jennifer Guthrie Ryan and High Stiles Golson
p. cm.
Includes bibliographical references and index.
ISBN 978-1-929490-36-3
1. Lowe family.
2. Scottish Americans—Georgia—Savannah—Biography.
3. Savannah (Ga.)—Social life and customs—19th century.
4. Savannah (Ga.)—Economic conditions—19th century.
5. Cotton trade—Georgia—Savannah—History.
6. Savannah (Ga.)—Biography.
I. Golson, Hugh Stiles.
II. Title.

F294.S2R93 2011
929'.20973—dc22

2010045205

Manufactured in the United States of America

First edition

For my grandchildren
Nikolai, Aidan, Tigerlily, and Abby
hoping it will help them chart
their own journeys through life

Contents

Illustrations

Preface

Genetic memory. Is the image of a place where our ancestors once lived imprinted on our cells? I know this place deep in my bones.

I HAVE BEEN SEARCHING FOR THIS PLACE ALL MY LIFE. I HAVE BEEN to castles in Cornwall, castles in Ireland, Lands End, and Cape of Good Hope. Wherever I have been, I have driven, sometimes for hours and hundreds of miles, to find the land at the end of that specific piece of my earth.

I have finally found the place for which I have searched. I am home. I know it. On a sunny February morning, the low winter sun blinding my eyes, white light blazing off the calm gray sea, I stand where I have stood before, maybe many times. A small search-and-rescue boat chugged its way from left to right. A pod of dolphins breaking the bow wave, they surely should not have been here at this time of the year, but they were. Seals would lie here sunning themselves in their season. I do not see them now, but I have seen them before.

I have spoken with them, heard their siren songs of the deep, and have been lured by their Lorelei cries to follow them to the ends of the earth. The black glistening rocks shone below, and quarrelsome gulls squawked and squabbled in their cliffside aeries. The castle stands alone and isolate across the deep ravine, inviolate and impregnable, built high on the perpendicular rock jutting out into the ocean, a huge ocean-liner about to sail off to a mystical destination on a magical journey. The land where it meets the sea reeks of antiquity; it is four hundred million years in the making, regurgitated one cataclysmic day aeons ago, a gout and spout of molten lava, deep purple in color, bound like plums in a pudding together with small pebbles and rocks to form a porous conglomerate about fifty fathoms high. A natural fortress for turbulent times, to see as the Norsemen approached in their dragon-headed raven-sailed longboats, predators of the sea. This is a fierce place embodying the stalwart and indomitable

The ruins of Dunnottar Castle today. This eastern point of Kincardinshire was an ancient defense against Norse invaders. *Courtesy Jennifer Guthrie Ryan.*

spirit of the Scot. Close cropped, grassy land slopes down to the vertical cliffs, a very safe place.

A mile or so down the coast through fertile dark clay soil lays *another place I know.* It is the ancient fishing village of Crawton, no longer functioning as a place for fisher folk and tenant farmers, but a place for holiday accommodation. On this day it is as it was. It is another place of deep and ancient meaning, a lava flow like an outstretched hand, four fingers and the thumb, sprawls clutching the sea in its greedy grasp, eternally washed by the ebb and flow of moon and tide. Seabirds wheel and squeal and deal in the daily doings of their brief existence, descendants of those birds my own ancestors carelessly robbed of life in a boys' way, as they clambered dangerously up the cliffs to gather the eggs, testing themselves and their courage or foolhardiness. It is almost a parody of a Scotsman's dream of home, with a babbling burn and gorsy yellow banks, granite rocks gleaming in the watery sunlight of winter.

The burn falls down the erect cliff, a waterfall splashing diamonds into the sea below, an overflow, a plenitude of crystal clean and clear water. An old ruin stands sentinel upon the cliff, over the hand in the ocean, perhaps used for worship or a school in days gone by two hundred years ago, providing the children with the tools of commerce and morality, taking care of their minds and souls, while hard work took care of their bodies. The lessons learned there in childhood preparing and equipping them to carve a future for themselves in lands over the ocean, that none could have begun to visualize.

A long, low, white-washed cottage made of stone—there is an abundance of stone and rock to build with in this area—stands a little back from the sea, slated roof now, but then it would have been thatched with a mixture of grasses and gorse. Holes in the roof to let the smoke out, a single room where the family conceived, birthed, lived, and died.

Another mile down the coast is a fishing village named Catterline. On the side of a steep bank and a running burn, a small and ancient churchyard lies asleep at the curve of the bridge, green and mossy. Brave snowdrops lie like drops of white blood in the swords of their dark green leaves cluster around the ancient gravestones, buried now beneath the turf, illegible. Old trees stand sentinel, guarding and shading the sleep of my people. This is where my ancestors lie buried. I went there to tell them they are not forgotten, that I remember them; and I thank them for giving me life—a life I love, a life of richness, sorrow, and pain turned to joy and love.

A woman named Catherine Croll, who gave birth to eight children in this very place, lies with three of her sons, two of them dying on passage back from Savannah, two hundred years ago. Her husband was James Low, a tenant farmer born in nearby Crawton, descendant of tenant farmers for as many generations as there are written records. James, who died at the age of forty-nine, leaving her a widow, set in motion the events that bring me here today. They hear me. They will sleep well tonight, snoozing eternity away in this serene and contemplative corner of my planet. They are safe and I am glad.

Acknowledgments

THIS PROJECT HAS TAKEN OVER TEN YEARS ON TWO CONTINENTS TO research, write, and revise. The individuals who have helped bring it from conception to fruition are myriad and in no way can be acknowledged in a linear fashion in order of importance. I shall attempt to give them all credit, as in a play, in order of their appearance. Having said that, there are obviously in any project certain people without whom it never would have been started, let alone finished. The person to whom I owe the most gratitude for her unfailing enthusiasm, friendship, and support is Mrs. F. Willson Daily, my dear friend Alice, a lynchpin of the Andrew Low House and Friends of Andrew Low. Her encyclopedic knowledge of the story as is interpreted is legendary. I have already given Stephen Bohlin, then curator of the Juliette Low Birthplace, credit for suggesting the idea of the book; and Alice from the very beginning helped me mold it into shape, constantly guiding me with her wisdom, wit, and good taste. The second person whose constant support as lifelong friend of my daughter in law's family, and who became my own dearest friend—shoulder to cry on, sounding board, and peer reviewer—and who steered me through the intricate meanings of Southern culture, habits, mannerisms, and culinary delights, is the much missed Joan Cobitz.

The early research in the Andrew Low House archives was helped considerably by then-curator Kara Briggs, who was always unfailingly supportive and helpful. Betty Tattnall at the Andrew Low House regaled me with tales of her intimate relationship with my great-grandfather as she frequently claimed to see him sitting in his easy chair by the fire, and as she smelled my great- grandmother's perfume in the upstairs bedroom. Catharine Varnedoe was instrumental in helping me accurately research the history of Southeastern Indians and the origin of the early rice plantation slaves from Sierra Leone. The wonderful staff at the Georgia Historical Society, particularly Jewel Anderson, Susan Dicks, and Mandi Johnson, frequently helped steer me to material both unknown and known, and boosted my morale when my energy began to falter. Gordon Smith frequently dropped nuggets of cheese around for me to pursue like a cat after a rat in hot pursuit, opening doors unknown before.

My first trip to Scotland resulted in unprecedented success commencing with the encyclopedic understanding of family genealogy of now retired Edna Christie at the Stonehaven Library, and the always cheerful head librarian Mrs. Kate Urquhart and her staff; the helpful folks at the Aberdeen Library, Fettercairn, Brechin, Angus Archives in Montrose, all of whom helped me develop pieces of the puzzle. I also made friends over the Internet on sites such as the Stonehaven group, and with all the family history center groups whose members generously help each other locate the information they seek. Above all, it is Violet Murray, who has dedicated her entire life to the task of grafting branches onto their proper roots, who helped me track down the requisite registry entries at the Aberdeen Family History Center. Alan Moir gave of his time and analytic ability, and incidentally turned out to be a distant cousin from the ancient past. I am also grateful to Pauline Linsley, who always found room for me in her "Wee Hoose" whenever I turned up on her doorstep; the staff at the various Edinburgh archives who steered me through the dusty stacks with unfailing accuracy and courtesy; the National Library of Scotland, which helped me find maps that would chart my course; and also to Dr. Charles McLean, who pinpointed the ultimate proof of land possession, Dr. Anthony Parker, who identified primary sources to check early Highland migration to Georgia, both of the University of Dundee,.

Eventually, when I reached Liverpool, many individuals were helpful—especially Paul Young, who spent hours of his time going out to photograph locations for me, as well as Bob Jones and Roy Rawlinson, historians and Civil War aficionados who led me to understand the extent of the involvement of Liverpool in the American Civil War. The faculty at Liverpool University, the Maritime Museum, the Liverpool Museum of People—all helped me trace the dramatic history of Liverpool's various incarnations and the role the Isaac Low Company played in its nineteenth-century story.

In Leamington I need to express my thanks to Lady Elizabeth Hamilton, who confirmed many of the local rumors about Willy Low's sojourn there; Peter and Rosalind Bolton, for their confirmation of several of my pet theories; and the archivists at the Leamington Library, who assisted me in tracing the arrivals and departures and social goings on of the Low family during their early sojourn there, and at the Brighton facility, who assiduously searched for any trace of the two older Low sisters. I must also make reference to the incomparable small town of Hay-on-Wye, home to thousands of used books where I spent hours searching for out-of-print gems to flesh out the portrait as it emerged.

Back in the States, further research at the special collections of the Woodruff Library at Emory University, the incomparable Southern Historical Collection at Chapel Hill, North Carolina, the Atlanta State Archives, and the South Carolina Historical Archives in Charleston and Beaufort, South Carolina, helped me weave the story into a coherent tapestry.

During the years of my research and writing, my friends and colleagues offered me unflagging support and assistance in the evaluation of my progress by reading and critiquing the evolving manuscript in its various stages. For that I thank Joan Cobitz, Elly Wininger, Barbara Martinez, and Statia Henderson. In Savannah, Betsy Cain always stood by for tea and sympathy often taken at the Sentient Bean. In fact many unnamed coffeehouses around the country offered me detachment and caffeine in equal proportions.

I must also thank my own family for their constant support: Alex, Melissa, Niko, and Aidan, and my granddaughter Tigerlily, who, although too young yet to understand the potential, hopefully will gain from my toiling in the family vineyard; my cousins, Mary Carr and her wonderful husband, Alf, and also Kitty McDuff Duncan and her son Colin, whose generous help in tracking down and separating truth from rumor was invaluable, especially their generosity in sharing the previously unread journals of Jessie Low Graham. My cousin Margaret Wrathcliffe introduced me to East Haddon Hall and the lovely churchyard where so many of the characters in this book are interred. Although I never met her in person, and on account of her recent death never will, my cousin Jane Davidson allowed me access to her voluminous correspondence covering the decades whereby she too tried to unravel the twisted skeins of history. And her only son, Christopher Davidson, and his family helped return many of the Low treasures to their current safe haven in the Andrew Low House and Museum. And most of all, I thank my friend and cousin, coauthor Hugh Stiles Golson, without whose unfailing support none of this would have materialized.

Jennifer Guthrie Ryan

2010

Introduction

I AM THE GREAT-GRANDDAUGHTER OF ANDREW LOW, JR., AND MARY Cowper Stiles. Today their home is an important monument to an era of Savannah history, operated as a museum by The National Society of The Colonial Dames of America in the State of Georgia. The purpose in writing and publishing this book is to correct the factual record and eliminate distortions and corruptions that have entered the conventional wisdom.

Writers have choices: This book promises to be somewhat of a hybrid—part historical biography, part personal quest. Both aspects are equally vital to the interpretation. The basic story is that of a very old nation, Britain, and a very new nation, America, and some of those who shaped the histories of both. The focus—the lives of individuals in a specific extended family. The purpose—to attempt to bring the past alive for the present grandchildren.

There would be no story to tell without the commitment to keep the flame of history ablaze by The National Society of The Colonial Dames of America in the State of Georgia. In 1928 the organization purchased the Andrew Low House in Savannah for use as their state headquarters. Through time, more and more acquisitions of the highest standards are being made, imbuing the house with a spirit and presence that encompasses the broader history of the United States of America and Great Britain. As a living museum, it stands as a growing memorial to a past we can all share.

In certain areas, however, imprecise recording has caused crucial errors of fact to enter the archives, making it difficult to ascertain accuracy and verify biography. Sparse details existed to document the early life and struggles of Andrew Low, Sr., who emigrated from Scotland to Savannah in 1800, or why. The interpretation currently commences with the arrival of Andrew Low, Jr,. in 1829 from Scotland, to join his uncle as a clerk in his thriving international cotton factorage firm. It fails to explain the origins of the Andrew Low Company and the Isaac Low Company on both sides of the Atlantic as the foundation of their epic story.

This is a serious insufficiency, as the key to understanding who these people were, and why they did the things they did, is to comprehend the forces and influences that drew both of these men to the opportunities of the New World, and is a microcosm of the story of America. It is equally valid to state that I, writing from my own place in time, am hostage to my own prejudices and imprints.

I have attempted to select primary sources to stencil my own interpretation on the facts, as I was able to uncover and prove them. Accuracy and integrity are the guidelines I follow. I do not hesitate to speculate on reasons for specific courses of action in the absence of empirical proof of purpose. That I retain as my prerogative. Think of this as being a journalistic endeavor, written from the duality of now and then, by one who has the right to tell the story.

The purpose is to return the two Andrew Lows to their rightful position amongst the stories of the titans of their day as two of the most innovative, courageous, and ofttimes reckless entrepreneurs of the nineteenth century. We have made a conscious decision in the main to use original spellings and sentence construction as much of the information comes from personal letters, diaries, and journals. We also decided to retain my own twentieth-century British way of speaking, as well as allowing others to tell their stories in their own idiom. This book is intended to be the definitive interpretation of the House of Low spanning three centuries.

Jennifer Guthrie Ryan
Taos, New Mexico
2010

I am descended from the Stiles branch of the family. The writing of the history of the Andrew Low family and its enterprises is long overdue. The popularity of Savannah as a vacation destination has called close attention to this city's history. In many cases the record is of full cloth. The Stiles and Mackay families fall into this category. Letters and artifacts were kept and revered in an Asian-like reverence for ancestry. The total Stiles-Mackay papers that exist today in archives and private collections probably exceed twenty linear feet—a huge amount of documents. With similar appreciation the furnishings and accessories of this extended family were dutifully cataloged and divided among descendants who have recognized and commemorated their provenance.

This was not so with the history of the Low family. Its record lay as threads and fragments of fabric. Although the descendants of Andrew and Mary Cowper Low continued the Stiles-Mackay tradition of saving letters and papers, there was no great personal archive from which to extract the history of the first Andrew Low and the enterprises he built on both sides of the ocean. Because of this void there was more speculation than truth in the interpretation of the House of Low.

Many years ago I began work with Mrs. F. Willson Daily of The National Society of The Colonial Dames of America in the State of Georgia. Mrs. Daily was serving as furnishings chairman for the Andrew Low House and was very interested in a new interpretation that would flesh out the family that lived in that impressive edifice. At that point there were only a couple of artifacts original to the house. After many years of building family interest in the Low House, we can now point with pride to the scores of family furnishings and artifacts that now define the site as the home of Andrew Low, antebellum cotton factor.

This quest for authenticity has reached across continents and retrieved important objects from distant hemispheres. With this quest came more connections and interest. By far the most significant contact came in the form of Jennifer Guthrie Ryan, Mary Low Guthrie's granddaughter.

Although I have met over a dozen of Uncle Andrew's descendants, I did not know my cousin Jennifer until I met her in 1999 at the Andrew Low House, at a proper reception held by its support group. Jennifer was recently retired from a lifetime career in documentary radio, film, and television journalism on a global level and was relishing the role of grandmother, doing radio in her home, Taos, New Mexico. Revisiting Savannah, where she had resided for a year in the 1950's, she happened to arrive on the day the Juliette Gordon Low birthplace celebrated their anniversary. She discovered she was related to half the individuals at the meeting; and during a conversation with curator Stephen Bohlin about the confusion inherent in Andrew Low's ancestry, he casually suggested she should write a book about the Lows. The following year she spent several months in Savannah, working with Alice Daily at the Andrew Low House and spending hours immersed in the Georgia Historical Society old newspaper collection in an effort to trace the continuity of the House of Low. The tug of family mysteries took hold and this project was born.

Jennifer was hooked on the importance of properly defining the Low family. Her journalistic instincts took over as she went after this "big story" with an experienced reporter's enthusiasm. She visited Savannah year after year, developing circles of friends and deciphering the secrets of Southern libraries and collections. And as her research grew, so did our friendship and collaboration. Jennifer's British education and two-world experience equip her well for researching in the U.K., diligently tracking down details in Scottish and Liverpool archives. She certainly understands English and Scottish culture and practices. With my background in Savannah's history and my training as a teacher of American history, we began to see we were yin and yang in this project. Jennifer could go after research with a journalist's tenacity. I could fit the outcome into the historian's template and also define the discussions needed to reach a proper conclusion. Jennifer's free-flowing prose, so replete with vivid imagery, could be tamed and framed by this former grader of student essays. We made the decision to collaborate, and I was drawn deeper into the project.

Be aware of this project's purpose. This effort is intended to correct the record and to catalog all relative information available at this time. It is an attempt to connect the dots and carry the family story across the centuries. It is not a precise history, where all statements are substantiated and all hypotheses tested. It was not created to win history awards and garner academic laurels. This work is for the ardent history student, the traveler in time who wants more, the casual reader who does not want to be bogged down in endless facts, but rather wants to place some perspective linking the past to the present and into the future. I think you will find it achieves that purpose.

Hugh Stiles Golson
Savannah, Georgia
2010

Part I

Scotland to America, 1600–1800

1

Genesis: Scotland and Georgia, 1730–1782

As long as there shall be one hundred of us remain alive, we will never consent to subject ourselves to the dominion of the English. For it is not glory, it is not riches, neither is it honour, but it is liberty alone that we fight and contend for, which no honest man will lose but with his life.
Declaration of Arbroath Abbey, Scotland, c. 1320.

THOSE INSPIRING WORDS COME FROM THE MOST TREASURED DOCUMENT in Scottish history, written by the earls and barons of Scotland to the Pope, asking him to recognize Scotland's independence from England.[1]

When the twenty-one-year-old Scot Andrew Low arrived in the New World on an autumn day in 1800, he had his life before him and his history behind him. Bridges had been burned over which he had no control; in front lay bridges he would build between the Old World and this New World of discovery. To understand his journey it is essential to peer backwards through the mists of time to fathom the influences and events that drove him to steer his personal ship of fortune into the future. For practical reasons Andrew Low soon became an American citizen, but remained a Scotsman at heart until his death.

The story of the kin of the House of Low starts back in Scotland at the latter end of the seventeenth century. A full understanding of the context of their heritage must necessarily start with knowledge of historical and commercial imperatives as trade began to dominate the agenda of empire. The advent of the industrial revolution offered unheard of opportunities on two continents, as did the American Revolution of 1776.

Andrew Low, Sr., arrived in Savannah in 1800 to found Andrew Low & Company. His nephew, Andrew Low, Jr., my great-grandfather, joined him in 1829. Two centuries later, I undertook a voluntary mission to correct the record and seek the truth. The next leg of my own journey would be to follow their footsteps.

These steps would transport me to the place, where, in another coincidence of connections, the father of the founder of the House of Low was born in the same year in far-off Scotland that the colony of Georgia in the New World was founded. It was there in Savannah that my cousin, historian Hugh Stiles Golson, would join in this search for our ancestors.

Soon after the birth of my grandchildren, I became obsessed with the necessity to pass on an accurate picture and understanding of our mixed heritage. This would assist them in the navigation of the complex and complicated world of the twenty-first century they would inhabit. They were born in America, but their lineage, through our Scottish and European bloodline, was a multifaceted and ancient one, shaped by a European history that was seldom taught in American schools, as well as an American history that was rarely debated in British schools.

The physical search for the truth about the roots of our Low ancestors in Scotland commenced on the second floor of a granite stone library surrounded by children, books, and computers, with dust motes floating in the sunbeams streaming through the windows. I was in the town of Stonehaven, the ancient capital of the county of Kincardine in the parish of Dunnottar on the northeast coast of Scotland, on a crisp winter day. The discovery of a spidery handwritten birth record in a faded scratched microfilm, the original parish record dating back more than two hundred and fifty years, provided the first clue. A "bingo" moment! My heart literally leaped! I had found the beginning of the line—"October 17th, 1732—John Low in Crawton had a son baptised named James. Witnesses Jas Low & Jas Gregory in Gallowton."

This is what I believe to be the accurate record of the birth of James Low, father of Andrew Low, Sr. The event is listed in the Old Parish Record of the Church of Scotland in Dunnottar Parish, Kincardineshire, Scotland. There is no verifiable record of a marriage preceding the birth of this man-child, and no mother's name is listed in the register, as was the custom of the times. She, my maternal ancestor, remains nameless to this day.[2]

The National Archives of Scotland at Edinburgh revealed a 1780 survey titled "Part of the Estate of Dunnottar." This vital document proved beyond any speculation that this particular James Low was a "tenant"—meaning in the vernacular of the times that he was a man of substance, roughly analogous to the "gentleman farmer" of English social status, farming a portion of land owned since the mid 1500's by the Keith family, nobility known as the Earls Marischal. The unavoidable assumption, therefore, is that the Lows had been feudal/vassal people of the Marischal family since the beginning of record keeping.[3]

Struggle for the Church and Throne

The period of time these early Low ancestors were living in Scotland was extremely volatile and unstable. Sporadic violent clashes between the Presbyterian and Catholic faiths were compounded by the constant battles for ascendancy between the Protestant English monarchs and the Catholic Stuart dynasty of Scotland.

Since the middle of the sixteenth century, Europe had been riven by religious conflict propelled by a reform movement led by a German, Martin Luther, a French-Swiss, John Calvin, and a Scot, John Knox. This puritanical anti-idolatry movement became known as Calvinism. The trigger was pulled in Scotland on May 11, 1559, when Scottish priest John Knox, practicing this new radical theology, preached a sermon that was "vehement against idolatry" in the church of St. John in Perth, Scotland, thereby initiating a chain of events that had a profound effect upon Scottish society. This movement inexorably led to the Protestant Reformation of the Scottish church, which had previously been predominantly Catholic. A convention held in January 1561 by Knox and others laid out for nobility and lairds the principles of their vision for spiritual reform of the church in Scotland.[4]

The crowns of England and Scotland united in 1603, when Catholic James VI of Scotland became James I of England. Revolutions and civil war disturbed the peace for another hundred years, when yet another dynastic crisis loomed. In an act that is still being argued by historians and citizens alike the two separate Parliaments of Scotland and England merged. The 1707 Acts of Union between the two nations made them one under the leadership of the Parliament of Great Britain, in which all members of both nations could vote.[5] Most Scottish merchants viewed the union through the prism of easing trade restrictions, but the decision was generally not popular with the rest of the country.

In 1714, through a series of royal deaths, the monarchy reverted to the Hanoverian line of Germany, and George I ascended to the throne.[6] Many in Scotland did not accept this arrangement, still recognizing the Catholic Stuart dynasty in the person of James II of England (and James VII of Scotland), now living in exile under the protection of the king of France.

When James II died in 1701, his son, James Edward Stuart, who became known as the "Old Pretender," was recognized by his father's court in exile as the heir apparent. Although this was no surprise, it was significant—to England's consternation Louis XIV of France also recognized him as the rightful heir to the thrones of England and Scotland. That was a very different kettle of fish in the teetering balance of power between European monarchies. In 1715 his followers, who dubbed themselves Jacobites (after

"Jacobus," the Latin name for James) mounted an abortive rebellion to return the monarchy to the throne of Scotland.

The story of the "15 Jacobite Rebellion" has not been as widely romanticized as the one thirty years later known simply as "The 45," but remains most pertinent to the story of the Lows for the singular fact that the laird whose land they farmed was Earl Marischal, one of the ringleaders of the uprising. The earl was forced to flee into exile, thereby forfeiting all his lands and estates. The times were most perilous, and tenants of rebellious landlords were themselves in as much danger as their lairds of retribution from a vengeful English Crown. To add to their peril, unlike the majority of Scots who were Presbyterian, much of the population of this region at that point in Scotland's turbulent history were members of the Episcopal Church, and were singled out as a focus of brutal persecution. For the Lows, who lived as tenant farmers on Marischal land, times would have been exceedingly precarious.[7]

Back in the present, my next discovery was even more exciting. The Stonehaven librarian, an immensely knowledgeable gray-haired woman named Edna Christie, about to retire after a lifetime of service assisting seekers of their roots from all corners of the diaspora, had an intuitive sense of the connections and where it all fit together. Unerringly she reached for a publication of the Scottish Genealogy Society compiled by bands of intrepid seekers who spend their weekends and holidays tramping through the graveyards of Scotland, taking rubbings off crumbling gravestones, hoping to preserve the heritage of this ancient land, home of a large proportion of America's early settlers. She located the final proof that this was the correct James Low, born in Crawton in 1732. I had been looking for Lows in the parish of Dunnottar through the birth of their children, but had drawn a total blank on any records of death and burial. It appeared to be a brick wall or a dead end.

She knew better from years of experience and looked in the adjacent parish of Catterline and Kineff, and there they were.[8] Not only did she find the place of their burial, but also she found irrefutable proof that it was the right family through one remarkable fact. The inscription also listed the death "en route by sea from Savanna" of two of the Low sons, brothers of Andrew Low, Sr. This was more than coincidence, and it was a cosmic revelation, an event that happens rarely in the painstaking drudgery of genealogical research. I was ecstatic.

The site at Catterline, where the family is buried, was originally an Episcopal church gifted to Arbroath Abbey by the bishop of Brechin in 1178. It had been at Arbroath Abbey that the famous Scottish clarion call of freedom was issued in 1320.[9]

The old church is no longer there, but the graveyard where the table stone still stands is well kept and accessible to visitors. Its location is probably where the old parish kirk stood until the eighteenth century, on the roadside just outside the fisher village of Catterline, and about a mile and a half from the fishing-fermetoune of Crawton, where James Low and Catherine Croll birthed their family of eight children.[10]

In the late afternoon I stood in that ancient graveyard with tears streaming down my face as I examined the weather-worn lichen-covered headstone. Still readable, carved into the side of the table stone were the words "Erected by their son Andrew Low—1836." A clear voice from the fog of time echoed my own clarion call to continue the quest to unravel a journey that took a young man in 1800 from these craggy cliffs of Scotland to the tidal marshes and river of Savannah in America, to seek his fortune. Proof that he never forgot who he was and where he came from.

The Settling of Savannah, 1733

King George II of Great Britain granted a charter on June 9, 1732, to the Trustees for Establishing the Colony of Georgia in America. Like many other colonial settlements necessitated by expediency, the original incarnation of Savannah was modest. There was a plan, the brainchild of James Edward Oglethorpe. A group of parliamentary reformers known as the Trustees, led by their president, the Earl of Egmont, received a charter to settle poor and persecuted people from England on territory just south of Carolina, a no-man's land according to the thinking of the times, claimed by both England and Spain. Rights of previous native inhabitants to the land did not enter the equation, although Oglethorpe contrived a good relationship with the Yamacraw leader, Tomo-chi-chi. His band was an offshoot of the Creek, and they controlled a small village on Yamacraw Bluff that served as a loading ramp for the Carolina Indian traders. Oglethorpe selected this place as the ideal site, and on February 1, 1733, the first settlers started their American adventure.

Pragmatic and philosophical at the same time, the experiment was designed to assist in defending the plantations of South Carolina against her enemies, especially the Spanish in Florida. The vision was utopian for its time—there was to be no slavery allowed, and the Indians were treated with respect; individual land ownership was strictly regulated to fifty acres, precluding development as a plantation system. Oglethorpe arrived armed with a blueprint that has resulted in the unique layout of the city to this day. Located on a sandy bluff, forty feet above a bend in the Savannah River, surrounded by a forest of pine, oak, and cypress trees, the town was to be set out in squares. Each square had four "Trust Lots" named for the Trustees of the fledgling colony and reserved for public buildings. Four "Tything Lots" flanked each square to the north and south with ten lots each to house the forty odd families who were part of the original contingency. General Oglethorpe did not forget the original military component of the venture and designed the town with defense in mind.[11]

According to historical accounts gleaned from documents of the period, the Trustees' quixotic vision contained the seeds of failure due to the inherent nature of humanity. They had deliberately chosen applicants who were self-acknowledged failures, unable to support themselves in England. In return for the Trustees' offer of transportation, food, supplies, tools, and land, these colonists were to comply with restrictions that probably would not have appeared onerous back in England, but proved unworkable on arrival. These constraints included prohibitions on rum and slaves, two of the elements that would have made life a little more bearable in this exotic and hostile land of heat, mosquitoes, and humidity.

The military nature of the enterprise necessitated a personal discipline not enjoyed by many of the original settlers. The outposts soon extended to a fort in Frederica for Oglethorpe's soldiers, and a lighthouse on Tybee Island to warn shipping entering and leaving the tidal river. A small community in Darien to the south sprang up, settled by Highland soldier-farmers, who served as the first line of defense against the Spaniards to the south from their fort at St. Augustine.[12]

Reality Versus Idealism

"A parcel of poor people ... incapable of living at home" is how William Stephens, secretary of the colony after 1737, characterized the first colonists.[13] Why Oglethorpe and the Trustees thought the new settlers would fare better in a hostile wilderness is unimaginable, unless they had fallen victim to their own idealism and propaganda. According to many sources, the founding of Georgia is most often seen as being a philanthropic undertaking, to find a home for the poor of England, and as such, Georgia was considered a "debtors" colony. It appears that the death of a close friend of Oglethorpe's, Robert Castell, in prison in England for debt where he unfortunately contracted smallpox, was the trigger. His death launched a parliamentary inquiry into prison abuses. The inquiry was led by Oglethorpe. This underpinned the compassion he felt for the underdog.

A most insightful account and analysis of Oglethorpe's character and motivations are to be found in a remarkable essay by Sir Keith Thomas, renowned historian of the seventeenth century and president of Corpus Christi College at Oxford University. He attributes Oglethorpe's humanistic views to the education he received at this small Jacobite college—an education grounded thoroughly in classical literature and philosophy and a personal fascination with the Roman Empire.

Sir Keith's essay gives us extraordinary illumination into Oglethorpe's views on Indians, slavery, Jews, philanthropy, colonialism, and what is today called "civic humanism," which for his time was radical. This lead him to admire the Indians as noble people who rejected trade as a commercial venture, using goods only for barter, and refusing to work for wages, as well as burning the belongings of the dead to prevent inheritance of property. His views on black slavery were equally at odds with prevailing sentiment, as he believed that their ownership would make their white masters soft and idle. He despised the institution on moral grounds, declaring it "an abominable and destructive custom." They certainly were not the prevailing views of the ruling elite of Britain and the plantation class in America. Britain's imperial might was not built on the shifting sands of philanthropy, nor motivated by idealism. Neither were the English ruling classes renowned for their compassionate views regarding Native Americans and Africans.[14]

Oglethorpe soon ran into criticism, accused by the settlers of running the endeavor with an imperial hand. From its idyllic inception in the far-off halls of power, the new enterprise fell into the more manageable and practical parameters of what was needed to keep the flags of the British Empire flying. This meant a professional administration supervised by the Board of Trade in London, run by those whose personal and commercial interests predominated in all corners of its far-flung ventures around the globe.

Oglethorpe's inclusive philanthropic sentiments extended to Jews. In the middle of the first vicious summer's fever season a group of Jews arrived on board a ship and asked to land and settle. Perhaps the reason he allowed their request was the fact that they had a doctor with them and that the settlement's only physician had succumbed to the rigors of frontier life and terrors of the "night miasma." Oglethorpe did so reluctantly on account of his knowledge of the Trustee's animosity to Jewish settlers, but this singular action was to make a vital contribution to the key role that Jewish merchants played as Savannah metamorphosed into a multicultural entrepot.

On the eve of his departure for London to solicit more funds in March 1734, a group of German Lutheran Salzburgers arrived. Henry Newman, secretary of the Society for the Promotion of Christian Knowledge (SPCK) in London, had negotiated their passage and acceptance. Oglethorpe obviously had a good relationship with this organization and stayed to help the new arrivals lay out a town they called Ebenezer. They, too, were fleeing religious persecution. SPCK emerges as a powerful influence in the Highland regions of Scotland as they evangelized the area to convert Catholic clan members to Protestantism and to eradicate the speaking of Gaelic, the language spoken by the Celtic Highlanders, in order to introduce English as a tongue that would benefit emigrants to the New World.

When Oglethorpe sailed in December 1735 with a second group of settlers bound for Fort Frederica on St. Simon's Island, the complement included John and Charles Wesley. These young sibling clergymen were fresh out of Oxford, where they created a stir with their "Holy Club." Out of that experience grew their belief that being a true Christian required a personal spiritual rebirth, and Georgia was to be their proving ground where the emotional experience would be taken to the Indians. Accompanying the Wesleys were Benjamin Ingham and Charles Delamotte. These were the spiritual founders of the later Methodist Church, but the harsh realities of frontier Georgia soon curbed their coltish enthusiasm.

The adage that when the cat's away the mice will play soon manifested its truth. Oglethorpe's obsessive need to micro-manage only functioned when he was actually in residence and in charge of the details. He also had obligations to the Trustees to continue selecting settlers, raising funds, and accounting for his progress thus far. Human nature being what it is, the records show the usual complement of complaints, ignoring of the rules, improper relations, neglect of basic commonsensical methods of agriculture, family squabbles, autocracy, nepotism, bribery, and corruption—on the part of the settlers of Savannah, from the top down. (Mills Lane, in *Savannah Revisited,* lists all these human frailties with great gusto in a fascinating account of how idealism must always give way to realism.)

Utopia Fades—Crown Colony

By 1743 the utopian vision had begun to fray around the edges. The settlers' focus had shifted to the colony across the river. In South Carolina a new arrival could have all the land that he could afford with slaves to work it; and the novelty of being the target of hostile Indians and marauding Spaniards, as well as cultivating their own land, had soon palled. South Carolina's economic success was based on rice, and the impoverished Georgians had only to gaze across the Savannah River estuary to see the golden glow of rice and the Africans who tended it. Records show that of six thousand or so settlers who had come to Georgia, by 1743 only a thousand or so hardy souls remained.

Oglethorpe returned to England and fought somewhat ignominiously for the Crown in the disastrous Jacobite rebellion of 1745.[15] This futile attempt to place the heir to the exiled Stuart dynasty, known today in song and legend as "Bonnie Prince Charlie," on the throne of Scotland culminated in the massacre of Scottish rebels at Culloden in the Highlands. Led by the army of the Duke of Cumberland, known as "Butcher," son of King

George II, this still-remembered event has contributed to Scotland's notorious hatred of the English. Oglethorpe's reputed reluctance to pursue the Crown's enemies was perhaps influenced by his own previous Jacobite loyalties. His reputation suffered, and he did not again participate in the Georgia experiment.[16] Events had proved his ideas unworkable, Georgia reverted to a Crown colony, and the installation of slavery led the way to a slave-based plantation system mirroring that of South Carolina. Savannah eagerly embraced mercantilism as her way to prosperity.

Parliament refused to further fund the sinking venture, which in desperation for labor by 1750 permitted slavery, and in 1752 the Georgia Trustees surrendered their charter to the king, a year ahead of its scheduled elapse. The Crown promptly appointed a governor, and Georgia's ideological illusion gave way to practical reality, and the colony was absorbed into the British imperial cosmos. Georgia, by pandering to the worst of human nature instead of rising to the heights of the best, missed an opportunity to mold the nature of what the United States would become. Successive Crown governors attempted to inject an English "tone" into the colony—code for aping aristocratic mores. Mercantile realism warred constantly with more socially desirable plantation idealism—the nation of shopkeepers battling the lords of the manor.

In colonial records, further indications show that the names of William Low and James Low appear in "An Index to English Crown Grants In Georgia 1755–1775." This is the period immediately following the arrival of the first royal governor to Georgia. The land grants were substantial ones on the south fork of the Newport River near Darien. Despite lack of biographical data in the records, this could indeed be the missing lead as to why Andrew Low, Sr., emigrated to Savannah instead of Charleston, or even New England or New Jersey, where other Lowland Scots from the same region had emigrated since the 1600's.[17]

Lead up to Revolution

The end of the French and Indian Wars in 1763, compelling Spain to cede Florida to Britain, extracted the cork from the bottle and a tide of emigrants soon reached Georgia. From three thousand whites and two thousand blacks in 1754, Georgia's population swelled to fifty thousand people by the end of the Revolution, half free and half slave. Those who came to fight from the North stayed to seek their fortunes in the frontier atmosphere that prevailed, amongst them many Irish and Scots who became known in America as "Scotch Irish," a terminology still derided by true Scots who claim Scotch is the pure whiskey they love to imbibe. Between 1790 and 1800 the population of Georgia nearly doubled again. The conditions and opportunities would have proved a magnet for those more interested in fighting for their own survival than establishing a nation.

This era of prosperity did not last long. The last and poorest British colony in the Americas did not have much time to get its own affairs in order before it was overtaken by what has become known as "The Revolution of 1776"—America's War of Independence.

As discontent in the northern colonies against the domination of their English king increased, in Georgia the situation was different. Shared interests in prosperity between the representative of the Crown and the increasingly prosperous planters and merchants kept matters on an even keel. Savannah was booming because most goods moved through the port and the city's robust trade was financed with British credit and banks. *Savannah Revisited* states that "Georgians were reluctant rebels ... led to revolt by pressures and propaganda outside the colony ... the people of Savannah were Englishmen first, then Georgians and only finally Americans." Events overtook complacency; and by 1775 revolutionary sentiment had taken root feeding the aspirations of the mob, resulting in the rebels taking control of the provincial militia.[18]

In January 1776 the by now helpless and powerless Crown Governor James Wright escaped to HMS *Scarbrough*, a British man-of-war guarding the entrance to the port of Savannah. In late 1777 all Loyalists were expelled from the state, and it appeared that Georgia was fully committed to the revolutionary process. The British were not at all prepared to give up though, and in 1778 they massed three thousand troops to recapture Georgia. In December the British took Savannah easily, a forecast of events in 1864, when Sherman's troops waltzed in and took her again. The pendulum swung back, and the English governor returned to administer his part of the state.

It was now that once again the broader picture of European global expansionist designs affected local affairs. In October 1779 a French fleet of four thousand men and twenty-two ships commanded by Comte Henri d'Estaing joined the American rebel forces and attempted to lay siege to Savannah. The Continental forces commanded by General Benjamin Lincoln joined d'Estaing with fifteen hundred troops, and the tide should have turned for the rebels at that point. As often happens the French and the Americans were unable to cooperate; and despite the fact that their combined forces outnumbered the British two to one, and despite a bombardment of artillery that damaged the town of Savannah considerably, a frontal assault on the British lines failed and the French sailed away.

The British soon consolidated their gains and under General Sir Henry Clinton moved forces down from the north, and captured Charleston and the entire Continental Army protecting it. Next to fall was Augusta, and concurrently a struggle ensued between the royal colonial government and the newly elected state government. Unfortunately for the British, they were never able to send enough troops to Georgia to restore it to its previous Crown status and thereby use it as an example to persuade other colonial governments to return to the royal fold. Savage guerrilla warfare in the backcountry marked that phase of the Revolution. By April 1782 General Nathanael Greene, commander of the Southern Department of the Continental Army, began to mount a new offensive and retook Augusta, thereby freeing upcountry Georgia from British control.

Enter Our Ancestors

Joseph Clay's origins date to the early Methodists in Georgia. John Wesley convinced his Oxford classmate, George Whitefield, to come to Georgia to create an orphan house they named Bethesda. Whitefield's variety of the Methodist way included emotional preaching, and two of his followers in London were shopkeepers from Beverley, the brothers James and Joseph Habersham. James would decide to accompany the charismatic preacher to Georgia, and after operating Bethesda for nine years James created Georgia's first merchant house. Success meant opportunity for other family members, and in 1760 his sister Elizabeth's son, Joseph Clay, joined his uncle in Savannah. James Habersham became a man of great wealth and importance, serving the colony as secretary and a regular member of the Governor's Council, as well as acting governor during the absence of Governor Wright during the Revolution.[19]

Clay was a prosperous Savannah merchant, but became a staunch oppositionist at the beginning of the conflict, and eventually served as paymaster general of the Continental Army. Revolutionary General Nathanael Greene sent his trusted colleague to Augusta to try to reestablish a state government. In July 1774 Clay helped draft the document that bound Georgia in resisting English tyranny. His most daring act had been to take part in the raid on the king's powder on the night of May 11, 1775, one of the acts that precipitated Georgia's participation in the rebellion against the British.

Some of the most desirable of Savannah River plantation holdings owned by Royalists, including Springfield and Vale Royal, were confiscated during the War of Independence and were purchased by prominent Revolutionaries at the cessation of hostilities—to the winner go the spoils.[20] In June 1782, in the town of Ebenezer, a land sale was held and Joseph Clay bid for the Springfield and Vale Royal, adding to sixty acres east of Musgrove Creek he already owned. It was there he built his home, where it would now have been at Bay and Fahm streets, in modern Savannah some of the most desirable town property. This elegant Georgian style mansion was the obvious work of the French-born architect

Adrian Bouchet, and the elements of this design would be mirrored in his later City Exchange, Savannah's most significant civic building. Clay also purchased further confiscated Tory holdings on the Savannah River and by 1785 owned a valuable stretch of property, beginning with town lots, and extending to the Ogeechee River. He also bought the land where the famous Ten Broek Race Course was laid out.

In 1804 Joseph Clay died intestate, and the vast holdings descended to his heirs, children of his wife, the former Ann Legardere, whom he had married in 1763.[21] The entire appraisement disclosed a worth of over $275,000, a considerable fortune in early nineteenth-century dollars. His sons-in-law—Joseph Stiles, William Wallace, and Thomas Cummings—administered the holdings and plantations. Through various legerdemain and sleight of hand to avoid the legal rules precluding administrators from becoming purchasers at their own sales, eventually the Vale Royal was quitclaimed to Stiles.[22]

The Bermuda-born Joseph Stiles was the fifth generation of his family to hail from the mid-Atlantic isle. Bermuda in the seventeenth century was comprised of about three dozen families who were involved in sailing and shipping syndicates that plied the Gulf Stream of the North Atlantic. On his father's side were important connections: Copeland Stiles, speaker of the Bermuda Assembly; Edward Stiles, wealthy Philadelphia merchant; and Debora Stiles Gambier, wife of the governor of the Bahamas and ancestress of Sarah Ferguson, the Duchess of York. His mother was from the powerful Todd family. Joseph's father, Captain Samuel Stiles, was well known in shipping circles. The Stiles family harvested the salt ponds of the Turks Islands, and it was here that the French Navy detained Captain Stiles during the Seven Years War. Captain Stiles's deposition of the matter, dated June 22, 1764, is filed away in the Bermuda Archives.

Captain Stiles saw opportunity in Georgia, a coast where he harvested live oak for his ships. He began a slow process of accumulating land grants in Georgia and shifting his family to that colony. When the Revolution broke out, he played a diplomatic game of seeming to be loyal to the king while smuggling armament and powder to the Americans. Family legend says he had a horse shot out from under him at the siege in October 1779. On that day he was allied to the French, who had detained him fifteen years earlier.[23]

When the British left, many of the original settlers who had supported the Crown or who were royal appointees also left hurriedly. This included two uncles by marriage—Basil Cowper and James Wright, Jr., son of the last royal governor.[24] On July 10 and 11, 1782, the British were forced to evacuate Savannah, not because they were threatened, but because they required their troops elsewhere to plug up more important holes.

With the departing British went those civilians who could not expect to prosper under the new political system. They included Loyalists, Tories, blacks, and whites. Some went to the West Indies, some to East Florida still under Spanish control, and some returned to England and Scotland. For some this was where their own ancestors had previously been sent into exile by the very British who had now lost control of their jewel in the crown of their New World enterprises.

2

Birth of the Buck: Scotland, 1766–1781

THREE MILES FROM THE CAPITAL TOWN OF STONEHAVEN, KINCARDINESHIRE, on rich volcanic soil bordered by a windswept cliff in the northeast corner of Scotland, pounded by the gales of the North Sea, stands Dunnottar Castle. When our first Andrew Low was born, the two major landlords in this region were Barclay of Urie, and the Keith family, owners of Dunnottar Castle. The name of the Barclay family is illustrious in Scottish history. The original David Barclay of Urie, during a period when he was imprisoned by the Crown in the mid 1600's, converted to Quakerism. His eldest son, Robert Barclay, is noted for writing the Quaker manifesto of the "Friends" beliefs called *Apology for the True Christian Divinity*. He was an associate of William Penn, the Quaker founder of Pennsylvania. In 1681 Barclay became one of the syndicate granted land in America that became known as East New Jersey. A year later he was appointed governor-for-life of the new colony. The family was reputed to have Jacobite leanings, but managed to avoid exile or forfeiture of their extensive landholdings. By far the most influential Barclay in Kincardine history was the fifth-generation Robert Barclay, renowned to this day as the architect of land improvement at the end of the seventeenth century that drastically changed the way agriculture was conducted in Scotland. He was known locally as "The Heaven-Born Improver."

Following the Jacobite rebellion of 1715, the English Crown forfeited the estates of the participants. By 1720 the appointed commissioners were seeking a purchaser. Scotland was broke, partly through its investment in the disastrous Scottish Trading Company at Darien in the Panama isthmus in 1698. Many of the interpreters of the past believe today that Scotland only acquiesced to the Acts of Union because England agreed to pay her debts; instead she confiscated much of her land. This was the time

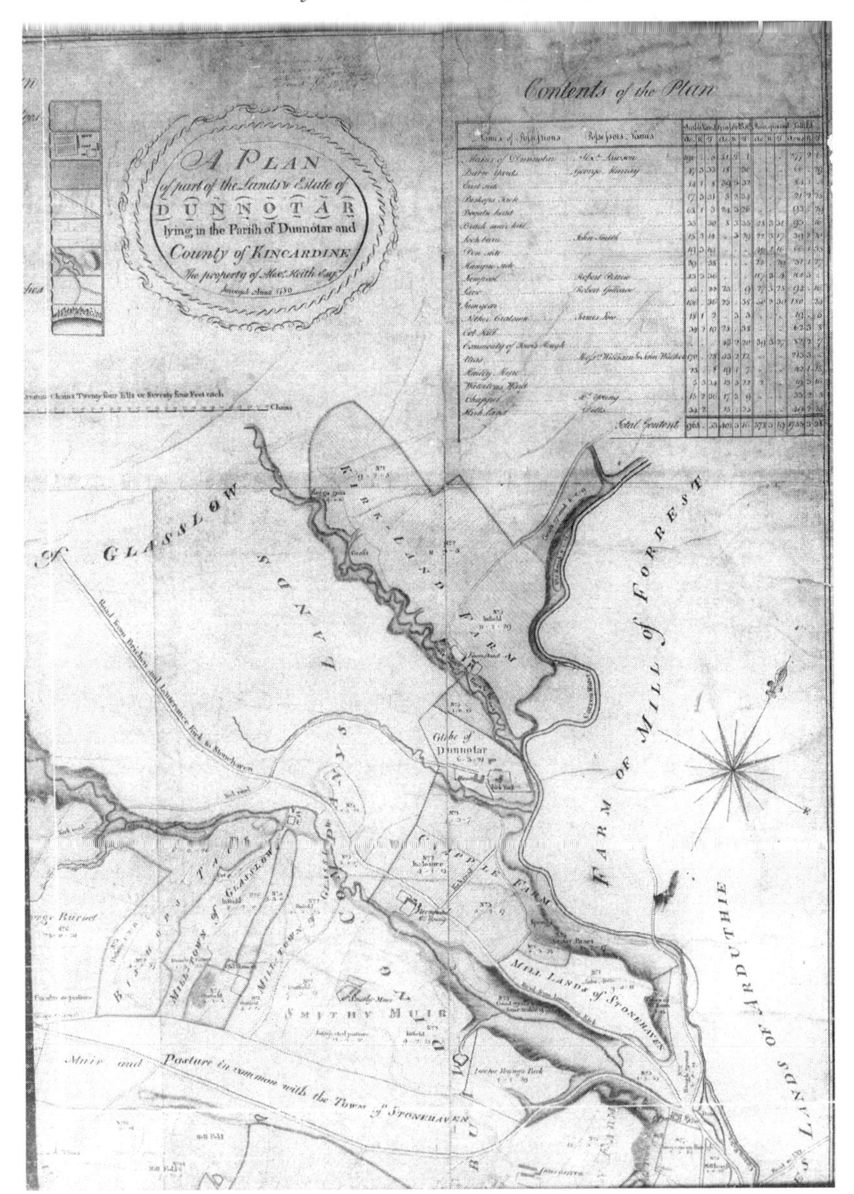

A map of "A Plan of Dunnottar, County of Kincardine" shows the Keith (Building Company) lands where the Lows farmed. *Courtesy National Library of Scotland.*

of joint stock companies, most of them also disastrous, as witnessed by the South Sea Bubble fiasco. Enter the York Building Company, a London-based, water-purification company known as the "Company for Raising of Thames Water in York Buildings." The company was sold to a set of new investors involved in the insurance-assurance business. When the subscription was opened, they raised 1,200,000 pounds for purchasing forfeited estates in Scotland. By October 1720 the company had purchased most of the Marischal estate in Kincardine.

The reality proved to be the impossibility of administering from London on account of active resistance from the tenants, poor roads, and indifferent overseers; the enterprise proved unworkable. By 1764 the English Crown had been forced to relent and returned the estates to the Keith-Marischal family, and it is an interesting fact that James Low married just two years after its return to the rightful owner—his landlord.[1]

In 1766 James Low, born 1732 in Crawton, married Catherine Croll of Fettercairn, an adjacent parish. Catherine Croll's christening records in 1743 show she was born to George Croll and Jean Milne. The Old Parish Record reads "Katherine Croll, baptised 5th, that day (May, 1743) Katherine, lawful daughter to father George Croll and spouse Jean Milne, was baptised Fettercairn." Her name is spelled with both a "K" and a "C." This record is a little unusual since it lists both the names of father and mother and place of birth. The marriage record also is unusual since it is registered in both Dunnottar and Laurencekirk. These four parishes where the preponderance of Lows are found—Fordoun, Dunnottar, Fettercairn, and Laurencekirk—are all within a ten to fifteen mile radius of each other in the county of Kincardine.

In 1767 the eldest son was born. They named him William, and as was usual for those times the children arrived at intervals of two years—the only girl, Jean, was the second born. Then came six more boys, the last being George in 1780. The young Andrew Low was born in 1779, the seventh child, and sixth son. James Low's premature death at the age of forty-nine in 1781, one year after the birth of his last son, left his widow with eight young children ranging in age from fourteen to a babe in arms—an event that changed the course of our story irrevocably.

Childhood Days in Dunnottar

If the gang of young Low boys had time to play, they had at their disposal a veritable magic kingdom. This part of the coast is very rugged, formed of plum-pudding rock, and contains several deep caves. The most remarkable stretch is an area named Fowlsheugh, about a mile long and fifty fathoms high. These cliffs were inhabited by seafowl of every description—gulls, coots, and kittyweaks—in numbers that provided limited employment opportunities in summer months to a few brave souls. They would climb down the perpendicular rocks, by the help of a rope tied round a man's middle, to catch the birds at their rest and in their nests. The feathers and down were in great demand, and the kittyweaks, whose flesh resembled that of a goose, were sold at high prices in the local market towns. A rent was paid, of course, to the owner of the cliffs, and the work only available during migratory months from April to September. It is quite likely that a brave or foolhardy boy could scratch a few pennies out of this trade; money to augment the meager picking of tenant farming would have been welcome in many a small crofter's cottage. In any event, later deeds certainly indicated a bold and often rash quality as the Low boys grew to manhood, ignoring danger or consequences. This is a character trait that is often the product of a harsh environment, where life was not held to too high a standard.

Crawton was a fishing harbor as well as a farming community. The fishing was of excellent quality, with cod, ling, haddock, whiting, and flounder the predominant catch for market, while lobsters and crabs were more often consumed in the neighborhood. Some kelp was grown and harvested every three years to allow it time to regrow, but was never the major industry that it was on the western shores of the Highland islands. A few miles to the north was Stonehaven, situated where the River Carron runs into the sea. The principal reason for its existence in the eighteenth century was as a well-protected harbor that vessels in distress could easily utilize. There was very little trade, except by a few small vessels used for supplying basic needs, bringing lime and coal from Sunderland and the Frith of Forth, and a few cargoes of wood, iron, and flax from the Baltic. The town, along with the rest of Dunnottar parish, labored under the stigma and economic hardship of having been part of the forfeitures of 1715 following the Jacobite rebellion.

The First Statistical Survey

Scotland has been most fortunate to have in its historical archives a remarkable compilation of facts, figures, and commentary known as "Statistical Reports," compiled from the annals and mindsets of "Ministers of the Church." Some two hundred years ago, on May 25, 1790, Sir John Sinclair of Ulbster in Caithness sent out his first circulars detailing social and economic conditions of the late 1700's, covering the period our focus lived their youth and formative years. The reports cover some 938 parishes, ministers of which were sent a questionnaire on local conditions relative to the national situation. It was one of the first examples of an attempt at a logical, cohesive, and statistical analysis, an absolute ingredient in any modern policymaker's portfolio, but unknown in those times.[2]

The timing occurred at a significant transition point that demarcates the Scotland of romantic myth, where loyal chieftains protected their warrior clansmen from outside harm in good times and bad, to the land reform revolution that took place in the last few decades of the eighteenth century. Up until then Scotland was predominantly subsistence agriculture—tenants and subtenants scratching a sparse living from malnourished cattle and sheep and a few crops for food, mostly oats and turnips. Changes in crop rotation, different grains, or more modern tools were viewed with deep suspicion; tenants had little incentive to improve either their land or their homes since they never knew when their tenancy would be abruptly terminated.

The flight of major landholders, Scots and English, to the brighter lights of England meant a more expensive lifestyle—clothes for the fair ladies, education for the children, and antiques for the townhouses. This necessitated higher incomes, and the obvious source was the land they owned, land that frequently brought them no more income than a few scrawny fowl and a bushel of oats. Naturally consolidation and modern methods of productivity were part of the answer to higher yields, both in the form of rents and income. The first casualties were the tenants and those even lower on the social scale, the cottagers, and the cotters. The methods employed ignored modern concepts of human rights. They were simply evicted.

Life was short, brutal, and harsh. Punishment for even minor transgressions was swift and barbarous, hanging and banishment being the severest. For the sons of the landed gentry the norm was inheritance for the eldest; for the rest of frequently large families, options included emigration—the West Indies, Barbados, and Jamaica being the favored destinations, to seek fortunes as planters and slaveholders—or into the service of the East India Company, then the army, the navy, or the church. Daughters were married off to the best prospects for the entire family.

For the children of tenants and cottagers the options were fewer and more drastic. As day laborers they could work on the farms, or in the burgeoning manufacturing sector. The other option was emigration. It was in this tumultuous time that the immediate ancestors are born. The 1707 Acts of Union opened dreamed-of opportunities, especially for the merchants of Scotland champing at the bit. They fretted against the restricted trade practices of the monopolistic East India Company, controlled by the exclusive establishment of England—the monarchy, the landed gentry, the military, and the politicians.[3] By the time the American colonies had enough of their British masters, had rose up and threw them out, the Scots had absorbed enough benefits of union with England to realize that they were better off with it than without it.

Legends and Myths

The land was saturated in the ancient glory days of Scotland's history. In all the literature and history of emigrants to America, Scottish pride has been legendary. The young Low boys' minds and hearts would have been as inundated with the romance and virility of their ancient heroes as they would have been buffeted by the storms and gales of long winters, when stories warmed the heart and lit the fires of the soul, as the smoky peat fires smoldered in the hearth. Scottish memories last forever; and loyalty, fidelity, devotion, and constancy are imprinted in the genetic code of these people, even up to the present day; and even if one was not of the lineage oneself, status was conferred by kinship and allegiance. They may have been tenants and subtenants, but they were also intimates of kings and inheritors of the mantle of glorious Scotland's splendid bloody history.

The Scottish Episcopalian belief was most prevalent in Kincardine, and, despite persecution, remained so for many centuries. An ancestor of the Marischal family built the fortress in Dunnottar during the contest between two Scottish claimants to the throne in the thirteenth century. The relationship between England and Scotland had soured when Edward I, king of England, tried to establish the Scottish king as his vassal and Scotland as a feudal appendage of England by appointing and backing a weak pawn, John Balliol. Scotland preferred Robert Bruce and rejected Longshank's puppet king. This led to an invasion of Scotland by English forces of such brutality that it was remembered with bitterness for centuries, and forms the basis of many of the legends of former Scottish glory that exist today. Robert Bruce claimed the throne and set into motion the beginning of the reign in which Scotland won her independence.

As a direct result of the ascendancy of the Protestant church, civil war broke out between Scotland and England triggered by the execution of Charles I by the English Parliament in 1649. This caused such a revulsion of feeling in Scotland that it revived some sentiment for the Stuart dynasty. The Scots, once again feeling betrayed by England, now changed sides to fight for the Crown against the English Parliament. Unfortunately for Scotland, she had not reckoned with the man the military called "Ironsides," the self-named Lord Protector, scourge of Ireland and the Roman Catholic Church, the Puritan Roundhead Oliver Cromwell. History has revised its opinion of Cromwell to some extent by recognizing him as an outstanding political and military figure of his day, but to the Scots he was their nemesis.

The Stuart heir, Charles II, was recognized by the Scots and returned from exile. Oliver Cromwell invaded and crushed the Scots at Dunbar. The young Charles fled back into exile, Cromwell and his generals swept into Scotland, and for the first time ever the unthinkable had happened. England really conquered Scotland and incorporated her into the English state and parliamentary system. This state of affairs lasted only until the death of Cromwell in 1660, and resultant political confusion in England led to the return of the English army to London, fed up perhaps with once again spending far too much time and money controlling their unruly unreliable subjects in the north. Charles II was invited back from exile and restored to the throne.

It is reputed that the Regalia of Scotland—meaning the Crown, Sceptre, and Sword—were deposited in Dunnottar Castle to preserve them from the English army, which overran the area during the civil wars of the period. The Scottish Regalia is as important to the concept and symbolism of the Scottish throne as the Crown Jewels are to the English monarchy, or the Declaration of Independence to the American republic. More than anything else, the symbols of office sum up the spirit of independent character that personifies Scotland. Some might call this character intransigent or stubborn, but to the Scots it spells one word—freedom. So precious are the Regalia to the traditions and history of Scotland that a clause in the 1707 Treaty of Union specifies that they must never leave Scotland. This mythology, encompassing the Marischal family, would definitely have been an integral part of the lore that was imbued in the young Low boys.

All these legends would have sparked the imagination of a young boy as would the poetry of Robert Burns, the patron saint and epic bard of Scotland, who also has ancestral roots in this spot of the nation.[4] If you grew up here, you would have been steeped in the sorrow and the blood of Scotland's glory days, seeing yourself as a martyr, a warrior, a poet, and a slave. This was fuel for the fires of imagination in an active boy's head. In some ways hardheaded and eminently practical in the ways of business, Scots are poets and troubadours in their hearts. They are born romantics, to whom deeds of old fan the flames of future adventures, and all things are possible. This is especially true after a couple of quaffs of the firewater brewed with the crystal clear water and barley grain of the Highlands!

The image on the fragile scrim that always fluttered behind the stage of mighty battles and minor skirmishes between England and Scotland was the reality of the Cinderella status of Scotland in England's eyes. Usually regarded as a nuisance and a pauper nation, peopled by uncontrollable outlaws, cattle thieves, and ruffians, she was constantly excluded from England's commercial imperial aspirations, useful only as fodder for her armies, through supplying the incomparable and greatly feared soldier warriors of the wild and indomitable Highland clans. Scots regarded themselves far more highly than England did them, and applied all kinds of imaginative strategies to level the playing fields, often most successfully.

The result was that the state of a man's material wealth bore no relation to his concept of personal pride in his own and his ancestors' achievements, even if survival was the only one that had any real value. A saying in medieval France, "that man is the cousin of the King of the Scots," was a derogatory dig at anyone boasting, but one that missed the point of the Scotsman's sense of self. His was not an expression of wishing for upward mobility, and a poor man did not aspire to the rank of baron, earl, or king. Rather he was expressing his equality through his own bloods' virtue and valor. This was a characteristic that took the Scot to the furthest corners of the known world in all capacities, ready, able, and quite willing to grasp any opportunity that arose. Perhaps here is the origin of the expression—a canny Scot—being both cautious and shrewd, knowing which way the land lies and the wind blows, pragmatic yet visionary. A can-do sort of person, tempered with a large dose of romanticism, idealism and a remarkable freedom of spirit, balanced by a notorious frugality in spending, and above all a risk-taker.

Death of a Father

In 1781 James Low died suddenly at the age of forty-nine. He was wrapped in a rented mort cloth and buried in the serene kirk yard at the fishing village of Catterline under a bed of snowdrops, a mile and a half from the small fishing and farming hamlet of Crawton, where he was born. Such a severe blow of fate would have changed the lives of this tenant farming family drastically. Providing the rental on the lease was paid, they would not under the law have been prevented from staying on the land as tenant farmers, and neither did the law prevent women from holding the lease. The widow Catherine could have returned to her Croll family in Fettercairn, or Milne family in Laurencekirk, and assistance would have been available from the parishes. But no records show that she ever received "poor relief" from any parish. She had a large extended kinship to call upon—many of whom, especially the Low family, were substantial farmers and traders; she could have had considerable moral and actual support. Family was one of the only constants in the shifting shoals of treacherous societal quicksand afforded to the Scot born at the cusp of feudal times. All of these factors would have had an insidious if not overt influence on the decisions the widow, head of the family of James Low, would now have to make.

3

The Widow's Mite: 1781–1800

CATHERINE CROLL LOW'S SCOTLAND WAS A COUNTRY IN TRANSITION. There is no visual record or written account of this remarkable woman, and the choices she faced can only be imagined from contemporary accounts of what her life might have been like when her husband died in 1781. Today the fields in Crawton are neatly demarcated by stone fences. They are ploughed many times into perfect rows, waiting warm and fecund under the turned soil in the winter rain for their bellies to swell with the cornucopia of seed planted for spring. In the winter the wind howls and the rain falls in driving sheets. Behind the double-glazed windows American and Scottish housewives, whose husbands work the Aberdeen oil boom, sit watching the "telly" and sipping their tea—warm and consciously oblivious to the weather outside prowling their newly renovated fishing and crofters cottages, searching for the way back in. If they did not nurture their obliviousness they would be forced to confront the primal fear that humans feel when the weather turns vicious and temperamental.

Below the cliffs the steel gray sea whips itself into a frothy frenzy, battering at the black rocks that prevent it from penetrating the land, and sometimes in its anger hurls its spume fifty, a hundred feet into the air to smash against the picture windows with their spectacular view. Occasionally in its rage it heaves manmade objects abandoned to the weather, such as ice chests left by careless summer holidaymakers in the rocky inlet below, to batter its way in to the comfort it is eternally prohibited from sharing. Outside the mud has already started its slow and inexorable slide down the hill, eroding more of the topsoil to drop into the hungry maw of the sea, waiting to be fed by the land.

In 1781, more than two hundred years ago, the weather would have been equally threatening, but the comfort level would have been nonexistent on a day like today. A long, low, stone-sided croft or farmhouse

Late eighteenth-century farmhouse that is typical of the tenant farm that Catherine Croll and James Low would have worked. *Courtesy National Library of Scotland.*

squatted with a thatched roof made from the gorse-like whinberry or whistle berry foliage that grew in profusion on the mossy, swampy, grassy headlands. A smoldering fire of peat would have filled the interior with stinging smoke as it blew back through the hole in the roof that allowed it to escape. Adults and children, outside animals and inside animals huddled together for warmth and security, wretched and wet, yet curiously serene in acceptance that everything passes, and only the one-hundred-year storms would have frightened.

Conversation would be desultory, mainly about the weather, and the children would have been forced by their mother to pay attention to the learning work, glued to their well-thumbed books. The whitewater fishermen would not be out on a day like this, no matter their need for food and money, their boats tied securely in the cove below. One of the reasons the fishing village at Crawton gradually died out was because the rocks in the small bay proved too dangerous for the new deeper hulled fishing boats of later years. The land today is extremely fertile under modern agriculture methods and so would have been then, with good drainage and rich topsoil, certainly sufficient to support a relatively large community of farmers and fishermen, millers and laborers, as neighboring ruins attest.

After James Low's death it is not beyond the bounds of possibility that if Catherine Croll, strong and vigorous at thirty-eight years old, was a wise and industrious woman she would have been able to keep her family together and stay on the farm. Her other options could have been taking in an experienced farmer as overseer or expanding her resources by soliciting weaving work for herself and her daughter Jean. If she put the two older boys William and David to work on the farm, she could have sent the fourth and fifth sons, John and James, to sea as apprentice mariners, and herself undertaken the responsibility of schooling the three younger boys—Alexander, Andrew, and George—to become merchants and traders. If the stars were in alignment she could have held on and remained on the piece of land her husband's forefathers had lived on long before we have records of any proof.

They would in all probability have walked to the Catterline school, or perhaps as they grew older to the Stonehaven school, or even boarded there; their older brother David appears to have purchased a part of the Barclay housing agricultural project known as the Links of Arduthie,[1] and sister Jean is reported to have died in Stonehaven. Another large family of Lows lived in a nearby Fordoun fermetoune called Pittengarden as subtenants.[2]

Hard Times Arrived

The year following James Low's death there was a famine caused by an almost total loss of the grain crop. It was followed by prolonged early frost and snow before harvest, prompting the local minister to report that the crop was certainly not sufficient to maintain the inhabitants. Relief was granted by the government, paid for with monies taken from the capital of the "poor fund" held by the kirks, as well as private benefactors. A period account by Archibald Cameron states:

> The worst year of the century was 1782. The summer was so wet and cold that the corn began to shoot only in the end of August. A severe frost in October followed by a heavy snowstorm in the end of the month, the crops—even such as had got beyond the green stage-were entirely ruined. Very little of the grain was fit for next year's seed. That "snowy hairst" was long remembered. To relieve the distress, meetings of the county gentlemen were held, and money was collected to bring supplies from England. With aid from Government, shiploads of pease and meal were imported to be sold or distributed. For the sake of economy, all idle dogs and other useless animals were destroyed, horses were fed on straw and bruised whins, beer was not malted, and other means were used for the saving of provisions.[3]

Cameron continues elsewhere:

> The large number reduced to poverty continued for years to depend on charity; and for the years 1800 and 1801, when the crops failed from drought, meal and provisions rose to famine prices, and the

> list of poor people was more and more increased. In the early part of the century, the farmhouses were wretched hovels, low, damp, and dirty; the people and the cattle were very much the same for accommodation. Where stones were scarce, the walls were composed, at least in the upper part of turf, or mud and straw. A long narrow building covered with thatch in the "ben" or (be in) and the "but" (be out) of the family dwelling; and a continuation of the "but" or kitchen, beyond a rough partition, held the cattle; so that even the snoring of the beasts could be heard at the fireside. In front of the house, only a step or so from the door, stood the dung hole—a deep area—filled with solids during the winter and stagnant water in summer, where pigs and poultry held riot and after nightfall people frequently stumbled.

To these dreadful living conditions, was added the milk of human kindness. When a house (byre) or barn required repair, the neighbors all gathered and gave a *love darg* (friendly turn) to complete the work, usually with the help of many hands completed within a single day.

The minister at Fettercairn reported "the numerous poor of the parish in 1792 had to be relieved entirely from the weekly collections at church and from fees from the use of the mort cloth, because the savings in the box had been used to buy meal." However, the kirk records extant in the Archives show no mention of any application for charity from Catherine Croll for herself or her family in any of the contiguous parishes. This is an indication she was a proud woman, trying to remain self-sufficient, not seeking charity.

My present-day dilemma is that the memories of those who lived are long erased. Speculation, instinct, logic, and intuition must take the place of first-hand knowledge. People do not move far from their comfort zones; people do not seek exotic solutions to survival problems. People seek help where help is to be found and in the close-knit communities of late eighteenth-century rural Scotland, the extended family offered the only salvation available, apart from poor relief under the supervision of the often condemnatory eyes of the church. There were no social safety nets. When drowning in a turbulent sea, you do not reject the tenuous lifeline for an ephemeral one that may or may not materialize later. You grab what is thrown you, and hang on for dear life.

An Embarrassment of Lows

The Low extended family was common and extensive throughout the Mearns, as the region was known of old, appearing in extant records as both respectable and disreputable members of the community, as these three examples will show. The Presbyterian Church predominated in this region and in Cameron's history, yet another Andrew Low was the first beadle in Fettercairn. The duties of beadle included "attending the minister at parochial visitations, summon culprits of all kinds to undergo church discipline." He was responsible for giving church notices after church services, to walk in front of funeral processions and ring a hand bell, to keep dogs out of the church and if they happened to get in, put them out as best he could. This he usually managed with a clip like a smith's tongs, which he kept to catch them—what the dogs were doing in the church was not recorded! His multifarious duties led him to be regarded as the best newsmonger in the parish—a sort of walking "agony aunt." He needed to be honest since he had access to the Kirk Session funds, and sometimes the beadle got carried away and borrowed those funds.

The beadle also got two shillings and sixpence extra pay every year for shoes to do the digging, presumably of the graves—most ordinary people went barefooted. This must be where I get my lifelong abhorrence of wearing shoes! "His money emoluments were two pence from each church collection, and half of each groat charged for his ringing of the hand bell at funerals." Cameron's contemporary account states that, "The occupation of beadle has always been associated with shrewdness and sharpness of wit." That pretty much sums up the character traits attributed later to Uncle Andrew Low, Sr.

At the other end of the scale of notoriety dwells another Low, this one the same John Low who shows up in the *Black Book of Kincardine* as the John Low who was transported to Virginia.[4] He also appears in current day records compiled by David Dobson, the unsurpassed contemporary digger of ancient ancestors.[5] Who would have guessed a quarter of a millennium ago, that the theft of some cattle would have resulted in more mentions in modern-day researchers' attempts to reconstruct the past, than the exemplary life of a Presbyterian pillar of the church!

According to Archibald Cowie Cameron, with information lifted almost verbatim from the revised *Black Book of Kincardine*, "in 1747 a John Low, at Easthill of Johnston (Laurencekirk), stole four oxen and a quey (cow) from Andrew Glen in East Mains of Balfour, and to escape punishment offered to give back a certain amount of his own cattle. Glen refused the offer, whereupon Low agreed to pay one hundred pounds Scots on condition that the theft should not be reported. This promise failed, and he petitioned the Sheriff to let him go off to America, never to return, on the grounds that he was a 'poor weak creature.' This prayer of petition was granted and in 1750 or so said John Low was transported to Virginia, and whether or not he is one of our ancestors remains unknown.

Another miscreant, yet another Andrew Low, is reputed to be the last man hanged in Scotland. This gruesome and infamous event occurred in the adjacent county of Angus, town of Brechin, in 1784, and the handwritten details of his trial for minor theft is riddled with corrupt witnesses; political chicanery and resultant hanging have passed down to the modern archives as a prime example of the brutality of the age. Both legends would have been the subject of much gossip and tittle-tattle around the peat fires on a wet-and-windy winter's night.[6]

Other Hazards

One of the hazards of the period under the microscope was the nefarious habit of the Customs Service apprehending local people going about the business of augmenting their incomes through a little illicit activity. The major ports along the northeast coasts of Kincardine and Angus were Aberdeen, Stonehaven, Gordoun, and Montrose, a stretch of coast that was renowned as Smugglers Coast. Smuggling was a time-honored profession before the Act of Union opened up opportunities for trade, which curtailed the activity to some degree. A man could earn far more from smuggling than from deep-sea fishing, or "whitefishing'" as it was called then, and with less danger and more excitement. It is said that more tobacco came from the colony of Virginia via smugglers than ever passed through the Customs House in Montrose, which until 1745 was Scotland's chief tobacco port. It is written that as the big ships majestically sailed down the coast on their last leg from America, it was only too easy to push a few bundles of the cargo overboard and let them drift in on the tide. Much in the same way, deliverance of marijuana and cocaine is accomplished today in the waters of the Caribbean. Not much changes when profit is the motive.

Add to the hazards of being caught smuggling was the real fear of being swept up by the press-gang, another reprehensible habit performed with great enthusiasm by the Royal Navy. Much of the population was heavily involved in ocean fishing and export trade to the Baltic. The fishing boats were stopped at sea and the best of the crew removed to serve in the Royal Navy. On land, the press- gangs roamed the ports and fairs and commandeered or "pressed" the younger men into service. The small cliff-top fishing and farming hamlet of Crawton would have been prime harvesting for the press-gangers. This would have been serious worry for the widow Low, dependent on her growing boys for help and support.

The only provable fact is that the widow would have been positioned as a member of a well-known yeoman family scattered throughout the entire region. The names of Croll, Milne, Nicol, Reid, and Low are multitudinous in the records of the Mearns of Old with merchants, blacksmiths, weavers, shoemakers, grocers, millers, lawyers, clothiers, farmers, crofters, and fishermen, part of the extended family community.

The Son's Tale: Influences, 1780–1800

Andrew Low was obviously far more influenced in his youth by the manufacturing sector than the agricultural sector. He arrived in America well schooled and well versed in the manufacturing, marketing, and possibilities of "dry goods." He chose a rapidly growing settlement in a nation where entrepreneurial and mercantilist instincts would give a cutting edge to the success of a young man with a pragmatic bent and sharp mind.

With our modern-day sensibilities we tend to think that poverty equates illiteracy, but the educational needs of young people were paramount in the Scotland of the late 1700's. Wherever the young Low boys enrolled, it would not have been out of the ordinary to walk up to ten miles a day, even at a very young age, to attend school. Old-timers told me that as children seventy years ago they walked five to seven miles to go to the parish school. I myself, as a young child in England, walked one-and-a-half miles each way each day, come rain come shine, to attend school before being sent to boarding school.

Paradoxically, education was universal despite the abysmal salaries and living conditions offered to the schoolmasters. Around a century earlier, during the reign of William and Mary, an act had been passed to ensure that each parish should have a school and schoolmaster.[7] It appears as though the parishioners benefited a great deal more from the law than the poor schoolmasters did, resulting in a literate and opinionated breed of back room philosophers, especially compared to many other European countries.

What was perhaps even more important, there appeared to have been an extremely modern concept of vocational schooling in eighteenth-century Scotland. One minister wrote in the statistical account for the parish of Kincardine, "the bulk of mankind have neither the time nor money to procure a liberal education; a scheme to instruct in agriculture, manufacture and commerce, brings practical instruction within reach to provide the people with various forms of knowledge, of which they are at present destitute." The result of this extremely enlightened view of education for the masses was a remarkable range of subjects taught. This curriculum included arithmetic, writing, book-keeping, mathematics, geography, and in some instances Latin and Greek. Often in fact, in these accounts of social conditions of the time, it was the more modest schools in rural areas that attract the most attention because of their excellence. Certainly the four younger Low boys had been the recipients of a basic grounding, if not a level equivalent to university learning.

This education was made available by true democratic principles to the lowest, not only as a privilege of the aristocracy and the moneyed classes.

The result was that young people of the eighteenth century emerged from Scotland better educated in the basics than most of their counterparts in other nations. This laid the foundation for Scots of lesser means and lowly birth to venture to the farthest corners of the expanding empire, well equipped to compete and lead in the industrial revolution that lay ahead.

We can only imagine how young Andrew's character was molded. In a new history titled *The Scottish Nation,* Professor T. M. Devine puts forward several fascinating theories surrounding these years specifically relating to the region in which Andrew Low lived.[8]

The times were changing all over the known world during the last few decades of the eighteenth century. We have already seen in America how the revolutionary act by the people in overthrowing their colonial masters released torrents of energy, especially in the area of commerce and trade. The French Revolution, according to Devine, was "sending political shock waves around Europe" as the common man commandeered the role of judge, jury, and executioner, feeding their mistress "Madame Guillotine" with an unending supply of bowed heads, mostly those of their former lords, ladies, masters, and mistresses. The streets of Paris ran with the blood of the aristocracy.

Scotland, again according to Devine, "suggested a society with a robust independence of mind and spirit based on the Calvinist inheritance of 'the equality of souls' before God." This liberation manifested itself in a rejection of ecclesiastical patronage, and dissent grew like weeds in stony ground. The church started to lose its iron grip on the manners, mores, and the souls of man.

In addition, the Acts of Union had opened up a vast panorama of possibilities that had never existed before, especially in overseas trade. During Andrew Low's formative years, Scotland was administered by a man named Henry Dundas, the London-based Parliament's "manager" or minister for Scotland. Dundas had also cracked the impenetrable shell of protectionism by being appointed as commissioner of the Board of Control of the monopolistic mercantile East India Company, later becoming its president. This opened up the India, Japan, China, Indonesia, and other Asian markets to hungry Scottish merchants, and they flocked like seagulls over a good catch, grabbing their share. Many a fortune was made as young men flooded into the "Honorable Company," in many cases repatriating their profits to their small slices of the homeland—a different form of local patronage ensued that had no basis in the church. Mammon superseded God.

Probably the most influential radicalization that could have affected Andrew Low's way of thinking and acceptance of societal strictures was that which occurred within the burghs. At that time, particularly in burgh towns of northeast Scotland that he would have been familiar with—Dundee, Aberdeen, Perth, and on a greater level Brechin—the merchant class was the dominant force. It was also corrupt and unresponsive to the needs of the rank-and-file of the common people, and murmurings of dissent began to expand into demand for electoral reform. The notion of man's control over his own destiny started to thrive like mushrooms in a dank cellar.

Devine suggests that "a mood of profound disillusionment" existed amongst the people toward their government on account of the loss of the American colonies. It spilled over into revulsion against authority and rejection of local controls. Although ironically for Scotland, the American Revolution was somewhat of a blessing in disguise, as their own sons and daughters were the bedrock of the rebellion that sundered the ties of colonialism. The loss of the colonial markets, far more devastating to the English traditional mercantile monopolistic status quo, had the opposite effect for Scottish merchants, unhampered by traditional ways of doing things, at least legally.

By 1790 the amount of newspapers available to the grassroots had exploded, creating a surge of accessible information and issues. An author whose work was to have profound influence on the reform-minded hit the mass market. In February 1791 Tom Paine published his immensely significant work titled *The Rights of Man.*[9] Paine's radical manifesto rapidly became a blueprint of reform for the man in the street. These new ideas were revelationary and revolutionary, and the Scots took to the concepts expressed like flocks of grouse rising from a highland moor or a pack of hounds baying after the stag.

Events in later years show that at a very early age Andrew Low was open to influences that expanded his mind and enabled him to go his own way. Perhaps this is not a far stretch, as the innate Scottish character tended to reject the bounds of the conventional—the ground was fertilized for the reception of such ideas by personal experience. If you did not help yourself, no one else was going to do it for you. The death of his father when he was a toddler would by definition have created somewhat of a need for self-reliance. Such a trait readily embraces the rejection of external authority and the acceptance of personal responsibility.

Judging by his choice of occupation, it is more than probable that it was either in Aberdeen or Glasgow that he received his own apprenticeship or exposure to market forces within the textile trade. By the time the young Andrew Low and his brothers were ready to join the labor pool, industrialization had created rapid growth in the population of the towns. This was particularly true in the city of Glasgow, where a vast underbelly of migrant and part-time workers was forced to the margins of society.

The old traditions of agricultural paternalism and clan leadership were buried under the avalanche of urban mercantile realpolitik. The appetite for reform, universal suffrage, and individual rights had been whetted, and in all probability would have had a profound impact on the desire for a young man to start anew in a place where "We the People" had succeeded in changing the rules, allowing a new economic order to emerge. Rather than stay and chip away at the manner in which rules were deeply enshrined, why not move on and make your own way? It is also now that the seeds of a lifetime involvement by the Low family in the cotton industry were sown.

Historian T. C. Smout describes the beginnings of an increasing importance of cotton on both sides of the Atlantic: "The industrial revolution may be compared with the Reformation (of the Church) as an event that stopped and turned the current of man's social life into new and unfamiliar channels: the crucial decades were the 1780's and 1790's. It was then that cotton grew with unparalleled speed from virtually nothing to become by far the greatest industry; it was then the pace of change in agriculture quickened so suddenly as to leave the laggard, and not the improver, as the exception who was laughed at by those who followed the rule."[10]

What is a proven fact is that the period of formation of character in this young boy, growing to manhood, coincided with the greatest social, political, and commercial revolution to occur in Europe and America since the reformation of religious structures a century before.

Voices of the Ancestors

Back in the present, I myself departed the shores of Scotland that time armed with few facts, immense speculation, and enormous respect for those shadowy figures that had become real flesh-and-blood people speaking down the ages. These are people whose genes I carry and have passed on in turn to my own children and grandchildren. Maybe the quest I have embarked upon will help the children make their own way.

The conclusion, based on the scant records available to us, must be that the four older siblings stayed in Scotland, while the four younger brothers moved into external careers, all of them eventually relocating to Savannah, where in one capacity or another they were part of Andrew Low & Company.

Catherine Croll Low managed to bring her entire brood to adulthood well educated and ambitious —no social security, no dole, no benefits, but merely the kindness of a benevolent landlord and the support of family. The eldest, William, father of my great-grandfather Andrew Low, Jr., became a merchant burgess in Brechin, Angus, in 1818. Jean, the only daughter, lived in Stonehaven. David became a tenant in Arduthie, on land belonging to Barclay of Urie. John became a mariner and lived in St. Nicholas, Aberdeen. James also became a sailor, later surfacing in Savannah as master of the "copper bottomed ship *Georgia*." Alexander came to Savannah as partner in the Andrew Low Company, and later married Mary Nicol, uniting two mercantile families in Scotland. George, the youngest, came to Savannah and worked for his brother as partner in Low, Wallace, and Andrew Low, Sr., became the founder of the House of Low.

My discovery of the memorial in the old churchyard in Catterline is a voice from the past. It is Uncle Andrew telling me that he was brought up in that spot and was honoring both his father and mother for the gift of his life and the tenacity and strength he needed to go out into the world. I wish I could show Catherine that tangible proof in the image of the mansion in Savannah, built by her grandson Andrew Jr. who she never knew, so she could compare it with her own life and struggles in that windswept, storm-lashed headland in northeast Scotland. What did she think when she stood, her seven children around her, her baby in her arms, on that day more than two hundred years ago, as she saw her husband's body laid to eternal rest in the dark rich loam of the land, embarking on the ultimate journey.

Our people are of Celtic and Viking descent; death to us is the final lifting of the veil between this world and the next, and they lived their lives every day in full knowledge of the flimsiness of that veil. Even in death the spirit is vulnerable and needs to be guarded against the forces of evil as it crosses the bridge between now and eternity. That is what Andrew Low remembered when in 1836 he memorialized his mother's memory and left his name inscribed on her tombstone for me to find. He was there then for the same reason I am here now—to honor our ancestors—and he has left me the clue that I too shall honor.

She died in 1804 at a relatively young age of fifty-eight, worn out and depleted, but secure in the knowledge that the path on which she had set her children's feet would carry them to the ends of the earth. I dedicate this work to her, my great-great-great-grandmother—great indeed were her deeds.

The twenty-one-year-old Andrew Low departed the shores of his native land in the year 1800. On the eve of his departure from his ancestral homelands, one can imagine the young Andrew standing on the rocky headlands crying in Scarlett O'Hara style, "I'll never be poor again!"

Part II

Savannah and Scotland, 1800–1829

4

The Sign of the Buck, 1800–1811

Throwing the Bones

I have an image in mind of that soft October morning so long ago; of white sensuous birds—egrets—drinking the brackish waters of tidal marshes, reacting to the magnetic pull of the far distant moon in its rise and its fall, its ebb and its flow, going about their everyday task of feeding the family. I see in my mind a beach, sparkling and white, millions of grains of sand, only the grains are not sand, they are tiny bones; each one with a miniscule mark showing exactly where it fits in the overall body. My job is to identify those bones and fit them together, into first the skeleton, and then as that form emerges, seeking the flesh and the vestments, that will slowly develop into the portrait I am seeking—to see the whole by examining the parts—for the most monumental task of all—telling the story to present and future generations. I am content with my task, because I understand that I am not alone, and all I have to do is to listen to the voices; trust the voices of the ancestors, whatever they have to tell me.

THOSE WERE MY THOUGHTS THE FIRST TIME I ARRIVED IN SAVANNAH two hundred years later, to try to discover the truth about events that had unfolded, and place myself in the mindset of an earlier period.

On Sunday, October 12, 1800, a twenty-one-year-old Scot named Andrew Low landed in Charleston, South Carolina, and headed for Savannah. Most of the ships listed that day came from Greenock, Scotland, and one from Liverpool, but the only record available to posterity—his application for naturalization—fails to identify the name of the ship or its port of embarkation.[1] One year later Robert Isaac arrived in Savannah. In his naturalization case file it reads "born, Glasgow, Scotland; Aged about 26 when naturalized in 1806." This would make his birth year 1780, almost exactly the same age as Andrew Low. They were two ambitious young Scots raring to make their mark. A new life, a new world.

Savannah in 1800, although already elegantly laid out in squares, was still relatively insignificant, a wooden southern frontier town snoozing on the banks of a mighty river. It had already sown the seeds that were soon to grow it into a bustling, raucous, wide-open multicultural port, dangerous and seductive, bursting with opportunities for go-getting and energetic men. About fifteen miles separated the port from the open Atlantic at Tybee. Savannah was built on a bluff, surrounded then on two sides by wet, low-lying rice fields in mosquito-plagued marshes, and on the north side by the Savannah River and even more rice fields on the Carolina side. The town was not a healthy place, especially for those Scots used to the bracing cold winds blowing off the North Sea, but most especially for women and children; the concept of sanitation had not yet surfaced, and in the steamy summer heat the streets of Savannah stank with refuse, rotting garbage, and waste of all descriptions. There were approximately twenty-five to thirty deaths every day—men, women, and children.

There are no records indicating why Andrew Low chose Savannah as a destination, but it is logical to believe that the possibilities of growth and wealth had seeped into the awareness of Glasgow and Liverpool mercantile circles. Savannah merchants had already established offices in the city of Liverpool, including Mein & Mein, the firm that Robert Mackay joined in 1798. There are records that prove the name of Low was already a familiar one in Georgia. The first census record show the name of Low scattered throughout the state, especially around Augusta; and the name of Low, many of them master mariners from New England, was well known up and down the eastern seaboard.

A decade before the town had begun to awaken from its somnolence, galvanized by the invention of the cotton gin. Eli Whitney of Connecticut invented this simple and affordable machine while serving as tutor on Revolutionary War hero General Nathanael Greene's plantation Mulberry Grove, one of the great Savannah River plantations. The estate, while initially growing rice in the marshlands that surround it, was also experimenting with cotton. This singular event was to change the economy of the South, fuel the industrial revolution in England, and prolong slavery in America for almost seventy years.[2]

A sidebar of history here lies in the extraordinary coincidence of a very young cornet who had served in the French Comte d'Estaing's forces during the siege of Savannah in 1779 against the British. His name – Henri Christophe of Haiti. He learned his lessons well and by the turn of the century was one of the leaders who steered his own country to freedom through the first and only successful slave rebellion in history.[3] Following the Haitian Revolution, the exodus of white French émigrés from Haiti to

Savannah in the early 1800's greatly inflated the population and shifted the cultural balance. Today they still have their own corner of the Colonial cemetery in Savannah as a monument to their flight.

Snapshot of the Day—Savannah

These are a sample of items in the daily newspapers, as Andrew Low arrived in Savannah: "Negroes for Sale: A Fellow, about 27 years of age, who is a house carpenter and cooper, his wife, a complete house wench, washer and ironer, about 24 years old, and their male child, about 6 years old. A field slave, about 26 years old, his wife, about 25 years old, a good house wench and their female child, about 6 years of age."[4]

Business opportunities abounded, and a great many tax collectors' sales and sheriffs' sales listed land and property, including Negroes, houses, and boats upon which the owners had defaulted in failing to pay their taxes. The Savannah of this period was a growing "entrepot"—perhaps the most multicultural of all cities and ports in the South, with the possible exception of New Orleans and Charleston. Settlers and immigrants came from Ireland, Scotland, Germany, and the West Indies. There was a sizable community of Jews as well, many of who were merchant traders. In addition, the Indian traders, many of them Scots, swelled the ranks and served the needs of the growing city on the river. The names of the merchants reflected diversity. Scottish names include McLeod, McCall, and Mackay. The French were represented by Machin, Monnox, and Drouillard, and the Dutch by Outterlide; Cohen and Sheftall were Jews, and there were many English and Irish names, such as Hunter, Thompson, Wayne, and Watt.

Privateering was rampant on the high seas. The oceanic passage by sailing ship took upwards of seventy days; and by the time news arrived it was already old and, much like today, usually bad. Europe was enmeshed in the Napoleonic Wars, and the newspapers spoke daily of the hatred and contempt felt by Bonaparte toward the British. Germany, France, Denmark, and England were still squabbling. Austria and Russia were having a go at each other. In the United States questions of trade continued to be the preoccupation of the day. America and England, by virtue of treaty, mutually stipulated free entrance into their respective ports, with complete protection to the privateers and ships of war of the two countries, and the prizes taken from their enemies.

My constant fascination with the rhythm of the lists of names and commodities available in the market of nineteenth-century Savannah takes me right back to childhood, and the melodic soprano voices of schoolgirls growing louder and louder as we reach the crescendo of John Masefield's poem "Cargoes." The poem starts with the incredibly exotic:

Quinquireme of Nineveh from distant Ophir
Rowing home to haven from sunny Palestine
With a cargo of ivory,
And apes, and peacocks,
Sandalwood, cedar wood, and sweet white wine.

It ends with the prosaic:

Dirty British coaster with a salt caked smoke stack
Butting through the Channel in the mad March days,
With a cargo of Tyne coal,
Road-rail, pig-lead,
Firewood, ironware, and cheap tin trays.

Every British schoolgirl worth her education can still to this day quote that poem and remember the dreams of adventure it always inspired: far away places with strange sounding names! [5]

The First Brick

Days after his arrival, a young emigrant Scotsman announced to the world in the pages of the *Georgia Gazette*, dated November 5, 1801:

> B. Fleming and Co. Muslin Manufacturers and Calico Printers, GLASGOW. Beg leave to announce to the inhabitants of Savannah, and its vicinity, that they have opened a small store in St Julian Street, nearly opposite Mr. Gibbon's brick building, where they have received, and are exposing for sale, on very low terms, for CASH ONLY; A neat assortment of muslins, consisting of jaconet, book, crepe, lappet, japan, draw-loom, tambor, needlework, mullmull, and fashionable stained muslin.
>
> Signed: ROBERT ISAAC. Agent for B. Fleming and Co. of Glasgow.

The Scottish city of Glasgow was one of the most progressive and prosperous cities of the burgeoning industrial revolution, with emphasis on export trade to the Americas in textiles and shipping. In his recent book *The Scottish Nation,* T. M. Devine states that it was the practice then of giant syndicates to open chains of stores in the colonies, sending out Scottish clerks and factors to buy and sell—the first franchises in America. One of these syndicates, based in Glasgow, was named Spiers Bowman & Co. This announcement certainly indicates that Robert Isaac knew Bowman Fleming & Company, and came out to Savannah specifically to open the store.[6]

Savannah was setting the stage for successful international trade. A city

Church Square (Johnson Square), Savannah, 1840. This view looks east and features the Bank of the State of Georgia (1816), the Nathanael Greene Monument (1830), and Christ Church (1838).
Engraving courtesy Hugh Stiles Golson.

government had been in place for twelve years, and military companies were organized to provide internal and external security. The business district of the town comprised the riverfront of wharves and storehouses, as well as the shops and offices of Johnson and Market (Ellis) Squares. Mansions of the merchants lined the western side of West Broad Street, as well as Broughton Street and Bank (Reynolds) Square. Immigrants and mariners were crowded into the plank-house neighborhood of Yamacraw to the northeast, and the Old Fort neighborhood to the east. Crude tenement rooming houses lined Bay Lane. The town was a contrast of decaying shacks next to elegant examples of Federalist architecture. The streets were sand or mud, depending on rain. Wagons of goods climbed the ramps paved with the cobblestones and bricks brought as ballast in the sailing ships, from the river to the stores around Market Square.[7]

The finest commercial building on this square was the range covering the southeast trust lot, a sophisticated structure built by Mayor Thomas Gibbons which was destroyed in the fire of 1820, but its replacement stands today. To the north of this range, across St. Julian Street, was the Fleming store, later to become A. Low & Company, the Sign of the Buck. This trust lot formerly housed the Calvinist church, Independent Presbyterian, which had built these stores as an investment after their edifice burned in 1796. This would be a logical place for newly arrived Scots to lease out store space.[8]

Six months later, in the *Columbian Museum and Savannah Advertiser* of April 27, 1802, Isaac published another notice stating that: "... the Subscriber being about to leave this place, has sold the remaining stock of goods of B. Fleming and Co. to Mr. A. Low, who is empowered to collect the standing debts, and discharge any accounts that may yet be unsettled by said concern. Robert Isaac, Agent for B. Fleming & Co."

Andrew Low Takes Over

This was how commerce was conducted in Savannah when Andrew Low went into business for himself. Negroes were bought and sold to discharge debts, food and drink was consumed in copious abundance, and lots of bargains appeared in fire sales, tax sales, and sheriff's sales, to satisfy unpaid debts. The pickings for an astute and energetic young businessman were plentiful.

These immigrant Scotsmen were educated men, targeted for trade, and taught the intricacies of keeping the books. Everything was done by hand, the books and ledgers in the countinghouses were paramount, meticulously necessary for keeping track of who owned what and who owed what and to whom; profit and loss were imprinted in their genes. These were not young men destined for military service, the church, or the navy as younger sons; these were not young men set to inherit the family estate. These were those with few prospects, who went out into the world to seek their fortunes, and to do that you were required to acquire a multitude of skills: no specialists need apply.

As the year 1803 waned, a partnership that was to take these two young men into uncharted waters was consummated. On December 14, 1803:

> Andrew Low (Sign of the Bucks Head) Respectfully informs his friends and the public, that he has entered into Co-Partnership with Robert Isaac, and that the business will now be carried on under the firm of Andrew Low & Co. Andrew Low embraces this opportunity to express his gratitude to his numerous friends for past favors, and hopes, that the variety which A. Low & Co. are enabled to keep, with the terms on which they can sell, will ensure a continuance of their custom. Those indebted to A. Low are particularly requested to order a settlement of their accounts; and are at the same time respectfully acquainted, that in order to enable them to sell cheap, A. Low and Co. have determined to deal only for ready Money.

A new and much improved Andrew Low surfaced; the most significant detail, the use of Scottish symbolism in the stag's head; metaphor for the leader, the Monarch of the Glen. This was not the emblem of artisan or trader, farmer or blacksmith, from the lowland country where Andrew Low is purported to have hailed; this was personal: a bold and challenging view of Highland Scottish confidence, denoting supremacy over all others. The red deer was a mark of Scottish pride. In another interesting coincidence, the estate of Fasque in Fettercairn, Scotland, belonging to the Gladstone family—William Gladstone later became Prime Minister of Britain—contained a famous red deer park, and the wild deer also ranged the slopes of the Grampian mountains looming over the Strathmore valley.[9] The village of Fettercairn was where his mother was from, where his oldest brother William Low was living, and where his nephew Andrew would be born. More than anything, the emblem represented the strong sense of self, epitomized by the Scots as a race.

It was also the crest of the Marischal's, Clan Keith of Dunnottar, where Andrew Low, Sr., was born. The Scottish Heirloom Company states that "Clan Keith are one of the most powerful of the ancient Celtic families and held the hereditary title of Great Marischal of Scotland, one of the most prestigious offices of state from the early twelth century. Throughout the history of Scotland, the Keith's are renowned for their fealty to the Crown and their valorous deeds reflect this loyal spirit. The crest of the Clan Keith is a stag's head, and the motto is Veritas Vincit, meaning Truth

Conquers." That was no coincidence. The Stag's Head became the House of Low's signature logo.

The firm was expanding and its owner showed a distinct flair for promotion and market savvy, changing his ads frequently, endorsing his procurement of goods, broadening his reach, becoming bolder, until he commenced ordering and shipping his own consignments instead of purchasing from other consignees.

The Family and Business Expands

George Low arrived in Savannah in January 1803. He was the youngest brother of Andrew Low Sr. and immediately went to work as a clerk in the Andrew Low Company. As early as this the Low family was consolidating their position by placing family members in the firm. These Scots retained an extremely close-knit society, clannish to the extreme, and trusting only kith and kin. On October 8, 1806, another new contender appears in the advertisements: "Co-Partnership. The Subscribers respectfully inform the public, that they have entered into a business, under the firm of Low & Wallace, and now offer for sale, at their Store, (the one formerly occupied by Messrs Burr & Hoyt, and formerly by George Buchanan & Co) the following articles . . . selected for them by the finest Manufacturers in England, Signed: George Low & Norman Wallace."

There are clear signs that Robert Isaac was already the resident Savannah partner, and it was Andrew Low who did the buying and selling in Britain, a pattern they adhered to throughout their partnership. With prescient foresight in a pragmatic preemptive move on August 12, 1806, Robert Isaac became a naturalized citizen of America in Savannah, as did George Low.[10]

Trade Tensions Increase

Free and unfettered exchange of goods was the lifeblood of economic prosperity for the young American nation, nowhere more so than in the Southern states. Merchants with a foot on both continents were buffeted uncontrollably by the constant gales of political change. Transatlantic business commenced to be affected adversely as the guns and dogs of war roared and rumbled between Britain and France, both of whom had considerable colonial trading interests in the adjacent Caribbean region. America patrolled her perimeters trying to look after her own sphere of interest, while flexing her newly independent muscles.

In hindsight, wars tend to start with a single shot, and on June 22, 1807, United States frigate *Chesapeake* was fired upon by British frigate *Leopard* and forced to permit removal of four of the crew claimed to be British deserters. The European "cousins'" fighting-sickness had infected

America, whether it cared to be involved or not. At the beginning of the nineteenth century the boot was on the other foot—when Europe sneezed it was America that caught pneumonia. The American newspapers had started to carry items with a distinctly anti-British feeling, presaging the trade and tariff wars that were forming like storm clouds on the horizon.

While the superpowers squabbled, well aware of signs portending trouble ahead, Andrew Low, Sr., made the decision to put down some roots, perhaps to prove to the authorities that, despite the time he spent in Liverpool, he also resided in Savannah. Thereby he avoided any potential nationality problems.

On July 7, 1807, the Savannah newspaper carried an item stating that certain persons had applied to become United States citizens, their declarations admitted by the Inferior Court for the County of Chatham. Andrew Low was on that list. He had decided his financial fortunes lay with America, and was not about to be penalized by his British status. This was a pragmatic decision. The thirteen applicants that day included Andrew Low, Alexander Hunter, and John Hunter. Low was proved correct when Britain seized naturalized U.S. citizens as part of their war strategy.

By Christmas 1807 a small announcement stated that on December 21 the ship *Perseverance* had landed in Charleston from Liverpool, and the captain informed the authorities that on the day he left, being November 13, a proclamation was issued by the British government declaring, "All enemies Ports in a State of Blockade." The British blockade was in retaliation for Napoleon Bonaparte's decree that "All Vessells and Cargoes bound to or from any of the British Ports are good and lawful prizes. All British manufacturers or produce to whomsoever it belongs or wherever bound, are lawful prizes." The U.S. Congress passed the isolationist Embargo Act on December 22, 1807, prohibiting virtually all commerce with foreign countries. It had become extremely evident that being a British citizen in America was a dangerous condition.

This fallout from the Napoleonic War between France and England was to have a serious effect on trade in America from the Southern coastal ports, particularly Savannah and Charleston, and all the way up the east coast, to New England and Canada. The effect was to cause the United States, several years later, to undergo its first real foreign policy decision since independence, and to finally sever the umbilical cord between infant and mother.

Andrew Low took action to protect his Savannah business, and on April Fool's Day, 1808, the following notice appears in the Savannah papers: "The Co-Partnership existing between Mr. Bowman Fleming of the City of Glasgow, and Andrew Low and Robert Isaac of this City (Savannah) under the firm of Andrew Low & Co, will expire by its own limitations on the first day of April, 1808. Those having demands upon the concern are required to render in their accounts to Andrew Low and Robert Isaac, who will carry on the business, after the above date, under the firm of Andrew Low & Co."

On that day, the two Scotsmen, now in their prime of energy and creativity, cut their own umbilical cord, and sailed under their own steam. By the end of the month the new partnership is offering at "far below cost a number of articles which are rather unfashionable—for Cash, Cotton, or good acceptance in town"—an excellent example of prevailing "going out of business—everything must go" marketing strategies employed effectively to move goods that are out of date or fashion. The House of Low once again was ahead of the curve.

Perhaps they felt that their suppliers in far off Glasgow did not understand the changing requirements of a fashion-conscious, socially mobile society forming in the steamy South, where a significantly different milieu was developing. It was partly to do with the vagaries of climate, but also because of the diverse and disparate elements that infused this gumbo mix. What is far more likely is that through their transatlantic connections in Liverpool and Glasgow, they saw how the burgeoning textile manufacturing sector of the north of England was changing. This change was caused by the shift in the manufacture of fabric, from wool to cotton. They had the vision to see that branching out into the export of the raw cotton grown in the South would be highly advantageous. Cotton factoring was on the way in, clothing on the way out.

There is no indication that Andrew ever owned a home in Savannah, although he did procure furniture and several slaves—two young females—which suggests he kept "rooms" in the English fashion, above the store. The Recorders Office also shows a purchase: "from Teresa Pine, milliner, to Andrew Low and Company, merchants; for $100:00 . . . one mahogany bedstead, feather bed, mattress, bolster, pillow and bedclothes, one mahogany tea table, six Windsor chairs, 1 pair brass fire dogs, 2 pairs plated candlesticks, one room carpet, six tablespoons and seven teaspoons, 1 pair sugar tongs, 1 pair salt spoons (silver) and two waiters (silver)."[11]

At the very least he planned on sleeping in his own bed and doing a spot of entertaining.

Slave labor provided the economic foundation of plantation life in Georgia in the early 1800's with rice, indigo, and cotton being the staple crops. In the cities slaves provided domestic labor and performed the heavy work of loading the ships for the river commerce. Andrew Low, steeped in the feudal sensibilities of his youth in Scotland at the turn of the eighteenth century, would have had no moral compunction or qualms about the institution of slavery. Although the landowners of Scotland did not own labor as chattel slaves, certainly many tenants lived at the whim of their landlords, as witnessed graphically by the massive Highland Clearances that led to waves of emigration to America.[12]

Two years later the firm took into copartnership another brother, Alexander Low, along with a James McHenry. A small notice, first seen June 18, 1810, appeared in an inside page, signed by Isaac and Low. It had been assumed, that because the notice of copartnership was first seen in 1810, that this was the year the older Low brother joined the firm.

In fact, in 1808, a notice of his membership in the Chatham Artillery shows up in the records, and both he and his brother's firm were delinquent in paying their taxes for 1807. So it is probable that Alexander was being groomed all along for service in the firm. There is no indication that he ever took out naturalization papers.

Expansion and Marriage

As the newspaper ads change, so it is possible to follow the progress of the growing firm. Trade restrictions, due to the imminent conflict between America and Britain, would have hampered rapid progress, but despite the brewing war—or perhaps because of it—Andrew Low was positioning himself for expansion. In his boldest move to date, Andrew Low bought Town Lot No. 1 of Frederick Tything, Derby Ward, which was on Johnson Square at the southwest corner, a highly desirable piece of property, central to Savannah's commercial district, and convenient to the waterfront area.[13] Here the Low firm would remain for the next sixty years. With stores on the street level, the upper floors probably housed the extended Low family. Andrew Low, astute as he was, must have worried about the effect the distant shock waves of European muscle-flexing would have on his own business.

On February 20, 1811, Robert Isaac put down more permanent roots when he married Lucy, sister of William Scarbrough of the firm Scarbrough & Taylor, in the Independent Presbyterian Church of Scotland in Savannah.[14] This was a consolidation of one of the older mercantile firms and one of the newer ones. In terms of social rules of the day, the paramount insight this marriage affords us is that the Glasgow-born partner in Andrew Low & Company was considered eminently suited for marriage into the family of one of Savannah's most prominent merchants and social arbiters. From that time on the fortunes of the two families were inextricably entwined.

By August 1811 their brand new brick-built store was ready for business. Located on fashionable Johnson Square, the center of the merchant trade and adjacent to City Exchange, the countinghouses of Bay Street, and the mansions sprouting on Broughton Street, it was impeccably

Johnson Square, looking south, 1890's. Andrew Low & Company occupied the building across the square, to the right of the shaft of the monument, after 1808. Two prominent hotels, the Screven House, left rear, and the Pulaski House, right center, still stand. *Stereo card courtesy Hugh Stiles Golson.*

situated. A notice states: "The Sign of the Stag, respectfully inform their friends and the public, that they have removed from Gibbon's building to their new store, south side of Johnson's Square, where they are opening a very extensive assortment of Fall and Winter Goods."[15]

Tensions Smolder

Savannah in 1811 was still very much a village that was both a frontier crossroad and a rowdy sailor's port. The population of five thousand was half white and half African and mixed blood. Only about a quarter of the white population was born there. The remainder came either from other parts of Georgia or regions of the United States, and the last quarter was born externally, Great Britain and France being the dominant origin.[16]

The business of Savannah was trade, and all other politics were secondary to the pursuit of profit. Profit still included trade from the various Creek tribes to the south and west, mostly in leather goods. The bulk and volume of trade then was rice, for in the last fifty years the entire Savannah and Ogeechee River estuaries had been cleared and gridded with canals and dykes for the cultivation of rice. The large African population was an outgrowth of this economy: West Africans knew how to produce rice, particularly those who hailed from Sierra Leone. A steady slave trade out of Carolina, the West Indies, and West Africa brought the labor in at the right price. The upper islands of the Savannah River—Hutchinson, Onslow, Argyle, and Isla—held the most profitable plantations. Each was a few hundred acres of wetland with a settlement of rice mill, overseer's house, and slave cabins. Thousands of Africans were bound to this small, wet world with little connection to the outside world.[17]

The port of Savannah was seeing an increase in its tonnage. Into the port came cargoes of finished goods from Europe and from the North. Cargoes of fruits from the tropics joined spices from Asia and rum from the islands, but the human cargoes dried up after 1808.[18]

Although Savannah was still a wooden town on its sandy bluff, it already featured examples of outstanding architecture. The City Exchange, Savannah's largest building, commanded the riverfront with its four-story prominence that rose from below the bluff to three stories over Bay Street. A massive hip roof was crowned with a steeple from which the city's watchmen called out the hour or rang the fire bell. The building was of scored stucco over native brick. Leading merchants built it as a venture, but the city government slowly bought up its stock to make the Exchange its city hall. That year the U.S. Customs and Post Office leased the basement and city government occupied the two floors over Bay. The second floor contained the Long Room, used for council meetings and public gatherings, and the mayor's office. The fourth floor was a series of rooms leased out to organizations such as the new Library Society and several militia units.

The riverfront also housed the stores and countinghouses of the merchants. Stone and brick buildings lined the base of the bluff, and gabled shake roofs stood on buildings one and two stories high. Many of today's Factor's Walk buildings can trace the origins of their lowest floors to this era. The eastern bluff along Bay Street was The Strand, a parade ground and public recreation area. The western bluff was given to commerce, the open area crowded with carts and wagons during business hours. The high bluff had no stone embankment to hold back the caving sands, and the north-south streets of the village ramped down to the waterfront with ballast and plank paving. Here at the foot of these streets were the sites of the public wharfs, with the private docks of the merchant companies found in front of their sheds and stores.[19]

In Savannah the terms of the blockade decree were published, showing that it included "neutrals" also. Smuggling was rife, plunder and piracy on the high seas the order of the day. The merchants of Savannah were in no mood to just lie down and play dead. Frustration was rampant. Free trade through the eastern seaboard ports of the United States was the arterial blood of commerce. Conditions were ripe to take matters into one's own hands in what was still a frontier society, a long way from passively taking orders from a remote government in far off Washington.

The embers were smoldering and the stage was set for what was to come.

5

The War of 1812: England and America, 1812–1818

Two French privateers docked in Savannah in the summer of 1811 for emergency refitting. The privateer crews proved restless in the restricted environment, and on November 14 broke into street fighting with crews of two American merchant ships, killing sailors on both sides. A rowdy sailors' brawl in the village of Savannah promised to derail complex international diplomacy.

The clashes occurred in Yamacraw Ward, a dense and crowded neighborhood of narrow streets and frame structures of all styles. Old Yamacraw's waterfront stretched from West Broad to Musgrove Creek, extending the capacity of the Savannah harbor. Yamacraw's principal arteries were the parallel diagonals, Indian Street and Mill Street. A narrow lane ran between Indian and Mill, and numerous cul-de-sacs and narrow side streets serviced a maze of structures and a diverse humanity not seen in some wards of the Oglethorpe plan.[1]

This was a ward of laborers and tradesmen, of the Reverend Andrew Bryan's African Baptist Church on Mill Street within the shadow of the tall Clay-Stiles residence. Many languages could be heard, from French and Spanish to Ibo, Dutch, and German. Freed slaves and mixed-bloods lived among Irishmen and Frenchmen. Runaway slaves frequently hid out among this diversity. In this rambunctious neighborhood, the city authorities frequently winked at violations of the curfew, liquor, gambling, and prostitution ordinances. Here the transplants of many lands catered to the tars and matelots, with shops, dance halls, and taverns and, of course, brothels. This was a world quite different from the ostensibly sober merchants on their squares.

The 1788 Charter for the City of Savannah called for aldermen elected from every ward. When this board first met they chose one from their number to serve as mayor for a one-year term.[2] Property, gender, and race qualifications for voters limited participation and favored the merchant class to hold civil authority. The mayor and aldermen directly managed the workings of the town from the criminal justice system to sanitation, from roads to building standards, from the market to the burial grounds.

The criminal justice system started with the "night watch," able-bodied men who were deputized and armed with lanterns, clubs, knives, and pistols. They roamed the town under the supervision of constables, searching for curfew violators and any criminal activity. Galloping through the streets was a common violation cited. Suspects that they apprehended were taken to their lockup off Courthouse Square, and the mayor sat as a court the following morning to dispense justice. Incarceration sentences were served at the jail on the south Commons. Savannah's applicable ordinances were simple and direct: a 9:00 p.m. curfew targeted slaves and free Africans as well as sailors who were expected to sleep on their ships. Citizens could be fined for entertaining sailors or Negroes after hours.[3] The homeless reported to seamen's bethels, missions, and the Savannah Poorhouse, where rotating clergymen preached their lost souls to sleep. The Poorhouse was on the grounds of the new Savannah Hospital on the Commons beyond the jail. In case of civil strife the mayor could call out the militia units to provide what muscle he may need.

Savannah's wealthy elite were syndicates of merchants, and the professionals who expedited their business ventures. Most of these trading houses had established ties with British-flagged merchant ships, and their operatives in Britain were partners or relatives. The proprietors of many of Savannah's top merchant houses were Scottish or English born. They were part of a network of relationships built on blood and loyal service. Work was a series of ledger entries where the art of the deal with friend and foe promised to bring in the big rewards. Most of these merchants were diversified into rice holdings and speculation in timberlands to the south. The Scots in particular had fought for their right to trade throughout the British Empire and outside, and they proved tenacious in their determination to maintain that right.

Based on the trade of companies such as Andrew Low & Co., the politics of the merchants would be Federalist and pro-British. A steady migration of northerners to Savannah only strengthened this position. The loyalty was to commerce, not any political party. This was typical of the earlier support in Savannah for the adoption of the Constitution, while inland Georgia rejected its pro-commerce leanings. U.S. foreign policy between 1801 and 1811 was a roller-coaster ride for American commerce.

France had cashed in her American empire in 1803, following her abandonment of Haiti. In 1805 Britain's Lord Nelson broke Napoleon's navy at

Trafalgar. The French emperor cut his losses on the high seas to build the Grand Army for control of the continent. Then the crafty Bonaparte unleashed an annoying Atlantic impediment with his Berlin and Milan decrees; French privateers could capture British cargoes, as well as cargoes of any neutral nation supplying Britain. This targeted the U.S.—its largest trade partner was Britain. France was the second largest trade partner.

Although Britain and the U.S. enjoyed strong trade, old issues still lingered. The old problem of the violent press-gangs was now played out on the high seas. The Royal Navy, always short on sailors because of strict discipline and poor pay, regularly stopped American-flagged vessels and kidnapped sailors to fill their personnel needs. Another aggravation came from the British presence in Canada. Western settlers were reporting that agents from Canada financed the hostility of the northwestern tribes. Nationalistic Americans were seizing an initiative by calling for the conquest of Canada. President Thomas Jefferson, always the theoretician and experimenter, took a novel and idealistic approach to the problem. He ordered an embargo on all U.S. trade. He theorized that the embargo would stimulate domestic commerce, and lead the nation to economic self-sufficiency. His "Dambargo" drove the nation into depression and left many bitter feelings toward the founding father in his political twilight.

James Madison's ascendancy to the presidency saw the banishment of the "Ograbme," as the self-imposed blockade was ridiculed in reverse by the new administration. The replacement bill ushered through Congress was the Non Intercourse Act of 1809, opening trade to all nations, save Britain and France. This badly designed legislation only succeeded in placing America's merchant fleet at the mercy of the feuding Europeans. In 1810 Congress replaced this law with Macon's Bill No. 2. The new law opened trade with whichever belligerent dropped its attacks on American shippers. Napoleon took the initiative and President Madison accepted it in November of 1810. Now the U.S. would impose nonimportation against Britain. By November 1811 President Madison and Secretary of State James Monroe knew that there would be an unavoidable war with Britain, and Bonaparte would have to be courted. It was time to reignite the passions of the Alliance with France that won America's revolution. The administration in Washington certainly wanted no incidents with the French.[4]

Trading became an adventure in evading the British naval ships for fear of boardings for impressments, and avoiding the French privateers who seized cargoes and stole stores of vital supplies. Flagging of the merchant fleet was an important consideration, for the Stars and Stripes attracted the predators. The Embargo of 1807 was intended to halt America's Atlantic trade, but the sorry state of the U.S. Navy allowed for blatant smuggling. The Non Intercourse Act revived the Atlantic trade, but for the syndicate that meant shipping English-bound goods through a neutral port. French privateers feasted during the short tenure of this law that lasted until November 1810. All of this changed with Bonaparte's acquiescence to Macon's Bill No. 2. Now the French were friends and trade partners and Britain was embargoed.

The syndicate in Savannah would have felt the sting of French thievery and defined their foe. Now the cursed French privateers were free to dock in the syndicate's homeport! Savannah had a legacy of trouble with French privateers. In the 1790's the frequency and number of these lawless ships who used Savannah as a rendezvous was increasing, and the local constabulary was overwhelmed and could not contain marauding armed gangs of French mariners. When the city marshall was threatened and a constable nearly killed, the night guard and watch were created. Then curfew laws were passed by City Council to tighten up on security and order.

The Merchants' Revolt

By 1811 conditions were ripe for trouble and it arrived with a vengeance. Whether the Savannah merchants were frustrated by the loss of trade, or whether the French privateers merely presented a visible target, the merchants took matters into their own hands. Perhaps they felt that acts of piracy committed in the West Indies did not permit the privateers to take refuge in neutral waters. Maybe they vented their anger on a target they thought they could not be held accountable for destroying. Maybe such an act could put a stop to the endemic smuggling created by the embargo, which was seriously hurting their legitimate business. Illegal activities were rife, and perhaps they merely wished to return to normal trade and transatlantic commerce that they all understood and could control. Whatever the trigger, the situation exploded into violence.[5]

The incident concerned the burning of the French privateers *La Vengeance* and *La Franchise* and consequent murder of members of the crew in November 1811; in the forefront of the outrage were brothers Andrew, Alexander, and George Low, as well as the local militia. This was an event that almost caused an international incident.

This dramatic affair represents one of the most revealing insights into Andrew Low, Sr.'s character in the records, as well as pointing to the strong family and colleague loyalty that existed amongst the merchant community of Savannah. These actions show how these Scots had no qualms about taking charge of events when pushed too far, and had little regard for the law, or patience with diplomacy. The newspapers carried heavy coverage, including the protests made by the French consul—an exciting and sensational story going way beyond romanticism, involving killing, destruction of property, and total flouting of international convention.

November 15th saw an organized march of sailors from two American brigs break into a riverfront riot that consisted of snipers, stabbings, cuttings, and bludgeoning, the removal of the French flag and its replacement by an American standard. One French privateer vessel was burned to the waterline before the mayor and militia restored peace and seized the second vessel. That day somewhere between four and eight people were murdered—the numbers vary according to accounts, but the burial registry lists only two French sailors and two American sailors. They ranged from eighteen to twenty-nine years of age. The cause of death for all four is officially "murder by persons unknown." The mayor ordered the arrest and detention of all remaining French crew and jailed them. Later that night the second vessel burned.

Newspapers in those days were the only real source of news and information and reprinted with impunity accounts of events from other national and international publications. Both the *Columbian Museum and Advertiser* and the *Republican and Savannah Evening Ledger* reported the incident in all its gory and glorious detail.[6] The French claimed the incident involved an unparalleled outrage committed against the flag of his imperial and royal majesty.

The hyperbolic account in the newspapers represented the French position. The syndicates stood accused! However, the syndicates were Savannah's economy, and Savannah would not give up her own. Savannah's position was markedly different. In direct contradiction of the French claim that these gentlemen were present, armed, encouraging and participating, each one had an alibi sworn to by a prominent citizen that this charge was a calumny. Naturally, the denials came thick and fast with each member of the accused providing a signed alibi affidavit, witnessing their whereabouts as to being somewhere else. Whichever or whatever was the actual truth, the story shows the degree of feeling running as high as the flames of war. This is an extraordinary tale, showing as it does the character of these men, perfectly willing to take whatever action they deemed necessary, and then stick together like sticky spurs to a pants leg in the aftermath.

Richard M. Stites, Capt. Chatham Artillery, provided Alexander Low's alibi:

> I do hereby certify, that Alexander Low, of the firm of Andrew Low & Co and George Low of the firm of Low & Wallace of Savannah, merchants, are members of the Chatham Artillery, under my command, and that on the afternoon of the 15th November last, they were on duty with me from the time of the alarm, between 3 and 4 pm until early the next morning; that their conduct during all

that time was orderly and exemplary; that at the sound of the alarm, the company met at the Laboratory, and from thence proceeded to the Bluff with their cannon, where they remained until dark, ready to obey the civil authority, the mayor being present; that not a man belonging to the said company was on board either of the French privateers, during that day, and to my knowledge the said Alex Low and George Low had no participation directly or indirectly in burning the said vessels, as was maliciously insinuated by a publication in the Aurora. Savannah 23rd December, Richard M. Stites, Capt. Chatham Artillery.

James Hunter, Lieut. Commanding, provides Andrew Low's alibi:

I do hereby certify that on the 15th November last, Andrew Low did appear on the Parade Ground of the Chatham Rangers on the drum beating to arms, between the hours of three and four o'clock in the afternoon; and that he remained under my command until about seven o'clock, when the Company was dismissed until nine o'clock, and at that hour he again appeared, and remained under my command for a considerable time after the La Vengeance privateer was on fire, and to the best of my knowledge and belief he was not engaged directly or indirectly in burning either of the privateers. James Hunter, Lieutenant Commanding, Savannah, 23rd inst, December 1811.[7]

During this fracas Robert Isaac, the more sober member of the team, seems to have been blameless, diligently and quietly doing his civic duty.

French pressure on the Madison government brought a promise by City Council to investigate and ask for indictments for the stabbing death of Cherry Chatuc, captain-at-arms of *La Franchise*, whose body was found on the bluff Saturday morning, November 16. The investigation deteriorated into a public meeting, which became sentimentally patriotic. The local leadership ranted about the importance of law and order, and they emphasized that the French pirates regularly challenged the curfew and threatened the night watch, and even the mayor. The American mariners were buried with honors from the Exchange. The French government recalled Mess. Le Marvis, its consul in Savannah, and demanded that the Madison government investigate and punish. City Council released the French prisoners, and promised a full investigation that conveniently dragged out until the advent of war in June of 1812. All locals accused of instigating the riot appeared in court with sworn affidavits that they were elsewhere. End of case.

This incident portrays fascinating aspects of the character of the participants. This was no schoolboy prank; this was murder and mayhem, and there is no record indicating any remorse. It was back to business as usual. Andrew Low & Co was on their way to building the biggest Emporium of Dry Goods the city of Savannah had seen. They were established and thriving. Then real disaster struck in the guise of war.

And in another place, on July 20th, 1812, a child came on the scene; a boy child, named Andrew, was born to William Low, Father, Katherine Reid, Mother, in Fettercairn, Kincardineshire, Scotland. The heir to the empire had arrived.[8]

The Trade and Tariff War, 1812–1815

A less competent administrative system seldom drifted, by reason of its incompetence, into war with a superior enemy.

—Henry Adams' biography of President James Madison

According to conventional wisdom, the war had three causes: Britain seized U.S. ships trading with France; Britain seized four thousand naturalized U.S. sailors; and Britain armed Indians who raided western borders. Although trade with Britain was not stopped until 1810, these trade wars would have a profound impact on the commercial health of the embryo colony of Georgia, especially the river port of Savannah, and most especially with those traders, like the Low Company, who specialized in trading with England and Scotland.

The sea was a most dangerous place to be on during those times, with privateers and plunderers of all stripes prowling the passages, marauding the waters. Rewards were offered every day for deserting militiamen. By June 18, 1812, America had had enough. Tired of being pushed around, the national honor of the new nation impugned, the Congress and President of the United States declared war on Britain, and for two years the battles raged all along the Eastern seaboard and on the high seas. The impact of the blockade of the seacoast and the seizing of ships on the merchants of Savannah was devastating.

The action in this little-remembered war, that perhaps more than any other sticks in the minds and craw of American citizens, was that the amphibious British force landed on the shores of Chesapeake Bay, advanced on and burned public buildings in Washington, D.C. This destroyed the fruits of three population census statistics, including those of Georgia. The Library of Congress and the National Archives went up in smoke, and valuable colonial records were lost. The advance was repulsed at Baltimore and it was here that Francis Scott Key composed the "Star Spangled Banner."[9]

The closest the war came to Georgia was when Royal Marines, under Admiral Sir George Cockburn, seized Cumberland Island and St. Mary's in January of 1815. Cockburn had ordered the burning of the District of Columbia during the previous year, and Savannah awaited attack. Simultaneously, the British Army under General Sir Edward Pakenham landed near the mouth of the Mississippi River. On January 8, 1815, they were defeated with heavy losses in the Battle of New Orleans by defenders under Major General Andrew Jackson, a good career move for him as he later parlayed his military reputation into the presidency. Before the war ended, most U.S. naval ships were captured or shut up in port, and the commercial blockade of the American coast was complete.

The conflict created unintended consequences for British immigrants doing business in the United States, as through no fault of their own they suddenly found themselves cast in the role of "enemy alien." Foresight of this potential calamity proved to be twenty/twenty vision for Andrew Low, his brother George and the Hunters for declaring their intention to become American citizens as they had done in 1807. Certainly there is no proof that Andrew Low did so out of burning sense of patriotism, for it appears to have been a purely logical business decision, thereby avoiding arrest and confinement during the unwanted, unnecessary, and inconvenient conflict.

The book compiled by Kenneth Scott documenting British Aliens in the U.S. during the War of 1812 outlines the conditions that had to be endured. He writes:

> On June 1, 1812, President Madison sent his war message to Congress, which on June 18 declared war. Subjects of Great Britain were henceforth enemy aliens and were to be dealt with in accordance with an Act of July 6, 1798, and a supplementary Act of July 6, 1812. Accordingly notice was promptly given that all British subjects in the United States were to report to a marshal of the state or territory of their residence ... the persons composing their families, the places of their residence and their occupations or pursuits, and whether, and at what time, they have made application to the courts as required by law, as preparatory to their naturalization.[10]

It was ordered that the notice to be published in the newspapers and that reports by the aliens were to be sent to the Department of State.

The war was a disaster for everyone and did not last too long, but for its duration the name of Low disappeared from public records. No more advertisements and their names virtually absent in the newspaper indexes. The river pilot John Low, no relation,[11] shows up in the Savannah records as being a "British Alien," but the others, with the exception of Alexander Low, were already naturalized, rendering them safe from incarceration. The probability is that Andrew, James, and Alexander Low spent the war years building connections in Liverpool and Scotland. Having by now a good indication of the energy and pragmatism of the Low family, it is hard to believe they just sat out the war, but there are no real records of that period to speculate.

The entire war lasted only two years, but it caused widespread economic disaster for the mercantile trade. Business sputtered to a virtual standstill in Savannah, with all goods going in or out either embargoed or seized. War at sea was a profitable business if you were winning, or controlled the shipping lanes, but while the powers-that-be were negotiating a face-saving retreat, it was almost total economic disaster for everyone else. The damage to trade was so enormous that it managed to bring everyone to their collective senses.

The major psychological impact of the War of 1812 is that it marked the end of a period of American dependency on Europe and gave stimulus to a new sense of nationality in the young America. It could also be seen as the launching pad for the "special relationship" with Britain that survives to this day.

Back in Business, 1814

By the end of November 1814, in Savannah signs of renewed commercial activity started to appear in the newspapers: Mrs. Pine announced that she had received a "Fresh assortment of Elegant Toys, including Dolls, Swords, Fifes, Sham Fights, Cannons and Soldiers, Tea Setts and Country Houses," and that "a few gentlemen can be accommodated with board." Miss Ester Sheftall in her emporium on Broughton Street offered solace to the ladies with hats and bonnets and elegant white Levantine silk, and the Planters Bank announced a small dividend and new elections for directors to be held January 24 next. New schools were opened and the principal of the Chatham Academy returned with his family to permanent residence and to superintend the academy.

By mid-December, news of the ongoing negotiations for peace spotted the evening newspapers, many of the sticking points concerned with the British propensity for fomenting dissention amongst the Indians of the Northern territories of the Canadian border lands. These burrs lie like seed pods amongst the scarlet blooms of war stories, exploding into profusion in their telling. Soon it was all over, the shouting and the shooting ceased just in time for Christmas. The Peace Treaty, negotiated in Ghent, Belgium, was finally signed December 24, 1814: like all wars one wonders why it started in the first place, with some winners, some losers. The signed treaty received full approval by the Senate in February 16, 1815, to popular acclaim, heading off a potential secessionist movement from New England.

Two weeks after the end of the war, Andrew Low's familiar Sign of the Buck reappeared, a little lopsided and somewhat coarser than before, with only twelve prongs instead of thirteen, but boldly pronouncing that he was a winner, definitely a survivor. "White and Blue Plains of a superior quality. Fine Broadcloth and Cheap French Laces, Coarse and fine white Flannels"—Andrew Low & Co. was back in business, and the little ship icons sailed back onto the pages once more. Savannah's lifeline had been restored.

The dogs of war were on their leashes, and the sharks could swim with the dolphins again. The world was in rags and riches were required. Everyone advertised "peace prices" and famous battles were hashed, rehashed, and totally trashed, in the coffeehouses and taverns of an exuberant city aching to get back into the thick of the commercial fray and the social whirl. America retrieved her honor and got on with the proper business of life, that of making money.

The passages were alive with the clinking of the countinghouses and cotton flowed in an endless skein across the Atlantic, filling the holds of ships of all nations, and Andrew Low's sights were set on his next target. He was one of the first merchants to recognize the future value of the cotton trade and capitalized upon that vision as soon as peace was declared. Shipping was coming and going at increased rates and every day another ship, a prize, a wreck, a forfeiture of war, was on the auction block, and Andrew Low & Co. it appeared had acquired the copper bottomed *Lucy* as well as the *Georgia*. Partnerships were dissolved and cemented; the minuet of winners and losers danced on the wharves and riverfront of Savannah. Patriotism and piety were running a close race. By the end of the year, Napoleon had given himself up as a prisoner of war, and the screams were to castrate the French poodle once and for all. The bulldog and the poodle were still yapping and barking at each other in a cacophonous din.

In Savannah, at the end of the War of 1812, the Andrew Low Company changed radically, switching from a focus on the retail end of the business of dry goods in their own store, to cotton factoring. This consisted of buying raw material in Savannah and middle Georgia and selling to the hungry mills of the north of England—as well as supplying whatever goods were required by the American merchants and planters who were enjoying a recovering economy. The Andrew Low Company now firmly established their foothold in the major industrial city of Liverpool in Great Britain.

The partnership between Andrew Low and Robert Isaac was to bring them wealth and prestige, adventures and tragedies, driven by ambition, blessed with vision. Whatever driving force brought them from Scotland to the river port plantation city of Savannah, took them now to the industrial and slave port of Liverpool in England, linking two cities, that on the tapestry of history are woven some of the most amazing achievements and dreadful accomplishments of the nineteenth century. They would take their place in the pantheon of merchant princes, the forerunners of the robber barons who made vast fortunes in the heyday of American expansionism in the nineteenth century and laid the foundations of twenty-first-century America's wealth, power, and prestige.

6

The Burgher's Son: Scotland to Liverpool, 1812–1818

On a cool October morning, after the summer's hot and humid air had receded for another season, I stood under the live oak trees in Lafayette Square in the old evocative city of Savannah, gazing at the elegant mansion that Andrew Low, Jr., had built, the barbed hooks of history piercing my flesh. The square was not one of the original squares designed by Oglethorpe, but had been laid out in 1837 and named after the Marquis de Lafayette, French hero of the American Revolution.

At that time, I knew none of the details that have led to this point in my quest to unravel the tangled skeins of misinformation surrounding Andrew Low's birth and early years. I had not yet traveled to Scotland to dig in dusty archives in search of the truth. I was about to enter the house, now a museum, for the first time. I was about to introduce myself to my own great-grandfather. I was not yet obsessed, but I was hooked.

The conventional wisdom in Savannah, for years, has had Andrew Low, Jr.'s father as John Low, born 1783, died 1876.[1] The result of this egregious error is that John Low is mentioned in most published sources as Andrew Low's father. This fact is wrong.[2]

The initial error has resulted in several books being written attributing the wrong parent and wrong birth year to Andrew Low, Jr. Examples include an entry in the International Genealogical Index from a patron submission form,[3] and numerous references in various Georgia Historical Society files from other genealogists and student researchers; all of them based on acceptance of the accuracy of the original assumption. It is essential now for our full understanding to introduce the protagonists that enter the timeline at this point, and map out the motives, influences, and unintended consequences that move our story forward. Armed with some speculative notes from other family members, I traveled back to Scotland to attempt to unravel the mystery.[4]

What I discovered literally revolutionized the existing history in America. Researchers and family historians all recognize the sheer euphoria that comes from one of those breakthrough moments. After hours of tediously poring over microfilm, indecipherable ancient registers, and lists of facts in myriad published books, trying to connect the dots—it happened. At exactly 4:59 p.m., one minute before the bell rang for closing, in the basement of the Aberdeen Family History Center, ignoring the "Silence" rule, I let out a shriek of joy! I had found the missing link. All the folks present smiled sympathetically—they had been there themselves. I was on the right path at last.

The connection was crystal clear—we had always known that Andrew Low, Jr., was the nephew of Andrew Low, Sr., founder of the House of Low in Savannah, Georgia, but now we also knew who his rightful father and mother were.

William Low—Katherine Reid—Parents

William Low, born 1767 in Dunnottar,[5] was first-born son of James Low, born 1732 in Crawton, and Catherine Croll of Fettercairn. The Old Parish Records show that William Low's spouse, Katherine Reid, was also born in Dunnottar in 1771. Andrew Low, Jr., my great-grandfather, was their youngest son.[6]

The absolute proof of Andrew Low's parentage is to be found in *The Services to Heirs,* or as the original volumes were called, *Inquisitionum ad Capellam Regis Retornatarum Abbreviato.* The document is a petition filed in 1858 of "Andrew Low of Liverpool, formerly of Savannah, sole surviving son of William Low, merchant of Brechin" to attest to that relationship for inheritance purposes after William Low died *intestate* (without a will) in February 1849.[7] His mother, Katherine Reid, died in Brechin, Scotland, in 1857, and it was following that event that the petition was filed.

By 1800 the family appears to have moved to Fettercairn, an adjoining town and parish. Fettercairn was the ancient capital of Kincardine before it was moved to Stonehaven in the late 1600's. It was a market town about ten miles from Brechin, the Royal Burgh City of Angus, in the neighboring county. The name of Reid was well known in Fettercairn, as James Reid became the first Protestant minister for the parish after the Reformation. The name Reid is a long and distinguished one including many ministers of the church; Alexander, physician to Charles I; Thomas, Greek and Latin secretary to James VI; and Thomas, the famous moral philosopher. Whether or not the mother of Andrew Low, Jr., was descended from the more famous names or from the extended family of Reid servants is unknown, but even carrying a famous parish name in the eighteenth century would confer a certain moral responsibility and even superiority regarding status and behavior.

There is no record of their actual marriage in any of the Old Parish Records; however, the births of all five of their children are registered in Fettercairn. William and Katherine had five children: James, born 1802; Jane, 1804; William, 1806; Mary, 1808, and Andrew, 1812.

The second birth records Katherine Reid as the spouse; the first does not. That is not unusual in family records as it cost money to record a marriage, and times were very hard at the turn of the century. Mandatory civil registration did not come into effect in Scotland until 1855; many marriages remained unrecorded. In light of social conventions, though, it would have been unusual for them not to marry. Andrew Low, Jr.'s birth record shows he was born in "Forewoodside," Fettercairn, Kincardineshire, on July 20, 1812, as was the first son; the three middle siblings were born at "Braeside." These could be names of a farm, croft, house, or area. Today there is a development called Braeside on the road to Edzell and Brechin.

The Merchant Venturers of Liverpool

Reconstructing history can be likened to forensic science at a crime scene. The clues scattered around are rarely connected. The face of the past starts with the skull a scientist painstakingly fleshes out around bare bones. One eminent historian has written that "revising interpretations of the past is intrinsic to the study of history."[8] Academics and historians are hampered by the necessity to adhere to known facts, but remain free to place their own interpretation based on educated imagination. I, too, am trying to see with my own mind's eye, and penetrate the mindset of probable actions and motivations undertaken by my ancestors, using my own genetic connection to connect the sparse crumbs of fact left on the landscape. I have some latitude to speculate, in order to string the beads of information, and create an unbroken thread from the prosaic words that dance across the abyss separating my time from theirs. There is no one left who remembers.

The scant empirical records of the family prove that life began to improve dramatically coinciding with the end of the War of 1812 and the rise in fortunes of the House of Low over the seas. It is during the enforced lull in mercantile activity of the war years that a convergence of interests commences between Savannah, Georgia , and Liverpool, England. There are sufficient details to allow an acceptable degree of informed speculation concerning relationships and connections within the parameters of conventions of the times. We cannot know for sure that events unfolded this way, but we can certainly contemplate.

The abolition of the slave trade by the British at the beginning of the nineteenth century severely depressed the economy of Liverpool, and many established merchants believed that the metropolis would be ruined.[9] Liverpool and her people were resilient, and determined to attract new avenues of commerce, especially in cotton, that eventually made the port one of the most important trading centers in the world.[10]

Liverpool, during the eighteenth century a major slave-trading center, was by the beginning of the nineteenth century the foremost Atlantic trading port with America, and would have been as familiar to the Andrew Low & Company partners as Savannah.

Several close associates, such as Robert Mackay of the Savannah firm of Mein, Mein & Mackay, had already moved his family there. The firm was already advertising in the 1807 trade directory known as *Gore's Advertiser,* with Alexander Mein, merchant, residing at 13 Rodney Street, a wealthy area of handsome Victorian terraced townhouses looking down the hill to the docks below. Today, after several incarnations of decay and destruction, they are gentrified again, located in the middle of the university area known as Mount Pleasant.

In 1809, on April 11, Elizabeth Anne Mackay was born to Eliza and Robert Mackay in Liverpool, where, according to Walter C. Hartridge's *Letters of Robert Mackay to His Wife,* they lived at 5 Stanhope Street.[11]

By 1810 a William Low(e), merchant, is listed at 6 Vincent Street in the Liverpool Street Directory, the connection confirmed as it is the same address listed for Andrew Low, Sr., several years later.

A successful merchant was required to understand the winds that blew on a global level inasmuch as they affected local conditions, and one of his daily tasks would be to peruse the pages of the papers to seek the details that coffeehouse gossip would later augment. No modern-day stockbroker ever threw the bones with more fervor, and inside information made and broke fortunes. The merchant was often looked upon with grave suspicion as a man who did not produce anything himself, but lived by the sweat of and toil of others. He was held in a certain degree of contempt by the landowners who grew the cotton and produce, and England was often derided as a nation of shopkeepers. A certain amount of envy was aimed at those whose wealth brought them a prestige that only money could buy, and whose money could buy just about anything he wanted, including a wife. Liverpool was replete with wealthy merchants.[12]

The dearth of records in Liverpool during the period of the war mirrors that of Savannah, as has been previously stated, and an absence of evidence does not necessarily prove evidence of absence. Like faded photographs, there are many gaps in historical records due to wars and other disasters, but life went on nevertheless. We are left with no real clues as

The gates of Fettercairn, Kincardineshire, today, framing the spire of its church. Catherine Croll Low was born and baptized here, as was her grandson Andrew Low, Jr., of Savannah and Leamington.
Courtesy Jennifer Guthrie Ryan.

to whether or not Andrew Low, Sr., spent those years in Liverpool or in Savannah, but from events that occurred immediately at the end of the war and from what we already know about his energy and shrewdness, it is inconceivable that he sat around idle.

Liverpool trade directory *Gore's Advertiser* picks up again in 1814, the year the war ended. An indication of an explosion in business was its increased size, being considerably larger than the prewar issues. William Lowe is still at St. Vincent Street, but the firm of Mein, Mein & Mackay has disappeared. Robert Mackay had by now returned with his family to Savannah, and was to die in 1816, while on business in New York.[13]

By 1818, father William Low had been granted a license to function as a "burgher" in Brechin, the ancient market seat and Royal Burgh of the County of Forfar, now called Angus, and only about ten miles from Fettercairn.

An Infusion of Wealth

Following the end of the war the fortunes of the Andrew Low Company rose precipitously, leading us to believe that several events had a hand in this change of fortune. The first was the appearance in 1815 of the American registered copper-bottomed ship *Georgia*, at the helm Andrew's brother, Master James Low. The second was the marriage in Scotland in 1816 of his brother Alexander Low to Mary Dyce Nicol, daughter of William Nicol, a well-known Kincardine naval surgeon. Her brother James Dyce Nicol, who later became a member of Parliament for Kincardine, was married to Catherine Loyd, daughter of a prominent Manchester banker; another cousin was William Nicol, listed as a "wealthy Bombay merchant," with possible ties to the East India Company, married to Mary Nicol's sister.[14] These connections could certainly have been the source of the infusion of money enabling the purchase of *Georgia*.

After their marriage, Alexander and Mary Nicol Low appear to have moved to either the farm or big house in Upper Criggie, St. Cyrus in Kincardine.[15] There is anecdotal indication that the property might have been owned by A. Low of Savannah, and had a connection to the Croll family. In 1818 Jane Fordyce Nicol, sister of Mary Nicol, married John Fleming, merchant of Glasgow and partner in the William Nicol Bombay adventure. Whether this Fleming is related to the Bowman Fleming connection of Glasgow that started the entire saga in 1800 is unknown, but possible.

These certainly could be construed to all be coincidences, or interpreted in the customs of the times, to be deliberate measures whereby marriages cemented business ties—mergers and acquisitions with daughters as the commodities. The inevitable result would have been that this access to international commerce elevated the ability of the House of Low in Savannah to expand its trade.

The Firm Expands—Isaac Low and Company

In 1818, for the first time there is an entry for Isaac, Low & Co., at 15 Water Street, Liverpool, and William Low is no longer listed, which is not at all odd because he now appears in Brechin, Scotland, as a merchant living on Pearse Street with a grocery business at the Cross, in the center of town.[16] The young Andrew would have been six years old at that point in his life and probably living with his mother and the other children in Brechin. So that is the proof; 1818 is the year the Andrew Low Company expanded into the Liverpool market in a major way and reduced their reliance on the retail business in Savannah, becoming primarily cotton factors.

The first record to indicate that William Low moved his family to Brechin from Fettercairn is the Burgher Record in 1818. On October 17, 1818, William Low was admitted as a "Burgess" and on the following day "James Low merchant in Brechin, a stranger," was also admitted.

> Brechin, October 14—1818: WILLIAM LOW, Merchant in Brechin, admitted Burgess, he having satisfied the Treasurer as such. (2 pounds).

> Brechin, 15 October 1818; JAMES LOW, merchant in Brechin, a Stranger, admitted Burgess—from (2 pounds).[17]

The second record is an interesting insertion. James Low could have been brother of Uncle Andrew, and master of the ship *Georgia*; the label "stranger" indicates that he was not resident in Brechin. Admittance as a burgess was a license to trade. The period is correct—it was just after the Treaty of Ghent at the end of 1814, when trade was allowed to resume between America and Britain, and business had started to pick up again. The Andrew Low Company of Savannah was expanding into Liverpool, and setting up the web of family connections to trade in Scotland as well.

We know absolutely nothing about the early life of the young boy other than the record of his birth and the deaths of two brothers during his childhood. In order to understand influences on the man who later had become the central figure in the story of the House of Low, it is essential to know something about the place where his formative years were spent.

Burgesses had played a central role in Scotland's commercial history. Prior to 1900, only citizens who took the oath of allegiance to the Crown and obedience to the Magistrates were admitted to the Roll of Burgesses. Such citizens had to be occupiers of property of a certain value, be of full age, and on payment of the fees for admission to the Roll. Burgesses are a matter of historical interest, and at one time they alone had the right to elect and be members of the Town Council. They alone had the right of free trade, and commerce, and the manufacture of beer and spirits, except on specified market days when all the town's populace might sell goods for payment of petty customs or market dues. It was a most advantageous position in feudal times.

At the same time, only Burgesses were liable to pay local rates, taxes, and levies made by the Crown. They were also liable to pay for the supply of arms and men in times of war or rebellion—they provided the officers, and paid for the men who performed the watch or local police force. Burgesses therefore enjoyed many privileges, but they also incurred substantial responsibilities. The Burgess Rolls of Brechin begin in 1712—older Rolls were destroyed during the 1745 rebellion.

The *Brechin Almanac and Directory*, printed and published by Black & Johnston at 40 High Street, seems to have commenced publication in 1885, but it lists obituaries much older than that, and one of them was for "William Low, Cross, 1849, aged 79."[18]

The Guthrie Family Connection

Andrew Low, Jr., certainly would have grown up knowing the name of Guthrie as a leading family and name in the town or burgh. David Guthries, three separate ones, seemed to have been provosts at various times in the 1830's; the role was equivalent to that of mayor today in many ways. The Guthrie Chalmers Company had offices in Brechin; the firm started in 1800 and originally more or less factored linen until they went into ship "adventures," insurance, and banking businesses, acting as agents for other mercantile firms.[19] The boy's training in and around the countinghouses, offices, and warehouses of his father would have given him a thorough grounding in the business. Socially some Guthrie's would have been equals, others lower in status—the tenant farmers for example. The others, sons and families of the lairds, were much higher on the social scale, just one rung down from the nobility.

A map of the Royal Burgh of Brechin in 1822 by John Wood shows Mr. Low's house on Pearse Street, neighbor to John Guthrie. The relationship between the Guthries and the Lows had already been established, with the extraordinary coincidence of the event of the hanging of an Andrew Low in 1784, the last man reported to have been hanged in Scotland. The coincidence lies in the man who sentenced him to death. Patrick Chalmers of Aldbar, the same Patrick Chalmers who took the young David Charles Guthrie into the embryo mercantile firm of Chalmers Guthrie, headquartered at 9 Idol Lane, London, which by 1801 was already a considerable one with offices in Brechin, Montrose, Dundee, and many other Scottish towns of the northeast region.[20]

When William Low moved his family to Brechin, he had five children to help with Low business. One very interesting clue emerges with the premature death (maybe of cholera, which was rife at the time) of both of William Low's elder sons, James and William. This left Andrew the sole surviving son. At the time of Brother William's death, he would have been ten years old.

7

King Cotton: Great Britain–USA, 1815–1829

THE RISE OF LIVERPOOL PARALLELED THE EVOLUTION OF THE COL-ony of Georgia through its Trustee period from 1733 to the advent of slavery in 1750, thereby opening the gates of a thriving trade between Savannah and Liverpool. It had risen from being a fishing hamlet plying the Irish trade in the late 1600's to become a great port city of wealth, serving the needs of a heterogeneous group of cosmopolitan merchants trading with their North American counterparts. Following the Acts of Union in 1707, the gates opened for the Scots as well, and they flowed in as easily as oil oozes through a pipe, or water flows into a vacuum, finding their own level. Local industries flourished, feeding the growing settlements of emigrants pouring across the Atlantic. By the end of the eighteenth century the African merchants had became the aristocracy of the merchant community, assuming positions of power on local and national levels. The trade they plied in some part paid for the American Revolution. If one examines the business, philanthropic, and social positions of the men involved in that great democratic experiment, non-slaveholders had become the exception rather than the rule.[1]

During the previous century the importance of the port of Liverpool lay in its position in the trade between the New World, European nations, and Africa. This became known as the "triangular trade"—exchanging sugar and cotton from the West Indies and the southern colonies of America for trade goods manufactured in England, which purchased black slaves from Africa. Liverpool's first slave ship sailed for Africa in 1709, when for the benefit of Liverpool merchants the first commercial dock in the outports was built. The slave trade transformed Liverpool into a great center of international commerce. It was a common saying in the town that its principal streets had been marked out by the chains, and the walls of the houses cemented by the blood, of the African slaves. The red brick Customs House engraved with a frieze of Negro heads bore terrible testimony to the origins of Liverpool's rise to the position of one of the most famous—or infamous, depending on the point of view—towns in the transatlantic mercantile world.

Liverpool boasted about the wealth engendered by the trade in black bodies, with one street known as "Negro Row." The fortunes of many slave-trading families in Liverpool became the foundation for banks, insurance companies, and new manufactories, especially those of the textile industry, rivaling their flourishing neighbor, the adjacent city of Manchester.

In 1771 an Act of Parliament authorized the building of another dock, called George's Dock, located at the foot of Water Street. This began the process of building docks in the river. A natural adjunct to trading in slaves was the need to build the ships to transport them. Liverpool benefited mightily from this necessity. The rebellion in the thirteen colonies initially had a disastrous affect on Liverpool's prosperity; many of the slave ships were turned into privateers, and the former slave ships preyed on the slavers. This did not help the planters, but it saved the necks of many a merchant and captain. The need to cut back on employment led to serious riots over wages. This resulted in severe property damage, unrest, and injuries, but also showed Liverpool to be well in the forefront of organized labor activities. The result was an increasingly sophisticated and radicalized workforce, inspired in part by the rebellion over the Atlantic Ocean, and works of men like Thomas Paine. His *Rights Of Man,* written at the time of the French Revolution, showed Britain's working class that they had as many rights as their bosses—only the slaves remained powerless.

In Britain, one of the leading figures in the growing cacophony of voices raised for the abolition of the slave trade—not to be confused with the institution of slavery itself, but rather the trading in human beings—was that of William Wilberforce.[2] Pragmatism was his strong voice, and although he abhorred slavery or claimed to, he insisted that evil though the slave trade was, economically it would be ruinous to abandon it precipitously. Much of the landed class, merchants, and planters on both sides of the Atlantic owned vast estates in the West Indies and the Americas. They relied on slave labor for their continuing profits. As the new century began, Wilberforce and his adherents recognized that despite their efforts, ten years after the formation of the abolitionist movement British ships were still carrying over fifty thousand slaves per year from Africa to the Americas—in 1798 almost 150 ships left Liverpool for Africa.

The climate was beginning to change due to the rise of democratic sentiment after the American Revolution, and acceptance in Great Britain toward benefits of slavery was fizzling out. In the United States, especially the Southern states of Georgia and the two Carolinas, the abolition movement was being fueled not so much by enlightenment as fear—fear of slave insurrections on the St. Domingue or Haiti model. Between 1787 and 1803 they all prohibited the import of slaves for varying periods, pragmatically repealing their own prohibitions at the times when the supply ran short. A new federal Act of 1800 tightened the laws regarding ownership or shares in slave ships, culminating finally in 1807, when the federal government prohibited the trade entirely—sort of!

By the beginning of the nineteenth century, Liverpool had another element in common with Savannah—the cotton industry. In Britain the industrial revolution and the rise of cotton were two principal reasons for the increase in both imports and exports: the import of cotton especially escalating dramatically. The export of coal and salt increased exponentially as well, and in the days when the only way to cross the "great ponds" was by ship, obviously the mercantile trade surged just as dramatically. On both fronts cheap labor was the key to merchants' profits. In the American South it was slavery that provided the hands and backs, and in Britain it was children and the working poor that provided the fodder for the factories.[3]

By the time Andrew Low & Company appear on the scene, Savannah and Liverpool had a relationship that reflected three-quarters of a century of mutually beneficial trading. There is no proof that, unlike Robert Mackay, Andrew Low indulged in the trading of slaves; there is plenty of proof that through his early experiences in the merchant trade he would have had a practical understanding of the relationship between cheap or free labor and the profit motive. The lack of social stigma attached to the trade in slaves at the end of the eighteenth century would certainly not have caused him to lose sleep. The requirements in Savannah would have made it imperative for him to have purchased or hired slave labor, and the record shows that indeed he did. None of them would have had moral qualms regarding the status quo of the institution of slavery. That is the way business was conducted then.

A Whiff of Steam and SS Savannah

As all black clouds have silver linings, and necessity is mother of invention for many reasons, out of this war evolved the need for pioneering inventions in the field of getting things to market—namely the advent of steam as transportation. The first steam-powered boat entered the Mersey in 1815, and in 1819, in a somewhat controversial claim, the first steamship to cross the Atlantic, the SS *Savannah*, arrived in Liverpool. She was built in New York, financed mostly by Savannah investors, including the

Andrew Low Company. The fact that she did not steam all the way across has mitigated the American claim, but nevertheless she was certainly the first, and it is uncontestable that these visionary men saw a need and filled it—that need was the faster you got things there, the more profit you would make.[4]

The Company—the good old boys, the Scottish syndicates—had other fish to fry; they had a vision, and it required capital and plenty of it. Back in Savannah, on Thursday, April 23, 1818, the Union Society of Georgia, to which belonged most of the city's leading merchants, celebrated their sixty-eighth anniversary, and after going through the usual business of the day, sat down to a plentiful dinner. It is not hard to conceive that during one of those courses of food, during one of the copious drafts of good claret, the idea of the extra profit that faster ships would bring came up.

Paddle-wheel steam-driven boats plied the rivers and inland waterways as well as the coast trade, and Andrew Low was already involved in a company called the Steam Boat Company of Georgia. "J. Hutchinson, Treasurer that year, announced that it declared a dividend of Twenty Five percent, or Sixty Two Dollars and Fifty cents per share, on the past transactions of the Company." This was an extremely high dividend; the Bank of Georgia paid only three dollars and sixty cents for the same period. Obviously, steam was the answer. Full speed ahead.

Friday morning, May 8, 1818, a small notice appeared in the *Columbian Museum and Savannah Advertiser*: "STEAM SHIP COMPANY: Yesterday morning a subscription paper was opened at the exchange, for the purpose of establishing a Savannah Steamship Company; and we understand the shares apportioned for this city were all subscribed before noon."

Full steam ahead! Well-known Savannah merchant William Scarbrough had formed a new company to invest in a new form of ocean transport powered by steam. They intended to build the first transatlantic steamship, and they boldly named her the SS *Savannah*. Andrew Low was one of the original subscribers, but it was Robert Isaac who became one of the first directors. The obvious reason for their risky investment could only be that the sole purpose of this new mode of transportation was to cut the time of the voyage by one third, and therefore gain a tremendous edge on your competitors.

The story of the SS *Savannah* has been told and retold and is famous to those who follow the ships and go down to the seas, but it is the fascinating puzzle of the jigsaw pieces from contemporary newspaper accounts that convey the emotional thrill of this giant leap in human ingenuity. With imagination we can follow the progress of the preparation of the great ship with the same excitement through the eyes of those reading about the momentous invention for the first time and the civic pride of the city that conceived her.[5]

On December 28, 1818, the Savannah newspaper listed the acts passed by the Georgia Legislature during their last session, stating it was not only proof of the industry, but also of the wisdom of the members who composed it. Item No. 60 was to incorporate the Savannah Steamship Company. So ended that year of 1818, with the vision a reality, the dream a substance, the era of steam had arrived, or so they hoped!

As 1819 dawned, the hopes of many of Savannah's merchants were pinned to the success of their great bold adventure and innovation, the first transatlantic steamship ever built. The intention was to provide not only the fastest manner in which to transport the prized cotton to the manufacturers of Manchester, but to create a magnificent new mode of elegant and luxurious crossing of the ocean. This was to be the precursor of the mighty ships of the line—the Queens of the sea—many of which have captured the public's imagination, especially the ones that turned into disasters, like the *Titanic*. Well, the SS *Savannah* did not sink on her maiden voyage, but she certainly sunk the hopes and dreams of her investors, especially William Scarbrough. They were just a little bit ahead of their time, visionaries waiting for the world to catch up.[6]

Her maiden voyages continued that spring; on April 15, she took a short journey to test her seaworthiness: "The steamship SAVANNAH, Capt Rogers, started yesterday for noon with a number of passengers aboard and came to anchor off Tybee at half past one o'clock, in consequence of thick weather and hope they can proceed this morning. May success attend her."

The *Charleston City Gazette* announced on 17 inst:: "the beautiful steamship Savannah, captain Moses Rogers, arrived here yesterday from Savannah. She made her run from Tybee lighthouse in something less than 11 hours. This novel spectacle drew a large concourse of spectators to the wharves, which cheered as she passed the city. During the day she was visited and admired by several hundreds of our citizens."

Not only were the citizens of Charleston fascinated: "April 29th, 1819. President James Monroe of the United States and suite arrived at Charleston on Monday last. They were to partake of a public dinner the next day. It was not known when or which route he will take for this place. The steamship Savannah, it was expected in Charleston, would be tendered to him."

Even then, in a much smaller nation, one did not just pick up the phone and call the President. One needed influence and the owners must have arranged this trip well ahead of time. It is in the details that triumph or tragedy lie, and the weather in this coastal port city was always the uninvited guest at the dinner party. Disaster could have cancelled the maiden voyage.

"On the evening of Saturday, May 15th, about 8 o clock, a violent gust of wind and rain, accompanied by thunder and lightning from the N.W. passed this city. It was of short duration, however, several of the shipping broke their masts from the wharf, which occasioned a dreadful cracking among the jib booms, spanker booms, riggings etc. the steamship Savannah injured one of her wheels. We believe the damage was not so great but it can be easily repaired."

On May 24 the great adventure finally began when she was cleared out of the Savannah River at Tybee, heading for St. Petersburg, Russia, via Liverpool. On the crossing, one ship's captain, seeing the smoke rising from her stacks reported she was on fire. On May 30, Captain Brown of the schooner *Union* told of seeing the ship at sea "with sails set and machinery in motion." The first news of her record-breaking trip across the Atlantic was on August 19, when it was announced that, "By the Brig Higson, at Norfolk 40 days from Cork, we learn that the Steamship Savannah, Capt Rogers, arr. at Kinsale, off Cork, on June 12th, after a passage of 21 days." That would place her in the Channel between Ireland and the west coast of England, headed for Liverpool. The *Savannah* arrived at Liverpool on 21 June after a passage of twenty-five days. Her arrival was heralded in the Liverpool papers:

> Among the arrivals in this port on the 21st we were particularly gratified and astonished by the novel sight of a fine steam ship, which came around about half after 7 pm, without the assistance of a single sheet, in a style which displayed the power and advantage of steam to vessels of the largest size, being 350 tons burthen. She is called the Savannah, Capt Rogers, and sailed from Savannah 26th May and arrived in the Channel 5 days since. Her model is beautiful and the accommodation for passengers elegant and complete. This is the first ship in this construction that has undertaken a voyage across the Atlantic.

That was about half the normal voyage, the concept was a huge success. A month later she continued her voyage to St. Petersburg in Russia. Czar Alexander was impressed enough with the new technology that he presented Captain Rogers with an iron settee, which now resides on the rear piazza of the Richardson-Owens-Thomas House in Savannah.[7]

Unfortunately the great ship never reached her investors' expectations and was never a commercial success, and only a year later was sold at auction for an undisclosed sum to a Captain Nathan Holdridge of New York. He removed her engines and operated her as a lowly packet plying between New York and Savannah—the elegant swan turned into an ugly duckling. On November 5, 1821, the dismembered vessel that carried so many hopes and dreams ran aground off Fire Island and sank. She was a total loss.

1820 Financial Disaster for Scarbrough

William Scarbrough was one of Savannah's most prominent merchants, who with his socialite wife, Julia, gave splendid balls, dinners, and parties that were an absolute must for Savannah's elite. Their lavish lifestyle was conducted in a goldfish bowl, at a magnificent mansion on West Broad Street, built by the well-known English architect, William Jay. The secret the public did not yet know was that William Scarbrough was grossly overextended financially and virtually bankrupt. Sometime between November 1819 and August 1822, the sheriff either advertised the home of William Scarbrough on West Broad Street for sale, or the deal was cut under the table.

William Scarbrough's house was sold at public auction, and it was Robert Isaac, partner in the Andrew Low Company, who purchased the property, although that detail did not appear in the newspapers at the time—perhaps giving rise to the rumors that his friends had come to his rescue. A product of the "good ole boys network!" This is yet another of the misconceptions regarding the relationship of the Andrew Low Company with prominent Savannah titans; the salvation of William Scarbrough has been credited to others. In this case, both fact and rumor appear to be true!

The city of Savannah is understandably proud of her colorful history. But, passed down the years, tales tend to become distorted by carelessness as well as by those who maliciously color the fine points with the shadow of their own agendas. In this instance, it is said and written, that it was English cotton merchant Godfrey Barnsley, married to the younger daughter Julia, who bailed Scarbrough out of the financial abyss, in which the great vision of the SS *Savannah* had dropped him. The truth is that it appears to have been the partners in the Andrew Low Company who saved his face and enabled the Scarbrough family to stay on in their magnificent home.

At the time it was reported that William Scarbrough took the brunt of the loss as the chief promoter and head financial man, and rumors spread that he was bailed out by his friends and partners through a deal cooked up to rescue him. It was whispered that Robert Isaac would purchase the house for $20,000 (although no indication appears concerning a marshal's sale) and the Scarbrough family would continue to live in it. Historian and former Savannah mayor, Thomas Gamble, in an article published in 1906, also says that it was sold in a marshal's sale. In his book, *Savannah Ahoy*, written in the 1960's, Malcolm Bell writes in the epilogue: "Fortune frowned on William Scarbrough. Beset by adversity that descended with the great Savannah fire of 1820 and the ensuing depression that wiped out land values, the prince became pauper and was forced to sell the West Broad Street mansion to satisfy a judgment held by Andrew Low and Co."

On August 28, 1822, Robert Isaac made a new will, and all became clear to those who had access to it. Robert Isaac was William Scarbrough's brother-in-law, so it made perfect sense for him to be the front man. In this will, he specifically states that he "purchased the House, the Furnishings and contents at Marshall's sales." Certainly, Robert Isaac never lived in the house, and he leaves the lot, the house, and the contents to his niece Charlotte Scarbrough, daughter of William Scarbrough, probably to protect her father from his creditors.[8] Since Isaac did not die for another decade, it is obvious that the purchase was not made for his own personal gain. It is also proven that after his bankruptcy, William Scarbrough worked for Andrew Low and Company at the Upper Darien Rice and Saw Mill undertaking in Darien, McIntosh County.

Isaac's own fortunes were inextricably tied into the fortunes of many others in his personal and business life, and what would have come to light following the reading of his will are the facts that seem to have been lost in the story that has been passed down to contemporary Savannah. The true account is how Andrew Low and Company rescued the Scarbrough family from financial disgrace following the economic disaster of the 1820 SS *Savannah* debacle.[9]

Death of Captain James Low and Fire of 1820

A tremendous loss for the House of Low occurred during the same period. In the Records of Chatham County a small notice, lost among the vast accumulation of property, much of it in the form of slaves, is the following:

> Inventory of the property belonging to the Estate of JAMES LOW, late of Savannah and deceased.
>
> | | |
> |---|---|
> | One half of Ship GEORGIA | $6660:67 |
> | 50 Shares of Insurance Stocks | 1000 |
> | 20 ditto State Bank do. 100 | 2000 |
> | 12 patent lights | 26 |
> | Total: | $9,690:67 |
>
> Sworn before me; M. Myers, Wm Taylor; Donald McLeod; Robert Isaac.[10]

This conveyed the news to the people of Savannah that sometime between June 19, 1819, when the ship *Georgia* sailed for Liverpool, and November 12, 1819, when she returned with a new master, Captain Varnum, the brother of Andrew Low had died on board. This news is also conveyed as corroboration, by the inscription on the grave in Catterline, which says, "James, died at sea on passage from Savanna (sp) 27/9/1819, aged 44" and remains one of the most crucial pieces of the proof in the puzzle, helping unravel the unfolding story.

Robert Isaac was a passenger on board the *Georgia* when she returned to Savannah from Liverpool.[11] "The Georgia has been lying off Tybee Island for the last 8 days." That notation meant that there was disease on board. The Tybee Island Lazaretto was a quarantine station. If ever there was sickness aboard, everyone had to get off the ship, and remain at Lazaretto Creek—that included slaves, passengers, and crew. The purpose was to use the two-story tabby brick building as a place where any sick slaves or seamen would be dropped before allowing the ship to proceed up the river to Savannah. They were left to see what happened and many died there.[12] Death and disaster stalked indiscriminately on land and at sea.

Ever since its early origins a century before, the mostly wooden buildings of Savannah had been extremely susceptible to fire and had burnt down several times already. Sometime during the night of Monday, January 10, 1820, fire broke out again, roaring through the streets and squares close by the Market. The town was devastated. It was the most disastrous conflagration Savannah had ever seen. One of those whose business was destroyed, among the first to announce their renewal plans, was Andrew Low: "ANDREW LOW & CO. Inform their friends and public that until their own store is rebuilt, they have rented the brick store on the opposite lot, lately erected by John Pray—where in a few days they will remove their goods, and open their countinghouse. In the meantime, persons having business with them, will please call at the house of Mr. James McHenry, Courthouse Square."Two months later, March 8, 1820, the following notice appeared on the front pages of the *Columbian Museum*: "ANDREW LOW & Co, have now their goods opened in the new brick store adjoining their old lot, and have just received by the Caroline from Liverpool, a variety of new goods, suitable for the season, which they offer at most accommodating terms. Casks London Porter, in bottles, and Crates of Crockery Ware, assorted."

And, just below that the momentous news of the extended empire: "The Undersigned, Having for several years past, had a commercial establishment in Liverpool, under the firm of Isaac, Low & Co, offer their services of the house to their friends and public, in the sale of produce, and other business, on commission. Liberal advances will be made on shipments. Andrew Low, & Co."

The great fire could not stop them. These men grasped adversity between their teeth and ripped it to shreds, picking the bones of tragedy, gluing it all back together. All the Kings horses and all the Kings men could and often did put Humpty Dumpty together again.

1820 Yellow Fever Epidemic

As a result of the economic boom treading on the heels of the war, foreign shipping had proliferated, especially from the Caribbean. Immigrant workers had flocked in, causing severe overcrowding in the tenement areas of the city. Fire was not the only serious danger that faced this town built between the ocean and the river, surrounded on all sides by swampy tidal marshes and rice fields under wet culture. That same year a terrible yellow fever epidemic devastated the city and its citizens.

Savannah's most desperate experience with the disease came in 1820, when the disastrous fire in January left part of the city in ruins, and extraordinary spring and summer rains had left standing pools of water in the craters and depressions left by the burning. The hot, humid months of July, August, September, and October were most dangerous, and those who could afford to left the city for cooler and more salubrious climates to the north.

At that time, the true origin of the cause of the disease was not known. Dr. William Daniell, who had actually gone through and survived an attack, became an observer and participant in the search for a cure for the sickness, believed to be caused by "qualities imparted by marsh miasma to an atmosphere, which thus impressed, impairs the capillary action of the skin and affects the equilibrium of the circulation." The *Savannah Georgian* of August 15 states "although our Health Committee and Medical Societies are silent on the subject, we are induced to believe that a pestilential disease of no mild character rages to a considerable extent in certain portions of our city." The newspapers, from August 15, 1820, through to the end of the epidemic around the end of September, wanted to believe that doctors and medical knowledge were adequate to combat the peril, despite the fact that three of the four physicians appointed to investigate the disease had died. It was not until the first frost arrived that the disease abated; it killed off the carriers.

At the beginning of the epidemic it was estimated that some 5,000 whites lived in Savannah, but by June due to a panicked migration, it was reduced to 2,500 and by September the number was further reduced and went down to about 1,500 inhabitants. This meant that the disease struck about one in five people mortally. The first symptoms of the disease were a jaundiced complexion and fever. Next, the victims progressed into a frenzied stage characterized by violent eruptions of "black bile." After this stage victims fell into a coma, with about half living through this final episode.

In a paper delivered to the Savannah City Council in 1821, Dr. William Waring[13] said that he believed that the fever was increasing because of crowding in the city. One of the reasons given for the excess deaths of this particular epidemic lay in the overcrowding caused by an influx of immigrants following the peace. Dr. Waring's account states:

> . . . these unfortunate Foreigners, for the inducements presented in the Southern Cities, came in crowds to the Southern Ports. In consequence of this great accession of strangers, without acquaintance with that kind of economy of living which is adapted to an unwholesome latitude—without money, and without conveniences—destitute of proper clothing, food, or bedding—gathering in throngs of 15 or 20, in narrow wooden buildings, with small yards—without caution, and without that considerate industry, which leads to the prompt removal of the daily products of filth, which drop from their immediate persons, a source of pestilence has been established, in addition to that which ordinarily existed. In the course of the summer of 1819, fifty Irish emigrants arrived in the same ship, not one of whom survived 'til the frost.
>
> The year of 1820 has been tinged with a deeper and more melancholy gloom. Our older inhabitants look back and tell us that these are not like former times . . . then, the common labor was altogether done by Negroes, and white laborers, collected in crowds, in small houses, were unknown. Then the population was thin, resident, and composed of natives, or permanent inhabitants, whose constitutions, manners and customs, modes of living and comforts, fitted them, in the best way, to perceive the means of health, and to preserve. All this has been changed, and everything has been introduced which can render a spot unfriendly to the human constitution.

It is an extraordinary medical document for its age and degree of understanding. We should never forget how things were, before things are the way we know them now. It closes with an explanation of the treatment Dr. Waring has employed and is a most remarkable document, as testified to by Dr. Lemuel Kollock, when it was presented to the Savannah City Council on 23 January, 1821.

Personal Tragedy Strikes Twice More

In early June 1826, George Low died on board the *Milton*, en route to Liverpool. Having lost one brother in 1819, Andrew Low now lost his youngest brother who had been a babe-in-arms at the time of the death of his father. Of the four brothers who came to Savannah to find fortune and a new life, two of them were dead, and the third had retired to live the life of a country gentleman in Scotland.

To compound those losses Andrew Low was about to lose the cornerstone of his life and business. An ironic and somewhat poignant notice appeared on July 7, 1826: "BREAST PIN LOST. A Scotch Pebble, set in gold, well known to many of the subscribers acquaintances, and having been the gift of a friend, a reward equal to its value will be cheerfully given for it by ROBERT ISAAC."

Since the war and the expansion into the Liverpool market, the Andrew Low Company had prospered mightily, had picked up the pieces resulting from a terrible fire, a disease epidemic, death of two brothers, and then tragedy struck again. The news was announced, as it always was in small abrupt stark notices in the daily columns of the Savannah newspapers. A notice published by the Society of St. Andrews.

> DIED: On Tuesday, the 16th October, 1827, of the prevailing Disease in the 46th year of his age, Mr. ROBERT ISAAC, of the longstanding and respectable firm of Andrew Low and Co of this city. Exemplary in every relation of life, whether as son, brother, husband, father or member of the community (all the consequences of a faith, pious and sincere, but not ostentatious, in the great truths of the Christian dispensation) His progress thro life and final exit, leave nothing for doubt in the minds of his bereaved and afflicted relatives and connexions, that he safely repose in the bosom of his Father and his God. The St Andrew's Society at a Special Meeting held at the City Hotel, on Thursday, 18th October. It was unanimously Resolved that the members of the St. Andrew's Society entertain the highest regard for the character and a lively and sincere respect for the memory of Robert Isaac Esq., their former Vice President, and that in testimony of their sorrow for his untimely death they wear crape on the left arm for thirty days. It was further resolved and the same be published. Wm Robertson, Secretary.

Robert Isaac's official cause of death was listed as yellow fever. As we have seen, yellow fever had occurred in spectacular epidemics throughout Savannah's history. The year Robert Isaac was stricken was no better, no worse than any normal year facing the inhabitants of the city.

Andrew Low arrived in Savannah from New York on December 24, 1827, on the ship *Howard*, six days sailing. During the forty-four days it took to reach New York from Liverpool, he had time to contemplate his options. For Robert Isaac's friend, confidante, and partner it was a most terrible loss, and one that would lead to a decision that changed destiny. At some point, to replace the partner who was irreplaceable, he searched his soul for a substitute. Robert Isaac had been like a brother to Andrew Low, and the only possible solution was to look for someone who might step eventually into the shoes of his friend. To move forward he would need to look back. Andrew Low had to pick up the pieces and restructure his thriving businesses. He did what any loyal clansman would do; he looked to family.

Andrew Low Picks Up the Pieces

The first action Andrew Low undertook was to temporarily take over the duties and positions previously occupied by Robert Isaac in business relationships and directorships. Robert Isaac had been the principal Savannah partner, while Andrew Low occupied the roving acquisition position, the traveling salesman, certainly in England and Scotland, but possibly also in other parts of Georgia. There has been no proof of Low ever owning a home in Savannah, having a wife or family there, but many pointers have him with fingers in business pies in Augusta and Darien, Charleston and Milledgeville, Boston and New York.

There is no indication of Low having a social bent, unlike his early contemporary Robert Mackay, who seemed to be as much at home on the dance floors of Savannah as he was in the countinghouses and wharves of the port. But Mackay was also the son of the wayward daughter of Godfrey Malbone, the wealthy and extravagant privateer of Newport. His social life reflected this heritage, not that of his Scotsman father. There is no indication of Andrew Low having the kind of upwardly mobile social life that William Scarbrough and his social butterfly wife Julia enjoyed and in many instances instigated.

There are many indications that when it came to demanding his rights in the halls of power, whether it was the Georgia General Assembly or the U.S. Congress, he had no qualms. There is absolute indication that he was perfectly capable of taking the law into his own hands, and in the process committing murder, some might say sedition, by instigating the burning of the two French privateers, prior to the War of 1812.

Soon after Isaac's death, Andrew Low, Sr., joins the St. Andrew's Society, another fraternal brotherhood in the family connections and socially conscious Savannah. Their annual meeting is on November 30th, St. Andrew's Day; however, he would not have been in the city for that particular meeting, but appears to have joined very shortly after, perhaps indicating that the membership was as much a business move as a social one. There would have been no opposition from the other members. The record also indicates that John Low joined at the same time.

Much of the confusion concerning relationships within the Low family through the years has focused on the similarity of names, a common practice in the nineteenth century where each generation of frequently large families carried the same names based on Scottish naming patterns. The main mix-up was between the two Andrew Lows and two John Lows.

One of the first decisions Andrew Low, Sr., made was to bring over to Savannah one of his nephews, now known to be John Low. This nephew appears to be the oldest son of one of Andrew Low's older brothers, also named John, who had been a mariner, married to Margaret Leighton of Dunnottar, and lived in St. Nicholas, Aberdeen.[14] Their eldest son John Low was born in Aberdeen in 1799, but at that time was living in Liverpool, where he was working as a bookkeeper and was married to Eliza Green Low. Eliza Green was the sister of Charles Green, who is soon to emerge as a prominent character in the unfolding story.

On arrival in Savannah, nephew John Low was named as one of two partners in a new subsidiary company, Low, Taylor & Co. On May 22, the firm commenced running the most poignant notice of all::

> The co-partnership heretofore existing in this city, between the subscriber and ROBERT ISAAC, under the firm of ANDREW LOW & CO was dissolved on the 16th day of October last by the death of Mr. Isaac. THE IMPORTING DRY GOODS business will be continued, and the affairs of the former concern brought to a close by the subscriber, in connexion with JAMES TAYLOR and JOHN LOW, under the firm of LOW, TAYLOR & CO, signed. AND'W LOW, Surviving Partner of Andrew Low and Co, Savannah, 21st May, 1828.

That took care of the retail end of the business. A further notice went on to indicate that the senior partner was spreading the load and fully intended to drive the vehicle down the road he was constructing.

> NOTICE—The subscriber having taken into Co-partnership MR. ROBERT HUTCHISON proposes to continue in connexion with him the transaction of a general COMMISSION BUSINESS under the same firm as heretofore, namely that of ANDREW LOW & CO. They will be prepared to extend the customary facilities to those disposed to make shipments to their friends in Liverpool, Messrs ISAAC, LOW & CO. AND'W LOW, Savannah, May 21, 1828.

In those terse terms, tragedy reveals and the future is mapped. One phase of an extraordinary partnership and one life comes to an end and another commences. The words indicate that Andrew Low, Senior, remained the principal partner and intended to continue the empire he and his friend had built. He brought into the dry goods, the shopping import and retail emporium facet of the business, two men: John Low, related to him by blood, and James Taylor, who, two years later, in 1829, married Charlotte, the niece of Robert Isaac's wife, Lucy, in her turn, the sister of William Scarbrough. A new player appears in the person of Robert Hutchison, who he chose to bring in as his agent to run the Commission business in Savannah.[15] William Smith was chosen to run the Isaac Low Company in Liverpool. It all stayed in the family.

In June 1829 the paper *Georgian* gave notice that the executors were selling Robert Isaac's "Negroes." It lists the names of all seven of them, indicating a way of life, the amount of servants required to run his household. On June 2, 1829, a notice in the paper that ran from March to June:

> EXECUTOR'S SALES; By J. Herbert: On the first Tuesday in June next, between the legal hours of sale, will be sold before the Courthouse, in the City of Savannah, seven Negroes, belonging to the estate of the late Robert Isaac, deceased, viz: Flora, a first rate cook and washer: Diana, her daughter, about 15 or 16 years of age; Cora, do. About 12 do; little Alex, her son, about 3 or 4 years of age—Adeline, a girl about 15 or 16 years of age; Annette, a girl about 12 or 13 do: and little Sampson, a boy about 6 or 7. Terms made known at time of sale: Wm Scarbrough, Wm Taylor, and Norman Wallace.

By then Lucy Isaac had moved to Liverpool, perhaps to be closer to her best friend and intimate, Andrew Low. Lucy Isaac never remarried, but she did remove her entire family to live in Liverpool, stating that she did not wish to expose them further to the health hazards in Savannah. She stayed a close companion to Andrew Low, Sr., for the rest of their lives.

Now two other pivotal figures enter stage left. First, in 1829, Lieutenant Robert E. Lee, a young West Point Army engineer, arrived in Savannah to devise the system of dykes and canals that would eventually form Fort Pulaski, and provided us with one of the central historical markers of our story further down the line. The second was the presumptive heir.

The Arrival of Andrew Low, Jr.

The first item in the *Port of Savannah Shipping News*, October 17, 1829:

> ARRIVED: Ship, Georgia, Varnum, 36 days from Liverpool, a full cargo of Dry Goods to A. Low & Co. Consignees, R. Campbell, R. Habersham, N.B. & H. Weed, A. Low & Co, Low, Taylor & Co, J. H.

> Reid, G. W. Owens, Stiles and Fannin, N. Wallace, and T. Young—Passengers: Messrs, William Scarbrough, Jno. Miller, and And'w Low, Jr. Maria Quigly, Edward Quigly, Terrence Quigly, Abraham Lewis, John Lewis, Henry Ross.

In that brief notice lays the seed of this book, and my own being on this planet. That was Andrew Low, Jr., my great-grandfather, a boy of just seventeen years of age, born in Kincardineshire. Educated in the rudiments of reading, writing, and mathematics—the rumor being that even at that age he had a flair for money and how to make it work, a trait that eventually became a very American hallmark, the not so subtle art of entrepreneurship. He was here to make his own mark on posterity. He was accompanied on this trip by William Scarbrough, who by now had become one of the cogs in the Andrew Low mercantile machine, rather than the leader of the great merchant prince class of Savannah society.

Andrew Low, Sr., understood the global politics of his time and how to manipulate and cajole those in power. It was perhaps those very qualities and a foot in both camps of England and America that had enabled the two firms to prosper when others had fallen by the wayside. Andrew Low, Sr., was an astute, hardworking, tough, manipulative, and ruthless man. He was instrumental in helping to put Savannah on the map of global trade during those years before the Civil War destroyed the heart and soul of the South.

Part III

Savannah–Liverpool, 1829–1841

8

The Merchant Prince, 1829–1836

THE YOUNG ANDREW LOW WAS THE ONLY SURVIVING SON OF Andrew Low, Sr.'s eldest brother, William Low. A letter written by his uncle a few years later indicated that he did not know his nephew very well. That would argue that he had not been apprenticing in the merchant trade in the offices of Isaac Low in Liverpool. There is no provable record one way or another, although it is obvious that he would have received his earliest training at the hands of his own father, a merchant of Brechin, in the parish of Angus, Scotland.

What traits shown by this young lad led his uncle to offer him a clerkship in the Savannah firm are unknown, but letters written by Andrew, Sr., to his agent Robert Hutchison, spanning the 1830's, show him to be a diligent, hardworking, and conscientious young man. So the fateful decision was made; Andrew Low, Jr., journeyed for the first time from Liverpool to Savannah. The heir-to-be was moving into a transatlantic enterprise that had become successful through the factoring of cotton. There was a sturdy foundation upon which to build hopes and dreams.

At the age of seventeen he would have been getting a handle on the national and global intertwining of the business. He had worked in the countinghouse of his Uncle's firm, sorting out cargo manifests, allotting space on the company ships, and organizing space for consignment shipments, both in and out of the port. His duties would include overseeing the operations of the ships tied up at the company's wharf, dealing with agents for other company ships, and working with the captains of both their own and other vessels.

Snapshot—Savannah 1830

As the first full year of the young Andrew's sojourn in Savannah began: "Salmon and Herring, Sugars, Ale and Rum, Pinto Port, Java Coffee, London Fish and Meat Sauces, Holt's Butter Crackers, Raisins and Currants,

Prime Beef and Pickled Tongues and Havana Cigars" all arriving on ships from exotic ports. Havana, Cuba, was a major player in the first part of the nineteenth century. Many languages would have been spoken in the port, especially Spanish and French from crews plying the Caribbean trade. Coastal trade was still a major part of the operation, as was interstate trade both north and south. There was a great deal of competition to keep clients happy, and a global understanding of supply and demand. Sensitivity to commodities futures would have been a key element of the success or failure of a company's annual business—decisions needed to be made on predictions for seasonal goods, as well as prices at market for raw material. He would need to keep up with trends and understand the economics of his trade.

If young Andrew was literary-minded, he might have bought a ticket for a "Raffle for Boydell and Nicholl's splendid quarto edition of Shakespeare's Dramatic Works, revised by George Stevens, with the prefaces of Pope and Johnson, illustrated by numerous engravings, and bound in Russian gilt extra—in nine volumes." This splendid work was to be raffled at the City Hotel the following evening and was valued at $400, which amount will be divided into 100 chances of $4 each. It could be seen at the Bookstore of T. M. Driscoll.

Or, if he were more sport-minded:

> To Sportsmen, the annual sports at Bonaventure, will be resumed tomorrow. Smooth Bore, Pistols, and Rifles admitted. Distance for shooting Turkeys viz. With Smooth Bore 100 yards, Pistols 60 ditto and Rifles 165 ditto. At 2 pm, two Deer will be introduced on the Rifle Ground and shot for at a distance of 300 yards. NB Dinner will be provided on the ground.
>
> It does not state whether the deer was the Dinner!
>
> And, Sports of the Season: There will be a shoot for a flock of fine fat Turkeys at the mile and half house on White Bluff Road Tomorrow, New Years Day.[1]

There was an abundance of activities offered the discriminating citizen that New Years.

Three years after his arrival Andrew Low, Jr., received cargo on the ship *Emperor* from New York, as well as in the name of Low, Taylor & Company. This appears to be the first trade conducted in his own name; he would have been twenty years old and already making his own decisions and his own money.

Low may have noticed a young U.S. Army engineer strolling the streets on his off-hours. Robert E. Lee of Virginia was assigned to the large construction project on Cockspur Island—the building of another coastal defense fort. This one was named for the Polish cavalry officer, Casimir Pulaski, who died during the siege of Savannah in 1779. Lee was a classmate at West Point Military Academy of Savannahian Jack Mackay, and he enjoyed the hospitality of Mackay's family home on Broughton Street.

In 1832 a daughter was born to William Henry Stiles and Eliza Mackay Stiles in Savannah. She was christened Mary Cowper Stiles.

In 1833 a young Englishman, Charles Green, arrives in Savannah. He was born in 1807 in Halesowen, Shropshire, England, a town that is now a suburb of the great industrial center of Birmingham, but by now his father Josiah Green had lived in Liverpool for many years. His sister Elizabeth (Eliza) Green was married to John Low of Aberdeen, who was the partner in Low, Taylor & Company, and Uncle Andrew's nephew, therefore cousin to Andrew Low, Jr.

St. Andrew's Society

Young Andrew was making all the right moves insinuating himself into the proper business and social niches of Savannah left vacant by his uncle's former partner. Savannah, then and now, was filled with civic organizations, ethnic clubs, and affiliations, many of them designed to assuage the homesickness of their members, and to bind them together into ever-tighter webs of loyalty. One of the most prestigious was the Scottish St. Andrew's Society. Not surprisingly, one of the first actions taken by the young Andrew Low, Jr., was to join. His name was read for membership in May 1831, and he was approved in August of that year. This action is very much in character, as it sustains his former Scottish roots and grafts them on his new Savannah social branches.

The Savannah St. Andrew's Society is the third oldest Scots society in the nation. The oldest is in Charleston. Although the Savannah chapter was not chartered until 1824, its origins can be traced back to around 1737. The "St. Andrew's Club," as it was originally called, often struggled during ninety-five years of existence, experiencing periods of low membership and times of inaction. On November 20, 1819, a group of men met to establish a "Charitable and Social Society" to be called "Savannah St. Andrew's Society." Five years later, with the signing of the charter on December 24, 1824, by Governor G. M. Troup, the Savannah St. Andrew's Society was acknowledged as an organization that had matured and was firmly established. The roster of membership shows that many of our ancestors and associates had been members: Basil Cowper, joined 1774; Robert Mackay, 1795; Robert Isaac, 1819; Norman Wallace, 1819; and Andrew Low, Sr., in 1827.In 1834 Andrew Low, Jr., became a steward of the St. Andrew's Society's annual celebration. That year the paper announced

"Festival of St. Andrew, the Anniversary of the birth of the Patron Saint of Scotland, was celebrated on Monday last, the 1st, inst. (30th of November falling this year on a Sunday)." This indicates to us that Sunday was a day of abstinence, a churchgoing day, and because toasting was an integral part of the celebrations, it would have been unthinkable to hold a toastless function, especially at the City Hotel.

At 4 P.M. the guests and members of the Society sat down to a sumptuous dinner, comprising the favorite national dishes, and every delicacy of the season, prepared by Captain Wiltberger, in his usual superior style. After the cloth was removed, several standard and national toasts were drunk; national comic and sentimental songs, and recitations were given, and the evening was spent with the greatest good humor and conviviality.

Toasting was a central feature of the celebrations, and the following standard toasts were given at every anniversary dinner:

1. The Pius and Immortal Memory of St. Andrew
2. The Kirk of Scotland
3. The King
4. The President of the United States
5. The Land O'Cakes
6. The Land We Live In
7. All Who celebrate the Day
8. Rob. Gibbs contract
9. Geordie McGregor's Malison
10. The Beggar's Benison
11. All the Bonnie Lassies That Whir Amongst the Heather
12. The Memory of Burns
13. Success to Benevolent Societies

Following all those raised glasses, no doubt filled with Scotch whiskey, it would not have been surprising had some of the members been a trifle befuddled. But they celebrated the business of the day in true Scottish style, and that year William Taylor was elected President, Robert Scott 1st Vice President, Norman Wallace 2nd Vice President, and James McHenry Secretary. It is not unexpected that young Andrew was made welcome; the list is also the roster of the business partners and associates of the Andrew Low Company.

First Signs of Dissatisfaction

The first concrete indication we have concerning Andrew Low, Jr.'s activities and his increasingly responsible position as a clerk at Low, Taylor & Company comes from a remarkable collection of original letters at the

Georgia Historical Society, written by Andrew Low, Sr., from Liverpool to his copartner and agent in Savannah, Robert Hutchison.[2]

A letter dated January 21, 1832, suggests that Andrew Low, Sr., is not too pleased with the performances of either nephew John Low or James Taylor, and would be pleased if his other nephew Andrew Low, Jr., were to prove worthy of his confidence:

> I am much surprised at the conduct of Jas. Taylor last year [1831]. I declined answering an insulting letter he wrote me from New York until Novbr. in a PS of a letter to the House of the 14th ultimo. He observed in consequence of my not going out to Savannah or answering his letter, that it was his intention to visit our debtors in the Country in May, and then join John in New Orleans to embark with him to this place, both of them seem to have abandoned their true interests. John has not sufficient knowledge of mankind to be entrusted with the management of a Dry Goods Business like ours, and Taylor's manner and temper is so disagreeable he is not a desirable Partner to be connected with, but it would be difficult to get anyone so well fitted to collect the debts due us. I have not had an opportunity to make myself acquainted with the character and Business Talents of my Nephew Andrew, his Cousin John and P. R. Yonge spoke favourably of him as being a steady, well informed young man. If I find he is well acquainted with the State of the accounts of the concerns which he ought to be as Bookkeeper, I will feel more independent of the services of J. Taylor, in that case he must promise more civil conduct in future or leave the concern. He will find himself mistaken in his calculations of my giving up the Business in favour of him and John and allowing my funds to remain with them on interest.

Reshuffle the Deck

Two years later Andrew Low, Sr., arrived to make what was the beginning of his final reshuffling of his business interests in the Americas. The principal reason for this business trip soon becomes apparent. On May 23, 1834, the following notice appears in the daily paper:

> Dissolution; The partnership, heretofore existing between the subscribers under the firm of Low, Taylor Co. of Savannah, is this day dissolved by mutual consent. The unsettled business of the firm will be attended to by Andrew Low and James Taylor jointly, and by the latter during the formers absence from the United States, who are hereby duly authorised to settle the affairs of the house... James Taylor is about to continue the Dry Goods business on his own account.

The three partners in Savannah—Andrew Low, Sr., James Taylor, and John Low—sign it. Andrew Low, Sr.'s letters of this decade show the underlying reasons behind this decision has to do with the changing climate of manufacturing in the north of England, although it may also have had to do with Senior's previously expressed dissatisfaction with the conduct of the two partners in Low, Taylor & Company.

This dry notice seems to dispose of the partnership with nephew John Low, although the letters also indicate that a John Low was doing business on his own account in Dundee, Scotland, and owned his own ship, a brig named *British King*, but whether this is the same nephew John Low is not recorded.[3]

By the time of the dissolution of the interim partnership young Andrew Low would have been five years in training, and deemed to be ready for greater responsibilities. He would have attained his majority in 1833; his star was on the rise.

Ships and Trains—Church and State

That same year Andrew Low, Sr., had informed his agent Robert Hutchison on a slip of paper that he had purchased a ship called the *Robert Isaac* for the sum of $18,000, and she is shown to be delivering a load of hay at the company wharf in Savannah on October 11, 1834. This was no river steamer, however, and she soon becomes one of the oceangoing ships of the Andrew Low Company.

It is now very early in his career that Andrew Low, Jr., shows exactly the same awareness of the importance of modern transportation that his uncle had shown in the steamship era. On June 4, 1835, a notice appeared in the *Georgian* listing the names of 1,100 shareholders in "The Railroad"; these included the name of Andrew Low, Jr., but not Andrew Low, Sr. The other names included most of Savannah's most upstanding and prominent businessmen. This venture was the Central of Georgia Railroad, Savannah's answer to Charleston's success in linking its port to upcountry produce. Charleston's venture called for a spur to connect to Augusta, and the fear was that Charleston would raid Georgia's interior if Savannah did not act. The Central was the brainchild of William Washington Gordon, who engineered an election to become mayor and then a member of the state legislation. These two positions gave him the ability to achieve a charter and obtain venture capital. Gordon's drive to complete the rail line led to his early demise—he died of exhaustion while supervising construction. His family's future would be entwined with the Stileses and Lows for generations to come.

A study commissioned by the owners of the Andrew Low House and Museum in Savannah[4] states that in 1835 Andrew Low, Jr., paid $80 on Pew

No. 9 at the Independent Presbyterian Church. This is the same church that Robert Isaac was heavily involved in, and it would be very much in character for the young Andrew to have been brought up in the more austere Presbyterian Church of Scotland although his grandparents, neither of whom he knew, were probably Episcopalians. Later on he became a member of Christ Episcopal Church. Membership in a church in Savannah during this era appears to be more of a social and business activity than a purely religious one.

One of the more fascinating facets of the story of both Andrew Lows is that of the social status accorded to merchants and planters in the nineteenth century. The new civilization of the Americas, at least in the Southern states, appears to have based their social consciousness on the aristocracies of England and France, the very imperialism and monarchical arrogance they had rebelled to escape from.

Consequently, in the Savannah social pecking order plantation owners seem to be at the top of the heap and merchants in second place. This would have been the antithesis of the social order in the Scottish burgh capital of Brechin, where Andrew Low's formative years were spent. Although nobility and landed gentry represented the powerful ruling class enforcing the laws there, the merchant class was a highly respected and an essential element of society.

It was in 1836 that Charles Green and Andrew Low, Jr., became partners in Andrew Low & Company in Savannah. That was the year Andrew Low, Jr., made his complete commitment to Savannah society by doing all the things that a young man would have been expected to do. It would make tremendous sense to be taken into the firm as a partner and would signify his uncle's faith and confidence in his nephew's abilities and his intention to stay and make his own fortune.

This first half-decade was one of intense growth for young Andrew Low. He found his own niche in Savannah society; he pursued his own interests as he metamorphosed from the rawboned and raw-brained youngster he had been, plucked from obscurity by his father's brother, that mythical figure from over the seas who had achieved wealth, power, and immense prestige in the new nation—the United States.

The man who emerged from the chrysalis of adolescence into the butterfly of young manhood completely reinvented himself. Did he do so out of necessity or expediency? Or was it because that is who he was evolving into as he matured on the streets, in the coffeehouses, on the parade ground, countinghouses, ships' holds, and great plantations of the Southern city of Savannah?

The indications are that the younger Andrew Low was expected to branch out on his own, find his own clients, create his own niche, and not just coast in the wind of another man's passing. There would probably not have been much tolerance or room in the competitive climate of Savannah of that day for unearned success; you would be expected to achieve your own merit badges. Authority was gradually being shifted to the next generation. This time the reins were being handed to a clansman, a member of the family, the son of one of Andrew Low's brothers, although from the terms of the senior Low's will it was obvious that he had a plethora of relatives to choose from.[5]

9

The Indian Affair: Florida, 1836

IN 1836 ANDREW LOW, JR., JOINED THE RICHMOND BLUES AND WENT off to fight the Indians in Florida for three months. Was militia service a dilettante act, a social commitment, or community necessity? An examination of this period and why the young men were required to volunteer sheds considerable light on the attitude the South held toward their civic responsibilities and way of life. The militia played a crucial role in the several occasions when the defense of Savannah was paramount. The role of the militia in colonial and post-independence America is a fascinating one—and one of the loose ends of contemporary culture in the ongoing right to bear arms and gun-control controversy.

Facets of the relations between Georgia and the indigenous peoples—first the Creeks, then the Cherokee nation—is from the perspective of twenty-first-century sensitivity a shameful saga of treaties broken and shameless land grabbing by European settlers. It needs to be treated as fairly as possible from the perspective of the realities and moralities of the time, with as little bias as is thinkable, working from hindsight. The importance to the story of the younger Andrew Low lies in its adventurous aspect, as well as carrying the seeds of the constant dilemma personified in the dual allegiances of his Scottish heritage and his American roots; they would come to a head during the wrenching realities of the War Between the States twenty-five years later.

The Colonial Militia

The concept of volunteering for militia duty in a citizens' army was one of the cornerstones of the American Revolution, fought in part at resentment in the colonies at having to pay taxes to support King George's army. In Britain, the original home of a large proportion of America's immigrant population, there was a profound distrust of the military. In fact, the last time the army was used in a direct intervention was during the time of the late 1600's Glorious Revolution of Scottish history. The British Declaration of Rights made a standing army illegal, unless it was authorized by Parliament, the reason being the British dislike of royal tyranny.[1] In Scotland the entire concept of vassal servitude to one's lord and master had been the foundation of the feudal system that had existed for centuries; but things had changed. Following the Acts of Union of 1707, the Scots had been excluded from the 1757 Militia Act, which created a force in England and Wales for homeland defense, but not in Scotland. The basic reason was the suspicion that Scotland was still infested by Jacobite supporters, hell-bent on restoring the Stuart king to the throne. The storm of patriotic indignation and national humiliation that erupted at this exclusion could not overpower the benefits of trade and political connections enjoyed by the nobility, landed gentry, and burghers. Although by 1797, when the English army was running short of men to fight its wars, especially in France and Ireland, news of a possible conscription for a Scottish home militia caused riots to break out in the rural Lowlands.

In Georgia the militia had been a fact of life from the very beginning, as the professional soldier-farmers from the Scottish Highlands brought over by General Oglethorpe established a military reality firmly in the hands and weapons of immigrant Scots. In an expanded Georgia, following the relinquishment by the Trustees of their charter, the power of an appointed royal governor to rule the colony with an autocratic hand gave him both command of the militia and the right to negotiate problems with the native tribes.[2] The role of the volunteer militia, as Georgia became the thirteenth colony to rebel against the British, is well documented.

This particular excursion was against the Seminole nation in north Florida, centered on St. Augustine. In February 1836 Andrew Low did what was expected of a young man in Savannah at that time—he joined the militia and went off to fight the "savages." The adventure lasted only a few months, but nevertheless, it was both a revelation and a turning point in his life.

Culture Clash or Ethnic Cleansing?

The colonization of native people in the Americas commenced during the sixteenth century by the Spanish, followed by the French, but ultimately it was the British who succeeded in gaining control of the southeastern Indians. The first successful colony was South Carolina, when 150 British colonists landed at the mouth of the Ashley River in 1670 and founded the trading town they called Charles Town. A lucrative trade in deerskins soon dominated the early colony, and inevitably trading currency included firearms. Some traders provided the Indians with guns and persuaded them to capture other Indians who could then be sold as slaves. The highly successful British proclivity for divide and conquer used for centuries of imperialism proved highly effective in dealings with people unused to such tactics, as they would arm one group of Indians and set them against any other group who threatened their conduct of trade.

These tactics eventually led to excursions south to raid Spanish missions, mostly run by Jesuits in their quest to save souls of the heathen while Spanish conquistadors sought the gold to fill the coffers of the Spanish monarchs and fill their own pockets in the process. British traders and merchants filled the gap in the middle. At that time the Indian trade was dominated by Highland Scots who appeared to have a remarkable affinity with their red-skinned brethren, possibly because their own clan-based feudal systems allowed them to comprehend and, in many cases, to assimilate into native culture.

An unsuccessful attempt by Scottish settlers under Lord Cardross at Stuartstown, now known as Port Royal, followed.[3] By the time the colony of Georgia became a reality South Carolina's traders, plantation owners, governors, and their proxy Indians had systematically destroyed Spanish missions all the way down the coast of Guale—as coastal Georgia was known then—to St. Augustine, taking prisoners. Men, women, and children became chattel slaves for resale, albeit at lower purchase prices than those of African slaves, the preferred labor pool. The usual platitudes were spouted to justify the practice of increasing abuses against the Indian peoples.

However, just as African slaves frequently rose up in revolt, the Indian people also struck back repeatedly. The Yemasee War[4] that broke out in 1715 was a concerted attempt by the Creek, Choctaw, and some Cherokee to regain control of their lives. Again, by divide- and- rule tactics the Carolinians were able to turn one nation against the other and in the end concluded a peace treaty with the Creek in 1717, leaving the rest to fight each other. This was a situation the British encouraged on the principle that if they killed one another, they would leave the settlers in peace.

In 1729 South Carolina became a crown colony, followed by the creation of Georgia in 1732. In 1736 the British, under the command of General James Oglethorpe, had built Fort Frederica on St Simons Island to defend the colony against the Spaniards. English Methodist ministers John and Charles Wesley arrived to compete with the Spanish Papist Jesuits to spread their Methodist version of the Church of England and convert the heathen to their Protestant God. They soon gave up and returned to the more soul-friendly fields of working-class England.

From then on Southeastern Indians were increasingly drawn in on one side or the other of the vicious battles between the French, the British, and the Spanish as they competed for total domination of the North American continent. In the game of "football" for control that ensued, with these powers scoring wins and losses interchangeably, the Indians scored a few goals of their own. After the American Revolution the pressure became even more intense as immigrants poured into the new world of milk and honey with no regard for the rights of those who had occupied it for thousands, possibly tens of thousands, of years. The indigenous Americans held such elements as the earth, sky, and its inhabitants sacred, and were culturally unequipped to deal with a people who viewed the same elements as commodities to be exploited. Above all, the land greed of the settlers knew no bounds and they drove the native people before them in their inexorable march to the west, like so many herds of cattle or sheep. If they got in the way they exterminated them like rodents. The conquest of the Southeastern Indians was not a quick invasion resulting in occupation. It was a long drawn out event that spanned three hundred years.

According to Charles Hudson in his book *The Southeastern Indians,*[5] "the ultimate conquest was achieved by the social system known as the Old South, a strongly hierarchical system of agricultural production using slave labor." Land hunger created a more subtle form of conquest by legislation and by treaties that caused forced removal of entire tribes in resettlement to other land west of the Mississippi, leaving their more fertile land vacant for settlers to grab, purchase, or win by lottery.

Much has been written, especially recently, as revisionist history reclaims and returns the rights and roles of both Africans and Native peoples into America's colonial past, but Charles Hudson's excellent chapter in *The Southeastern Indians* explains concisely what happened next:

> The final assault against the Southeastern Indians came in the 1830's. Seldom in modern history has one people's aggression against another been so unforgiving, so relentless, and marked by such terrible results. The world of the Southeastern Indians changed greatly before 1830, but what happened after 1830 virtually brought it to an end.

Our story deals with two aspects of that terrible destruction: with the Seminole nation as a microcosm of resistance of a people who fought to the death, and the Cherokee nation, whose betrayal by the white European settlers is a blot on the American escutcheon to this very day.[6]

By the time we pick up the story, the greed to acquire land had reached epic proportions. The need for black labor to pick and prepare the cotton had exploded, and the Indian people had become nothing more than a nuisance to be dealt with in order to appropriate their land to grow more cotton.

The Seminole People

The Seminole were descended from Creek who had moved south into Florida after the original indigenous inhabitants had been enslaved and killed. By the 1800's they were living in scattered permanent towns in northern Florida around the St. Johns River, just north of St. Augustine. They had become more and more independent from the Creek Confederacy, and the white settlers began to call them Seminole which, according to Charles Hudson, is derived from the Spanish word *cimarron*, meaning "wild runaway." Another element of their population was a large contingent of escaped black slaves. The Seminole, who numbered approximately six thousand at that time, like other native tribes owned black slaves. They appear to have treated them better, allowed them more latitude and considerable freedom. In fact, the descriptions of these Indians' attitude toward their African slaves resemble more the slavery that had existed in Africa itself before the Europeans introduced the element of commerce, resulting in chattel or property ownership with no rights or freedoms included.

Unlike the Cherokee, who were forced off their land because the settlers needed it for expansion, the land the Seminole inhabited was not as valuable. Hudson says, "what the whites wanted from the Seminole was not their land but to gain possession of the blacks who lived among them and to close off Florida as a place to which their own slaves could escape and find refuge." Greed and fear appear to have been the motivations.

The Seminole fought two wars against the United States. The first was in 1816, when the army invaded Spanish Florida and attempted to capture the blacks living amongst the Seminole. Later that same year, the feared Indian fighter Andrew Jackson, nicknamed "Old Hickory," later President of the United States,[7] also invaded Seminole country, wreaking havoc and leaving devastation in his wake. That war ended in 1818, and the following year the United States purchased Florida from Spain, which left the Seminole under the official jurisdiction of the federal government.

In 1832 the government pressured a group of Seminole leaders to sign a treaty stipulating that the Seminole would give up their Florida lands and move west to unite with the Creek. The majority of the Seminole did not want to move, did not want to merge again with the Creek, and above all did not want to deliver their black slaves and brothers into slavery again by whites. In addition, the spurious leaders who had signed this treaty did not represent the will of the Seminole people, and they considered it had absolutely no validity.

The Indian agent, a white man named Wiley Thompson, tried to get them to migrate voluntarily by telling them the army would kill them if they did not. Instead, Osceola, the Seminole leader, turned the tables and on December 28, 1835, killed Thompson and a companion. A second war party moved out of the swamps and attacked a company of troops moving through dense scrub forest of central Florida near Ft. King, under the command of Major Frances L. Dade, killing eight officers and 102 enlisted men. Only three of Dade's men escaped alive.

This massacre could not go unchallenged, and the Second Seminole War had begun. It immediately turned into a guerilla war, a version of nineteenth- century Vietnam on American soil. The Seminole just melted away into the swamps they knew like the back of their hand, and the U.S. Army sent in several thousand troops to wage a scorched-earth campaign against the Seminole homes and food sources, but they caught few Indians. It was into this hostile environment that the volunteer militia regiments from Georgia and South Carolina were called out to join the professional soldiers in the increasingly one-sided battle in the swamps. The American soldiers began to suffer more casualties than the Indians. It seems as though the Second Seminole War never really ended, it just faded away, causing many casualties and destroying many professional careers in its course, another parallel with Vietnam. Hudson writes "The war lasted six years; cost the lives of 1,500 American soldiers, twenty million dollars, and incalculable death and misery for the Seminoles," not to mention more betrayals and broken promises, and jealousies between the professional army and the militia commanders. It broke the back of the Seminole nation as they moved into the inaccessible interior of the Everglades. Nobody won, but the Seminoles definitely lost.

Andrew Low's Role in All This

The regional newspapers elaborated on the immediate actions taken: "General Duncan Lamont Clinch, the US Army commander in Florida, with a small federal detachment and five hundred Florida militiamen, immediately took reprisal action by attacking the Seminoles along the Withlacoochee River. The Seminoles severely mauled the Americans and disappeared into dense foliage." On January 1, 1836, President Andrew Jackson appointed Major General Winfield Scott, commander of the Eastern Department of the U.S. Army, to personally supervise the Florida campaign. The War Department, however, could not provide the number of federal troops General Scott felt were necessary to accomplish his mission. Reluctantly Scott issued a call for state militia volunteers to fight alongside those federal troops available to him.

A call from John Eaton, the governor of Georgia, went out to volunteer regiments of the Georgia militia to defend the Georgia-Florida border from Indian rampages. Two weeks later, the following notice was published in the state capital of Milledgeville, January 13, 1836: "The Commander-in-Chief, under existing circumstances, will not order the Militia of Georgia, or any part of them, to march beyond the limits of the state—but he earnestly invites such of the Volunteer Corps as are willing to go to the relief of their suffering fellow-citizens of Florida, immediately to signify to him their readiness for such service."

The Phoenix Riflemen from Savannah immediately volunteered to guard the federal depot at Picolata, located at the site of a traditional Indian crossing on the St. Johns River, a few miles inland from St. Augustine, a historic Spanish town and fort on the Florida coast. The volunteers got more than they bargained for, as on arrival at Picolata they were mustered into federal service. Limited to a one-month tour, Savannah's Phoenix Riflemen were released by General Scott and returned home. Several other volunteer militia regiments formed for service in Florida, but on reaching Picolata most of them refused to be mustered into the United States Army because of the length of service required of them.

Starting in late February the trials and triumphs of the Southern militia troops can be tracked on a day-by-day basis from dispatches in the field. It was not Boy Scout camp; this was real warfare, pitting relatively untrained volunteers and regular soldiers under the command of conflicting generals with their own political agendas, against Indians fighting not only for their lives, but for their very existence.

Bravo Georgia!

The aspect of the story that is most interesting to us is the fact that Andrew Low, Jr., was one of those who answered the call to duty. Full coverage is given to this aspect of the Indian Wars in the Savannah papers partly because of the "massacre" of Major Dade's troops that had taken place and the arrival of Captain Bones with a detachment of Hussars, including Andrew Low, Jr.[8]

It is important in the examination of the maturing of this young Scottish emigrant, more used to counting coins than bodies, to understand that he would nevertheless have had his head filled with romantic fantasies of warriorhood from his Scottish boyhood in Kincardine and the Stuart cause. Whether this foray into battle truly represents a profound emotion, or whether it was the "right thing to do," is open to interpretation. Certainly several of his fellow volunteers, Edward Purse and William D. Berrien, were from Savannah top-drawer society. Peer pressure or business acumen could have played a role, or was it to appear courageous in the eyes of the young ladies? Many published poems attested to the fact that the fashion was for the ladies to go into print with their admiration.

In February of 1836, Andrew Low, Jr., was twenty-four years old and had been in Savannah for a little over seven years. Perhaps the most important aspect of his military duty was that it could easily have ended in his death—this was not turning out in dress blues on a Sunday morning in Parade Square, preening for the young ladies! This was to actually fight with the volunteer militia in the Indian Wars.

The first we hear in public that Andrew Low was involved was a notice dated February 15, 1836, in the Savannah *Daily Georgian*, apologizing for not including his name in the list of volunteers who had responded to the call to defend the homeland: "We have published from time to time the names of our citizens pressing on to Florida. In our last the name of Mr. Andrew Low, Jr. should have appeared among the little, but gallant band who embarked last week from St. Mary's with General Charles Floyd."

Someone was obviously looking after the interests of the young man. On February 23 the arrival was announced in the *Georgian* in a reprinted article from a Florida newspaper:

> Jacksonville Courier, 18th inst: Bravo, Georgia!!!!! Yesterday touched at our wharves the Steamers Santee, Tomochichi and Florida, having on board five volunteer companies from the counties of Monroe, Babb, Hancock, Morgan and Putnam—in all upwards of 400 men, all prepared and eager for a battle with the warriors of the brave chief, whose beautiful name, Osceola, signifying in the Indian language "the rising sun" is so descriptive of his own rising to be the great warrior of the Seminoles. All those on board the three steamers were bound for Picolata, thereon to march into the Indian nation. Judging from their martial and favorable appearance we think these Georgia sons will do their duty bravely and heroically on the day of battle.
>
> We give below a list of the few volunteers who arrived at this place on Friday evening in the last week. They came from St. Mary's in an open boat belonging to one of their number. This small band, only ten in number, is, we are told, composed of not only the most wealthy—but of the bravest hearts—of the elite of Campden, Chatham and Glynn counties, Georgia. They go on to join their brother volunteers from Georgia. They left yesterday on board the schooner Ariel for Picolata. We understand that the Georgia volunteers will form themselves into a regiment, at the head of which it has been suggested that General Charles Floyd will be placed. He is a gentleman extensively known, and is admired by all hands, that he possesses great military experience and skills, and is as brave as Julius Caesar.

The company Andrew Low joined was known as the Richmond Blues, led by two officers from Augusta, Captains Bones and Robertson. The roster of names included Robert Mackay, Jr., proof that at that very early stage of his life in Savannah, Andrew Low, Jr., would have bonded with a son of the Mackay clan, sharing not only a Scottish heritage, but perhaps forging a connection that can only be tempered in the crucible of combat.

The journey from Savannah to form into companies was quite hazardous, especially as the small group from Savannah embarked from St. Marys, a small port on the coast of Georgia just above Amelia Island, and wended their way in a rowboat down to Jacksonville before congregating at Picolata.

The next reference to Andrew Low's militia service was published in the Savannah newspaper on March 10, 1836:

> Capt Bones's company of Richmond Hussars arrived here (where 'here' was is not ascertained accurately, but probably was Fort Drane) Thursday last, from Picolata—Col. Dubignon commanding the following gentlemen, on their way to join the Glynn and Campden volunteers, had the advance on the march. Capt. Gates, commanded the detachment. John Dubignon, Robert Mackay, John Rudolph, James Morrison, Joseph Dubignon, Andrew Low, Jr., P. M. Nightingale, Jas. Gould, Thos. Bourke, Robert Scott, W. D. Berrien. Immediately after our arrival at Fort Drane, we were ordered to proceed next day as an escort with wagons to Picolata. The Glynn and Campden volunteers accompanied us on this service. General Clinch speaks well of us, in a general order, which was read before our company and bids us an affectionate farewell. As there is no immediate prospect of meeting the common foe, we are not sorry to think that home will soon break upon our view.' Adieu. Ps. Col Dubignon and his little band seeing no chance of a fight come with us.

From this little account it sounds very much as though these particular Georgia volunteers spent most of their war service marching across north Florida from Picolata to Fort Drane and back again—"they marched them up to the top of the hill and marched them down again" as the nursery rhyme says.

The next announcement appears in the *Georgian* on May 3, 1836:

> The steam packet Florida, Captain Hubbard, arrived yesterday morning from Picolata via Jacksonville, freighted with the gallant corps of Capt Robertson and Captain Bones, from Augusta, whom, officers and men, we welcome back to their native States, after the perilous campaign they have encountered. Their conduct, and that of all the brave volunteers who sacrificed their comforts at home for the perils of the camp, must ever be a source of the most unmixed gratification to those, whose names are more than ever identified

> with the country, from whose bosom they have sprung. We regret that those gallant men returned so much earlier than was expected thereby depriving our citizens of the opportunity of making some preparation for their reception. Messrs. Andrew Low, Jr., Wm. D. Berrien, Edward Purse and Wm Reed, of this city, returned with the Richmond Blues.

Their term of duty was only about two months; nevertheless it had been potentially a very dangerous and literally very real experience. Despite the apparent fact that all they sacrificed were the comforts of home, it could have been different and was for many of the volunteers. These militia forces were much more than toy soldiers. There is no further indication that Andrew Low remained a member of the militia; perhaps enough was enough.

The same day the young volunteers returned to pick up their lives again, the Chatham Artillery celebrated its fiftieth anniversary. According to the Savannah *Morning News* of Tuesday, May 3rd: "This corps was established in 1780, and is the oldest volunteer Association in the state, and the second in the Union. It is also the only Artillery corps in Georgia."

It was also the corps that young Andrew Low's three uncles—Andrew, Alexander, and George—had belonged to during their escapade with the French privateer, *La Vengeance*, in 1811, almost thirty years before. Membership was also a major social element denoting the status of a young male, as the article in the newspaper attests to:

> The members deserve much credit for the spirit with which they have sustained a corps, so honorable to the pride of Georgians. Yesterday they paraded in unwanted strength, having recently received many additional members who, though young in years, bid fair to be honorable representatives of the esprit de corps, which originated in their Association fifty years ago. Escorted by the Georgia Hussars, Lieut. Kollock; Phoenix Riflemen, Capt Bowen; Republican Blues, Lieut. Miller; and Savannah Volunteer Guards, Lieut. Bayard; they proceeded under the command of Capt Stephens, attended by their fine band of music, to the Unitarian Church, where, after an impressive address to the Throne of Grace by Rev. E. L. Bascom, an Oration replete with patriotic sentiment and glowing with eloquent allusions. The plaudits with which the youthful orator was frequently interrupted evinced the pleasure, which swelled the bosom of his attentive auditors. After the exercises in the Church, the corps, with their usual precision, fired in Monumental Square a salute of fifty guns, which was succeeded by a National salute from the Guards, who thereby commemorated their thirty-fourth anniversary. Dur-

> ing the day, the Guards, the Blues, and the Riflemen also exercised themselves in target practice. In the evening, a splendid Ball was given by the Artillery in the Exchange, which was attended by a gay and fashionable assemblage.

No doubt the returned heroes attended and regaled the "fashionable assemblage" with their own tales of exaggerated derring-do, leaving many a young lady with fluttering heart behind her fan.

Andrew Low, Jr., picked up the threads of his life. Several months later the young man made his only recorded foray into local politics, when on September 3 he ran on the Young Man's Ticket for alderman. He was unsuccessful, placing eighth out of fourteen and receiving 175 votes. He was more successful in the St. Andrew's Society, and on November 30, 1836, his name appears as secretary, announcing that the anniversary meeting will be held at the City Hotel on that same day.

10

Passing the Baton: Savannah–Liverpool, 1836–1841

In the early nineteenth century, on both sides of the Atlantic merchant adventurers were the risk-takers and entrepreneurs of the commercial world, competing for stature with the inventors and innovators of the new industrial age. It is at this point that the personality of the inheritor of the empire starts to emerge, and although the record shows several more trips by Andrew Low, Sr., to oversee his business interests, more and more we see the younger man coming into his own.

Ours is the story of an older man moving on as his young nephew moved up, and two of the pre-eminent cities—Savannah and Liverpool—linked with a thread of cotton speckled with red dirt, picked and baled by black hands, spun and woven by white hands.

In November 1836 an itinerant artist named George W. Conarroe visited Savannah for the purpose of soliciting portrait commissions from leading citizens. A small notice appeared in the *Daily Georgian* stating: "Mr. Connaroe [*sic*] from Philadelphia begs leave to inform the ladies and gentlemen of Savannah, that being on a professional visit to this city for a few weeks only, he renders his services to them. He may be found at his room on Broughton Street one door from the residence of Wm. B. Bulloch, Esq. where specimens may be seen and his terms made known."

Several merchants of the city took advantage of the offer, among them Andrew Low, Jr. It is fortunate for posterity that he did, as this portrait, which now hangs in pride of place in the Andrew Low House and Museum, is the only one extant.[1] He would have been twenty-four years of age at the time, and is the only true likeness we possess of how he looked in his youth. The portrait shows a young man in his prime, the dark red hair of his Scottish heritage, piercing hazel eyes, a sensitive, sensual mouth, clean shaven with a long curved well-shaped jaw, which has been passed down to his descendants.

The Cotton Factor

The factorage system was a British import. For centuries British factors had acted as bankers and agents for colonial clients. The principals of these great far-flung mercantile houses resided in London, Bristol, Liverpool, Edinburgh, and Glasgow; their clerks toiled in the warehouses and stores of Virginia, the Carolinas, and Georgia, not to mention Java, Sumatra, and Hong Kong. Their sons captained the ships and fought Britain's wars—they were the heart of both the oak and the lion. Initially in colonial times, when commercial rice and cotton production began in the crown colonies of Georgia and Carolina, planters at first used existing organizations, as commission merchants bought the raw materials outright or consigned it to London.

The vagaries and fluctuations of the marketplace built trust and integrity between the planter and his factor, which is why respectability and reputation for the factor was an absolute and the key element in their relationship. Many cotton factors were also speculators with an interest directly opposed to the planters. Both required a profit to survive, and everything depended on accurate bookkeeping and good credit in the triangle of growing, transporting, and marketing of cotton. The factor was above all the planter's banker. Credit and access to capital was the factor's lifeline. He was also enslaved to his marketing contacts. He needed to be able to take risks and speculate in futures; he also needed to be circumspect, with a moral rectitude enough to create schizophrenia.

The plantation system was a never-ending spiral, requiring more and more land, more slaves, more investment resulting in more credit, more risk, and more dependence on each other. No little wonder then that these families, merchants, and planters only trusted their own. Rarely has commerce resulted in such cooperation and synergism on all levels; and the books are filled with as many accounts of relationships that did not work, as much as those that did. It was also a relationship that shackled both in a form of economic bondage—the production of cotton. Cotton slavery sucked everyone into its maw and absorbed much of the energy of two nations for almost a century. It also made a few enormously wealthy and created untold miseries for uncounted many.

The relationship between the factor and the planter was paramount. The planters would come down the river in their pirogues or small river schooners or later on in the steamboats, hungry for company, hungry for money, hungry for drink, and the only place they could get what they needed was from their factor. The planter would make his way to the factor's countinghouse, the factor would receive the lists of supplies they considered necessary and unload the bales of cotton they had brought.

They would go over the accounts and balance the books. Then the factor would provide the planter with a wad of money to give him a brief interlude, and he would go off to the tavern and drink himself into a stupor, maybe go to a whorehouse—celebrate and unwind from the tensions of life on a rice or cotton plantation. In Savannah the wealthier planters would stay at the Pulaski House, the Screven House, or at the home of an associate or family member. But without the credit extended to them from the factor they were helpless. The factorage and banking business traveled parallel paths. The factors owned the planters, and the banks owned the factors.

The insurance and banking business were equally symbiotic and co-dependent. Agents from the great European insurance companies traversed the state like traveling salesmen, digging up the dirt on all aspects of a prospective or current client's business and personal affairs; did he drink, was he an adulterer, was he a good family man, a lecher, a reader, profligate, quick tempered? With the accumulated information, credit reports would be prepared, blunt, raw, and direct—because it was on these reports that a company had to make a decision whether to trust a man enough to take on his business. Andrew Low & Company was in the forefront of the business of banking and insurance, acting as agent for prominent insurance companies. The House of Low was represented on the boards of several banking establishments, as well as deeply embedded in the factorage business.

Savannah and the Savannah River plantations were, in the context of the greater world, a very small pond. To the ego-driven planters and merchants striving to outdo each other, competition between them ruled the day. The very British notion of one-upmanship was not an abstraction; it was the reality that governed their behavior and shaded their decisions, whether business or social. Where to attend church, who to marry, where to build, what size home to build, where to locate the business, all feature in the constant jockeying for position. The few who rose to the top and held on to their rank and maintained a leadership role for a lifetime—such as the Gordons, the Andersons, and the Lows—were often ruthless, always visionary men who saw what needed to be achieved, and then set out to achieve it. The factors, when Cotton really was King, ruled the top of the heap; it was their homes that were the largest and most magnificent.

Financial Panic of 1837

But there were lean times, too. In 1837 a financial panic shortly after the election of President Martin Van Buren, as inexplicable in simple terms as any modern-day stock market collapse, can be traced to lack of confidence that initiated a nationwide depression, causing commodity prices to plummet and severely restricting access to capital and credit. This triggered a crisis in the banking business, resulting in a massive economic meltdown on both sides of the Atlantic.

At the height of the depression a letter written by Andrew Low, Sr., to Robert Hutchison goes a long way to express the unpredictability of survival. Although difficult to read in modern terms, it is an essential component of appreciating how he dealt with the vagaries of business, how economic distress affected him personally, along with his friend Mrs. Isaac, and the operation of both the Savannah and Liverpool businesses.[2] These letters, written at the height of the crisis, during the period of July to December 1837, shed a great deal of light on how the company handled its affairs during this tense period, and it is clear that the company suffered, poised on the brink of bankruptcy. Andrew Low, Sr., struggled mightily to keep the company affairs in order and afloat. The old man had iron resolve and refused to panic as lesser men were doing.

The newspapers daily carried tales of doom and gloom as the entire cotton-growing South was affected. In Liverpool things were dire, as by now so much of the commerce was involved in the cotton trade, funneling the raw materials through to the industrial mills of Manchester, Oldham, Bolton, and other centers of the spinning and weaving trade. From the New Orleans *True American:*

> The news from Liverpool is truly discouraging. From no quarter whatever is there any hope. Confidence will suffer even more than hitherto. Every puff of wind that comes across the waters now will sink that delicate thermometer a degree at a time. Now and then, the innate energies of our people lift up the immense pile of ruins, that have overwhelmed them beneath, and we can almost fancy that they will succeed in freeing themselves from their horrid situation, but you look again and all is as quiet as the grave. Our levee, once the most animated scene in the country is now deserted, and where thousands were engaged in the business, now tens and twenties straggle along, looking the very picture of the times—sad and hopeless. It is true that piles of Cotton, are here and there but they are comparatively worthless. The steamboats are getting into the habit of coming into our ports without manifests, this is a serious evil. The fear, we are told, is that the produce which comes by them consigned to the broken houses, will be seized by the officers. How devoid of courage are men who are not guided by the high principles of commerce.

These articles explain and describe the tenuous and fickle nature of the world markets, with the risk for next year's crop undertaken by the factors and merchants. The elder Low understood these vagaries as he understood his heartbeat; the younger Andrew Low was just learning the dimensions of the swings of fortune that would be his own heartbeat for all of his life.

Somehow they managed to weather the financial storm and by December of 1837 Andrew Low, Sr., arrived in Savannah to patch the pieces together again; the phoenix once more had risen from the ashes. One of his solutions was to attempt to sell or charter several of the ships the company owned, the *Governor Troup* and the *Robert Isaac*. It appears that the markets had not yet recovered sufficiently for that avenue to be successful.

On December 5, 1837, per Express Mail from New York, Andrew Low, Sr., wrote to his agent:

> I have had the ship Rob't Isaac advertised for charter but T & M think that the season of the year and the state of the Money Market here leaves little hope of being able to obtain an offer for her or the Governor Troup, which I much regret, and only now hope we may be able to obtain a loan from the Bankers in Savannah on their security until their return in the Spring when T & M think they will sell to much more advantage as money is expected to be more easily obtained, altho it is most important we should be able to send early aid to our House in Liverpool to meet its engagements for the payment of the Railroad Iron and the Iron Boat.
>
> I sincerely thank you and Mrs. H. for your kind invitation to be your guest but having accepted Mr. & Mrs. Robertson to Lodge with him I cannot with propriety now decline it, the more so as he expects and reasonably for me to pay a fair proportion of House expenses—with best respects to your Good Lady and all friends. I am Dear Sir, yours truly Andrew Low.

The last sentence in this letter is extremely illuminating, as it is further irrefutable proof of the fact that Andrew Low, Sr., never owned his own home in Savannah, although he certainly at some time may have lived in the two upper floors with long cast iron balconies over the Johnson Square Emporium. Even in Liverpool he resided only as a boarder in several homes in well-to-do neighborhoods housing many of the cities wealthiest merchants. The letters also hint at a more than close relationship between Andrew Low, Sr., and Mrs. Lucy Isaac, although there is never any hint of impropriety.[3]

The decade of the 1840's was to prove pivotal for both Andrew Lows, and it started with a presidential election.[4] Unfortunately William Henry Harrison's presidency was short-lived. Harrison, ninth President and Whig, served only thirty-one days. He was the son of Benjamin Harrison, one of the signers of the Declaration of Independence. Harrison, although born to a wealthy and elitist family, was elected on a "log cabin and hard cider" populist theme. Previous roles in government were superintendent of Indian Affairs and governor of Indiana Territory. He was responsible for putting down a Shawnee uprising at Tippecanoe, Indiana, in 1811. The newly inaugurated President died of pleurisy, complicated with disordered liver and bowels. All the best efforts of the best medical skill were of no avail.

Both the older Andrew Low and the younger one were supporters of Harrison, and their sympathies lay with the Whig element of politics, although neither of them appears to have been much involved. Andrew Low, Jr., had made his mark on Savannah society at the age of twenty-nine, having been in Savannah for twelve years. He was well established in his own right by now, walking more in the footprints of Robert Isaac than his Uncle Andrew

Back in Liverpool, as reported in the *Georgian* on May 26, 1841:

> Death of President Harrison—Public Meeting in Liverpool. A general meeting of American merchants, shipmasters, and others was held on Friday evening, at half past 7 o'clock, at the Grecian Hotel, Dale Street, to adopt such measures as might be thought appropriate to express their grief at the death of William Harrison, President of the United States. The Chairman opened the proceedings by briefly stating the object for which the meeting had been convened. He said there was no distinction of party on the present occasion but that they were assembled in a foreign country, as Americans, to resolve upon the proper mode of expressing their respect for the memory of their deceased President.

This is an interesting sidebar since it does seem to indicate that in Liverpool, at least, the senior Andrew Low was considered to be an American.

Bowing Out

That same year, on May 6, 1841, the older Andrew Low wrote his last will and testament in Liverpool. In his will he left his brothers, nephews, nieces, grand nephews, and grand nieces provided for with an annual stipend, and he left to "my nephew Andrew Low, residing in Savannah, my property in Johnson Square and all my holdings in the State of Georgia and Florida."[5]

With that detailed document, all the family relationships become clear. To ensure that the stipulations of his testament be carried out, he appointed both his nephew Andrew Low, Jr., and partner Charles Green as executors. Secrets and lies are often part of the social fabric or survival mechanism, and the practice to deceive is also inherent in the social mores and manners of the day, especially in a family torn between two worlds, one a nation growing up, the other a nation winding down.

The conspiracy theories that have grown through the ensuing 150 years regarding the reluctance of Andrew Low, Jr., to reveal his origins could have been clarified through a close examination in Liverpool and Scotland of the business aspects of the family relationships. He would have merely been fulfilling the terms of his uncle's bequests by forwarding money back to the family following his uncle's death. Andrew Low, Jr., as one of the executors, would have had to be in close contact with his Scottish family and multitude of cousins. Low, Jr.'s own family, mother and two sisters, were still living in Brechin in Scotland.

January 31, 1843, Andrew Low, Jr.'s name appears in a notice to procure additional motive power for the Central Rail Road and Banking Company. He was a contributing director of this corporation's affairs. This was not merely a Savannah company; this railroad was the lifeline for the planters and businesses up-river and in the interior of the state. Here we see a close working relationship with W. W. Gordon, Jr., on a project that would bring development to the town while opening markets for the Low firm. The fact that Andrew Low's name is so prominent in the affairs of the company is an excellent indication that his status in the business community has grown, and the shareholders have confidence in his abilities. An accurate barometer—he has taken over the reins of power of the Andrew Low Company in Savannah.

Mays's *Interpretive Plan Proposal* lists the purchase by the Andrew Low Company of a slave named Cyrus, age sixty, from W. P. Clark in 1843 for the sum of $450. This is an odd purchase, the age being high for productive work. Andrew Low, Jr., would necessarily have made the purchase as his uncle was already living in Liverpool. Also to Andrew Low & Company. from William B. Bulloch in 1843 "For $750 a mulatto Woman named Sarah aged about Twenty and a Negro boy named Robert aged about nine years." Then to Andrew Low & Company, from Wylly Woodbridge in 1844, "Tom $398.92." This has always been assumed to be the Thomas Anderson Milledge who remained with Andrew Low, Jr., for the rest of his life, emerging as a friend as much as a slave or servant.[6]

We leave the first part of our story in Liverpool with the reference to Andrew Low, Sr., of Savannah attending a commemorative evening to mourn the death of President Harrison of the United States. The company he was in that night was of the highest order: merchants, professionals, diplomats, and the cosmopolitan cream of an international crop. These were the men and the women who ruled the world in the middle of the nineteenth century on both sides of the Atlantic. He was now a man who had earned his fortune and position and not inherited it. He was a man who during his life had faced hazards of health, dangers to life and sanity, and odds beyond our comprehension today—no safety nets, only family to fall back on, just pure undiluted strong Scots spirit. There is no physical image of you. I have not even been able to locate your burial ground. In the years that I have tried to trace your existence, I have grown to love you and above all respect your indomitable spirit. The Sign of the Buck's Head, the Monarch of the Glen. I salute you.

Part IV

Savannah, 1844–1860

11

The Crown Prince: Savannah, 1844–1849

By January 1844 Andrew Low, Jr., was fully assimilated socially and commercially in his new community. No record has been found of his taking out naturalization papers; by now there was no pressing reason to do so. It is unlikely patriotism entered the picture; pragmatism was the ruling arbiter of these men's decisions.

The next logical item on the agenda would have been marriage. Andrew Low was ready to start his own family. He chose as his bride a young woman named Sarah Cecil Hunter. The register of the Christ Church of Savannah records: "Married, No. 2587. On Thursday evening January 18th, 1844 Andrew Low, to Miss Sarah Cecil Hunter, daughter of the late Alexander Hunter."

Alexander Hunter was a contemporary of his Uncle Andrew, naturalized on the same day in 1807 along with John Hunter, the same who had been Andrew, Sr.'s commanding officer during the *La Vengeance* murder and mayhem episode in 1811. The name of Hunter has been entwined with the name of Low throughout the nineteenth century. Hunter was a prominent name as merchants in the Kincardine region of Scotland, and Hunters are buried in adjacent plots in both the Brechin and Catterline graveyards where Andrew Low, Jr.'s parents and grandparents are interred. It is not too wild a speculation to suppose that there had been a long-term connection in both countries.[1]

Sarah Cecil Hunter's mother was Harriet Bellinger of South Carolina, descended from one of the original English crown land grantees. Harriet Bellinger married Alexander Hunter in Savannah on March 30, 1809.[2] The South Carolina Historical Society in Charleston uncovered a chart that indicates she was the daughter of Barnaby Bull Bellinger.[3]

The young couple was married in Christ Episcopal Church on the

Sarah Cecil Hunter married Andrew Low, Jr., on January 18, 1844.
This portrait was probably done after the wedding.
Courtesy The National Society of The Colonial Dames of America in the State of Georgia.

evening of January 25, 1844. He was thirty-two years old, she a few years younger. The portrait painted eight years earlier, in 1836, the only one extant of him at any time of his life, shows a reddish sandy-haired slight young man, with strong comely face, a sensitive mouth, and straightforward eyes looking at the portrait painter without fear or shyness. He faced the artist as he would face life, taking it as it came. The only extant portrait of her shows a woman with a face that was neither startlingly beautiful nor plain, a woman with a serene calm demeanor gazing at what life was to bring to her—an ambitious husband, children, and a secure position in Savannah society.[4]

Edward Anderson's Diary

The husband of one of Sarah Hunter's best friends, Sarah Anderson, was an ambitious young man and an inveterate journal keeper. Notations in Edward Anderson's diaries show us a contemporary word sketch of Mr. and Mrs. Andrew Low from the day they married as well as a portrait of the Savannah of that day.[5]

Edward Clifford Anderson married Sarah McQueen Williamson, a niece of Mrs. Robert Mackay (Eliza McQueen), so she would have been cousin of Eliza Mackay Stiles. Anderson's diaries, written through his lifetime, are extraordinary in their obsession with descriptive details, almost as though he was writing them for posterity. One startling and revealing detail leaves us with the unmistakable impression that the groom had been somewhat dilatory in his consummation of the marriage:

> 1844—Miss Sarah C. Hunter was married on the 25th of January to Andrew Lowe. They moved down the same night to his Domicile opposite the Catholic Church. The engagement was a protracted one and placed her, I thought in rather an awkward position. It appeared to me as though the gentleman was not altogether certain of his mind and was holding off for some contingency. Sarah and myself attended the wedding. There were very few present except her own immediate family.[6]

Whether this marriage was a love match or a business arrangement may never be determined, and shows a certain degree of vacillation on Andrew Low's part, but the marriage would have been advantageous for both; a good alliance in terms of social acceptance and a comfortable one in terms of family relationships.[7]

Anderson's journals, written a century and a half ago, reflect the contemporary feelings and pride of Savannah's residents in their lovely old city, its origins, and frequently turbulent history. This pride is still reflected in the organizations in the present day, dedicated to the preservation of its architecture, its frequent reenactments, and traffic-stopping parades where civic souls dress up in eighteenth-century gear and relive the glory days of their colonial heritage. One of the single most obvious manifestations of Savannah's pride is the manner in which the citizens use their excellent archives on Whitaker and Gaston streets, at the top end of Forsyth Square, known as the Georgia Historical Society.

With its many exhibits, lectures, book publications, knowledgeable archivists and librarians, who daily with unflagging enthusiasm and Southern courtesy treat all visitors alike; scholars, genealogists, tourists, schoolchildren, and overseas visitors seeking information on the early days of the Methodists, the treatment of slaves, the black church, the military history of the city's multiple fortifications, to nineteenth-century manners, mores, and recipes. It is all there, and is a refuge for many who prefer to live in the past than the present. It is here that I have spent many hours of my own time and life carefully stitching the threads of my family's tattered tapestry back into a glowing living picture.

The Family Expands

Life must have appeared bright and sparkling that first year and soon saw a son and heir on the scene. A son named Andrew Low III was born on December 4, 1844, almost exactly nine months from the wedding night. He was baptized next spring with magnolias perfuming the air. Andrew Low's friend and partner, Charles Green, and his wife's sister, Elizabeth Hunter, stood up for the baby in the simple ceremony in Christ Episcopal Church.

We are extremely fortunate to have first-hand accounts of some aspects of their activities in the form of various letters in the Anderson Papers of the Southern Historical Collection at the University of North Carolina, Chapel Hill. It contains a remarkable find—a letter written by Sarah Hunter Low to her friend Sarah Williamson Anderson, dated July 14, 1845. It gives us a brief and penetrating insight into the lives of a fashionable young couple.

Sarah Hunter Low is staying in a boardinghouse in Newport, Rhode Island, and is writing to her friend, who has been ill, to suggest she come and spend a few weeks with them. She writes that she was seasick on the passage of six days to Newport. She raves about her first visit to New York, shopping and sightseeing. In New York they stayed at the American Hotel, and the first person they saw was Sarah's husband, Edward Anderson. She begs her friend to join them, saying that she is beginning to feel homesick, and dreads the departure of her husband, Mr. Low, who sails from Boston for Liverpool soon. They are staying at "Whitfields, not the most fashionable hotel but comfortable and neat, it is a large house but has few boarders"—probably money was still tight. She says if Mr. Low were to remain they would go to the Atlantic House, a new hotel. In one lovely little passage she talks about going bathing in the sea of which she was nervous, and how Mr. Low ducked her unmercifully saying he wished to cure her of her "cowardice." The conclusion drawn must be that the Low family—mother, father, and small son—were doing exactly what most Savannah people of means did if they could, which was to escape the brutal heat and humidity for cooler climes up north. Andrew Low would

Sarah Low and her daughter Amy by Cornelius Durham, ca. 1849. Mrs. Low died shortly after this image was made. *Courtesy The National Society of The Colonial Dames of America in the State of Georgia.*

have taken the opportunity to conduct business in New York and Boston before sailing for Liverpool, leaving his family to spend the summer in a more hospitable place than their hometown.

A daughter followed in short order. "Baptized, on Sunday, November 15, 1846, Amy, born August 7, 1846, daughter of Andrew and Sarah C.

Low. Sponsor Mr. J. Higham and Mrs. Edward Anderson." Life was still extremely good for the Low family.

A second daughter joined the family on October 22, 1847. Her birth appears in the Christ Church records thus: "Baptized: On Sunday July 2nd, 1848 Harriet Ann, born October 22nd 1847, daughter of Andrew & Sarah C. Low. Sponsors, Mr. and Mrs. Crowden."

Family Life in Those Times

Through a book, *Men, Women and Manners in Colonial Times,* by Sydney George Fisher, we are provided with a reasonably contemporary portrait of the world they would have inhabited in Victorian times, even though it had been written about a slightly earlier time. Despite improving conditions by the mid nineteenth century, this world had few safety nets.

Children were the currency of the future and the women bore the brunt of the dangers inherent in childbirth. The mortality among infants was appallingly high; putrid fevers, epidemic influenzas, raging small pox, whooping cough, typhoid, to name just a few, carried off hundreds of small children. The laws of sanitation were mostly disregarded, because the cause and effects were unknown. Drainage was still extremely poor; disinfections, other than a scanty sprinkling of vinegar, unthought of; isolation of contagious diseases impossible; and the mere accomplishment of surviving was a feat in itself. The history of many families is one of suffering, distress, and unfulfilled hopes as sons and heirs and, more often than not, beloved wives fell victim to procreation. Many men went through two or even three wives. Death was an equal opportunity employer, visiting the black slave quarters, the Indian villages, the plantation mansions, and the townhouses and shantytowns of rich and poor alike, masters and slaves, bosses and laborers. In spite of the profoundly held Christian beliefs of the ruling class, occult and planetary influences played a role in matters of health and life for all strata of a society thrown together in the melting pot of just literally making it through the night.

Children were dosed with all matters of patented medicines. Advertisements for all manner of drugs and nostrums predominated the classified pages of daily newspapers. Who dare not try anything that could protect from the miasma of the swamps that surrounded Savannah? In *Child Life in Colonial Days,* descriptions of domestic remedies included "Venice treacle," a nasty and popular compound traditionally invented by Nero's physician; it was made of vipers, white wine, opium, spices from the Indies, liquorice, red roses, tops of germander, and Saint-John's-wort, as well as some twenty other herbs, juice of rough sloes, mixed with honey. Mithridate, the ancient cure-all of King Mithridates VI, was another dose for children. There were forty-five ingredients in this.

The ideas in *Thoughts on Education* (1690) by philosopher John Locke would still have found favor in early Savannah society, forming part of the indispensable household advice to be followed in desperately adverse conditions. The book remained on many an old-time library list and among the scant volumes of a single book shelf, and was one of the most widely circulated books, along with the Bible, of self-help volumes. The notions of the English philosopher appealed to American parents because they were, as the author said, "the consideration not what a physician ought to do with a sick or crazy child, but what parents without the help of psychic should do for the preservation of a healthy constitution."

In fact his advice stands up to modern-day knowledge to a remarkable degree. Locke strongly counseled learning dancing, swimming, and playing in the open air. In his dietary advice he counseled against "flesh eating" until the child was two or three years old. For breakfast and supper he advised "milk, milk pottage, water gruel, flummery and similar 'spoon meat' or brown bread and cheese." Between meals he prescribed dry bread as snack food, and advocated the washing of the feet in cold water at frequent intervals. Life, however, was different in the colonies than it was in the mother country, and in many of the settlements native food crept into the diet as a matter of necessity. The plentiful cereal foods, including rice in Savannah, were considered a suitable diet for young children. "Samp, hominy, suppawn, pone, succotash" were many foods made from Indian corn and cooked in Indian ways that found their way into colonial kitchens. Baked beans were definitely on the diet.

Savannah was extraordinarily fortunate to have a remarkable collection of medical men to call upon. William R. Waring, M.D., and his descendants have left a prolific number of rare pamphlets that help us comprehend the dire health hazards that faced everyone everyday, regardless of status, stature, class, creed, or race. Dr. Waring was one of the most prominent physicians to practice in the first half of the nineteenth century in Savannah. The city owes much of its successful prosecution for dry culture of rice fields to this physician, a change that affected more for the permanent prosperity of the city than all other measures combined.

Sanitation was another serious hazard facing the citizens. Alderman James J. Waring published an informative tract on the *Evil and Remedy of the Privy System of Savannah.* In it, the relative values of sewage disposal in the British cities of Rochdale, Edinburgh, and Glasgow were considered to improve the sewage system of Savannah. He points out that since the waterworks of Savannah was established in 1853 and the sewer system not established until 1872, the water closets very generally put into houses after 1853 were forced to connect by waste pipes, dry wells, or closed and sealed midden vaults. These were putrefaction beds, connected by pipes to the interiors of houses, which in turn drained down into the water table. Regular privies, about 3,500 of them, were built with retaining walls of very porous brick and open porous sand bottoms, draining laterally and downwards to the water level.

These privies fill slowly with solid excremuta, the liquid portion being filtered away laterally through a very porous homogenous sand soil; hence the difficulty, if not impossibility, of proper emptying by any process of pneumatic suction, such as is prescribed by the present ordinance. No mild language can fairly describe the nauseating abomination of these middens. Even when clean, the saturated brick sides give off as much odor as the full vault. When it has proved that modern science has proven beyond refutation that the germs of such diseases as yellow fever, typhus and typhoid fever, diphtheria, etc. are the fungi or pathogenic bacteria of putrefactive beds and putrefactive fermentations, the grave question of how to deal with this pressing evil comes home to each of us.

Many of the diseases that attacked the city and the river plantations appear to have been local and containable in origin, but nevertheless were part of the very real terrors of life that faced Savannah in the 1840's.

Annus Horribilis—Tragedy Strikes

There was a son and heir and two daughters. Cotton was in great demand on the Liverpool markets and the future looked bright. It must have seemed to the young couple that they had the world in their hands.

On June 11, 1847, Andrew Low purchased Lots 13 and 14 on Lafayette Ward from the Inferior Court of Chatham County for the sum of $3,000, and he and his wife retained the services of John Norris, well-known eastern architect, to design a magnificent Greek Revival mansion in the classical style for their growing family.[8]

Tragedy struck with a vengeance. A little over one year later, on September 1, Friday, 1848, the *Georgian* newspaper in a short stark notice declared: "DIED; On Wednesday morning last, Andrew, son of Andrew and Sarah Low, aged 3 years and 9 months."

Death certificate states "croup" as cause of death.[9] Andrew was attended by the most well-known Savannah physician of the day, Dr. Richard Arnold, first secretary to the American Medical Association. Death of young children was very common, and in one of the first compilations of mortality statistics for one year, croup was the third highest known cause of death after dysentery and scarlet fever.

Despite the terrible loss of his only son, life went on; he had a family to support, and an expanding business to run. In December 1848 Andrew Low purchased Lot No. 2 east of Lincoln Street, in a sheriff's sale (Deed, Chatham County 3F277). It had a wharf for loading cotton onto ships.[10]

As in some terrible Greek tragedy, the blows continued to fall. On or about February 23, 1849, Andrew Low's father, William Low, merchant of Brechin, in Angus, Scotland, died. In March of 1849 Lucy Isaac's will was filed in Liverpool; she had died on March 13, 1849. Andrew Low, Jr., was named executor of her will as was Robert Hutchison. She named her son Robert Bruce Isaac as heir. It is apparent that the Lows took care of the financial affairs of the family of Uncle Andrew's partner Robert Isaac, and this responsibility was accepted by and passed on to Andrew Low Jr.

The worst cut of all! Another brief notice encompassing a lifetime of sorrow states: "Died: In this city on Sunday morning, May 20th, 1849, Sarah Cecil, wife of Andrew Low, and daughter of the late Alexander Hunter, aged 31 years."

And just above that notice another: "Sexton's Report of Internment's for the week ending May 23, 1849. Sarah Low, 31 years, childbed, Savannah resident."

Nine months later, giving birth to the child meant to replace the loss of their son, Sarah Hunter Low died. Andrew Low at the age of thirty-seven was left bereft of his wife and unborn child, a widower with two small daughters to care for. Sarah Low was buried on that Sunday, May 20, 1849.

Robert Hutchison writes to his own pregnant wife Mary in graphic sadness of the death of Sarah Low:[11] "Poor Mrs. Low had a miscarriage on Tuesday and a dead infant had to be delivered by surgical assistance. She is very ill."

His next letter says he is nervous for his wife because of Sarah Low's death. Childbirth was a serious hazard for women in those days,[12] and in the southern states the percentage was even higher. In five years Sarah had born three children and was pregnant with the fourth. His letter of May 20 gives details of her death:

> Poor Mrs. Low died at 1.o.clock this morning and is to be interred this evening. She was very generally esteemed and her death is much regretted. I join sincerely in this feeling for I thought her a remarkably happy amiable and rational character and had hoped you and she would have become good friends. Poor Low and his two little orphan girls are to be pitied. She had overcome the first shock of the miscarriage but during several days the kidneys had refused to perform their functions and hence the fatal issue. She died insensible but yesterday she was conscious of her hopeless condition and took leave of her husband and family firmly and composedly.

Sarah Hunter Low was buried in the Old Brick Cemetery on South Broad, now called Colonial Cemetery on Oglethorpe Avenue. The kind of ordeal that faced her two little girls, with their aunt Elizabeth Hunter and their father comforting them, as they saw their gentle mother put in the earth, is recounted through the memories of another little girl at the funeral of her own father. Sarah Low's burial would have followed the rituals of the burial of W. W. Gordon seven years earlier.

In 1924 Caroline Lovell recorded the memory of her aunt, Eliza Gordon Stiles, concerning the burial of the former mayor and father:

> She was five and dressed in deep black with long black pantalettes reaching to her ankles. She walked behind the hearse, holding the hand of her oldest brother, George Gordon. Her father, William Washington Gordon, was a very prominent man in Savannah . . . all the militia companies of the city marched in the funeral procession from the Presbyterian Church along South Broad Street to the Old Cemetery. Aunt Eliza said she felt very proud of her position until she happened to see a long black box and asked her brother what it was. "Our Father is in that," he replied. At this Aunt Eliza shrieked, "I don't want my father to be in that! I don't want him there!
>
> I was very naughty," she said, "and my brother was very much ashamed of me, but I was taken to the cemetery, and when every military company fired a salute over the grave, I almost died of fright, as I thought we were all to be shot.

Eliza was kept in deep black for three years—her mother wore mourning the rest of her life.

In his *Reminiscences and Recollections of Old Savannah*, Charles S. H. Hardee points out that the grand oaks of Oglethorpe Avenue were preceded by Chinaberry trees. These exotics, then known as "Pride of India," formed an arch under which the funerals proceeded to the cemetery's main gate at Lincoln Street. Vehicular traffic stayed outside of the two rows of trees. In his *History of the City Government of Savannah* Thomas Gamble recounts that the city's sextant met funerals at the gate. Carrying his staff of office, he led them to the gravesite.

Tragedy continued to strike the widower. The last and final loss occurred when, on August 31, 1849, following three months of illness, listed on death certificate as *morbus lividis*, Andrew Low, Sr., died at 20 Nelson Street in Liverpool.[13] The death certificate lists only Elizabeth Stripling, wife of John Stripling mariner, whose home it was, as present at death. He left sums of money to his surviving brothers William, who was Andrew Low, Jr.'s father and had actually predeceased his brother by six months, and John and Alexander, as well as various named nieces and nephews, grandnephews and great-grandnephews. It was his favorite nephew Andrew Low though who inherited all of his estates in Savannah and was named executor for the remaining beneficiaries in Scotland, all of them family members. Father, son, wife, and uncle—all in the space of one terrible year.

The 1849 Savannah City Directory lists Andrew Low, Jr.'s residence at 3 Parade Square, possibly a rented house while awaiting completion of what would have been their new home on Lafayette Square; it was close by so they could several times daily have been able to oversee the progress of construction. The location appears to be in Jasper Ward, on the side of Madison Square, a mere block to the west.

In the ward was located the United States Barracks with a parade ground covering a square of about one-and- half acres as well as the Female Asylum. Population was 213 whites and 131 colored in 33 dwelling houses, 22 of brick and 11 of wood.[14]

Adding insult to injury, a few months after Sarah's death on July 7, 1849, John Norris, the architect hired by the Low's to construct the magnificent home Andrew and Sarah planned on moving into together, placed an advertisement stating that the almost finished house on Lafayette Square had been vandalized and damaged. Notices appeared in the *Savannah Georgian* on July 7, 1849:

> Wanton Meanness.—Some miserable miscreant, some nights since, broke into the new dwelling of A. Lowe [sic], Esq., being erected on the South side of the city, and cut off the leaden pipe in bathing room, thereby flooding the upper rooms with about 500 gallons of water. The ceilings of the second story were very much injured and defaced, and the fancy work also. A reward of $200 is offered for the conviction of this mean act. It is to be hoped he or they will be detected and summarily punished. We learn the dwelling has been plastered in the most expensive and tasteful manner, and the dwelling itself is one of the most ornamental and substantial in the city. We regret we have among us wretches who could be guilty of such meanness.

Some say that people were angry with John Norris because he was importing workers to construct buildings; some say it was because it was built on the site of the old jail and jail grounds.[15] In the constantly evolving Savannah of the nineteenth century, jealousy and envy were more likely reasons for vandalism than sympathy for historical nostalgia. Whatever the reasons, the timing was appalling, and it would have been certain that Andrew Low could not have given his full attention to the building of his home as his life collapsed in tatters around his ears.[16]

It was a widower and not a contented husband who eventually occupied the magnificent mansion in Savannah planned and designed for

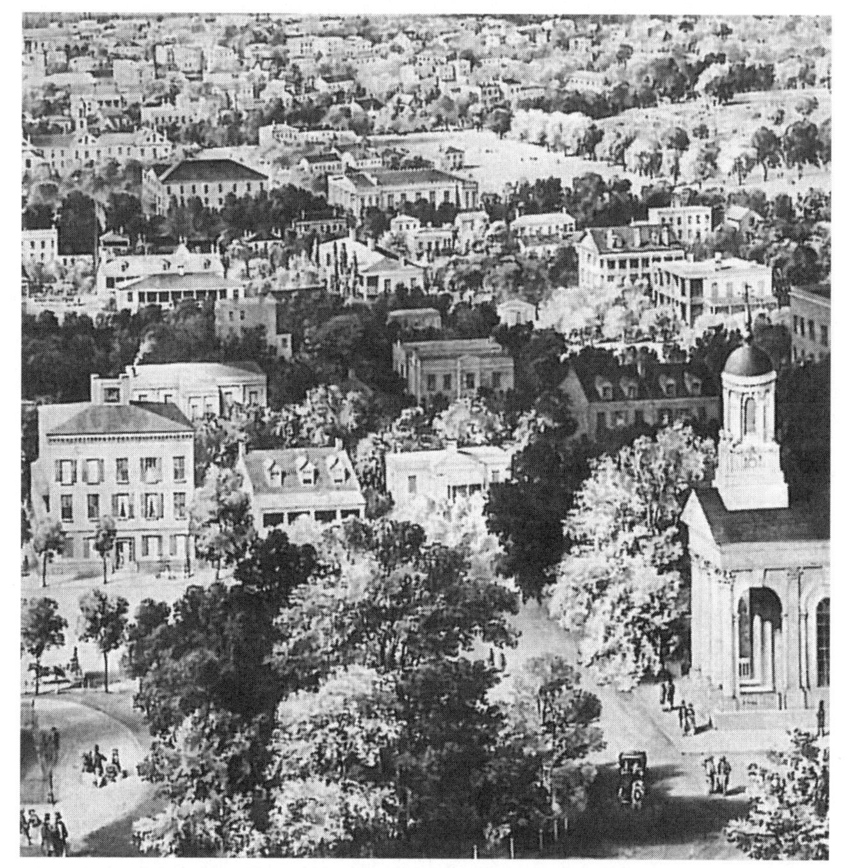

In this detail of the Smith and Hill engraving of 1854, the Andrew Low house sits above the church cupola to the right. This is the only image of the house with its original parapet roof line. *Engraving detail courtesy Historic Savannah Foundation.*

a thriving happy family. The small truncated group, comprised of his two small daughters, Amy and Harriet, and his late wife's sister, Elizabeth Hunter, moved into the new home sometime in 1850. A decade that had opened with such hope and promise ended in tragedy and loss.

The Census of 1850 gives a revealing snapshot of that pivotal moment of time for Andrew Low. It shows him, "a Male, born in Scotland, aged 37 years, responsible for Females, Amy, aged 4 years, Harriet, aged 2 years and Elizabeth Hunter, aged 35 years." It also shows him as having in his household "eleven (11) slaves; 6 Black Males, 24, 30, 43, 50 and two aged 62; 5 Females, 2 Mulattoes, ages 32 and 50, and three Blacks ages, 31, 32 and 40." One of the difficulties encountered in tracing genealogies of Africans in America in this period is that the pre–Civil War Census does not identify blacks and mulattoes by name, only by gender, age, and color. Only the white members of a household are identified by name.[17] When the census figures were gathered, he had moved his diminished family into the house on Abercorn Street on Lafayette Square. At that time the rear building, now the Girl Scouts Headquarters, would have been the carriage house and slave quarters, so there would have been room for some of the household of cooks, children's nurses, house servants, washers, and seamstresses, men and women employed also as carriage drivers, gardeners, and laborers.[18]

This amount of household help, whether slaves or servants, would not have been unusual at all for a man of substance as Andrew Low. It appears as though at least half of these Low slaves were inherited from Andrew Low, Sr., and/or the Robert Isaac estate. This indicates either a degree of humanity or a consciousness of the value of property on the part of Andrew Low and his wife in dealing with slave life in society at the time.

The institution of slavery in plantation life would not have touched the family other than peripherally, and that year certainly he had had a great deal more on his plate to agonize over than whether enslavement of other human beings was moral or not. To his class it was a convenience and the way of life of the South. His churchgoing at that point, probably to the Christ Episcopal across the square, would not have been a seminal part of his life, but more a social convention for business connections; and the anti-abolition Christian evangelistic preaching that might have affected his actions later were still in the future. Like his uncle before him, he would have been as tuned in to vagaries of European politics as they affected trade in northern England, as he would have been to the rumblings of imminent conflict over the way of life in the North and the South of America.

By 1850 Andrew Low had become a wealthy man in his own right, having inherited all his uncle's Savannah real estate and business operations. He would have been in a position to devote most of his time and energies to developing his business interests, drowning his sorrows in business affairs and perhaps even at that point, the bottle, certainly settling into a more sedentary life and putting on weight. Although no concrete proof of such has emerged, later letters from his then future mother-in-law, Eliza Mackay Stiles, appear to indicate that he enjoyed spending hours in the evenings sitting on the second story porch of his new home mellowing with good Scotch whiskey. It would be unusual if he did not, for both the times and his own inclinations.

He never appeared to be a truly intellectual man. As many of his associates of the time, he would have been socially well placed merely, if not for any other reason, because of his money and position as one of Savannah's leading cotton factors, and well on the way through his own shrewdness to becoming Savannah's wealthiest merchant.

Like his uncle before him, he was intensely focused on the question of

The Andrew Low House today. The exterior was restored to its original stucco tint. The deep-eaved roof was probably added prior to Willie and Daisy's wedding. *Courtesy The National Society of The Colonial Dames of America in the State of Georgia.*

acquiring wealth and retaining it. Savannah's rapid growth in the 1840's resulted in a relentless demand for increased municipal services, and the city fathers decided to impose an income tax of two-and-one-half percent on the most obvious source, those who had the most money—commission merchants, factors, and other professional men. By the end of the decade, this powerful class of citizen had had enough and legal action was taken to repeal the income tax. Andrew Low was prominent amongst those who lobbied against the hated tax, and the city council got the message. By March 1, 1851, it was abolished.[19]

Andrew Low Travels to England

In 1851 Andrew Low sailed on a ship for England with his daughters Hattie and Amy and left them there as was proved later in letters that have surfaced. On May 30, 1851, a notice stated that the "Arctic Steamship sailed from New York for Liverpool on 24th inst with 149 passengers on board. The World's Fair was the attraction for most of them. Among the passengers are Mr. Andrew Low, and two children, Miss Low and Miss Rippon, Savannah."

That brief notice is all the empirical proof we have that Andrew Low was reorganizing his life. There are many tantalizing snippets of information, a few facts, and much speculation; the only thing we really know is that he took his two small daughters to England, and returned without them.

Conventional wisdom has it that at the end of this trip he left his two daughters, Harriet and Amy, at school in Brighton, a rather racy but fashionable watering hole for the gentry on the south coast of England. They would have been five and four years old, even for those times a little young for boarding school, but he had limited choices. A later governess to the Low children named Emma Visick had an aunt, Suzanne Clarence, who lived in Brighton with what would have been one of the prime requisites—a healthy bracing sea climate. There is no record in the Brighton Local History Records of Harriet and Amy attending one of the many schools for foreign children, or of Mrs. Clarence running one. English literature is replete with instances of young girls and boys placed in boarding schools. Children were sent home to school from India at a very young age, six being quite common.[20] The custom would have been for younger children, especially girls from a wealthy family, to be placed as boarders with a suitable chaperone or guardian; and Mrs. Clarence's letters to her niece show her to be a devout Christian woman with strong ideas regarding the proper upbringing of children.[21] I myself can attest to the practice still operating one hundred years later. I was only seven when I was sent to boarding school.

His mother, Katherine, and two sisters were still alive at that time and living in the granite stone house on Pearse Street in Brechin, Scotland, a cold, wet, and, for small girls used to the southern softness of Savannah, an unbearably inhospitable place. Andrew Low, Jr., now on the death of his uncle, as the head of his household reverted to just Andrew Low, never showed any inclination to inculcate his daughters in the Scottish Presbyterian traditions of his own upbringing, To the contrary he was already commencing his transformation to wealthy English merchant and gentleman, preparing his daughters for a more genteel future. It would have not been in character for him to re-locate his two small daughters in either Scotland or Liverpool—both locations in Victorian times, considered less socially acceptable than the home counties and the southern coast.[22]

In 1853 William Makepeace Thackeray, famous English author of many mannered books of the period, including *Vanity Fair,* on one of his occasional visits to the Southern states, which he featured in many of his popular novels, was invited by Andrew Low to stay. This was his first visit to Savannah, and the author writes, "We have struck up a kinness because he has two daughters in Europe whom he goes to see each summer."[23]

A second letter written during a later visit in 1856, indicating that at the time of his first visit Amy and Hattie were back in England, perhaps in school, may be the only reference to their location in the records.[24] Andrew Low had already commenced a triple identity—hardheaded Scottish business man in Liverpool and Savannah, and English squire in England.

12

High Cotton: Savannah, 1850–1860

A PHRASE HAS ENTERED COLLOQUIAL LANGUAGE IN THE SOUTH—"living in high cotton"—meaning living well or better than others. It is based on the premise that when picking cotton, the higher the plant the less pain in the picking, the less bending down low back-breaking work. The merchants and plantation owners lived the life of "high cotton" prior to the War Between the States. After the war they sang the song of "bend down low" for many a long year.

Andrew Low's marriage to Sarah Hunter, daughter of old friend and associate of his uncle, was both predictable and acceptable. She was the link between the older generation and the younger. With her death and the wealth of his uncle he was free to reinvent himself, to walk down whatever road fate and life led him. Fate arrived in the shapely form of Mary Cowper Stiles.

As a widower of thirty-eight years of age, not young but certainly not yet old, the affluent eligible Andrew Low would have been extremely well received in the front parlors of mothers wishing to marry their daughters off, and into the bargain align their own fortunes with that of the growing Low empire. There is no record of exactly when and how Andrew Low met and proposed to Mary Cowper. There is plenty of proof that the Lows were on intimate footing, socially and commercially speaking, with Stiles and Mackay friends, associates, and relations. Savannah, at least in terms of those "that mattered," was still a small town. It would be reasonable to think that perhaps Benjamin Stiles, the brother of William Henry Stiles, and a not-too-successful Savannah businessman in his own right, could have been the initiator. Another mutual acquaintance was Mary Cowper's uncle, William Mackay. Acting as he frequently did as her father's agent, he was well aware of the abysmal state of his finances. We can only speculate, as it goes to the heart of why, other than money, the Stiles family married their vivacious, sophisticated, and only daughter to a man they would have found seriously lacking in social graces. Andrew Low's feelings toward Mary Cowper are indisputable and understandable—he was bowled over.

Not everyone welcomed the proposed match. With his courtship of the comely young woman Andrew Low became entangled in a web of closely connected family relationships, riddled with the normal amount of protectiveness, suspicion, and distrust. So commences the third phase of our story: time and place to introduce the other ancestors that make up our gene pool—all descended from planters, slave traders, merchants, and politicians—in the accelerated pace of America's evolution, considered to be colonial aristocracy.

Through the years of the existence of the United States of America, from colonial possession to revolution and independence, it was the practice of individuals to record their family's progress through privately published books, letters, journals, and diaries to show the following generations where they had come from, and hopefully help them know where they were going. The Mackays and Stiles have left us a rich heritage.[1]

The Stiles Family

When Joseph Stiles married Catherine Clay in 1793, the marriage united two of Savannah's oldest and most prominent families. Five children were born. William Henry was the third, born in 1809. William Henry's oldest brother was Benjamin Edward Stiles, merchant and planter, who was married to Eliza Mackay Stiles's sister, Mary Anne. The next son was Joseph Clay Stiles, trained in law and partner to young William Washington Gordon. The death of J. C. Stiles's young bride left the barrister depressed and aimless, and on a visit to a family holding south of the town an old African retainer advised him to "look to the Lord." Like Saul on the road to Damascus, the scales fell from his eyes and he felt a mighty urge to preach. His first efforts were aimed at slaves on his father's plantations, but his fervor caused the concern of owners and led his father to direct him to proper theological training. Joseph Clay Stiles seemed to have inherited the religious drive of his great-uncle Habersham and the mighty Whitefield, for he became a leading Presbyterian theologian and cleric.

Joseph Stiles paid a great deal of attention to his sons' education, sending both Joseph and William to Yale University. In 1823 Catherine Clay Stiles died suddenly after taking the wrong medicine for a headache, leaving the fourteen-year-old William Henry motherless. This probably accounts for his leaving for university two years later at age sixteen. It is at Yale that William Henry honed his skills as a debater and declaimer. The subjects he chose for his participation show a lively, even contentious mind.

The family's personal fortune was threatened by the prohibition by the

City of Savannah of wet rice culture on Joseph Stiles's lands near town. This seriously affected the potential prosperity of the family and constituted a basis for many decisions made by Stiles. But it was a public relations no-win situation for the plantation owner and undoubtedly created a dilemma for the public figure of the politically oriented son of the landowning father. The reality was that the continuation of wet culture created serious health hazards for the community, and that was no position for an upcoming public figure to take, selfish private rights over the public good. By 1825 there was an increase in the epidemic fever rate, and the town passed an ordinance preventing the wet culture of rice within one mile of the city. A major battle was carried out in the pages of the newspapers, and despite their personal influence, the problem of the rice cultivation on Vale Royal and Springfield became a serious public issue.

After leaving Yale William Henry returned to Savannah and entered politics by supporting Andrew Jackson for President. It was in the Democratic Party that William Henry Stiles made his own political mark. It would appear on the surface to be a contradiction in terms—he was slave owner, landholder, and, for the new nation, an aristocrat. For a Georgian and a Southerner, perhaps such contradictions were relative, since the vote was relegated to those who held the power (white male property owners), and the acquisition of land was essential for continued prosperity.

His father had by then remarried, a much younger woman, Margaret Vernon Adams, and he had seven children by that union, much to his third son's chagrin. Part of William Henry's discomfort with his father's new family may have come from a situation reported by Margaret Vernon Stiles in her memoir, *Marse George*: "Grandfather [Joseph Stiles] asked Uncle Dick Wylly for his sister's hand in marriage, and a short time later, his son, William Henry Stiles, came and asked for the hand of the young lady. Her brother replied to this second proposal, "Margaret has already accepted your father!"

The narrative, organized by historian Walter Hartridge, continues with a flattering portrait of the old bridegroom: "Joseph Stiles was at the time a fine looking man, much younger in appearance than his fifty-five years, with broad shoulders, a high, intelligent forehead and flawless teeth, a man in the prime and vigor of life. Margaret's eyes were deep blue, and her chestnut hair, lustrous and beautiful, reached almost to her knees."

A very different picture emerges from a letter written by the catty Mary Telfair. Her ridicule was probably a sample of gossip that chagrined the proud William Henry:

> What does Ann Wallace think of her Uncle Stiles's dereliction from common sense? He is in a few days to become a married

> man—His choice a young silly girl who I suppose is dazzled by his *filthy* lucre, for I can think of nothing *clean* attached to him—We have often discoursed upon the *insanity* of widowers but this exceeds all that has ever occurred in the annals of foolish matches—I understood he is *a devoted Love.* A man who for forty years has never left his own domicile except to walk over his fields & attend Church drives up daily in his Barouche to the door of his *fair Enslaver* and basks the whole morning in her smiles. Have I been too severe upon the old Man dear Mary?

In other letters she refers to the young bride as "old Mrs. Stiles" and cracks about the senior Joseph, "I hear he goes to *Roost* with the Fowls at seven o'clock—how terrible to be condemned to the pillow for so many wearisome hours."[2]

Paths Commence to Converge

Robert Mackay's son, John Mackay, had attended the U.S. Military Academy at West Point with the later-to-be-illustrious-Confederate-general Robert E. Lee. He was a classmate and a frequent visitor to the Mackay home, especially as his duties brought him to Fort Pulaski to perform engineering work in his earlier career. When Lee was assigned to the garrison at Cockspur Island in the Savannah River in 1829, he naturally renewed his friendship with the family, and a warm relationship developed among them. There are many rumors of a relationship between the young Robert E. Lee and his friend's sister, the young Eliza Mackay; this gossip, which in view of Lee's fame most probably, became much embellished in the telling.[3] The reality lies in Lee's flowery prose and excessive use of metaphors. His letters to the young Eliza Mackay are charmingly flirtatious in a courtly tradition—flattering pretenses of an older brother's charming college friend—pleasing to any young woman of any era. By 1831 he married Mary Custis, the daughter of George Washington's adoptive grandson, George Washington Parke Custis.

Whether it was because Lee was turned down by Eliza, or because it appeared a more advantageous alliance for an ambitious military man, is grist for the continuing rumor mill. Eliza Mackay began to be courted by William Henry Stiles, and they were married on January 7, 1832, the service officiated by the brother of the groom, the Reverend Joseph Clay Stiles. The couple's almost daily correspondence throughout their lives is proof positive of an endearingly close devotion. These stories are all told through the letters that exist in collections at various universities, archives, state, and national historical societies, especially since Robert E. Lee later became such a tremendous hero of the Confederacy and a towering historical figure even in modern times. Loyalty was one of the South's most admirable qualities, and he remained to his death a friend of the Stiles and then Low families.

On November 15, 1832, Mary Cowper Stiles was born to William Henry and Eliza Mackay Stiles. Andrew Low, Jr,. had been in Savannah for three years, and would have been nineteen years older than she.

William Henry's Rise to Prominence

William Henry Stiles had political ambitions and his own prestige and the prestige of his family were important to him. He may well have served as the earpiece for public sentiment. By 1833 he became Solicitor General of the Eastern Judicial District of Georgia, and was also elected to the Savannah City Council by a landslide. The dry culture legislation faded away, and the irony was that had the city pursued a lawsuit it would have been prosecuted by William Henry Stiles as Solicitor General. One can only assume that many strings were pulled in the Havana cigar smoke–filled rooms used by the Madeira Club, and by the mercantile factors and plantation owners in the their dingy countinghouses and offices along the waterfront; here was the city's true lifeblood that pumped and flowed up and down the arteries of the river. Anything that threatened the financial well-being of the good old boys was infinitely more threatening than a health hazard. "Can't make an omelet without breaking eggs," they would have harrumphed into their whiskeys.

One of Stiles's first actions on behalf of the council was to take subscriptions in the newly created Central of Georgia Railroad and Banking Company, of which Andrew Low was later a director and one of the original subscribers. The railroad connected Savannah to both Macon and Augusta.

In February of 1836 Stiles was appointed United States District Attorney for Georgia. That same month Andrew Low, Jr., went off with a small band of volunteers to fight the Seminole Indians in Picolata. Georgia politics were never clear-cut, especially in and around Savannah; and it was amongst the shifting currents of Jacksonian democracy and states rights that William Henry attempted to launch his personal ship and head for his personal star. During the 1830's William Henry's penchant for straddling the political fence became clearer–he carefully avoided being labeled as either a "states rights" man like many Southern movers and shakers, or a "nationalist" as personified by the policies of Andrew Jackson. He succeeded in establishing himself as a public figure in Savannah society.

It appears on the surface that Joseph Stiles favored this son, and by the time of his death in 1838 through the gift of land and property he had increased William Henry's personal holdings considerably. W. H. was elected the Democratic candidate for Chatham County to the state legislature in 1840. His actions in the legislature continued to make it difficult to classify him politically. His stands were consistent with his social standing and economic background, and also with the planter class, which dominated the Whig Party of William Henry Harrison; but his personal background appears to have conflicted with the Jacksonian views of the masses of small farmers that dominated the Democratic Party.

A change in residence to Cass County in north Georgia resulted from the inheritance that had improved his economic lot, and he was free to develop the land as a separate unit, disconnected from the Stiles's low country land. Secondly, he wanted to move his family—by now including Mary Cowper, William Henry, Jr., and Robert Mackay Stiles—to a healthier atmosphere away from the notoriously unhealthy Savannah area. Ironically, much of the unhealthy aspects of the area were caused by the wet culture of the Stiles's own plantations!

He was perfectly prepared to fight for his own rights, but also perfectly prepared to take whatever steps necessary to protect the rights and health of his own family, while blissfully ignoring the effect his actions were having on other people's families. Exacerbating the problem of health, his wife Eliza suffered from asthma and the northern climate of Cass County was infinitely better for all of them. For the next twenty-five years Stiles would switch his residence back and forth from Savannah to Cass, based on political opportunities.

His actions often seemed to illustrate the inconsistency of trying to rise through the ranks of a party that was not congenial to his own background. Was it for principle or expediency because that was where he could be elected? Or was he seen as a spy in the opposing camp, supported by his network of bankers, factors, and aristocratic planters, all united to preserve their own interests in the halls of state power? That certainly makes sense in hindsight. He was amiable and got along with everyone.

That brief biographical history does not begin to explain the contradictions and inconsistencies in William Henry Stiles's positions, nor does it attempt to analyze his ability to play the good-old-boy game with finesse and flamboyance. He appears to have been able to weigh and balance all sides of his public posture in terms of what he could gain for his own agenda.

The Cherokee Land Grab—Trail of Tears

America's attitude toward the indigenous peoples they found when they arrived is written clearly from the beginning, referring to King George:

> He has excited domestic Insurrection amongst us, and has endeavored to bring on the Inhabitants of our Frontiers, the merciless

> Indian Savages, whose known Rule of Warfare, is an undistinguished Destruction, of all Ages, Sexes and Conditions.
>
> —Declaration of Independence, August 2, 1776

In 1829 gold was discovered in Cass County, Georgia, on Cherokee lands. By then the Georgia legislature had started passing legislation that carved up Cherokee lands in northwest Georgia, including Cass County. William Henry Stiles purchased a considerable amount of land in the 1840's: some by lottery, some from speculators, and some through political influence.[4] It has been said that William Henry was first attracted by the Cherokee lands when he was sent on a special mission to pay off some of the Cherokee claims in North Georgia, but an examination of the records fails to reveal such a situation. The prices which William Henry paid for his lots indicate that they were obtained under widely varying conditions. Although he paid less than fifty dollars for some, he paid as high as $3,600 for one group of four-and-one-half lots. It seems very likely that he had taken possession of some parcels of land before he had a clear title to them and that later he had to pay a premium price in order to establish title and retain the property. This conclusion is further supported by the fact that some of the men from whom he purchased land were known to be speculators.[5]

Mystery surrounds the methods employed by William Henry in acquiring his land. He purchased some lottery chances, but there is no record of his being lucky in any of the drawings. He acquired land over a period of sixteen years, although most of his deeds were dated in 1844, 1845, and 1852, the years of his Washington legislative and Vienna consular service, and most of his lots were in the heart of the land vacated by the Cherokees. It is not likely that the finding of the gold had been William Henry's primary motive in selecting his property. Their location along the Etowah River indicates that he was interested in farming. Some of the lots were described in the original surveys as "first quality river" and "Indian improvement."

Although an examination of the records does not reveal that he purchased land prior to 1844, newspaper reports clearly indicate that he was considered a resident of Cass County before that time, and certainly would have integrated himself snugly into the patronage system of land distribution and speculation without scandal. There is no proof that William Henry Stiles was involved in influencing legislation despite his having an inside track through his connection with Wilson Lumpkin, former Governor of Georgia, and later Indian agent for the federal government.

Still another factor that must have influenced his move to Cherokee country was his political ambition. His interest in politics had already been established in Savannah, where he had made a creditable showing for a young man in his early thirties. This experience in politics had been in an old community where the political alignments were well established. Neither William Henry nor Eliza Mackay ever mentioned political opportunity as a cause for the move, but later activities clearly demonstrated that it had entered into the decision. Stiles must certainly have reasoned that, with his Savannah background and experience in politics, he could rise further and faster in a new section where ability and experience were at a premium and alignments were sufficiently fluid to enable him to cast his lot with either the States Rights or the Union element of the Democratic Party.

Whatever his reasoning, his transfer of residence to North Georgia was accompanied by political success. The Democratic Convention met in Milledgeville in June 1842, to nominate candidates for Congress, and Stiles was nominated, and then elected member of the Twenty-Eighth Congress in Washington for the State of Georgia during the presidency of John Tyler. He served on the Post Office and Post Road Committees.[6]

Washington and Vienna

Eliza joined him in Washington and soon became a vital part of the social scene in the city. First Lady Julia Gardiner Tyler was the talk of Washington. Many thought she had crossed the line of propriety when her likeness was used to advertise her father's soap products. But when the young model was rescued by the widowed President from a boating disaster, courtship followed. When the First Lady paid her welcome call to Eliza Stiles at Hewitt's boardinghouse, used by the Georgia delegation, it was a comedy of errors. The following passage is from a letter to Catherine Mackay from Eliza Stiles, dated March 18, 1844. Colquitt and Harrelson were also congressmen, and one of Harrelson's daughters married John B. Gordon, Confederate general:

> I had just come home and was sitting in Mrs. Colquitt's room with my pelisse and bonnet on, when a servant told me a lady in the parlor wished to see me. So down I went as I was and introduced myself to a very sweet looking lady—not pretty but with exceedingly pleasant and unpretentious manners. She did not tell me who she was, and I had not the remotest idea, but she shook hands, was very glad to see me, seemed to know all about me, talked of William Henry, and my not coming sooner, and while speaking, Henry rushed in with "Mother! Do come to the door and see the President's carriage with four splendid horses. Please Mother come, they are splendid." I whispered I could not, and sent him out. While he was asking this

Henry and Bobby Stiles in Washington, D.C., in 1844. This is how they looked when the First Lady paid them a surprise visit. *Courtesy Hugh Stiles Golson.*

in came Mrs. Hewitt, fresh from the kitchen, with a *very* soiled cap and an old shawl dragged round her shoulders, and altogether looking like destruction, and took a seat the other side of the lady. I then thought it was some acquaintance of hers, and kept expecting the contents of the splendid carriage momently to be ushered in, all the while feeling quite ashamed of the appearance of my landlady. At this moment in comes Henry again, more in earnest than before, imploring me to go only for one minute before the splendid horses were gone. Some other company called to see other ladies, and at once it struck me my visitor *might* be Mrs. Tyler. So I asked her, and she apologized for not telling me sooner, but had sent her name by the servant, and thought surely I knew.

It was very unpleasant and I tried to make amends, but everything would go wrong. Mrs. Hewitt asked her if she wished to see her on business she would take her into her private parlor. Mrs. Tyler looked rather amazed, and said no, she did not wish to see her, but was very polite, and anyone would suppose then that the woman would have the sense to vanish, but not her. And some time after down came Mrs. Haroldson [sic], looking like a real sallow cracker, dressed outrageously, and after a reasonable visit to her, and regrets from Mrs. Tyler that she was going away soon after my arrival, but hoped I would go and see her first, she rose to depart, (they move

Eliza Anne Mackay (Mrs. William Henry Stiles). This 1849 watercolor, done in Vienna, shows the diplomat's wife, who relished her time in the Austrian capital. *Courtesy The National Society of The Colonial Dames of America in the State of Georgia.*

to Philadelphia to live in ten days) and was followed to the door by me, Mrs. Haroldson [sic] and Mrs. Hewitt, and there we saw the beautiful horses, and two ladies seated in it waiting for her. She was dressed very plainly indeed, and much muffed up, looks sick, and says her health is very bad. You would have been delighted with her gentle and unaffected manner. Mrs. Haroldson [sic] asked me if I was not ashamed of my cracker friends when I had such grand

The Honorable William Henry Stiles, Vienna, 1848. Mr. Stiles had one hundred copies of this engraving printed, as it was the custom at European courts to exchange signed likenesses. *Courtesy The National Society of The Colonial Dames of America in the State of Georgia.*

company. I told her yes, of my cracker friend, and cracker child, and dirty landlady, and stupid servant.

Eliza became enamored of life in the national and international arena. The records prove that William Henry occupied a great deal of his time in securing political patronage for his friends and acquaintances, although he appears to have played a very minor role in the legislative affairs of the nation while a member of Congress, concentrating mostly on local Savannah and Cass County interests.

William Henry Stiles always lived beyond his means; his time in Washington was no different, especially considering the requirements of his extravagant wife. In 1843 the Georgia legislature changed the procedure for electing congressman by dividing the state into districts. This placed Stiles and another Congressman, John Lumpkin, in the Fifth District.

By January 1844 Stiles had begun to lobby for the post of consulship to Havana, his efforts endorsed by John Lumpkin in an extraordinary letter to President Tyler. This desire was based on the opportunities he felt would be afforded by combining private business with the public office, and perhaps his fear that he would lose reelection. His opponent was better known in the new district, and was the son of Wilson Lumpkin, a former governor and power broker in the county, district, and state. Stiles also lobbied for a posting to Liverpool, feeling that the cost of living might be less there than his other preference in Havana, perhaps influenced by his business acquaintance with Andrew Low, whose English offices were there.

It is far more likely, though, that it was his friendship with another Englishman—a son-in-law of William Scarborough, Godfrey Barnsley, who was also a neighbor in Cass County—that triggered that brief interest in Liverpool as a consular situation, or possibly the memories of his mother-in-law and his wife Eliza who was born there.[7]

In a letter from Congressman Stiles to his wife he worries over the pros and cons of what course to lobby for and which posting might prove the most advantageous financially:

> I received last night, My Dear Lib, your favor of the 9th from Savannah I am glad to hear of your arrival there. If my letter to brother Benjamin that 'I could have been consul at Liverpool' it certainly stated more than I intended to say, I do not yet know that I can be consul at Havana, I only meant that I could have applied for it. But whilst the facilities of business would be much greater in Havana than Liverpool, and as my expenses would be much less in the former than the latter place, and as the Havana consulship is generally given to a Southern man, there was a greater possibility of succeeding, hence I propose to go directly for it. The living or business might be cheaper in Liverpool than Havana, but I would have to entertain so many strangers and strangers of a higher order in Liverpool than in Havana, that I could make more in the latter than the former. But, I am happy to tell you and tell you privately I am trying for both, trying for Liverpool with Mr. Polk. It is uncertain whether the Senate

will confirm the man that Mr. Tyler put in the consulship last summer, and if they do not my colleagues mean to place my name for it, but if they should confirm him, then Havana is my only chance. Again, if I got Liverpool I could never expect to see Georgia for four years, whereas if I got Havana I could come home once at least every year to see to my affairs.' yr husband William Stiles.[8]

He was offered neither, but went to the far more prestigious diplomatic post in Vienna instead. Eliza returned to Georgia, but came back to Washington on William Henry's request to attend President Polk's inauguration. Many Georgia friends attended the event, sixteen of them being the Stiles's guests. An announcement was made in April by the new government of President Polk, who had been Secretary of State under Tyler's administration, of Stiles appointment as chargé d'affaires to Austria. The Savannah *Georgian*, commenting on the event, was high in its praise of Stiles and observed that public sentiment would approve the appointment.

From 1845 to 1849 the entire Stiles family resided in Austria, hobnobbing with the rich and infamous, the literati and the glitterati. That is where Mary Cowper and her two brothers spent their formative adolescent years in the courts and major cities of Europe, a far cry from rural north Georgia, with her playmates being the children of intellectuals and royalty, not slaves and farmers.

Mary Cowper Stiles

Her mother's Austrian diaries imply that like most teenagers, lovely and spirited, she had her share of fanciful fantasies about the opposite sex and they about her. Anecdotes extrapolated from these diaries indicate that Mary Cowper may have had a crush on her tutor, Mr. Kollman, although the interpretation could also be taken as the other way around.[9]

Contemporary portraits show her to be a remarkably independent attractive girl, but also a dutiful daughter, obedient and compliant with her parents' wishes. The diary reveals that on February 13, 1849: "Mary has grown exceedingly and is much improved in appearance, indeed were I to write all the fine speeches which are continually made about her, and it were to fall in the poor child's hands, her head would be quite turned."

She was sweet sixteen, poised and well-mannered, making a wonderful impression on those who met her. Several entries indicate more than a passing interest in the young girl from interested mamas with sons to marry off.

A young Austrian count sent Mary a present of a ceramic Swiss cottage saying he would rather live with her in that humble dwelling than with

Mary Cowper Stiles in 1849, when her father was U.S. chargé d'affaires in Vienna. *Courtesy The National Society of The Colonial Dames of America in the State of Georgia.*

all the people he lived with in the palace, and on meeting the same young nobleman's mother in Ischl, in the Tyrol Mountains, Eliza wrote: "Countess Wurmbrandt ran up to us, exclaimed at Mary's having grown so immensely, looked at her hair, and said it was delicieux; her easy grace and perfectly polished manners delighted Mr. Stille, who said it was a great treat to meet with such a person occasionally and seemed very glad to have made our acquaintance for this reason as well as others."

Despite all this admiration, Mary managed to keep her head on straight and retain her down-to-earth ways and affectionate nature. It was an entry in the autumn of 1849, when the family was slowly traveling back home to Georgia, that give an intimation that Eliza Stiles feels that the future may not be quite as bright as the past four years had been:

> We heard from Mr. Mackay, and Mama has lost 3 Negroes from cholera but they say nothing of it being yet in Savannah. William still scarcely able to write and we must be as economical as possible, the brickyard yielding little or nothing now and our place in Cass having gone pretty much to decay. I almost dread to go home to trouble, after leading such an easy life for three years.

And finally on October 19th, Friday, 1849:

> . . . went on board the steamer to arrange our baggage . . . well, my journal draws to a close, for this is my last day in England and on board ship I shall never be able to write, so goodbye journalizing and agreeable traveling—all the disagreeables are to come now,'til we reach home and then happiness will dawn again.

But it never was to be as happy again for them as a family, although the records show that the family rallied around to help as much as possible. Eliza Stiles's mother, Mrs. Robert Mackay, records as part of her estate:[10]

> Savannah, 8th March 1849—a list of Property owned at this time by me—The House and Lots in Broughton Street. The lot in Baker County—names of a family of Negroes that I gave in Savannah 1842 to my Daughter Mrs. Stiles to assist in educating her children: when the estate is divided these are to be valued with the rest but are to be a part of her portion. These remain at Mr. Stiles Plantation and have been sent thereto suit my convenience.
>
> Nancy William Justine
> Simon Sinai[11] Dido
> William Rhina Jack
> Nicholas Thomas Matthew
> Princes Martin Eliza and infant
> Milly MaryAnn Pompey
> Jacob Monday Sophy Monday Sally

These notations of African slaves with only Christian names to identify them are recorded in the plantation ledger the same year the Stiles family returned from Austria to run their north Georgia cotton plantation. Confronted with the desire to shore up their costly lifestyle, this loaned labor indicates that they were helped considerably by Grandmother Eliza Mackay from her own Grange and Sedgebank plantations. These would have been the people my great-grandmother Mary was brought up with before she married Andrew Low and managed her own large house and family. This ledger is also a record of the Africans who served the Mackay and Stiles family.[12]

The entries, along with details of Eliza Stiles diaries as she brought presents of shawls and scarves for the "servants" before her departure from Europe, illustrate the complicated relationship in the antebellum South between owners and humans viewed as property; many of them also were seen as treasured friends as well as slaves. The descriptions conjure up the relationships between the Scots and their "tackmen" in feudal days. It also shows that the knowledge of their value to the estate was a basic consideration, as was the income derived from their "hiring out."

Return to a Different Reality

William Henry returned to America, to rural north Georgia, with a deeper perspective on international affairs. As a young man he had determined on a career as lawyer-planter-statesman and on the surface had done well, holding office on the local, state, national, and international stage, building alignments and alliances on all levels, gliding smoothly through the barbed-wire thickets of political and diplomatic intrigue. By 1849, due to the fact that the hoped for upgrading to minister had not occurred, his diplomatic career was over. His salary as chargé d'affaires was insufficient to sustain a high living lifestyle in Europe while simultaneously running an agricultural plantation in America.

Mismanagement of the estate at Etowah Cliffs in his absence by his older brother had left him on the edge of financial disaster. Benjamin Stiles had reluctantly taken over the management of the plantation, but he had no talent for it. Earlier disorder in his own personal affairs had landed him in jail in Savannah resulting in his having to sell some land in Chatham County.

It was now that William Henry Stiles attempted to retrieve his financial fortunes by acquiring even more Cherokee lands in Cass County. He acquired at least 1,440 acres of land in the third, fourth, and seventeenth districts of the third section of the Cherokee country. He apparently hoped to sell the land at a profit to emigrants flooding in from South Georgia and Europe. The collection of William Henry Stiles papers at the Robert Woodruff Library at Emory University contains at least sixty letters and deeds that attest to the buying or selling of land.

The mystery remains as to where the money came from. When he returned from Vienna, his political clout had vanished along with his pocketbook. His first task was to mend his political fences and increase his holdings. Somewhere along the way, he must have had access to both patronage in the purchase of land, and access to money to buy it.

Eliza Mackay Stiles had emerged as an extravagant socially conscious

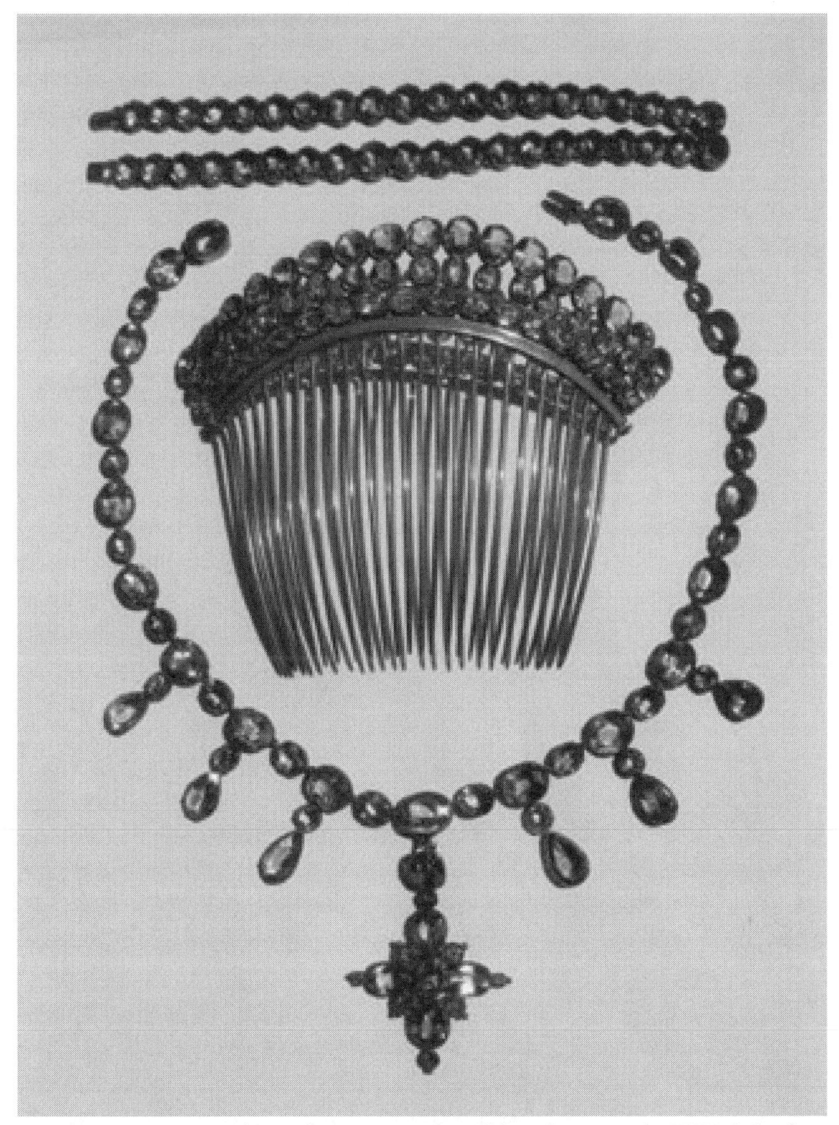

Empress Maria Louisa's amethyst set, purchased from her estate by W. H. Stiles for his wife. Inherited by Katie Low. *Courtesy The National Society of The Colonial Dames of America in the State of Georgia.*

and ambitious woman who certainly realized that an ample supply of money lubricated the wheels of life. The portrait of William Henry as an ambitious politician with little party loyalty but much personal resourcefulness had already emerged.

It is impossible to account for Andrew Low's progress in those years before he married his contemporary's daughter without examining William Henry's own progress. Was there a pact between them? Did William

Watercolor of Mary Cowper Stiles, probably done by her mother while in Europe. *Courtesy The National Society of The Colonial Dames of America in the State of Georgia.*

Henry sell his daughter for a "mess of pottage"? Was Mary Cowper a lovelorn loser in the romantic stakes, or herself a pragmatic chip off the old block? All personal descriptions of her show her to be strong willed, even headstrong, a tomboy, skilled in the arts of country living, which at that period in north Georgia was truly frontier living, primitive and dangerous. She excelled at horseback riding and shooting, equally if not more so than her two brothers. No namby-pamby miss was Mary Cowper.

It would appear apparent from existing documents that the extended elite families of the Clays, Mackays, Habershams, McQueens, Wallaces,

Elliotts, and Stiles were among the aristocrats of Savannah. It would also be self-evident that their own ancestors' rise to prominence was scratched and fought in the dirt and degradation of early colonial power-grabbing, Indian trading, land acquisition, and frontier diplomacy. But an entire century had passed; time has a habit of accelerating in such circumstances and yesterday's parvenu is today's aristocrat.

Mary Cowper's childhood summers were spent on her father's plantation, Etowah Cliffs, in Cass County in northern Georgia. The neighbors were a large extended family of Elliott cousins who adored her and lived close by at Summerland. To alleviate the winter monotony of country life there were frequent visits to Grandmother Eliza Mackay on Broughton Street in Savannah, doted upon by her maiden aunts Sarah and Kate, and widowed Uncle William Mackay, whose wife and two children had tragically died in the wreck of the steamer *Pulaski* in 1838.

Not until Andrew Low had proved himself capable of amassing huge wealth would he have been accepted, and even then would have been looked down upon in the parlors and bedrooms of women. He wielded real power in the political and business arena, but was denied considerable authority in the social theater. A daughter was expected to be obedient and subservient to the needs of the entire family. Mary Cowper was William and Eliza Stiles's most valued asset in those stakes.

13

Lovely Manners: Savannah, 1854–1860

RETURNING TO AMERICA FROM ENGLAND, WHERE HE HAD GONE IN the spring of 1851 to leave his two young daughters, Andrew Low's own letters indicate that he had already commenced courting Mary Cowper by the summer of 1852.

Rumors still swirl around in the Savannah gossip mill regarding this match, due first and foremost to a series of nineteenth-century romance novels, written in the late twentieth century! The plots focus on Andrew Low and Mary Cowper Stiles as two of the central characters in a quartet of books, set in Savannah, using factual figures in fictional settings. Eugenia Price's *Stranger in Savannah* alleges Mary Cowper 's parents forced her to end her infatuation with a Stewart Elliott to marry "old Andrew Low."[1]

The source of this entire premise appears to be based on a factual letter in the Mackay Stiles Collection from a real person—a cousin, Mary Elizabeth Huger from South Carolina, to Aunt Kate Mackay, dated January 1854. She writes:

> News has reached us here in South Carolina through a friend of his first wife, Sarah Hunter Low, that poor little Mary C. Stiles is definitely engaged now to Mr. Andrew Low—a match made and approved of by Mary Cowper Stiles parents, who have shut the heartbroken damsel up in their castle by the Etowah, until Blue, or rather Redbeard comes back from England to claim her.

The contents and context contained in the letter is used by a fictional character, Natalie Browning, to try and persuade a real character, Eliza Stiles, not to allow her real daughter Mary to marry a real Andrew Low, a real event based on fictional messengers![2] This fable placing my great-grandparents in a romance novel became a pivotal point of frustration in my own quest to uncover the truth. This was my real great-grandmother and grandfather, and this version of their love story had become, rightly or wrongly, engraved in stone, and constitutes the basis many people think they know about Andrew and Mary's relationship. The plot lines of the Savannah series bear only a barebones skeletal resemblance to the lives of Andrew Low and Mary Cowper, mixing fact and fiction to such a degree that it is impossible to extricate the truth from the embellishments.

My initial motivation had been to authenticate who Andrew Low's parents were. I was troubled that the record was wrong in several aspects, starting with an egregious factual error vis-à-vis his parents. That mission had been accomplished. But it was at this stage that my own involvement in the research veered away from hard-fought journalistic objectivity to hard-to-control emotional subjectivity. Now, I was truly disturbed at the portrait presented in Savannah of a young girl forced to deny the young man she loved to marry a licentious old man. The research early on led me to eminent historian Walter C. Hartridge's extensive collection at the Georgia Historical Society and a loose piece of handwritten paper that read:

> MARY COWPER STILES 1832—1863: Mary Cowper Stiles (Mrs. Andrew Low) was an unusual character. A radiant beauty, she had the disposition of an angel. She was thus described by her sister in law, (Mrs. Henry Stiles): She was very athletic, a splendid horsewoman, and said to be a better shot than her brother. Like her mother, she was practical and a fine executive, and adored her up-country home. Unfortunately, she was dominated by the powerful character of her mother, and yielding to family pressure, broke off her engagement to Stewart Elliott, the man she loved, and married rich old widower Andrew Low of Savannah. She was gentle and affectionate, and was not altogether unhappy in her short married life. Caroline Lovell.[3]

We have a description to summon up an image of what Mary Cowper looked like at that the time from her niece Caroline Couper Lovell's book, The *Light of Other Days,* of a portrait that hung on the walls at Etowah Cliffs, painted from life in Vienna:

> Aunt Mary is perfectly beautiful. A fine, tall, upstanding girl, with wonderful amber-colored eyes, a piquant nose, and a most entrancing mouth. Her hair is amber colored too, and waves down on either side of her face, ending in graceful curls, which fall to her shoulders. She wears an evening gown of sky-blue silk, trimmed with a fringe,

which is cut very low off her shoulders. It seems strange that such a beauty was a genuine outdoor girl, who was said to ride and shoot even better than her brothers! [4]

It is obvious that the description of Mary in descendant Caroline Lovell's book is correct[5] because this portrait remains for us to see for ourselves, but there was no mention of a forced marriage or even a rumored engagement to Stewart Elliott. The trail is still not clear, but undoubtedly that was where the contemporary gossip started, because it may have seemed a more sensational story than the more prosaic truth borne out through the course of her subsequent relationship with Andrew Low. Unfortunately all the principals are deceased so I cannot ask them personally, and can only document the trail of breadcrumbs that baked half a loaf of misconceptions.

If love was lacking on her part, money certainly was not on his. It was reported about this time that Andrew Low's annual income was $250,000, making him the "wealthiest man in Savannah."[6]

Letters From Andrew Low to Mary Cowper

Written in the flowery language of the nineteenth century from an older man to his young bride to be, there exist two letters; these are among the most intimate for me to read as they are very definitely ardent love-letters written by my great-grandfather, Andrew Low, to Mary Cowper Stiles. They speak directly to the rumors that have been passed down the years that not everyone in the family sanctioned this marriage.

> Savannah 24th, Nov'r 1852: A thousand thanks my own dearest Mary for your valued letter of 19th but which only came to hand yesterday, in the evening I had the pleasure of talking with your father . . . from whom I heard of your well being and was gladdened to my heart by your kind messages—you see thus far I am Mary dutiful in my correspondence. . . . I could convey my thoughts and feelings to you but they would always be the same—how dear you are to me, would you become, my dearest Mary, tired of so repeated a theme—you know I promised not to be so exacting, but you know also the real happiness you deserve, and hope you too will write often—I am really sorry that what has conferred so much happiness upon me, has thrown a gloom upon your Aunt Kate's spirits—she loves you very much and I believe that very affection makes her look kindly upon me. . . . I believe however the gossips continue to criticize our poor selves—some have given their approval, while others I dare say have something ill natured to say—let them talk, much good may it do them—fill your Mother with my affectionate regards and duty,

that I am not at all afraid or wish her harm, to remind her of my promises—I write regards to Henry and Robert. Believe me my darling Mary I remain yours with devoted affection, And Low

(PS) don' t you think my calligraphy is improving."[7]

The tone of this letter, dated one full year before Mary Cowper supposedly was pining for the romantic wastrel Stewart Elliott, certainly indicates that the May/December marriage was causing a considerable amount of gossip in Savannah's parlors, but some of it surely would have been elicited from envy as well as malice. The tone of Andrew Low's devotion is inescapable.

The courtship of Mary by Andrew Low continued without obvious roadblocks as recorded by a cousin Leila Elliott, who was staying at Etowah Cliffs in late 1853: "When we arrived at Etowah Cliffs, Aunt Eliza's place, we met there Mr. Andrew Low who was courting our cousin Mary Cowper Stiles. They became engaged that fall."[8]

The second letter from Andrew to Mary that remains to us was written a year later from Baltimore and shows a marked degree of attentive understanding, signifying a caring and comfortable familiarity with each other. Dated 8 Decr 1853:

> After writing you my dearest Mary on Monday, I met at the club with a number of friends whose kind civilities have been calculated to make my sojourn here most agreeable. . . . I found at the hotel invitations for me, for Miss Emily Harper's wedding and for the grand reception immediately after at Mrs. & Genr'l Harpers—as it was to be a grand affair I determined to remain a day longer and be present—it took place last evening at St. Paul's at 8.0 clock—the church was nearly filled, as many were present from Boston, New York, indeed everywhere. Savannah was represented . . . the bridal party was a pretty sight, one of the bridesmaids from New York was particularly good looking—and the bride is a very gentle and interesting girl—the poor thing was very much overcome, no wonder—the knot was soon tied and she was a wife . . . my own Mary was often present with me, and for one hour of quiet conversation with her in the park, I would gladly have exchanged all those scenes of changes and excitement and enjoyment. . . . I leave this afternoon for Washington where I will remain tomorrow and the next day—after that en route for home, which providence willing I expect to reach on Monday night—and now my dear Mary I have kept writing you of all my doings since I left Savannah and my next to you will be from that place. I suppose about that time you will be going to Roswell, of course you will. I am to address you there, and how long you stay

with her, not long I hope, for I am very anxious to see you again. Goodbye and God bless you my own darling and with affectionate regards to your Mother and the Boys. Believe in me—Andr Low.

This letter is fascinating in its detailed and thoughtful descriptions of things that would please a young woman's heart, especially as she would have already been in the throes of planning her own wedding. The letters from Andrew to Mary prove that they were already officially betrothed, and on the surface the courtship seemed acceptable to both parties. It was written on the eve of Mary Cowper's visit to Roswell, Georgia, where she was to participate in the wedding of a dear friend as bridesmaid. It is entirely logical that the rumors enshrined in Eugenia Price's pot- boiling romances originated at Mittie Bulloch's wedding.

Mittie Bulloch and Theodore Roosevelt

In late December of 1853 the marriage of Southern belle Martha "Mittie" Bulloch to Theodore Roosevelt of New York took place. Mittie Bulloch's sister was married to Roosevelt's brother. She later became the mother of Theodore Roosevelt, Jr., the future President of the United States. Mary Cowper Stiles was one of the bridesmaids at the Bulloch affair. The wedding was also attended by Mittie's half brother, Daniel Stewart Elliott, reputed to be a rather wild young blade as well as an accomplished musician with an artistic bent. One version of the story is recounted in David McCullough's *Mornings on Horseback*. This account was a sixty-year-old recollection of a member of the Bulloch family.[9]

In David McCullough's account he speculates that Elliott fell madly in love with one of the bridesmaids at the wedding without actually naming Mary Cowper Stiles as the "bridesmaid" at the center of the rumors. The Bullochs lived at Bulloch Hall, Roswell, about thirty miles from Etowah Cliffs. This was the town founded by Roswell King, former overseer on the Pierce Butler estates in coastal Georgia, with whom the original Andrew Low Company did business.[10] The Stiles family had returned to Cass County from Austria in December 1849, the same year that Mittie's father, James Stephens Bulloch, died suddenly of a heart attack. The entire family were forced to live permanently and under more adverse circumstances in Roswell rather than splitting their time between sophisticated town and rural country life. Mittie Bulloch talks about riding with Henry Stiles, who was rumored to be courting her sister Anna, and she recounts choosing Mary Cowper as a bridesmaid. The inference is obvious that they were all close friends.[11]

Daniel Stewart Elliott was Mittie Bulloch's half brother, so it is more than probable that from the time the Stileses returned from Europe all the young people would have been thrown together. It is also more than evident that Stewart Elliott would in no way, manner, or form have been considered a suitable husband by Mary Cowper's parents. If, as is rumored, that Stewart Elliott made a play for her at Mittie's wedding, it is easy to construe that William and Eliza Stiles would have nipped such a romance very firmly in the bud.[12]

A good decision as it turned out, as several years later he killed the son of a prominent Savannah doctor in a duel and was disgraced. At that point he was married to Lucy Sorrel, related to the Moxley family that Charles Green had married into.[13] Whether that event occurred because of inherent flaws in young Elliott's character or whether it was the result of unrequited love nipped in the bud is for the readers of romance bodice-rippers to determine. It makes for good fiction in any event.

The recounting of the event of Mittie Bulloch's wedding does clarify the realization that Mary Cowper Stiles also knew Mittie's brother James Dunwoody Bulloch extremely well from childhood, and that alone can provide a reasonable motivation behind the events that unfolded almost a decade later. On June 3, 1854, James Dunwoody Bulloch resigned his commission in the United States Navy and set in motion a predictable chain reaction. It is inconceivable that the inevitability of the coming conflict would not have been discussed extensively at both Mittie Bulloch's wedding and, six months later, at Mary Cowper Stiles nuptials. Both of them were marrying outside their traditional Southern heritage, the first to a Dutch northerner and the other to a man who although born in Scotland had become English in temperament—both of these exquisite Southern belles had a profound effect on their respective husbands and the direction of their lives.[14]

Marriage in Victorian times was contracted for many reasons other than romantic love, and while it is reasonable to suppose that the Stileses would not have forced their daughter into a completely loveless match, it is also provable that Mary was a practical young lady who understood fully the benefits that wealth and position could bring to her and her entire family. Her duty would have been quite clear, as would the alternative. It is odd that a marriage contract between Mary Cowper and Andrew Low has never surfaced, but if in fact it did contain some settlement of debts, it would not be at all surprising if along the way it simply disappeared.

The fact that the rumors of an arranged alliance have persisted through the chronicles of both the Stiles and Bulloch extended families through the succeeding years does indicate that there may have been some element of truth to the tale of love lost. The record also shows that the match was productive and satisfactory to all participants. Mary Low's short married life proved to be a relatively happy one, and indisputably a most

Etowah Cliffs, William H. Stiles's estate in Cass (Bartow) County, Georgia. The original house was the clapboard wing to the left, with the stucco-over-brick additions completed in 1852. The Etowah River is down a rock face to the left. The carriage entrance is to the right. *Courtesy The National Society of The Colonial Dames of America in the State of Georgia.*

prosperous one with a devoted husband who denied her nothing, and provided her with the best that money could buy, commencing with a magnificent wedding and a luxurious European honeymoon.[15]

Andrew Low married Mary Cowper Stiles at Etowah Cliffs on May 17, 1854. She was twenty-two years old and he was forty-two, three years younger than her father, William Henry Stiles.

The Wedding at Etowah Cliffs

The marriage took place at the Stileses' Cass County plantation home, Etowah Cliffs, located on the banks of the Etowah River in red clay country. It was a brilliant and dazzling affair. The wedding party traveled up from Savannah on a special rail car loaned for the occasion by President Richard R. Cuyler of the Central of Georgia Railroad,[16] and Savannah's preeminent minister, Bishop Stephen Elliott, married the couple. As was normal the wedding announcement appeared in the newspapers, in this case the *Savannah Morning News*: "1854, May 27. Married at Etowah Cliffs on the 17th inst by the Rt. Rev. Bishop Elliott, Mr. Andrew Low of Savannah, to Miss Mary Cowper, only daughter of Hon. Wm. H. Stiles."

Mary Cowper's cousin Leila Elliot Habersham writes:

> My cousin Mary Stiles was married that spring at Etowah Cliffs on the 17th May, 1854 to Mr. Andrew Low and a large party, 30 in number, came up from Savannah to attend the wedding & we had a right merry time, Fred and I being of the party. Mary was very lively &

Fred greatly admired her & she too being very fond of him, they were great friends all their lives. We all, with the bridal party, returned to Savannah in a car sent by Mr. Cuyler on purpose to bring us down. My sister Phoebe did not go up to the wedding as she was getting ready to spend the summer in Europe with Mr. & Mrs. Andrew Low who had invited her to accompany them on their wedding tour.[17]

Judging by all reports the affair went off splendidly. One letter written the same week, from a relative to Eliza Stiles on May 25, 1854:

> May 25th, 1854. Don' t know whether to congratulate or condole with you my dearest E, certainly the former when I think of your having gotten through so wonderfully with such a great undertaking. Robert told us he had never seen a country party go off so well, that there was nothing to be desired or regretted and that this is the unanimous opinion of the whole company, there is no dissenting voice, everybody enjoyed themselves excessively, so you may feel rewarded for all your trouble.

In a letter from Eliza Stiles to Mary Low, addressed to Vienna, where she was traveling on her honeymoon, we are able to view the perspective from both sides of the family; dated Etowah Cliffs, September 9, 1854, there is one poignant line ... most of the rest is gossip and requests for purchases: "Ask Mr. Low if he is not tired yet of his young wife, I will gladly take you back again if he is."

The tone sounds quite depressed, and maybe this is an indication that she at least was not terribly thrilled with the marriage, or just desolate to have lost the company of her only daughter, or more than likely remembering happier times for herself during their sojourn in Vienna.

The Family Starts to Grow

The newlyweds spent the summer in Europe, and it is believed that the portrait of Mary Low that now resides in the family parlor of the Andrew Low House was painted in Paris during their long honeymoon.[18]

In September, while they were still in Europe, one of the periodic hurricanes that still afflict the coastal areas hit hard. A notice in the *Savannah Daily Morning News* on 9 September 1854 states: "From Abercorn to Bull Street nearly every tree is blown down. The few that still remain standing are limbless and leafless—nothing but naked trunks remain to tell the truth of the gale—it will require years to replace the beautiful trees which now lie prostrate in that street."

Eliza Mackay writes to her husband that in the September hurricane the "tin rolled off roof of Mr. Low's house and it is leaking badly."[19]

Mary Cowper Low, 1854. Probably done in Europe on her wedding trip. Andrew Low displayed this portrait on an easel with a black drape in his Leamington home. *Courtesy The National Society of The Colonial Dames of America in the State of Georgia.*

The children arrived in quick succession. In the middle of summer, on July 9, 1855, Catherine Mackay Low, to be known all her life as Katie, was born at Etowah Cliffs, Cass County, Cherokee country, on her grandfather's property. Bishop Elliott baptized her on Christmas morning in Christ Church, Savannah.

Before the marriage in 1853, the English novelist William Makepeace Thackeray stayed in Andrew Low's Savannah mansion and in a letter mentioned that he and Mr. Low had much in common, including missing

William Makepeace Thackeray. Engraving from a drawing by Samuel Lawrence. The celebrated author brought his lecture tour to Savannah in 1853 and 1856, and on both occasions he was the guest of Andrew Low on Lafayette Square. *Courtesy The National Society of The Colonial Dames of America in the State of Georgia.*

their children. He specifically said that Low had told him his two little daughters were away in school in England; he would have been referring to Amy and Harriet, the two small daughters by first wife Sarah Hunter Low. A second Thackeray letter written on the "Feast of St. Valentine' in Andrew Low's house, February 1856, comments:

> I write from the most comfortable quarters I have ever had in the United States … [I had] a famous good dinner, breakfast etc, and

Writing desk by Edward W. Hutchings of New York, collection of the Andrew Low House. At this desk William Makepeace Thackeray penned letters to his daughter as well as chapters for his novel *The Virginians. Courtesy The National Society of The Colonial Dames of America in the State of Georgia.*

leisure all the morning to think and sleep and read as I like. The only place in the States where I can get these comforts—all free gratis—is in the home of my friend Andrew Low of the great house of A. Low and Co., Cotton dealers, brokers, merchants—what's the word? Last time I was here, he was a widower with two daughters in England, about whom there was endless talk between us. Now there is a

Andrew Low visiting his daughters Amy and Hattie in England, 1856. *Courtesy The National Society of The Colonial Dames of America in the State of Georgia.*

> pretty wife added to the establishment and a little daughter, number three, crowing in the adjoining nursery. They are tremendous men these cotton merchants.[20]

Thackeray's description of a Savannah he knew and loved made no mention of the tensions bubbling below the surface and in retrospect shows unawareness, a tragic parody of the realities of the turbulence to descend in a few short years. "It is a tranquil old city, wide streeted, tree-planted, with a few cows and carriages toiling through the sandy road; a few happy Negroes sauntering here or there, a red river with a tranquil little fleet of merchantmen taking in cargo, and tranquil ware-houses barricaded with packs of cotton,—no row, no tearing northern bustle, no ceaseless hotel racket, no crowds drinking at the bar."

Already awaiting a second child, the happy family sailed on June 26, 1856, as reported in the Savannah newspaper, "among the passengers on the Niagara, which sailed from Boston to Liverpool on the 18th, were Andrew Low and family, of this city." There is a photograph dated 1856 taken in England, of a bearded, sombreroed, swashbuckling Andrew Low with his two pre-teenaged daughters, Amy and Harriet, so it is likely that they were formally introduced to their new stepmother on that visit. But the trip was obviously too much for her physique to bear.

Back in Savannah, five months later, on November 8, 1856, a premature child was born and died and is listed in the Directory of Cemetery as buried in the Mackay Lot in Laurel Grove.[21] The child was only one day old. The *Diaries of Eliza Stiles* written in Austria indicate that Mary was not a terribly healthy girl, suffering from headaches, fevers, poor circulation, and constant dental problems. The bearing of children would have been a severe physical burden.

Death of His Mother

June 6, 1857, Katherine Reid Low died, aged eighty-six. She was mother of Andrew Low and is buried with her husband and children in the kirkyard of Brechin Cathedral, in the county of Angus, Scotland, under a handsome tablestone, fully engraved. The records show the entire family, with the singular exception of Andrew Low, Jr., buried in the graveyard of Brechin Cathedral. The street the house is on, the burial, and the records show a substantial family supported with funds either from family or business connections. On a sunny autumn day I visited the splendid graveyard embracing the granite walls of Brechin Cathedral, necklaced with scattered flower beds growing red, orange, and yellow flowers in rich dark soil, surrounded by a stone wall and stately yew trees, evocative of the passion of Christ. The massive studded wooden doors sadly are locked against intruders and would-be robbers. Located in an advantageous position adjacent to the graveled path leading to the entranceway, the gravestone of the Low family, a raised tablestone, is engraved with the names of the bones interred beneath:

> TS (Tablestone) William Low, Merchant, 2.2.1849, aged 79; wife, Katherine Reid, 18.6.1857, aged 86; son, James, 13.9.1819, aged 17; son, William, 29.5.1822, aged 15; daughter Mary, 7.4.1888, aged 79; daughter Jean, 11.10.1879, aged 74 (husband William Mill, cabinet maker, 31.5.1869, aged 61)[22]

I have found the resting place of my ancestors once more.

Conventional wisdom in Savannah has it that after the death of Andrew Low the executors of his estate discovered that he had been sending money to relatives in Scotland, although the same wisdom declared that his children knew absolutely nothing of his Scottish family. The size, magnificence, and position of the tombstone in the Brechin Cathedral graveyard indicate that some surviving relative was paying for its upkeep, and Andrew Low was the only surviving child other than his sister Mary. It is difficult not to draw the conclusion that he was fundamentally involved in upholding the family's resting place in his ancestral home.

Andrew Low traveled to Scotland on August 18, 1857, to file a petition with the Scottish Courts in Forfar (Angus) to claim his right of inheritance as the sole surviving son of William Low, Merchant of Brechin, who had died eight years before. At the time of his mother's death he still had two living sisters, but whether he informed his wife about his Scottish relatives is still unknown, although it is inconceivable that he did not, especially since they named their oldest daughter Catherine. It later became obvious that his two older daughters, Amy and Harriett, had at no time been in the care of their Scottish relatives.

I have spoken before of the superb manner in which Scotland has preserved the record of its ancient and modern history, and the National Archives of Scotland—now known as the Scottish Record Office in Edinburgh—have the most astounding and extensive collection of documents that with tenacity and energy one can trace and track down almost any event that ever occurred in Scotland. Thus, I was able to find out that when William Low died in 1849 he died intestate, which is why the disposition of his estate was held up until the death of his widow in 1858.[23]

Eighteen months later a second child was born to Andrew and Mary Low in Savannah; it was a girl, my grandmother, born January 25, 1859. Named after her mother, Mary Low was born in Lafayette Square.

The Census for 1860 is the first proof in Savannah records of the place of Andrew Low's birth, albeit misspelled—"Head of House—Andrew Low, 40M, Kingverdshire, Scotland."[24] One interesting aspect is that Hattie and Amy were listed as being in Savannah on the day the Census was taken, which was usually the beginning of the year, which could mean they were on holiday for Christmas, and would also account for why they do not show up in the 1860 census for Brighton, England, where it is supposed they were at school, or even in the rosters of the many foreign students in school in the fashionable seaside spa town, but the clues still point to Brighton as the most likely location.

On August 3, 1860, the heir apparent arrived. William Mackay Low was born in Newport, Rhode Island, replacement for the son Andrew Low had lost twelve years earlier.[25] It was during this summer in Newport that Mary Low showed her own interest in exploring the past, and spent her leisure time transcribing letters and journals describing the colonial heritage of her Malbone ancestry.[26]

Many years later Katie Low's godmother, Sidney Stiles Elliott, wrote to her with details of that summer in Newport. In a letter dated May 6, 1892, Savannah: "You know your Mother spent the summer of 1857 in Newport & saw a great deal of Mrs. Littlefield and the Brinley's, & they gave her these old letters & she became much interested in the Malbone family history generally and used often to talk to me about it."

Obviously Andrew took his family out of Savannah for the worst of the summer heat and humidity when disease was most dangerous. By then, Mary Low had conceived and borne four children in six years, three of who had survived.

It was not all business, and we find another excellent example of Andrew Low's extensive interests when on February 17, 1860, he presented a gift to the Georgia Historical Society Anniversary Meeting titled "An account of the first settling of the Colony of Georgia." This was an original and valuable colonial manuscript written by Peter Gordon, Bailiff of the First Settlers, which had come into Low's hands by a circuitous route emanating from Chester Castle and Liverpool, to the Richardson family, then to Maxwell in New Orleans, and then to Andrew Low. This gift is an interesting insight to his character and shows either that he was interested in the history of the colony or was attempting to parade his culture by indicating that he knew the value of such material. Nothing shows that he was a devious man, and it is most likely that under the influence of his wife he had more time and inclination for such matters.

The Meaning of the Marriage

One rumor has it that Mary Cowper's father had borrowed a considerable sum of money from Andrew Low to purchase land in northeast Georgia, rebuild Etowah Cliffs, and repair the brickyard or to finance the resuscitation of his political career, although no real proof has surfaced. No marriage settlement has been located although it is nonsense to suppose there would not be one. Whatever the reasons, it was obvious that on the part of Andrew Low at least the marriage was a love match. On her part, she proved to be a responsible and dutiful wife and held her husband in high regard and great affection, and treated her children as the reason for her own existence.

Eliza Mackay Stiles in many of her comments has left a distinct impression that she did not care too much for Andrew Low, although she obviously respected his position and enjoyed his money. She intimated he drank too much for one, and there is probably a degree of truth that he liked his whiskey—he was, after all, a Scot. His Uncle Andrew had formed the Madeira Club that continues today in a revived form. She often admitted though that he was a good, kind, and attentive husband and father. It is also obvious from the letters that the spinster Mackay aunts, Eliza's sisters Kate and Sarah and their friends, did not much care for the marriage, in fact often downright disapproved, but there is no indication that the parents were anything but satisfied. Andrew Low, after all, provided the wealth they lacked.[27]

Eliza Mackay Stiles was a snob and social climber, no more, no less than others of her status were for the times. To her credit she appears to have had a sense of irony, if not humor, and there are indications in her own diaries and letters that she felt that Washington society looked down on the Stileses for being "crackers," the South's pejorative term for tenant farmers. Ironically Andrew Low's own ancestors from Scotland would have fallen into that category as far as Savannah society was concerned, and she is quite amusing in her analysis of her actions and reactions to Washington snobbery and social protocol. She was as complicated an individual as all the others, and they all played the parts history allocated them with great gusto. All of them emerge as very real, sometimes irritating, often admirable, sometimes despicable products of social attitudes that made these individuals who they were in the context of when they lived.

Other family members in later years, even centuries later, have indicated that Savannah society rather looked down on Andrew Low and despised his strong Scottish accent. A note discovered in the Walter C. Hartridge Collection of the Georgia Historical Society taken from a conversation with Mrs. Frank B. Screven, a Stiles family member, states:

> Andrew Low of common Scottish origins. His Uncle, who kept a store in Savannah (very common) sent for him from Scotland. AL taken into store *not socially received. Later became a cotton merchant and married well twice (Sarah Cecil Hunter & Mary Cowper Stiles). The family later moved to England. Moved in highest social circles, but as Americans, not Scottish Lows. Ignored Low relations etc. except one, General Low (cousin) that they 'recognized.'[28]

Neither Andrew Low's words nor actions ever indicated that he felt himself socially inferior to Savannah's self-proclaimed colonial gentry. It is far more likely that it was his own children's generation who did not consider their origins aristocratic enough to boast about, or Savannah society who looked down on the family of "a common tradesman who had married well—twice!"

That attitude on the part of Savannah society certainly can be laid at the door of Southern culture and the tensions that always existed between the mercantile class and the plantation class. Those descended from the British aristocracy who founded many of these plantations along the Savannah River and Charleston, South Carolina, would have considered themselves a cut above the upstart, albeit most successful interloper merchants, many of them of humble origin from Scotland and northern England. These personal tensions are an integral part of the warp and woof of these relationships.

For me writing about these people—my people—from the vantage point of a century and a half in the future, there are also personal tensions, brought on by the need to truthfully recount the historical actualities of then, and my own legitimacy and beliefs of now. The theme of privilege was paramount, and the advantages the Low family enjoyed would have created envy in their communal circles, their social life entwined with his business travels. The summers at the Stiles plantation home in northeast Georgia, on the banks of the Etowah River, the slave quarters nearby; summers in Newport where William Mackay Low was born, visiting Mary Low's Malbone relatives, all illustrate the way wealth and privilege paved the path for those who could afford it—lives of the rich and famous.

The naming of Godfrey Malbone in records of 1732 in the context of traffic in Gold Coast slaves, and Rhode Island as the leading slave-trading state of the eastern seaboard, points to the comfort level the family would have had with the institution of slavery, and most certainly owning slaves would have been viewed, not through a contemporary revisionist prism but a nineteenth-century reality. The Mackay family ownership of Grange and Sedgebank, former Clay and Stiles ownership of Vale Royal and Springfield—all labor-intensive rice plantations along the Savannah River; and in the 1850's the ownership by William Henry Stiles of a cotton plantation in Cass County and in Southern Georgia, made the Clay, Stiles, and Mackay families leading plantation owners, thereby by definition, a slave-owning dynasty.

Certainly having a cultured, educated, beautiful hostess in the splendid house on Abercorn Street would have enhanced Andrew Low's social status. The house on Lafayette Square was magnificent, and his wealth allowed them extensive international travel for business and pleasure. The arrival of four children in fairly quick succession would have under normal circumstances made for a very productive marriage and happy times. But these were by no means usual times and the dogs of war had begun to growl. The Low family became caught up in one of the epic sagas of American history and found themselves inadvertently playing key roles in the unfolding drama.

Competition Between Green and Low

The 1850's saw an intensification of the notorious rivalry between Andrew Low and Charles Green, partners in the Andrew Low Company. The letters from Andrew Low, Sr., to Robert Hutchison indicate that the two firms, Isaac Low & Company in Liverpool and Josiah Green Company of Liverpool had business dealings. The indications from Charles Green's obituary are that following his arrival in Savannah in the late 1820's or early 1830's, following several other positions and one failed partnership known as Butts & Green, he entered the firm of Andrew Low and Company in Savannah in 1836.

By the 1850's Charles Green's status as a prominent and prosperous businessman in Savannah matched that of Andrew Low, and by April 1851 he had commenced building a magnificent mansion almost next door to Andrew Low. So although it is pure speculation to think that the partnership was never basically a personal choice for either men, rather a decision made by Andrew Low, Sr., when he reorganized the firm following Robert Isaac's death, it is quite likely that their partnership was a matter of convenience rather than closeness, and competition was their minuet. Certainly they could not have been more different in temperament. Green was flamboyant and reckless and Low steady and pragmatic, although his marriage to Mary Cowper demonstrates a strong sense of self-confidence and romanticism.[29]

It was now in the early 1850's that the same architect John Norris, who had designed Andrew Low's simple but beautiful mansion on Lafayette Square, constructed the Green House in Savannah. The Low House combines a Greek Revival entrance and interior with a crenellated parapet and mock casement windows.[30] Conventional wisdom has it that Green intended to build a house to outdo his partner Andrew Low. Norris' patrons included many of the leading men of the era, and it was here that public rivalry between Andrew Low and Charles Green seemed to have begun.[31]

Mills Lane's *Architecture of the South* states: "In 1853 Norris designed a mansion for Charles Green, an English born cotton merchant, across the street from the new St. John's Church on Madison Square. The finest surviving Gothic Revival house south of Virginia, Green's mansion is a luxurious blend of elaborate design and sumptuous materials, including a massive cast iron entrance and porches, shutters and windows which slide into hidden wall pockets."

The location was a mere stone's throw from the house on Lafayette Square belonging to Andrew Low, and when the trees were bare could be seen from Andrew's beloved upstairs piazza. When Green's house was being built it was the talk of the town. *Savannah Morning News*, April 26, 1851: "A splendid mansion, also in Gothic style, has been commenced on Madison Square. It is to be the residence of Charles Green, Esq. Madison Square promises to present one of the more imposing views in our city. The army of fine edifices, form with the noble forest trees surrounding them, a prospect to be equaled in few cities of the Union."

Green was also secretary of the "back-to-Africa" African Colonization Society, the organization set up to repatriate African slaves. This was not as peculiar as it appears on the surface given Charles Green's occupation. He was a devout Presbyterian, but was also a patron and supporter of St. John's Episcopal Church, built next door to his mansion on Madison Square, of which the influential Bishop Elliott was rector at that time. Green also built and supported the small Presbyterian Church in Vint

Hill, Virginia, on the grounds of his estate in Prince Edward County.[32]

By the end of the 1850's both Andrew Low and Charles Green separately and as partners in the Savannah-based Andrew Low Company and the Liverpool-based Isaac Low & Company were two of the principal merchants on both sides of the Atlantic. On April 7, 1853, the papers issued the Registry List of Voters and conspicuous by their absence are the names of Andrew Low and Charles Green. This is one indication that neither of them ever took out naturalization papers.

Part V

Savannah–Liverpool–Leamington, 1860–1872

14

Our Peculiar Institution: 1858–1860

NERVOUSNESS EMERGED IN THE INFLUENTIAL BRITISH PRESS REgarding the possibility of secession of the South from the North in America, harming Britain's textile industry. "America could ruin her, by withholding one year's supply of cotton, yet this tremendous power is dependent on the retaining of the present institutions, which is being denounced by professed patriots."[1] That stark statement explains the dilemma.

The British regarded America as the chief obstacle to a worldwide acceptance of the doctrine of free trade. As viewed by the British free trader, the one bright spot in America was in the Southern states, where cotton interests—seeing no advantage from protection since their market was in Europe—attacked American protectionism flowing from the manufacturing Northern states.

Adding to the tension, the dependence of British cotton manufacturers on Southern cotton created conditions where the attitudes of British traders were bound to have a powerful influence on governmental policy, despite British antipathy toward slavery. The stage was set for a type of internal civil war in Britain between competing interests; trade versus philanthropy, slavery versus prosperity. This was a situation with many levels of complexity.

Britain's relationship with America was extremely intricate; on the one hand America was viewed as a haven for emigration, and on the other there was an almost universal British criticism of American social customs and habits of life. This was rooted deeply in Britain's notorious xenophobia. In Great Britain popular public sentiment leaned heavily toward abolition, fueled by the romantic sentimentality of books such as Harriet Beecher Stowe's *Uncle Tom's Cabin* and *Life on a Georgia Plantation*, written by Fanny Kemble, English actress-wife of Georgia plantation owner Pierce Butler.[2] The writings in the popular press of the times could be construed as being rabidly anti-American. This, however, was a somewhat misleading conclusion. Even the working classes were divided between their emotional rejection of the enslavement of Africans to the growing of cotton in America and their own economic dependence on the manufacturing sector at home. Self-interest or self-preservation usually prevails under these conditions, however reluctantly.

The timing of the formation of the Isaac Low Company was dictated by the beginning of an immense expansion in the cotton trade that lasted until the early 1860's. Liverpool dominated the import market of raw cotton from America, mainly the South, and a great deal of it was from Savannah. Andrew Low, Sr., had positioned his company with enormous foresight at exactly the right time in history. One interesting aspect shows that the cotton trade became more and more concentrated in the hands of fewer and fewer merchants and factors. The records show Isaac Low & Company as one of the thirty leading importers of goods in Liverpool from America and Africa.[3] It is now that Andrew Low literally came into his own, unique amongst his associates inasmuch as his business was peculiarly bi-oceanic, transatlantic, and global in nature.

The Cotton Factor

Factors and commission merchants were a powerful element in Savannah business and government. It was frequently said that if cotton was the king, then the cotton factor was the power behind the throne. The cotton factor was much more than the middleman in the cotton trade. He was banker, purchasing agent, and often advisor to the planter. He was also the one that took much of the risk, as it was he who chartered the vessels, dealt with the captains, and was responsible for insuring the cargo. Ships frequently were lost entering and departing ports on both sides of the Atlantic, where dangers lurked in terms of squalls, rocks, and other shoreline hazards. On December 6, 1852, the ship *DeWolfe* went ashore near Sapelo Island, all cargo lost, consignee Andrew Low & Company. This stark reminder points to the considerable risks involved in shipping by sea, at that time the only way available over the oceans. The rise of the marine insurance business was an integral part of the success of Andrew Low's business activities, and by now the Andrew Low Company was involved as agents for the Royal Insurance Company of Liverpool.

The strands of the cotton trade between Great Britain and America were tied extremely tight during the decade prior to the Civil War, especially in the South, where New Orleans, Mobile, Charleston, and Savannah formed the pivots of a constantly revolving wheel of cotton. The threads extended across the Atlantic, winding down the streets of Liverpool, spewing into the maw of the mills of Manchester in the industrial north.

In April 1850 Godfrey Barnsley, an English cotton merchant who lived in Savannah, wrote ruefully: "It is rather astonishing on weak nerves to meet with such great men as Mr. A. Low, Jr." Several other Savannah merchants engaged directly in shipping to Liverpool, such as Englishman William Battersby, who built the Barbados-style residence just south of Andrew Low's home.

Another prominent name of English extraction was Edward Molyneaux, one of Liverpool's leading cotton merchants.[4] Molyneaux's magnificent mansion on Gaston Street in Savannah is now the exclusive Oglethorpe Club, but during that period he was the revolving British consul in Savannah, a role that was handed to whichever British merchant cared to undertake the responsibility of looking after the affairs of British citizens in Savannah.

The records indicate that Andrew Low was a member of a prominent banking company, Joshua Dixon & Company in Liverpool; he also was corresponding banker for W. Peabody, Baring Company of New York in the South. Alliances formed from the 1820's by marriages in England and Scotland between British members of the Nicol, Duckworth, Loyd, and Low merchant and banking families continued to be a major factor in the network of commercial interests that provided the foundation for the consolidation of the wealth of these merchant traders.

Low was a Director of the Iron Steamboat Company, Director of the Central Railroad and Banking Company, and a subscriber to the Jacksonville & Alligator Plank Road Company. Andrew Low, Jr., understood clearly that the railroads reduced the dependence of trade on the river traffic and that improving the roads delivered the goods to the railhead faster. He played a seminal role in the building of the Central Railroad, spearheaded by William Washington Gordon, grandfather of Juliette Gordon, who later married William Mackay Low, his only surviving son; once again this cemented a family and a business interest and two continents.

The role of the factor has been caricatured and frequently vilified in the accounts of antebellum Southern life. The traditional aggrandizement of a plantation elite, stemming from a self- proclaimed descendency from British aristocracy, and that class's aversion to trade as an honorable way of life permeated the culture of the South. Merchants and factors were viewed as "Shylocks in frock coats" yearning after respectability, which has a Hogarthian humor. The fact was that they also incurred much of the risk, had an impressive collective head for business, accrued financial power and credit worthiness—many of them were Scots with all that race's reputation for canniness.[5]

Political Background and the Stiles Influence

By January 1850 the slavery question had begun bubbling in earnest and the Fugitive Slave Act fueled the fires that were heating the pot. On the national scene, the entry of California and New Mexico as free states was connected to the concerns of the South going back to Henry Clay's infamous Missouri Compromise. This law was passed by the U.S. Congress of 1820 that had prepared the way for the admission of Missouri as a slave state, but furthermore limiting slavery to areas below the southern line of Missouri. This new situation could easily repeal the Compromise.[6]

The old alignments broke down in Georgia, resulting in the formation of the Constitutional Union Party and the Southern Rights Party. The Southern Rights was made up of those who opposed the repeal of the Compromise and who were mostly members of the Old Democratic Party. William H. Stiles played a key role in Georgia's response to this threat, as they saw it, to their sovereignty. Once again he showed his remarkable agility in holding several positions at the same time, and wound up nominated as the candidate for the pro-slavery Southern Rights Party for the Fifth Congressional District of Georgia; he was defeated 2–1 by his opponent, Colonel Chastain, representing the Constitutional Union Party. The close of the year 1851 marked the low point in the political career of this ambitious man.

He was not the type to accept defeat as a permanent state of affairs and proceeded to mend his political fences. The 1852 election was a struggle for power among various factions and parties. Stiles identified himself with the "Regular" Democrats, and despite residing in his Fifth District Cass County home, started to lobby again in the First District in Savannah; he appears to have had the support in Washington of Franklin Pierce, the current President. This indicates that he was still extremely good at maintaining his "you scratch my back, I'll scratch yours" approach to his own political survival. He is mentioned as a possible candidate for governor of Georgia, and a future member of Congress to further Savannah's interests. By the end of 1853 he might well have considered his reentry into politics complete, since he had aligned himself successfully with the faction of the Democratic Party that had gained ascendancy in Georgia, and reestablished himself as a politician in Chatham County without damaging himself in Cass County. This was no mean feat.

The Battle of 1856

The presidential election of 1856 shows the disproportional influence the small city of Savannah held over the national politics of an expanding nation. The chairman of the Democratic National Party was a Savannahian,

John Elliott Ward. Ward entered the international stage as America's first minister to China. He and Savannahian Commodore Josiah Tattnall observed a battle of the Second Opium War when the British seemed to be losing. Ward asked the naval officer if they should intervene. The commodore answered in the affirmative, saying, "Blood is thicker than water!"

In 1856 the Democrats nominated James Buchanan, William Henry Stiles's old friend. Buchanan was Secretary of State when Stiles was posted to Vienna, and all of his official dispatches from the Austrian capital are addressed to Buchanan. The American Party, also called the "Know Nothings," were a remnant of the divided Whig Party; and its national chairman was Savannahian John MacPherson Berrien, who in the last act of his career shepherded the nomination of former President Millard Fillmore.

The other remnant of the Whigs was the "Free Soilers," who morphed into the Republican Party. In 1856 they nominated the heroic "Pathfinder of the West," John C. Fremont. Fremont was born in Savannah in 1813, the illegitimate son of a French dance instructor and the runaway wife of a Virginia planter. His birthplace was a tenement in Yamacraw owned by the Gibbons family, within sight of the Stiles mansion where William Henry had been born three years before. Savannah's native son on the U.S. Supreme Court, James Moore Wayne, whose birthplace was also a stone's throw away in Yamacraw, also manifested Savannah's disproportionate influence on national government. Surely no other Southern town held so much national sway in this critical year.

The American Party was antiforeign, pro-nativist born, and chauvinistic, foretelling the white supremacist movements of the twentieth century. Stiles became a bitter critic and won a seat in the Georgia House of Representatives, leading the ticket in Chatham County. Coinciding with Stiles return to Savannah politics and resultant success, Andrew Low married Mary Cowper Stiles at Etowah Cliffs in May 1854.

Christianity's Role in Slavery

Another strong influence on Andrew Low following his marriage would certainly have been Stiles's older brother, Joseph Clay Stiles, who became a hell-and-brimstone evangelical preacher following his conversion and embrace of Christianity on the death of his wife. He also fits into the wheel of connections as his second wife was the sister of Mrs. Barrington King of Roswell. Joseph Stiles traveled and wrote extensively on the question of slavery and political and national conscience. The Reverend Stiles followed the line of the Second Great Awakening that Africans had souls and needed Christianity, but freedom and equality did not enter his reasoning.[7] Although J. C. Stiles's generation was one of the first to recognize that Africans had souls like white men and were in need of the Word, like most

Southern clergymen he espoused the philosophy that enabled Christianity to condone the institution of slavery based on the biblical interpretation of the "Curse of Ham." The Reverend Stiles preached that abolition was the folly of the day. A copy of a rare pamphlet in the Georgia Historical Society called *National Rectitude the only True Basis of National Prosperity—An Appeal to the Confederate States*, published by the Evangelical Tract Society of Petersburg, also written by the the Reverend J. C. Stiles, D.D., in 1863, has "Andrew Low, Esq." written in ink on the outside and has bolstered the theory that these ideas had resonance. For Andrew Low to keep his own personal copy all his life, it must have influenced him.

One of the Reverend Stiles's books was *The Voice of Our Fathers*, published by Rudd and Carleton of New York City.[8] The small book blames the North for the troubles facing the country, and tries to make the case that the Founding Fathers intended slavery to continue in perpetuity. Portions of the text present the reader with an extremely subjective contemporary mind-set for the times:

> That the institution of slavery has long been dying out in the North is undeniable; but the very causes which worked decay at the North wrought invigoration at the South. The cold climate of the north, uncongenial to the African constitution of the Negro, shortened his days, and diminished his strength and value, while the warm climate of the South, more suitable to his physical nature, proportionately augmented his powers, both of labor and enjoyment. In like manner it has been demonstrated that the commercial, manufactural, and skilful avocations of the North could extract but profitless service from the contracted intellect of the Negro, while the agricultural pursuits of the South found, in his remarkable physical endurance, even in a sultry climate, an exact provision for her simple culture of tobacco, indigo and rice. Thus, that very intellectual and physical structure of the slave, which so naturally worked out his rapid disappearance from the North, must exert an equal power to secure his permanent value at the South.

He goes on to point out, correctly, that the great Founding Fathers—Washington, Jefferson, Madison, Mason, Randolph, and probably every other prominent delegate from the South, despite their stated opposition to slavery—were themselves slaveholders, and apart from Washington, none of them had freed their slaves following the adoption of the Constitution of the United States.

Two things therefore, are perfectly clear. On the one hand, the Fathers had no reason to expect that their principles of opposition to slavery would work its speedy banishment from society; on the other, they had great reason to expect its sturdy endurance—for there must have resided somewhere in that institution a mighty power of self-preservation—since it did so long and so perfectly paralyze all the adverse efforts of the mightiest men of the nation, North and South.

He makes the case by quoting Southern politicians of Georgia and the Carolinas that "Slavery is justified by the example of all the world, since in all its ages half of mankind have been slaves—it is a blessing to the subject, for it civilizes the savage and converts the pagan—to the whole Union, for the more slaves, the more the produce, and therefore the more the carrying trade—the more consumption, and therefore the more revenue to the treasury of our common country."

Stiles's plea must have resounded in the ears of his family and friends, slaveholders and producers of consumer goods.

> To us of Carolina and Georgia, slavery is as necessary as a home, in this latitude; for who else upon earth could cultivate rice and indigo in our sultry swamps?

These publications by Joseph Stiles represent the duality of thought that many white Southerners felt in those times. Abhorrent though it may seem today, then it was truly believed that to be antislavery was anti-deistic and immoral, and that they were constitutionally guaranteed their sovereign rights, which included slavery to maintain their way of life.

Somewhat naturally many of the enslaved of African descent in the South did not feel the same way about their manifest destiny. One slave narrative written in London prior to the Civil War by William and Ellen Craft, both born in different towns in Georgia states:

> It is true, our condition as slaves was not by any means the worst: but the mere idea that we were held as chattels, and deprived of all legal rights—the thought that we had to give up our hard earnings to a tyrant, to enable him to live in idleness and luxury—the thought that we could not call the bones and sinews that God gave us our own: but above all, the fact that another man had the power to tear from our cradle the new-born babe and sell it in the shambles like a brute, and then scourge us if we dared to lift a finger to save it from such a fate, haunted us for years.[9]

Somewhere within those criteria would have been the yardstick with which Andrew Low judged his own personal interests, which by now would have been extremely influenced by the alignment of the house of Low with the house of Stiles.

Slavery in the South

In the inhospitable climate of the sultry South unsuited for European physiques, black African slaves were brought in by the tens of thousands to work the fields and swamps, particularly the rice fields. They were predominantly from Sierra Leone, whose people were familiar with the cultivation of the crops. Out of the subtropical marshes, river banks, and tidelands of the coastal barrier areas the slaves, under the whip, carved out vast plantations along the Low Country's many rivers, especially the Savannah River. In the doing, the slaves also built a way of life the self-styled aristocracy of this new land took upon themselves: mansions in town and pillared and porticoed estate houses on the riverbanks. Slaves were the true wealth of this new experiment in agriculture based on the labor of chattel slavery.

Although the feudal systems of land distribution in Scotland had created a virtual economic slavery, men still retained the right to their own souls and received the solace of the Scottish Church to salve the hardships of daily toil in the fields. To these transplanted Africans the Christian God was the god of foreign devils who believed that to whip them, to enchain them, to own them was the will of this god. In an ironic twist of history's river the Christian God soon appeared in their songs, their language, and their hopes for freedom, maybe for self-preservation, maybe a calculated irony, but the spiritual symbolism of master and slave merged, with totally opposite meaning.

It proved necessary to bring in blacks because the original indigenous inhabitants of the land saw no reason to work the land for profit, only as an equal partner in the quest for survival. Eventually the Indians of these areas would all die out, a euphemism for massacre and genocide, in their fight against enslavement, loss of land, and newly introduced diseases, some inflicted deliberately, some acquired involuntarily, brought over by the settlers, ranging from measles and chicken pox to the more deadly small pox and syphilis.

Peace after war brings its own form of depression, both personal and national; the Revolutionary War for independence in America was no different. War changes everything for winners and losers, and it takes a while for things to settle down one way or another, not always according to the plans of the winners.

The price of slaves fell off sharply, and at the end of 1794 George Washington advised a friend to shift from slaves to some other form of property. He wrote: "Were it not that I am principled against selling Negroes as you would cattle in a market, I would not in twelve months hence be possessed of a single one as a slave. I shall be happily mistaken if they are not found to be a very troublesome species of property ere many years have passed over our heads." Fewer prescient words have been spoken.

The *Draft Documents of the Declaration of Independence* are an illuminating revelation of the ambivalence felt by the men who drew it up as an instrument to make all men equal and establish democracy as a universal human right. Jefferson indicted George II for a "cruel war against human nature itself, violating its most sacred rights...in the persons of distant people, who never offended him, capturing and carrying them into slavery in another hemisphere, or to incur miserable death in their transportation hither." Fine words, but deleted because the South was going to have to depend on slavery, and because many in the North were engaged in that trade, or at the very least benefited from the labor provided by the commerce in human bodies and souls.

History of Cotton

Probably no single plant that is not a drug containing life-altering substances, like the opium poppy, cannabis, or coca plant, has caused quite as much human misery as the fluffy innocuous white fruit of the cotton plant. In America before the Civil War the production of cotton was the reason for the existence and perpetuation of black-African slavery. This institution led to a fratricidal war, a residue that exists to this day of bitterness and incomprehension, and a continuing need for America to heal the wounds inflicted by her past.

Cotton had long been grown in Asia, South America, and some in the West Indies—although in that region sugar was the dominant export crop, that sweet sorrow that built the mansions, fueled the estates and made palatable the lives of European powers from the 1400's to the 1800's. Cotton also created a hell on earth for Africans enslaved to grow it in the brave new world. In newly independent America, efforts were made to grow and manufacture cotton as an economic force at home. Thomas Jefferson, another slave-owning Founding Father, promoted its growth in the Southern states.

By 1780 the growing industrial revolution was changing the way of life in northern England and in the northern states of America. In Scotland, small mills and home weavers sprang up as land reformation techniques increased the profitability and yield of the raw materials of agriculture. In the period 1783–90, Britain's cotton imports jumped from 9 million pounds to 28 million pounds.

Very little of it came from the American South despite the fact that they could certainly grow it, the factory system demanded it, and they urgently needed a profitable cash crop. The only thing they could not do was to clean it quickly and efficiently.

Then along came Eli Whitney. The entire story of the invention of the cotton gin and Whitney's subsequent travails to secure a patent has been recounted in countless histories of the South. It was of such a simple design that it proved impossible to control, and homemade cotton gins and gin factories sprang up all over the South. It literally revolutionized the agricultural and industrial world, and set into motion dynamic forces that were completely uncontrollable or unforeseeable. It is not too far fetched to state that it was on the backs of this single invention that American contemporary might rests—as Atlas carried his globe, so America should carry her cotton gin.

Inadvertently it also changed the course of Africa's history, and the direct and indirect effect in America and England was unimaginable at the turn of the century. Fortunes were made, millions of lives lost to the fields and the mills—misery and prosperity in equal measure played host.

What the new technique required was labor, lots of labor—neither voluntary nor involuntary indentured servitude, or emigration could fill the fields with enough hands. The only profitable solution appeared to be the continuation of African slavery. By the mid 1800's thousands of slaves were cultivating cotton on hundreds of thousands of acres of Southern land, and half a million workers, many of them children, were spinning and weaving in English cotton mills of the North. Simultaneously, humanitarian forces for the abolition of human slavery coalesced.

This does not mean that the question of slavery was all one way in the South. In the 1820's there were as many if not more antislavery societies in the slave states as in the free states, but economic uncertainties and financial crises of the times changed the tenor of the debate. By 1859 loyalty to the South became a barometer of a man's allegiance, and patriotism to the Southern cause a guide to the denunciation of the abolitionist call for emancipation.

The romantic conventional wisdom has it that the South was peopled by an effete planter aristocracy living off the backs of the enslaved black, while the North was peopled by hard-driving, ruthless robber barons, living off the sweat and toil of the immigrant—elements of truth, vast dollops of myth and legend, north and south of the Dixie line. The entire nation fell prey to its own propaganda, victims of their own illusions.

The reality was that the relationship was both symbiotic and parasitical; one grew off the other, depending on the other for its survival; both were exhausting each other, using and abusing each other, depleting human, emotional, and spiritual resources. Cotton culture above all was about enslavement—to its laborers, to its credit system, to the bankers, and ultimately to the factor or commission agent—a one-stop shop for money-lending and marketing of the product.[10]

Slave Labor and the Factory System

Many historians focusing on the international cotton trade as primary causes of the Civil War refer to James Henry Hammond as one of the trigger mechanisms. Hammond had been editor of the *Southern Times*, governor of South Carolina, and in 1859 senator for South Carolina. He was also a large plantation owner, having acquired vast cotton fields along with a bride. His cotton credentials were impeccable—he was an ardent secessionist.[11] On March 4, 1859, he made his position abundantly clear in a key speech. A Southern contingent in Congress was struggling to modify the Missouri Compromise of 1820 and pave the path for the Kansas Territory to attain statehood based on slavery. That was the trigger for the secessionists and they were prepared to go to war over it. They were not interested in compromise. Senator Hammond asked:

> Would any sane nation make war on cotton? Without firing a gun, without drawing a sword, should they make war on us, we would bring the whole world to our feet. The South is perfectly competent to go one, two or three years without planting a seed of cotton ... what would happen if no cotton were furnished for three years ... this is certain, England would topple headlong and carry the whole civilized world with her, save the South. No, you dare not make war on cotton. No power on earth dares make war on cotton. Cotton is King!

Southern secessionists not only believed that England's need for cotton would prevail, but so would similar needs of the North. Ironically it had been the hardships caused to manufacturing by the 1807 embargo of Britain against America's east coast ports that had caused an explosion of manufacturing in the northern states of America. A contemporary historian/journalist, Edward Baines, wrote:

> The first cotton mill was erected in Rhode Island by 1790 by Samuel Slater, under the firm of Almy & Brown an English mechanic who, having worked in an English textile mill before emigrating, constructed from memory a mill for spinning cotton. ... As late as 1807 there was not in the States more than 15 mills, producing about 300,000 lbs of yarn a year. The embargo of 1807, the differences with England, and above all, the war of 1812, gave a great stimulus to the manufacturing interest, and led the Americans to indulge the desire of supplying themselves with the cottons and woolens their population desired.

By 1831 a report of the Committee on Manufacturers of the U.S. Congress stated that in the 795 mills there were about one and quarter million spindles, 35,000 looms, all consuming nearly seventy- eight million pounds of spun yarn. There were 18,539 male workers and 38,927 female. The entire economy of the town of Lowell, Massachusetts, depended on cotton manufacturing. Northern politicians advocated going to war to prevent the South from seceding, a position that was politically motivated to protect their home interests and prevent the South from monopolizing the supply of cotton for the foreseeable future. The textile manufacturing mills of the Union had almost as high a stake in the production of the raw cotton of the South as did Britain.

Conditions in the mill towns of the north of England resembled another form of servitude under the most horrible conditions with wages paid to factory workers below subsistence level, in dirty ill-lit drafty buildings with no sanitation, working six days a week, frequently forced to clean the machines on a Sunday after attending church. The appalling circumstances where the cotton was spun and woven into cloth left about as much to be desired in terms of human misery and degradation as the Southern plantations where the cotton was grown, giving rise to much literature of the social environment incurred by both sectors of cottons dominance.

The plight of mill children during the Victorian era has been well documented in literature and in modern times in film and television. Many of them were orphans or the children of laborers who could not afford to feed or clothe them. The children literally were owned by the mill owners who worked them fourteen to sixteen hours a day, many of them as young as seven years old. One description taken from a firsthand account of ten-year-old apprentice Robert Blincoe, one of a hundred apprentices in a mill in Derbyshire in 1815, reads:

> We went to the mill at five o'clock without breakfast, and worked until eight or nine, when they brought us our breakfast, which consisted of water porridge with oatcake in it and onions to savour it with, in a tin can. This we ate as best we could, the wheel never stopping. We worked on 'til dinner time, which was not regular, sometimes half past twelve, sometimes one. Our dinner was thus served to us. Across the doorway of the room was a crossbar like a police bar, and on the inside stood an old man with a stick to guard the provisions. These consisted of Derbyshire oatcakes cut into four pieces and ranged in two stacks. The one was buttered and the other treacled, and plain milk or buttermilk. We made our choice, drank down our milk, and ran back to the mill with the oatcake in our hand, without ever sitting down. We then worked on 'til nine or ten at night without bite nor sup. When the mill stopped we went to

the house for our supper, which was the same as breakfast, oat and onion porridge and dry oatcake.[12]

Neither the mill owners of Britain's great industrial northern machine, nor the merchants and plantation owners on either side of the great divide, appear to have suffered from an overabundance of social conscience, but we owe it to history to take all factors into consideration instead of oversimplifying the conflict or institution. Senator Hammond summed the situation up neatly for the ruling class:

> In all social systems there must be a class to do the mean duties, to perform the drudgeries of life: that is, a class requiring but a low order of intellect and but little skill. Its requisites are vigor, docility, and fidelity. Such a class you must have or you would not have that other class which leads progress, refinement, and civilization. Fortunately for the South, she found a race adapted to that purpose to her hand—a race inferior to herself, but eminently qualified in temper, in vigor, in docility, in capacity to stand the climate, to answer all her purposes. We use them for the purpose and call them slaves. . . . I will not characterize that class at the north with that term: but you have it; it is everywhere; it is eternal.

Some historians have argued that it was misuse of "King Cotton" diplomacy as an economic weapon that caused the disaster that was to come. By their decision not to ship cotton abroad, the secessionists brought their own houses down about their heads. True or not, they felt that the drying up of the tentacles of cotton markets would be an unmitigated disaster for Britain and America, North and South alike. Instead of looking forward and dominating the market, the Confederate leaders looked back to their own struggles for independence in 1776, figuring that if it withheld the cotton Britain required to keep its mills operating, she would intervene on the side of the South, the French would follow, and the Confederacy would triumph.

The leaders of the Confederacy based their hopes on several assumptions. The first, the basis of their own sense of Anglophile self, was that they felt they would have the support of the British upper classes that they thought of as being closer to a civilized South rather than an egalitarian North. Secondly, they believed that Britain would welcome the separation of a weakened nation that would constitute less of a threat to its own economic domination and social systems undergoing great stress. They believed that British merchants would embrace the concept of dealing directly with the South instead of siphoning off profits through Northern intermediaries. Thirdly, the ace in the pack, the winning hand, and the firmly held belief—the overwhelming final consideration that would force Britain's hand was cotton! Britain's greatest industry was cotton manufacturing. Four million of her twenty-one million people derived their living from it. They were economically and socially addicted to it, and they could never give it up.

Savannah—Defiance or Arrogance

During the decade leading up to war, several bizarre events occurred over the slavery question, which illustrates the mind-set of the elite of the city that some would call arrogance and others insensitivity. Savannah's defiant nature is well illustrated by several incidents as war over the question of slavery loomed as a certainty. One of them, the 1859 saga of the yacht *Wanderer*, with Captain Semmes[13] at the helm, owned by Charles Augustus Lafayette Lamar, better known by his initials, C. A. L. Lamar, a prominent banker in New York and Savannah, and a godson of the Marquis de Lafayette. What happened to its African slave cargo is an excellent insight into what some Savannah businessmen thought of as their right to continue in the business of slaving and profit, and parallels the earlier story of the French ship *La Vengeance* in terms of lawlessness. There is no evidence that Andrew Low had anything to do with the incident, but he certainly had business dealings with Lamar, who was married to a Nichol, and probably related to the Low family. Contemporary newspaper reports indicate the adventure derived considerable support from plantation owners desperate for labor.

On December 14, 1858, the Savannah newspaper reported: "Since Saturday the city has been filled with rumors to the effect that the yacht Wanderer has landed a cargo of Africans on some of the islands on our coast, and that they have been conveyed into the interior. Three sailors have been arrested, are now in jail. The ship is still at Brunswick."

Dec. 17, 1858. The *Augusta Dispatch* states:

> The two hundred and seventy seven of the cargo of Africans recently landed near Brunswick were brought up the Savannah River, and put ashore yesterday evening about 3 o clock at the mouth of Horse Creek, three miles below this city on the Carolina side. It is supposed that the Wanderer acted only as a decoy boat and that the vessel that brought them is still at large. Citizens of our city are probably interested in this enterprise, and those brought up the river are supposed to be their share of "the spoils" and have been distributed on their plantations.

Several months later federal marshals captured the slave-ship *Wanderer* and the trial, which occupied the greater part of the year following, became the town scandal as well as a topic for national discussion as it involved men of impeccable social and economic standing in the community. John Norris's customhouse held the federal courtroom where the drama played out. The fact that a prominent Savannahian was known to be the owner of the ship and the backer of the expedition to Africa to engage in illegal slave-trading only added zest to the proceedings. And when the *Wanderer* was put up for sale by the government, this same citizen, C. A. L. Lamar, bought it back for $4,000 and took a party of friends on a cruise to the West Indian islands, flying the pennant of the New York Yacht Club. Was this unmitigated gall or an astute business deal? It depends on your view from the bridge!

Lamar died in 1865 in a manner that was not totally unexpected. Two weeks after Lee's surrender at Appomattox, Lamar was in Columbus, Georgia, where he was killed by Union forces for sniping at them. A descendant's story says that when his sister-in-law received the news, her comment was: "Good. Now Caroline will not have to worry about more children!"

In the same vein was the sale of Pierce Butler's slaves at Ten Broek Race Course in 1859. The Butler plantations overseer, Roswell King, had had business dealings with the Andrew Low Company from the early 1800's, and it was in Roswell, north Georgia, that Mary Cowper had been bridesmaid to Mittie Bulloch when she married Theodore Roosevelt in the early 1850's. Mr. King's daughter-in-law was sister to the wife of the Reverend Joseph Clay Stiles. The Andrew Low Company, and the Stiles, Mackay, and Butler families had intimate knowledge of each other's doings. By the end of the decade Butler was in serious financial straits, and to dig himself out of the hole he arranged to sell his most valuable asset—slaves: "March 14, 1859—over the course of one week 450 slaves from the Butler plantation were sold at auction on the Ten Broek Race Course in Savannah, for a total of $300,204, or an average of $700 per head, to pay off Pierce Butler's debts. Purchasers came from Alabama, South Carolina and middle Georgia."

The Ten Broek Race Course was formerly a Stiles property and part of Vale Royal Plantation. This large slave auction was well monitored by Horace Greeley's reporter and posted as a sensational article in the *New York Tribune.* The sale was also covered in the *Times* of London. The story would have reverberated in Liverpool. Ironically, many of the slaves sold that day returned as free men and women to Butler's Island after the Civil War. Some of those sold would have been descendants of those sold to Butler by Robert Mackay and William Mein in the early part of the century, from whence comes the legend of the group of Ibos who drowned themselves rather than submit to slavery.

1860—Prelude to War

1860 was a presidential election year, and the various states were holding conventions and nominating candidates for the presidency and vice-presidency. As the time approached for the national conventions, the political atmosphere was charged and volatile. Legislation of the most extreme antislavery character was being enacted by Congress at the same time the African slave trade was flourishing. Previous years' reports show the price of slaves rising all over the South as the constraints on legal importation tightened. On both sides of the Atlantic abolitionists were on the rampage. The great issue, which divided the country, was the question of the extension of slavery in the western territories. Southerners felt that the time had come when they must take a decisive stand for the protection of their way of life.

At the Republican Convention in Chicago Abraham Lincoln of Illinois was nominated President, Hannibal Hamlin of Maine for Vice-President. Their platform opposed the extension of slavery in the Territories.

The Democratic Convention was held in Charleston, S.C. The Southern delegates seceded rather than adhere to Stephen A. Douglas' "Squatter Sovereignty" doctrine and surrender their rights. There was no balloting at the convention, which passed a resolution to adjourn to meet in Baltimore on the 18th of June—at which time Vice President of the United States, John Breckenridge of Kentucky, and Joseph H. Lane of Oregon were nominated for President and Vice President amidst the wildest enthusiasm and excitement.

In the general election, November 1860, Abraham Lincoln was chosen President. Lincoln, a staunch abolitionist, had won on a platform committed to limiting the scope of slavery while maintaining the union. In quick retaliation South Carolina seceded from the Union in December, and Georgia immediately followed in January 1861. Less than three months after Lincoln's election four more states seceded as well (Alabama, Mississippi, Louisiana, and Florida) and initiated the process of uniting in a new nation, having adopted the name of the Confederate States of North America.

The *Daily Morning News* of February 11, 1861, carries the following announcement: "Jefferson Davis of Mississippi has been unanimously elected President of the Confederate States of North America; A. H. Stephens of Georgia was unanimously elected Vice-President."

This dispatch appears March 12, 1861: "The permanent Constitution for the Confederate States of North America has been adopted." The die was cast.

The Shot That Began the War

Georgia was no laggard in playing her part in the rapidly changing conditions, and it quickly took steps to secure state fortifications for the new government. Governor Brown immediately issued orders to Colonel Alexander R. Lawton, commanding the 1st Regiment of Georgia Volunteers, to take possession of and hold the federal Fort Pulaski on the Savannah River between Tybee Island and the city. Mary Low's brother, Henry Stiles, took part in this adventure. The news of this action threw the people of Savannah into a paroxysm of excitement, for here at least was the first step in actual war. It was followed by a far more threatening step taken by South Carolina troops in firing upon the federal army post at Fort Sumter in the harbor of Charleston on April 13. This act marked the start of open hostilities against the federal government by the seceded states. Military activities now claimed the full attention of the entire citizenry of Georgia and Savannah, in a frenzy of enthusiasm, prepared to play her part in the now inevitable conflict.

Patriotic ladies assisted in many ways with the feverish preparations engaging the local troops. The *Daily Morning News* of April carries the following items: "Savannah ladies make cartridges for guns. In five days they made 4,000 cartridges." The popular excitement and enthusiasm in the South at the outbreak of war "equaled that which marked the start of the French Revolution," even infecting the "Negroes who knew that they were the object of contention"; and it is an interesting sidelight to learn that many of them boasted that their masters could "whip the world in arms." William Henry Stiles raised a regiment, the 60th Georgia, of which he assumed the colonelcy.

The valiant citizens of Savannah rallied to the cause. Among them were Andrew and Mary Low, Charles Green, and the Isaac Low Company of Liverpool. In June, Bishop Stephen Elliott of Savannah, a friend of the Stiles family who had married the Lows at Etowah, said: "The conflict in which you are about to mingle is one waged upon the holiest grounds of self-preservation and self-defense ... we are fighting to drive away from our sanctuaries the infidel, and rationalistic principles which are sweeping over the land and substituting a gospel of the stars and stripes for the gospel of Jesus Christ."

God was on the side of the South. There is absolutely no doubt about where the sympathies of the Stiles associates and friends lay. And that is where things stood on both sides when Andrew and Mary Low entered the fray.

15

Recent Unpleasantness, 1860–1862

THE STORY OF BOTH ANDREW LOWS IS INEXTRICABLY WOVEN INTO the story of two vibrant and powerful cities. One has a female personality —Savannah, personified by the fictitious character of Scarlett O'Hara, the sultry, sulky Southern Belle, capricious and wayward, rewarding her suitors with favors, but stone-cold hard and heartless when it comes to her own survival; the other is the masculine Liverpool, personified by the swashbuckling entrepreneur, blockade-running, Rhett Butler. Liverpool and Savannah are the lovers and the enemies, imbued with strong individualities, and they are the two hands that held in a straight line the skein of cotton connecting the Andrew Low and the Isaac Low companies.

Liverpool is the rambunctious, stormy, gale-ridden, male-dominated city on the Irish Sea in the North Atlantic. It is peopled by adventurers of all kinds, rapidly rising to prominence in the African, Atlantic, and West Indian slave trade as Bristol's power waned and British dominance took over from the Dutch and the French, who had in their turn superseded Spain and Portugal. Liverpool was in the eye of the storm of the antislavery forces under the guidance and leadership of the passionate advocate for reform in Great Britain, William Wilberforce. Despite the crocodile tears shed over the plight of the black slave in America, by the middle of the nineteenth century the British Empire had subjugated a goodly portion of the world's people in the islands of the West Indies, on the subcontinent of India, and especially across Africa. The culture of imperialism, with its consequent attitude on the part of the British that the white man was superior to the black man, prevailed.[1]

Andrew Low's influential friend Thackeray, who had traveled extensively in the South, especially made his views known to the general public, declaring that the black man would find it difficult to survive after abolition as he was not equipped to compete with the white man. Despite the vehement abolitionist sentiment in many quarters in Britain, the more hard-nosed reality was commerce. And in Liverpool, commerce was spelled with two t's—cotton! It was also paradoxically a hotbed of support for the Confederate secessionist position, mostly for economic reasons. Loyalties were divided.

In America the role that Liverpool played in the struggle for the soul of the South has not been as widely known as it is in England. The City of Liverpool today remains an authentic museum of Confederate sympathy with many sites, commemorative events, and celebrations remaining a magnet for those from all over the world interested in America's War Between the States.[2] Liverpool's support for the Southern cause almost precipitated a third Anglo-American war.

In 1861, when the skies darkened with the storm clouds of war, British merchants and factors of the cotton-spinning and weaving towns of the industrial north had had the foresight to stockpile the raw material and were convinced that they could ride the conflict out. Many of the influential political and chattering classes assumed the possibility of a Confederate victory, and many openly hoped for one.

The Blockade

In April of 1861 the Lincoln government imposed a blockade on all Southern ports, an act that in Britain was viewed as an unprecedented breach of international law although they themselves had engaged in the same activity during the War of 1812. It was unprecedented for a belligerent to blockade its own ports, but the Northern response was that the South was in rebellion and was not an independent nation; therefore, the blockade was legal because the federal government did not recognize the secession of the South. This convoluted interpretation was unacceptable in the halls of power in London.

A misplaced use of language in defining the reasons behind the blockade was probably the responsibility of the undiplomatic U.S. Secretary of State William H. Seward, but the result was that it forced the British to recognize the belligerency of the South, resulting in a royal proclamation by Queen Victoria that the blockade was to be respected.

In order to adhere to the appearance of nonalignment, the British government passed the Neutrality Act, prohibiting active assistance to either side in the fratricidal spat over the ocean. Lord Russell, the Secretary of Foreign Affairs, made the British point of view perfectly clear by stating in the House of Commons: "We have not been involved in any way in that contest by any act, or giving any advice in the matter: and for God's sake, let us if possible, keep out of it." This was a sentiment easier said than done, with so much at stake and diplomatically inexperienced leaders in America.

This royal edict gave Liverpool merchants and shipowners all the justification they needed to break and blatantly ignore the blockade, since their position was that the blockade was as detrimental to their legitimate trade as it was to the South. In fact, Liverpool merchants made fortunes supplying both North and South, and blockade-running activities paralleled the excitement and profit of the heydays of the prohibited slave trade. Many a countinghouse lawyer had a field day debating obscure legalities of commerce between a neutral and two belligerents, and the dubious legality of the British government interfering in legitimate trade between British subjects and the seceded Southern states.

Almost immediately ships began to be bought and built in the shipyards of Birkenhead at the mouth of the Mersey River, expressly made to run the blockade and ship war supplies to the beleaguered South upon whose soil the battles were being fought. The quid pro quo was a continuing supply of the cotton desperately needed to keep the mills of Manchester grinding.[3]

The Confederate States at the outset of the war had no navy. The Lincoln government naturally retained all the war ships of the U.S. Navy. Nothing daunted, President Davis met the situation by taking steps toward instituting the revival of the traditional eighteenth-century manner of waging war, the act of privateering or capture of enemy vessels for one's own use.

On April 17, 1861, North America was galvanized as the telegraph flashed the news from Southern headquarters in Montgomery, Alabama, that President Davis had issued a proclamation inviting applications for letters of marque and reprisal. Because of the high adventure and gain that such an enterprise promised, merchant vessels quickly rallied to the call. The seeds of a way to beat the odds had been sown, and Savannah had already shown that she was not at all averse to lawless behavior; in fact, it would have been her patriotic duty to flaunt a Union blockade, except they had no ships to do so with. The answer was to quickly purchase some, in Liverpool if possible.

Commodore Josiah Tattnall, a native Savannahian who had won distinction in the United States Navy, was now in the Confederate service. He was appointed commodore in March 1861 and set about organizing a navy, initially composed of a river steamer and a few tugs mounted with such guns as could be procured. The valiant "Mosquito Fleet," as it was affectionately nicknamed, patrolled the waters from Port Royal southward, intending to aid vessels coming from England with war supplies for the Confederacy. This was the humble beginning of the Confederate Navy, destined, in the course of the war, to become famed for the spectacular exploits of some of its cobbled-together warships, and the awesome brand

The CSS *Alabama*, Southern commerce raider, was commissioned by Savannahian James Dunwoody Bulloch from Laird's shipyard of Liverpool. John Low served as an officer on its last mission. *Courtesy Hugh Stiles Golson.*

new Liverpool-built CSS *Alabama*, commissioned by a local Savannah hero, James Dunwoody Bulloch.

Somewhat naturally, the Confederate government's scheme to withhold cotton from the market began immediately to leak like a sieve as personal interest took precedence over national interests. At home everyone got into the act, where Union soldiers traded with Southern civilians, exchanging cotton for supplies. As the price of cotton in America reached astronomical heights the pressure to trade reached bursting point and cotton reached out and corrupted both enemy and friend alike. The Union blockade of Confederate ports spawned a cottage industry in blockade-running, exchanging arms for cotton.[4]

Britain did not violate the blockade and remained neutral, or at least that was the official position. But as in everything, especially love and war, timing is the whole thing. The architects of King Cotton diplomacy had failed dismally in one aspect of their diplomatic blackmail strategy. The reality was that Britain was awash in cotton in 1861. A feast, a glut, not a famine in sight.[5]

Britain went into the beginning of the Civil War period with great stocks of raw cotton and manufactured cotton goods. She had bought heavily of the American crops of 1859 and 1860, and before May 1861 had received 1,650,000 bales of cotton. These were added to the nearly 600,000 bales she had at the end of 1860, to say nothing of a large inventory of Asian cotton.

Andrew Low around 1860. He is heavier and his beard has grayed. *Courtesy The National Society of The Colonial Dames of America in the State of Georgia.*

Therefore, in fact, the potential scarcity of cotton on the market and natural laws of supply and demand would have had the effect of raising profits for mill owners who had the foresight to stockpile. This, too, would have applied to factors and to some extent plantation owners as well, although their foresight would have been limited by their ability to actually grow more cotton. In the beginning the lack of cotton being exported brought wealth rather than hardship to Britain's cotton sector. This state of affairs did not last long and was perhaps another miscalculation of those who thought the war would be over in a short time.

The Cast of Characters

The Confederate government had already sent several agents to Europe, headquartered in Liverpool, to purchase arms, ships, and materials of war before Northern forces blockaded Southern ports. This key task was to be spearheaded by Captain James Dunwoody Bulloch of Savannah. Bulloch had resigned his commission as a U.S. naval officer in 1854, the year of Mary Cowper's marriage to Andrew Low. Before being selected by the new Confederate government as their purchasing agent in Europe, Bulloch had served as colonel in the Georgia Hussars and selected as his assistant master mariner John Low, a former merchant navy officer from Liverpool, England. Twenty-five-year-old John Low had been running a ship chandler's business in Savannah with his partner Robert Hardee, and had joined the Georgia Hussars as a volunteer until he was seconded to work with Bulloch for the Confederacy in Liverpool, the city he knew extremely well.

Another Savannah resident, Major Edward C. Anderson, formerly a United States naval officer, had joined the Confederate Army and was allocated the grave responsibility of fueling the supply pipeline to the rebels. In Liverpool the agents were instructed to cooperate with Charles Kuhn Prioleau, a Charleston cotton broker at Fraser, Trenholm & Company, who operated as bankers to the Confederate government in Europe. The company also financed the supply of armaments and other essential goods in return for cotton. They participated in blockade running, built vessels for the Confederate Navy in Liverpool, including the *Alabama*, assisted in the floating of Confederate loans, and encouraged support for the South throughout Europe.[6]

In May 1861 Edward Anderson departed for Liverpool aboard the sleek schooner *Camilla*, formerly the famous racing yacht *America*, arriving in Liverpool on June 21 where he states that his first task was to deliver his letter of introduction to Charles Prioleau. There he found James Bulloch and Caleb Huse, the other purchasing agent; neither of whom knew of his coming nor his instructions. He then immediately delivered his other letters of introduction to Isaac Low & Company's offices, and rejoined James Bulloch and Capt Huse at the Queens Hotel.

The next day he left for London, where he found Edmund Molyneaux, the British consul at Savannah, lodging next door to Mr. Yancey, one of the Confederate commissioners in England. Molyneaux proved very useful to the conspirators despite his position as one of Her Majesty's Consuls, a position he neatly circumvented by offering his assistance personally to Anderson, but not to the Confederacy. Part of this assistance was a letter of introduction to his brother, Captain Molyneaux of the British Navy. Another Liverpool merchant who was helpful was Joseph Battersby, brother of Savannahian William Battersby. By early August Charles Green—partner in Andrew Low & Company—and his son Charlie arrived in Liverpool and met with Edward Anderson at the offices of Isaac Low Co., where Green asserted "with a great air of mystery" that he was officially working for the Confederate War Department and was authorized by Governor Brown to make purchases for the State of Georgia. He produces a document in his own handwriting by removing a silver pencil case, which by unscrewing the head revealed a hollow cavity containing a roll of fine tissue paper covered with hieroglyphics that Green assured Anderson were instructions in cipher!

These somewhat ostentatious tactics were later confirmed to some degree in the "Case of Charles Green" in the *Official Records of the Confederacy,* which include a letter dated July 1, 1861, from L .P. Walker, Confederate Secretary of War, Richmond, specifically authorizing Green to associate himself with Major Anderson and Captain Huse in the purchase of arms and munitions of war. He is instructed that being a British subject he should be able to ship the goods under British colors, to which suggestion Charles Green replies on July 2: "My plan would be to ship the cargo as British property, under a British flag, with a clearance for Saint Thomas or to Matagorda, where the cargo could be deposited in default of an open Southern port."

He requests the secretary to give him a password to identify him to the Confederate agents in England as he plans to destroy the communications he has received. Green is obviously getting into the spirit of things. He was refused a password but, as we have seen in Anderson's diary, he was given a fair amount of money to further these aims.

The threads that tie all these relationships together were tenuous yet curiously intimate, involving marriage, family, friendship, and commerce. Green's sister, Eliza Green Low, was living in Liverpool at the time. Eliza Low was the widow of the late John Low, nephew of Andrew Low, Sr., brought into the organization to head Low, Taylor during the period immediately following Robert Isaac's death in 1827. The stage was set and the cast of characters waited in the wings.

James Dunwoody Bulloch was brother to Mittie Bulloch Roosevelt, a great friend of Mary Cowper Stiles Low. Edward Anderson was married to Sarah McQueen Williamson, best friend of Andrew Low's first wife, Sarah Hunter Low, and related to the Mackay family. They lived very near to the Low's house in Lafayette Ward. John Low was Andrew Low's cousin, the son of another Andrew Low, who in turn was son of Uncle Andrew's brother John. Edward Molyneaux, an English merchant, shows up peripherally as well in this saga, making some extremely devious decisions to protect his standing as the official British consul for Savannah, while surreptitiously assisting the Confederate cause in Liverpool.

Letter to My Grandchildren

The Lows' personal involvement commenced very shortly after the successful Confederate victory at the Battle of Bull Run at Manassas, Virginia, causing a sweeping surge of confidence in the ultimate outcome and prospects for victory and a quick end to the war so everyone could get back to business. Leaving their children at Etowah Cliffs with their grandmother Eliza, in July 1861 Andrew and Mary Low left Savannah for England, moving north through Union lines and sailed on the *Anglo-Saxon* from Quebec to Liverpool on August 10, 1861.

Afterwards Andrew Low claimed that the reason he had gone to Liverpool at that time was to dissolve his partnership with Charles Green. True or not, certainly their relationship had become increasingly competitive since Green built his mansion on Madison Square. But it is inconceivable that he did not know that his partner was already in Liverpool, purporting to be acting on behalf of both the Confederate War Department and the State of Georgia.

A most valuable document has been passed down to posterity to tell the story of Andrew and Mary Low's active participation on behalf of the Southern cause. The source is "Letter to My Grandchildren," dated July 1862, from their grandmother Eliza Mackay Stiles that starts thus:

> My Dear Grandchildren: But particularly Katie, who is now girl enough to remember some events which are now happening. I will try and write down all I can recollect to have heard of scenes your Mother passed through last fall and winter, some with and some without your Father. As little incidents soon fade from the memory, this scratch [sic] may help your Mother to recollect when you are grown, things which happened now and she can give you the

Mary Low visits Amy and Hattie at school in Brighton in 1861. *Courtesy The National Society of The Colonial Dames of America in the State of Georgia.*

Garnet pin given to Eliza Mackay by Lt. and Mrs. Robert E. Lee upon her marriage to William Henry Stiles in 1832. *Courtesy The National Society of The Colonial Dames of America in the State of Georgia.*

account more in detail then, with the help of these lines to freshen her memory.

This document confirms that on arrival in England the Lows went down to Brighton and spent time visiting Hattie and Amy, staying at the fashionable Albion Hotel on the boardwalk opposite the pier. They then went up to London. Eliza recounts her recollection of Mary's version of Andrew Low's meetings with Confederate Agent Major Edward Anderson in London, who was there purchasing weapons for the Confederacy. They then went back to Liverpool and spent much time in the company of Captain James Dunwoody Bulloch, who had already moved there with his family, along with other agents of the Confederacy. Eliza's letter makes reference to the purchase of the ship *Fingal*, which was soon to depart in an attempt to run the blockade into Savannah or Charleston, carrying guns and ammunition for the Confederacy.

Dispatches were given to Mary Low to deliver to General Robert E. Lee, who had been appointed commander of the Army of Northern Virginia, the Confederacy's largest. Eliza Stiles's diary entries would have been bonus enough to tell this portion of the story, but there was to be another, equally important document to draw from.

The original handwritten transcript of the *Diary of Edward Anderson* at the University of North Carolina provides startling new details that prove Andrew Low was involved up to his neck in the purchase of arms and the *Fingal*. However, when evaluating any of these records one has to keep in mind that everyone was lying through their teeth, trying to salvage their own reputations and attend to their own agendas, as well as deliberately keeping secrets from the enemy—which in this case was the United States Government. It is a fascinating tale of espionage, and one might even say treason—depends on your view from the bridge and whose side you were on.

The Fingal *Escapade*

In early August news of the utter rout of federal forces at Manassas arrived. Anderson writes: "This news created an immense excitement all over England, and especially in Liverpool where there were a large amount of American merchants, and amongst them a goodly sprinkling of Confederates. Later on some of the excited celebrants drove to the country where they hoisted the Confederate flag on Charles Prioleau's house."

In his memoirs titled *The Secret Service of the Confederate States in Europe* James Dunwoody Bulloch writes that he sent pertinent details to the Secretary of the Navy regarding the commissioning, through John Laird's shipyard in Birkenhead, for the building of two Confederate warships, the *Alabama* and the *Florida*, estimated to be finished by June 1862. He further informed that it would probably be necessary to purchase a steamer and return to the Confederate States with military stores, as well as for further consultation and reconsideration of his instructions, and pointed out that their activities were seriously hampered by lack of available funds.

One of the problems was the attitude of the British government, which employed private detectives to vigilantly monitor the activities of known Confederate agents, especially in Liverpool and London. Sending communiqués by letter was extremely hazardous, which made it most advantageous to impart plans through trusted envoys above suspicion. Bulloch was one of the Confederate leaders who believed that more cotton should have been shipped to Liverpool in the first year of the war, and if so done would have strengthened the Confederate financial picture immensely.

Andrew Low and Charles Green were obvious candidates for recruitment, both of them wealthy cotton merchants with impeccable connections in both Liverpool and Savannah, both of them British subjects and despite their known Southern sympathies through marriage, less overtly suspicious, on the surface anyway. In fact in the lull between the storms, immediately after secession in December 1860, and the attack on Fort Sumter in April 1861, any sensible merchant with cotton in his warehouse and a ship to sail it in took on full cargoes and sailed, loaded of course on private account. This is no doubt when and how the 50,000 bales later reported by the federal authorities to be the property of Andrew Low in Liverpool arrived there. The Confederate government was operating as an independent nation, not an insurgency.

By August 19, 1861, Anderson recounts that on his arrival in London he received from Charles Green the sum of five thousand pounds "on account of the Georgia funds entrusted him by Governor Brown for the purchase of arms and ammunition," and a letter delivered by Green announcing Andrew Low's arrival in England. He reports that he purchased 10,000 muskets for the Confederacy, dined with the Consul Molyneaux and his family in his rooms on Jermyn Street along with the Consul's British naval officer's brother Captain Molyneaux, and received letters from his wife Sarah brought over by Andrew Low.

On Sunday, August 25, Anderson took the train down to Brighton, where he met with Low, his wife, and two daughters. The next day the Lows and Anderson went back up to London for more meetings with Confederate agents where Anderson also successfully negotiated the purchase of 4,000 Enfield rifles. What could appear more innocuous to surveilling secret agents than a Sunday afternoon family outing on the seacoast? Agents of the U.S. government attempting to intercept these arms shipments were following them day and night.

Their main problem at that moment was how to ship to the Confederacy some of the arms and ammunition they had been successful in obtaining. The normal shipping channels were extorting such enormous freight charges for shipping that in effect it amounted to a prohibition. So Edward Anderson took it upon himself to stretch his mandate a little and called a meeting to seek what he felt was the only solution, namely to purchase a vessel of their own using the public funds entrusted for the purchase of fundamental war supplies.

> On Monday September 2, I decided to bring the matter to a conference, and accordingly invited a number of gentlemen to meet

with me on the subject, to get not only their advice but their tangible aid as well. Mr. Green had secured a room at a small Tavern not far from the Exchange, and one o clock pm, Andrew Low, Mr. Prioleau, James Bulloch, Mr. Green, and myself assembled there.

The conspirators agreed to purchase a ship. James Bulloch agreed to loan all the money he could spare from the Navy fund, amounting to some ten thousand pounds, and that very same evening Bulloch departed for Glasgow on the mission to locate and purchase a suitable vessel.

He was unsuccessful so they engaged the services of an agent who found them the *Fingal*; she was a "new vessel of 800 ton and was represented as one of the finest class of iron built ships, with engines built by Thompson of Glasgow, built on the Clyde for the Highland trade." The price they paid was 17,500 pounds sterling. Everybody involved understood the importance of this voyage because the *Fingal* was to be the first ship to run the blockade solely on the Confederate government's account, although many private blockade-runners were reaping a handy profit on their owner's account. In fact, to this day the *Fingal* remains of historical interest to Civil War buffs, especially as her subsequent career as the Confederate ironclad *Atlanta* gave her a certain prominence. For our purposes, however, it is the participation of Andrew Low in her purchase and ownership that is of paramount interest.

During the month of September, Anderson met in London several times with Andrew and Mary Low, where the cargo for the *Fingal,* still in Glasgow, was being assembled. Anderson recounts some seriocomic occurrences as private detectives and secret agents watched him constantly. Both the British Foreign Office and the U.S. War and State Departments would have very carefully documented the meetings between Andrew Low, Charles Green, Anderson, and Bulloch in both London and Liverpool.

By October 3, 1861, they were all back in Liverpool for the final arrangements, and Anderson, Bulloch and his family, Andrew and Mary Low all dined together at Mrs. Danley's. Writes Edward Anderson in his diary Friday, October 5: "In the evening Bulloch called at my rooms, as did Mr. And(rew) Low. We held a secret conference. We wrote out a short dispatch for the Richmond Govt. to be carried across by (Henry) Hotze."

A last minute hitch occurred when, on Saturday October 6, Bulloch received word from their agent Byrne in Glasgow that "by order of the Foreign Office in London the *Fingal* would not be allowed to take aboard her cargo in the stream." Consequently, they were forced to change plans and unload the cargo, which had already been loaded on a chartered ship in London for passage and transfer to the *Fingal* in Glasgow. By now the

American minister was making every attempt to foil the departure of the ship, laden with supplies for the Confederacy. As Britain was neutral, all of this had to be manipulated through opposing diplomatic channels prohibiting the vessel from obtaining the necessary clearances. The American minister was Charles Francis Adams, son of John Quincy Adams.

On October 9 Anderson reports that he settled up his accounts with Charles Green and handed over to him the papers connected with the purchase made for the State of Georgia. Certainly these diary inserts indicate that Green was functioning on an official level as authorized purchasing agent on behalf of the State of Georgia through the governor's office. On the same day, John Low arrived and reported to Anderson, who sent him immediately to Greenock to report to the *Fingal*. Low was a very experienced master mariner despite his young age.

James Bulloch's version describes fully his confidence and admiration for John Low's part in the adventure as well as his subsequent illustrious career on several Confederate warships, including the notorious CSS *Alabama*. The *Fingal* was carrying Enfield Rifles and other war supplies designated for delivery to the Confederate War Department, Navy Department, State of Georgia, and the State of Louisiana.

This was to be an auspicious day for all because they also received news of the arrival in Savannah of the blockade-runner *Bermuda* with her cargo of Confederate munitions.[7] The coconspirators adjourned to the Angel Tavern and Prioleau, Andrew Low, James Bulloch, and Edward Anderson drank a toast to one successfully concluded mission and prayed for the success of another.

The following day, October 10, 1861, Edward Anderson makes his final entry regarding the movements of Andrew Low and his wife. He writes: "Andrew Low and his wife sailed today in the steamer North Briton for Canada. I have sent several messages on tissue paper by Mrs. L sewed up in the trimmings of her bonnet. A letter from Huse informs me that Mr. Hotze will join the North Briton at Queenstown."

Eliza Stiles writes in her diary her version of the dangerous game they were playing: "Dispatches or rather duplicates of them were given to your Mother to bring over to General Lee or the Government and she had them so completely concealed they never would have been discovered, but by the time she got into the Southern Confederacy they were valueless."

Eliza also explains the somewhat sinister sounding Mr. Hotze.[8]

> While in London, Mr. Low met a bearer of dispatches from the Confederacy to Capt. Bulloch and Anderson. This young gentleman was from Mobile, a Swiss by birth, but spoke English perfectly, and is united to the South in feeling. He is editor of a paper in Mobile,

> was in the Army, and volunteered to go to London to serve his country. When your parents sailed from Liverpool the steamer touched at Londonderry to take the mail from London a day later, and this Mr. Hotze, who had been strictly watched in London, was afraid to sail in the steamer from England, so he disguised himself by shaving his beard and speaking very little, and then in broken English, and he went over to Ireland, and joined the vessel at Derry. He kept very much aloof from the Southerners, of whom there were several on board, and your Father did not discover who he was for some time, altho' he had met him in London. When he did recognize him they agreed not to know each other, and Mr. Hotze was Mr. Muller when he left London, as his passport averred. There were so many Yankees on the North Briton that all the Southerners kept very quiet for fear of being informed against, and arrested when passing through the States for home.... Mr. Hotze brought back dispatches, the same your Mother agreed to bring, he passing for a foreigner, and stopping to see Quebec and Montreal as a stranger, and came though New York and Baltimore. He had a lady friend, who concealed him several days, and then helped him across the Potomac, and the dispatches were delivered successfully to the Government.

The Fingal *Beats the Odds*

The day of October 10 dawned inauspiciously with news that the American minister had obtained an order to send an official to Glasgow to ascertain the ownership of the vessel and cargo. Anticipating this, the conspirators had already instructed the agent Byrne to transfer the ship and her entire cargo to John Low for one shilling sterling, and when asked by the government agent, to announce the fact that the "venture" belonged to Mr. Low. This was done and when the agent arrived demanding to know to whom the vessel belonged, without the slightest hesitation he was told that it had been sold to a Liverpool merchant, and his name was Mr. Low. All the information the agent was able to solicit was name, rank, and serial number, and was forced to hurry back to Liverpool to try to find out exactly what was going on, and who this Mr. Low was. It is still somewhat unclear whether "Mr. Low" was in fact cotton merchant Andrew Low or naval officer John Low, but as the merchant Low had already fled the coop, it is presumed that the officials were checking the Low who was actually still in town.

What was going on was that John Low had hastily returned to Liverpool, collected all the luggage of those who were intending to sail on the *Fingal*, which included both Anderson and Bulloch, and went to Lime Street Station to catch the London train to Edinburgh to put the watching agents off the scent. Fortunately for everyone John Low had never been seen by the agents with either Anderson or Bulloch, so they were not looking out for him. Anderson was helped during this charade of getting everything ready for shipment on the *Fingal* by Charlie Green, son of Charles Green, who had accompanied his father to many of the meetings in London and Liverpool.

By now the vessel had dropped down the river and was anchored off Holyhead. That day passed filled with anxiety, waiting every moment for news of the seizure of their precious ship. The weather refused to cooperate and by Sunday, October 13, a gale was blowing full force. It continued without abating throughout the following day until the evening of October 14, when it subsided and started to clear.

Things seemed to start going right, but then at four in the morning John Low in great excitement burst into Anderson's room in the hotel where they were staying to tell him that the *Fingal* had entered the outer harbor of Holyhead, unfortunately in the process running over and sinking an Austrian brig loaded with coal. Disaster!

They woke up the landlady, paid their bill, and immediately left the hotel for the pier where a ship's boat from the *Fingal* was waiting for them. When they arrived on the deck of the ship, they found an English customs officer on board making a report of the collision. Matters looked desperate. Anderson knew that if they stayed where they were, a representative of the sunken Austrian ship would certainly demand damages, the case would wind up in court, and as the *Fingal* was laden with arms and ammunition, they would end up spending the rest of the war tied to the dock in Holyhead harbor, or worse languishing in an English gaol.

Taking immediate action, Anderson urged the customs official to cut his own small vessel loose from the *Fingal* on the pretext that as they were faster they would probably tow him under as they turned to enter the inner harbor. He persuaded the officer that they would meet him at the dock where a proper report could be prepared at leisure out of the danger of the fierce wind. The English captain thanked the American profusely for his courtesy, got into his boat, and pulled ashore. They were either incredibly lucky, the customs officer dim-witted, or everyone knew exactly what they were doing. We, in any event, will never know as no one ever told.

The *Fingal* immediately fired up her engines and headed out to sea. The fox outwitted his pursuers, and James Bulloch, Edward Anderson, John Low, several passengers, the ship's English crew, and illicit cargo set sail for the Savannah River via Bermuda. The exciting story of the *Fingal*'s tension-filled voyage is told in full by Edward Anderson in his diary, including the manner in which they again outfoxed the British and the Yankee consul in Bermuda, where they needed to resupply with coal. James Bulloch's

Memoirs also contain a detailed account of the voyage, especially the cooperative attitude of the British crew, sailing on an American ship under the British flag, intending to run the Union blockade into a Confederate port. Not much legal about any of it from any one's point of view!

Assisted greatly by the usual morning mist off the marshes on November 12, 1861, the *Fingal* passed by Tybee Island, slipping through the mouth of the Savannah River with a cargo of war supplies. Passing Fort Pulaski, the crew fired a gun and hoisted the Confederate flag. They struck a mud flat in the tidal river, and seeing them aground, Captain Charles Olmstead, commander of the fort, sent a boat to inform them that their luck was unbelievable as the day before a large Union fleet had attacked and driven the Confederate troops out of their position surrounding Port Royal, not many miles away in South Carolina, and had occupied the area with a strong enemy land force. It became immediately apparent that their ease in slipping up the river had occurred because the Union vessels blockading off Tybee Beach had gone to Port Royal to assist in that operation.

Eliza was still at Etowah Cliffs, where she was taking care of the children of Andrew and Mary while Colonel Stiles's 60th Georgia was stationed at Camp Lawton near Savannah and included his sons Robert and Henry. The numerous letters they wrote each other almost on a daily basis form an astonishing portrait of how things were. They show clearly how the entire undertaking in the South was viewed in the beginning more as an adventure governed by the usual rules of social engagement than a war. One letter from Colonel Stiles to his wife, dated October 13, 1861, recounts rather petty social mundane details of the horses and uniforms they hoped to have and how the young men were jockeying for positions as officers: "Robert has not yet got a position in the Regiment but I think will be able to secure one—there are several sources from which he has expectations, but he is so minded on living here that he is slow in working himself up. Then there are one or two young men, who are willing to give $500 or $2,000 for a Lieutenant position in the Regiment. This having gotten out amongst the Companies they have become spoiled and I do not think they will give up their positions unless forced to do so by the strict discipline which I mean to enforce."

The whole thing is still a game of sorts, a dress-up romance of the battlefield, with church sermons for the troops on Sundays attended by admiring young ladies. The game was abruptly halted with the Union advance into their own backyard; the war had come home.

Colonel William H. Stiles saw his first action in November during the bombardment of Fort Walker on Hilton Head by the U.S. Navy. The Atlanta newspaper reported that he had two horses shot from under him while guarding the road to the rear of the fort. His regiment was part of the retreat from Hilton Head, and he described the engagement to his wife on Novemebr 17 from Camp Lawton: "We all escaped from Hilton Head wonderfully. . . . I do not think the enemy will attack Savannah, nor in fact venture on the mainland for some weeks, until they are well fortified at Hilton and have stronger reinforcements of land troops. The people are pouring into Savannah ready to fight, all they wanted was arms, and the arrival of Bulloch & Anderson with the arms from Europe was most opportune. I think there is no difficulty now in having armed men enough to meet them altho they are but poorly drilled troops."

Colonel Stiles underestimated the adversary. The intention had been to load the *Fingal* with cotton out of Savannah's warehouses and return immediately to Liverpool. Before this could happen the Union Navy drove the Confederate troops off Tybee Island, and with Tybee's capture the enemy bottled up Savannah. The fully loaded *Fingal* was stuck, unable to exit, and the prediction that Savannah would be sealed up for the remainder of the war was fulfilled. James Bulloch's *Memoirs* and the Savannah newspapers both detail the attempt to get her out of the Savannah River that included both John Low and Edward Anderson's son, Midshipman Edward M. Anderson. The Confederates later converted her to an ironclad warship and renamed her CSS *Atlanta,* where she performed several deeds of valor before being sunk.

John Low, upon the recommendation of Captain James Dunwoody Bulloch, was appointed a master in the Confederate Navy and accompanied Bulloch back to Europe, going on to serve in the Confederate Navy as an officer on the infamous CSS *Alabama* .[9] Edward Anderson remained serving the Confederate Army in several key roles for the duration of the war. James Dunwoody Bulloch returned to Liverpool, where today he is an icon for Confederate aficionados.

It was an amazing adventure, and clearly shows Andrew Low and Charles Green in it up to their necks. Whether one of the quid pro quo's in this entire episode was because they anticipated being able to ship cotton back to Liverpool from Savannah on the *Fingal* has never been proven, but certainly it takes no long stretch of the imagination to believe that would have been a powerful incentive and totally in both men's characters; neither of them were known to operate their business practices for altruistic purposes.

The Plan Goes Badly Awry

The *Fingal* arrived safely in Savannah; unfortunately Andrew and Mary Low and Charles Green and his sister Eliza Green Low did not. In early November 1861 a trigger-happy federal captain boarded the *Trent,* a

British ship out of Havana, in clear violation of international law, and forcibly removed two Confederate agents, Mason and Slidell, en route to Europe to attempt to establish relations with England and France. They were taken to Fort Warren, a federal prison in Boston harbor, for interrogation. The incident almost brought Britain into the war, and the arrogant Union Secretary of State W. H. Seward had a tough job smoothing troubled waters. Andrew Low was not so lucky and possibly was made a scapegoat for Seward's inexperience in diplomatic affairs. The Savannah newspapers reported the event in November 15, 1861:

> A dispatch from Nashville states that Robert Bunker, ex-Mayor of Mobile, and Andrew Low, Merchant, arrested in Cincinnati, were taken to Fort Warren in Boston harbor, on the 5th, by order of Seward. Both gentlemen had recently returned from Europe and were arrested on suspicion of having important information for the rebels. We have reason to believe that the Andrew Low named above is of the firm Andrew Low & Co. of this city. Mr. Low recently sailed from Europe on his return to Savannah.

Then on November 18.

> We have been furnished with the following dispatch received by a gentleman in this city from Richmond. Charles Green, and sister, and Mrs. Low, have been arrested at Detroit, charged with aiding the rebels. Mrs. Low was sent to Washington City. Her husband was previously arrested in Cincinnati.

And that piece of news is where the confusion commenced, and is the source of the many erroneous reports that have filtered down through the succeeding century and a half. The Mrs. Low who was arrested with Charles Green was his sister, Eliza Green Low, widow of John Low [10] of the firm Low & Taylor set up in Savannah during the reorganization of the Andrew Low Company following the death of partner Robert Isaac thirty years before. She was not Mary Low, wife of Andrew Low. Colonel Stiles wrote two days later to his wife:

> My Dear Lib ... do you see that Mr. Low has been taken ... Mr. Green with him and his sister. She was taken to Washington, Mr. Green carried to Boston, where Mr. Low is. I feel much concerned about Mary. I hope she has by now gotten safely to you but I must confess I feel exceedingly anxious. Write me the moment you have any tidings of her. Without knowing anything of where she is we cannot do anything for her relief. I hope she is with the Wallace's in New York.

Eliza's Version of Events

In her "Letter to My Grandchildren" Eliza Stiles makes no mention at all of the arrest of Green and his sister, but goes into length regarding the arrest of Andrew Low and Mary Low's ordeal. She starts this part of the tale telling about dispatches that Mary Low had agreed to bring back to the Confederate forces:

> . . . your Mother, by your Father's advice destroyed the dispatches she had before setting out on her journey home . . . they were determined to come through Cincinnati and Kentucky. They were five days in Cincinnati trying to obtain permission to come through the lines but were refused by General Sherman, and Mr. Low had taken tickets to set off Monday for Baltimore that they might try to come that way. On Sunday your Mother went to church leaving your Father at the hotel, not very well, and on her return you may imagine her surprise to find several men in her chamber with her husband and all her trunks open and unpacked . . . the Marshals told her that her husband was under arrest, but after examining the luggage and finding nothing to convict your Father, the Marshall telegraphed to Mr. Seward at Washington to say he saw no reason for the arrest. An answer came to take Andrew Low immediately to Fort Warren.

Obviously not knowing what to do with Mary Low, who was in the first stage of pregnancy, the federal marshals agreed to allow her to travel with them to Harrisburg, Pennsylvania, where she then had to leave her husband to continue his journey in custody; and she was allowed to take the train to Baltimore, where the city was under martial law. She left her trunks at the rail depot, and took a carriage to seek her long-time family friends, the Glenns. Fortunately Mary Glenn was at home, alone as it turned out; her own husband, Wilkens Glenn, was also incarcerated in a different prison, Fort McHenry.

Meanwhile Eliza and the family at Etowah Cliffs still did not know her daughter's whereabouts, and had only the newspapers to scour to try and find out what had happened and where Andrew had been sent. They learned that Andrew Low had been confined at Fort Warren and Aunt Elliott wrote to her friend, Mr. Gray of Boston, to ask him to reassure Andrew Low that his children were all with their grandmother at Etowah Cliffs and quite well.[11] Eliza complains ". . . this Mr. Gray did have the humanity to send him, but without a word of kindness that he owed it to our family and is related to you children."[12]

Captain Dimick, the commander of the prison, allowed letters to pass freely between husband and wife, and it was from those letters that some of the details of the conditions of his incarceration were revealed: "Your Father was obliged to occupy a small room with seven other gentlemen, who were however very pleasant companions, but he made his own bed, and was not allowed to walk on the ramparts or look at the sea."

Mary Low stayed in Baltimore for almost three months while her well-connected friends pulled all the strings they could to get her passage back home. She was finally given permission to travel and released through enemy lines to return to her mother and three children at Etowah Cliffs.[13] She eventually arrived home at the end of January. On January 23, 1862, one of the Elliott girls at Summerland, beside herself with joy, recounts her cousin's arrival in a letter to her sisters in Savannah:

> My dear Sisters: The whole family have gone over to see Mary Low with joyful hearts, we received the news at the breakfast table that she was at the Cliffs having been driven out by a boy in a buggy, & that is all I know. I am so glad for her sake and for Eliza's, her children are all well and look so—I saw them yesterday afternoon when I went to call . . . the girls have just come home having had a delightful visit. Mary L in excellent spirits and her Mother so happy and the children enchanted with their Mother.[14]

Eliza's description reads:

> Uncle Henry and myself were seated at the breakfast table, the rest of the family had not yet come down. The surprise and joy and thankfulness we felt at seeing her and having her home, I am sure Katie can well remember. Little Gordon was born on the 11th and your Mamma unpacked all the pretty and useful things she brought for us, we could hardly think that so much could be put into one trunk. When she had been home ten days she determined to go to Savannah to see her much loved grandmother and took Katie with her.

After his arrest Andrew Low remained in Fort Warren federal prison for three months and then was released on parole and allowed to go to Baltimore, where he waited until he was given permission to go back to Georgia. During the entire period of both his and Charles Green's incarceration, influential people on both sides of the Atlantic from the very top diplomatic and government echelons in both Britain and America, from the North and the Confederacy, to the merchants and bankers needed by both sides, pulled strings for his release.

Official Records of the Civil War

The *Case of Andrew Low, Mrs. John Low, and Charles Green* is to be found in the *Suspected and Disloyal Person* section in the massive multi-volumes of the government *Official Records of the Civil War* with other references in several different categories. It makes fascinating reading, and the first fact we learn is the official reasons the federal authorities arrested Andrew Low and the others.

From these documents it is possible to reconstruct a facsimile of events, at least from the perspective of the Union officials. It appears that the arrival of the couple in Cincinnati caused great concern in secret agent circles, and a telegram was sent to Secretary of State Seward:

> Sir: Mr. Andrew Low, of Savannah, with his wife is enroute for Georgia. He was one of the rebel commissioners to receive subscriptions to the Confederate loan at Savannah. He is a partner in a leading cotton house in that city and is supposed to have had an interest in the steamer Bermuda that ran the blockade off Tybee Island, Georgia coast. Mrs. Low is the daughter of W. H. Stiles, of Georgia; formerly minister to Austria, and the family all rank rebels. It is for you to determine about his arrest. I have no doubt of his being an agent at Liverpool this summer. Mr. Low has a sandy head, dark red, and looks like a Scotchman or Englishman.[15]

There was, of course, an element of truth in all these allegations, but the only one Andrew Low admitted was that certainly he had been one of the rebel loan commissioners for the State of Georgia, an action, as he was a merchant banker residing in the South, he looked upon as a community commitment rather than a treasonable act against the federal government. In addition, he had refused to take the oath of allegiance to the federal government as he was unwilling to take sides against the actions and community of which he was a part. The placement of his name as commissioner for the Confederate loan consisted only in his being named in a list of prominent businessmen of Savannah who were expected to discharge their duty in furthering subscriptions to the cause. The list he claimed was made out in Richmond, and his name was inserted without his knowledge or assent; he submitted to this after it was done, but took no other measure. Like Britain, he claimed he was neutral!

Despite the fact that from Cincinnati U.S. Marshall A.G. Sands stated to Seward that no treasonable papers had been found, Seward ordered his arrest and he was taken to Fort Warren in Boston, as was Charles Green, who had been arrested in Detroit with his sister Eliza Green Low. Mrs. John Low was initially taken to Greenhow House Prison in Washington, D.C., on November 10 before being released and allowed to proceed three days later to the Green family home in Virginia. Mary Low was not arrested and allowed to proceed to Baltimore.

Immediately Andrew Low engaged the services of a prominent New York lawyer, W. M. Evarts, and Charles Green took his case to Lord Lyons, the British foreign representative in Washington, specifically asking that certain business papers taken from him be restored immediately for remittance of promised funds to clients. At the end of November Seward received a letter from State Department official Seth C. Hawley that ensured Andrew Low's incarceration for several more months. Hawley had been importuned by a group of prominent Bostonian businessmen to look into the case of Mr. Low. He did, and came to a conclusion diametrically opposed to their purpose in enlisting his assistance. He wrote to Seward on November 28, 1861:

> Mr. Low is a banker of the first rank in the South, of English origin; has a branch house in England; is the corresponding banker in the South for W. Peabody, Baring & Co; is very rich and commands a very rich and moneyed circle at home and abroad. While last in England he was on his own account proprietor of 50,000 bales of cotton in Liverpool on which he has realized the advance growing out of the rebellion, making a large fortune by that operation. He is able and influential and is one of the commissioners for the Confederate loan. He pretends he has not accepted but does not pretend that he has declined, and unquestionably has so far undertaken the trust as to lend his influence to the enterprise.

If that was not damning enough Hawley goes on to say:

> . . . the man who can raise the money to carry on a war is of more consequence than he who commands the armies. Mr. Low, if at liberty, wherever his parole may place him, if disloyal could be dangerous. He is valuable as a hostage; is guilty of treason if he has acted as commissioner, as I assume he has, and in case of being driven to set up the *lex talionis* he would be worth a thousand common men. I consider him the most important man in Fort Warren—to keep—unless it be Slidell. I deem it probable that all this is known to your Department, but out of abundant caution I write this lest some of the facts might not have reached you.

The response from Assistant Secretary F. W. Seward to William Evarts was crisp and to the point: "I am directed by the Secretary of State to inform you that the release of Mr. Andrew Low at the present time is deemed inexpedient."

Perhaps fortunately for Andrew Low the confusion surrounding actual details appears to have been as inaccurate then as they remain today. Despite the fact that all the major characters in the drama were followed incessantly by agents of the government in London and Liverpool, and the fact that Andrew Low and Mary Low had indeed attended many meetings of the chief conspirators and agents of the Confederacy—all that seemed to have escaped attention. The Feds consistently mixed up John Low with Andrew Low, the blockade-busting *Bermuda* with the *Fingal*, which was never mentioned, and used letters in Charles Green's possession naming Andrew Low as a pretext to maintain both their imprisonment. Seriously flawed intelligence!

Persistent rumors of a serious rift in the relationship between Andrew Low and Charles Green continued. General G. Moxley Sorrel in his book *Recollections of a Confederate Staff Officer* affirms the truth of the rumor when he writes:

> When General Mackall was exchanged out of Fort Warren he told me of two other prisoners, civilians, Andrew Low and Charles Green. The latter had married my cousin, and both were Englishmen of the regular holdfast, energetic type. They constituted the most important business house in Savannah, were making quantities of money, but had quarreled and were about separating on the worst terms when Seward's detectives, suspicious of their movements (they had both married in Savannah and were truly Southern and Confederate) clapped them in Fort Warren. There by the irony of fate they were the sole occupants of the same casemate, these quondam friends, and now bitter non-speaking enemies. The situation was difficult and rather enjoyed by some gentlemen outside who knew of the partner troubles.

In England an extract from the proceedings of the British Imperial Parliament Records, dated February 10, 1862, in relation to the arrest of three British subjects in America was brought to the attention of Earl Russell, the Secretary of Foreign Affairs, by the Earl of Carnarvon—some serious strings were being pulled on both sides of the Atlantic. Two of the British subjects were Andrew Low and Charles Green, the third an impecunious Irish laboring man who had inadvertently got caught up in the war machinery while endeavoring to locate a relative in Harper's Ferry.

The Earl of Carnarvon stated that the petitioners request for release had been denied by U.S. Secretary of State Seward unless they first consented to take the oath of allegiance to the Government of the United States, an act we know that Andrew Low refused. The noble Earl Russell's response was a marvel of diplospeak:

> I am unable to say whether or not these persons may have been engaged in these conspiracies. We all know that during the time in which the United States have been divided there has been much sympathy shown in this country on one side and on the other …

> Lord Lyons has shown himself to be a vigilant British minister in that respect; and I trust your Lordships will not think that those cases have been neglected by the government of this country.

By February 1862, Andrew Low's Boston friends had succeeded in convincing Seth Hawley to continue to lobby Seward for his release. Part of the rationale for securing a well-known cotton merchant's release with ties to both Southern sources of raw material and British distribution network would have been that the cotton feast had turned to famine. In America the manufacturing mills of the north eastern seaboard were suffering as much by now as the north of Great Britain from lack of cotton, and slack trade due to the blockade of all Southern ports. Money flows quicker than blood and both were afflicted with arteriosclerosis of their trading veins and arteries.

On February 1 Seth Hawley wrote his report to the Secretary of State where he expresses the belief that "circumstances have transpired that have created the impression that Mr. Green and his family are active traitors," and that had prejudiced the case against Andrew Low. He refutes that notion and states: "A careful scrutiny, however, shows that Mr. Green and Mr. Low have dissolved partnership and separated their business interests for the future, and that such differences and divergences have occurred to preclude the idea of any sympathy in business or other transaction."

He then goes on to laud the character of Mr. Low as represented by his business associates and recommends parole to live in New York. The response was immediate: Secretary Seward instructed Colonel Justin Dimick of Fort Warren, in Boston Harbor on February 8, 1862, to release Mr. Andrew Low to proceed at once to Baltimore for a period of sixty days and then voluntarily return to imprisonment again in Fort Warren. Andrew Low was not the kind of man to agree to voluntarily return to prison, and once out and safely in Baltimore he turned to the War Department for disposition of his situation. On March 7, 1862, he wrote his own letter to General Dix in Baltimore to whom he had been ordered to report.

In this letter he confirms that his visit to England had been of a private nature to visit his two young daughters who he had in school in Brighton and to dissolve his partnership with Charles Green. The response was dramatic, and four days later L. Thomas, the adjutant general, by order of the Secretary of War ordered General Dix to "discharge Mr. Andrew Low from the conditions of his present parole and furnish him with a pass to enable him to go beyond the lines of the U.S. Army upon his engaging upon honor that he will render no aid or comfort to the enemies of the United States."

The reason given by Andrew Low in his letter to Union General Dix in Baltimore requesting a change to the conditions of his parole was that "I carefully avoided doing anything in England in violation of my neutrality. My sole business there was of an urgent, private nature, viz, to attend to arranging dissolution of my co-partnership and to see after the welfare of two young daughters I have at school in Brighton. Abundant evidence has been furnished the commissioner of the State Department, Mr. Hawley, by friends who were aware of all my actions, movements and opinions."

He was also instructed to report to the Secretary of War at the end of three months "unless during that time he shall effect the discharge of a political prisoner whose exchange shall be satisfactory to the Secretary of War." There is no record found to show that an exchange of prisoners was effected, but by the end of the three-month period Andrew Low had returned to his family in Georgia.

There can be very little doubt that everyone involved knew exactly what the Low Company partners involvement was, but it was by then deemed expedient to release them to continue procuring cotton, which all sides needed by 1862, including the British and especially the North.

Andrew Low Returns Home After Release

Following months of extensive influence peddling and string pulling by friends and colleagues in New York, Liverpool, Savannah, and other centers of international commerce, both Andrew Low and Charles Green were released about three months later in the early summer of 1862 and returned to take up their normal activities in Savannah. In the case of Andrew Low, he went to Cartersville in Cass County, to be reunited with his family and try to rebuild their shattered businesses.

On May 16, 1862, not knowing where her husband was, Mary Low sat down and wrote a letter to him.

> My own dear husband. What can I say to you if this should ever reach you. Savannah will be in the hands of the Northern troops, & you will have the satisfaction of hearing from my Grandmother & Aunts who will remain there under any circumstances it being impossible for the former to be moved anywhere, she is so feeble. I am thankful to say that I am still well but so distressed at not hearing a word from or of you since the first of March. Our dear little children too are remarkably well, there are eight of Mother's grandchildren in this home all under seven, Katie being the eldest. Maggy had a dear little girl born ten days ago, they are both doing well. If I only thought any of my numerous letters would ever reach you I could write with so much more satisfaction but I feel I am writing to no purpose. My

dear old grandmother talks of you daily and longs to see you once more. She is only able to go downstairs once a day now. Aunt Elliot and Phoebe go down on Tuesday to stay with her for a short time, but longer if necessary. Mary Elliot's baby is four weeks old so she can be left, her mother in law is with her. Of course, the men belonging to the two houses in Cass (Barstow) are away from home, eight in number. Not one seed of cotton is planted in this county, only provisions. I long to have your approval of all I have done since we were so shamefully parted on 7 November last. I never can forget it. Mama and Grace are both with me. Celia is taking care of her husband who is thought by all of us to be dying. It would be some consolation to me to know where you are and on what terms. If I thought you were in England I could almost be happy and certainly resigned. Tomorrow is our eighth wedding day. I trust I may hear something of you before night. If anything should occur before this goes, Mother will add a line. Words of love from all the children and your truly attached wife M. C. L.

Etowah Cliffs, May 16th.[16]

The letter was obviously never posted because they were reunited two weeks later when he arrived home on June 3rd, just three days before his daughter, who they named Jessie, was born. They had then been married eight years.

Those stark bones hide an exciting fleshed-out dramatic tale of intrigue, espionage, conflict, and tension told in the words of the protagonists themselves to a very large degree through letters, diaries, journals, and official records of the Civil War. The entire episode covered about six months and shows how influential the Union Army and the politicians in Washington considered Andrew Low to be.

16

Guns and Roses, 1862–1863

On June 5, 1862, two days after Andrew Low returned to her at Etowah Cliffs, Mary gave birth to a baby girl, Jessie. This was her fourth living child, and her sixth pregnancy in eight years—one born premature and one who lived only a day. For Andrew she was his fifth daughter. The child's godfather was Confederate general and family friend Robert E Lee, but as he was otherwise engaged on the battlefield, a cousin of the Stiles, Percival Elliott, stood in for him.[1]

Life turned to thoughts of the future. Like many others in those terrible times, the family was not to find much peace and little joy as events began to unfold with increasing impact. As the war increased in brutality and horror, the full ramifications of what may initially have seemed a romantic and honorable enterprise began dissolving into a tragedy of epic proportions, and a way of life disappeared forever. In a letter Mary Low wrote to her husband—not knowing whether he was still in prison in Boston, in Baltimore, or back in England—she mentioned that all the men in the family were away, and that there were eight children all under seven years of age under the roof of their grandmother's home. This would have been a normal situation throughout the South; with the men away at war, the women ran the farms, the plantations, the businesses, and the homes. The Mackays, the Stileses, and all their extended family were no different.

From a revisionist viewpoint the causes and reasons for the euphemistically named Civil War, more accurately the War Between the States—focusing on military aspects and the abolition of slavery—have diminished and minimized the layered complexity of Southern culture, and portray many young Southern men as foolish fops. In reality if the conflict is examined from the perspective of the times, such attributes as honor and chivalry prevailed, personal characteristics way out of fashion in our cynical age where social safety nets exist that did not exist then.

These families provided their own safety nets as a matter of their

General Robert E. Lee, ca. 1863. This old family friend and his wife continued their correspondence with the Stiles and Mackays throughout the war years. *Courtesy Hugh Stiles Golson.*

heritage and upbringing. The loyalty to the Southern cause of men such as Robert E. Lee was rooted in their allegiance to state, to family, to friends, to honor, to duty—and never let it be forgotten that much of the militia were volunteer—their basic obligation to their communities, and not necessarily to the institution of slavery. Slavery was a brutal institution as we recognize it today, and morality is a clearer shade of black and white compared with yesterday's multi-shades of gray. What was marginally acceptable in 1860 must be seen as egregious violations of human rights in this new millennium.

Great Britain as War Enters Second Year

In the last few months of 1861 contractors providing goods to the Union and those on both sides of the Atlantic engaged in the cotton trade were becoming enormously enriched, basically by less production and more profit. The prices of stockpiled raw cotton continued to rise, and speculators and blockade-runners on both ends found more and more imaginative ways to beat the blockades as these unanticipated riches continued to line the pockets of those willing to take the risks. Cotton was not only king, it was the currency of the realm, and the streets of Liverpool swarmed with Confederate agents and southern merchants, watched closely by Union and British secret service agents determined to stop the rot.

If the speculators were getting rich, mostly everyone else was beginning to feel the pinch. In the northern region of England, almost completely dependent on cotton from the South, the situation was reaching calamitous proportions. Small shopkeepers were reliant on the wages of the mill workers on short wages. Manufacturers, short of capital, had to pay exorbitant prices for the yarn to spin his looms, meaning higher credit and bad debts and unemployment. This was still at that time caused more by the glut than the famine but that was soon to change.

Groups of idle workers hung out on the street corners, but even now the feeling was still of optimism rather than pessimism. Hard times were here, but hard times were no stranger to workers used to the vagaries and fluctuations of the industrial revolution. By the time of Andrew Low's arrest at the beginning of November 1861, there were only forty-nine mills stopped throughout the whole of Great Britain, and 119 more on half-time, and less than 10,000 hands out of work, a mere fraction of the disaster to come.

By the beginning of 1862 the situation had deteriorated considerably. The uncertainties of the relationship between Britain and a split America, with a federal government in the North and a secessionist government in the South, contributed to the increasing decline of the manufacturing trade in the northern region of England. Now a novel twist emerged—the mills of North America were suffering from a cotton famine as well, and by the second week of January 20,000 bales of imported Southern cotton had been reexported from England to New York and Boston, at a steep profit too, for in Manchester manufacturers could only afford 1 shilling (12 pence) per pound while it was sold for 18 pence in America. It is an ill wind that blows no one any good. To put the flow of raw cotton into perspective—by April 1862, during the previous six months, the quantity arriving from America was only 11,500 bales, while in the corresponding period of the preceding year arrivals from America had amounted to 1,500,000 bales, more than one hundred times the quantity now trickling in.[2]

By mid-year the situation was grim; pawnshops were crammed with furniture, wedding rings, and clothing of the penniless workers; their funds in benefit societies, trade unions, and savings banks had been heavily drawn upon just to provide necessities for their families, and there was no longer a single ray of hope that things would get better soon. There was terrible suffering among the working men and women of the manufacturing industry, and a sense of hopelessness had set in along with a profound sense of repugnance over their plight, and a reluctance to place themselves as applicants for relief. They were a proud people, the British. Charitable agencies had been established for their relief and the government was taking steps to alleviate the distress, but the entire working population of Manchester, Blackburn, Preston, Wigan, and other mill centers of the textile trade in the north, where production had virtually come to a standstill, was living on a mere fraction of their normal income.[3]

The cotton trade was bombarded with rumors causing panic and euphoria in equal parts as news filtered in of battles won, battles lost. Tales of how the now desperately needed cotton was being burnt and used for ramparts in the South abounded, and anger in the ranks of the workers soared at the stockpilers and manufacturers, still making their own profits by selling the cotton back to the merchants and traders of the North. By the beginning of the second half of 1862, the stock of cotton in Liverpool had fallen to 180,450 bales; at the corresponding period of 1861, it had been 1,108,650 bales, while in 1860 it had been as large as 1,297,030 bales. This lack of supply naturally caused prices to rise to astronomical heights. If you had cotton to sell, you had money to spare

The records will not show clearly who was making money off this buying and selling, but I believe it safe to say that probably the Andrew Low Company and the Isaac Low Company would have had few scruples about turning a profit if they could. During this period Andrew Low and Charles Green were held prisoner by the Union forces in Fort Warren, so it is hard to see how they could have had much access to markets and speculating, unless they employed surrogates working on their behalf. Isaac Low Company was still operating with impunity in Liverpool despite its American partner's absence.

The *London Times* wrote: "No crisis in modern times has been so anxiously watched, nor has any European war or revolution so seriously threatened the interests of England."

To some extent the war did have the effect the Confederacy originally aimed for though. It sharply divided Britain along class lines with, generally speaking, the upper and merchant classes pro-Confederate and the working class pro-Union. The equality nature of the American Republic's democratic ideals threatened the British establishment's Tory mind-set, which feared the spread of egalitarianism at home. A collapse of the American democratic system would not have been anathema to either the commercial interests or the landowning upper classes that ruled Britain.

For the unofficial voice the London *Morning Post* wrote in February 1862, "if the Union should win the war democracy will have achieved its greatest triumph since the world began ... and who can doubt that democracy will be more arrogant, more aggressive, more leveling and vulgarizing ... than it has ever been before." Nearly all the leading English newspapers and magazines expressed sympathy for the South and hostility to the North, and with them stood the Establishment—the aristocracy, the Established Church, universities—although intellectuals were sharply divided—between those who saw the struggle as the way to emancipate the black, and those who saw abolition as a way to speed the spread of democracy into Britain, abolish the class system, and give working class men the vote.

In 1862, following the Confederate invasion of the North and Lee's victory at Bull Run, the British, testing the wind, considered offering mediation. Before that happened the news came of the Union victory at Antietam, changing the possible outcome, and the offer was postponed by Parliament. By October 7, 1862, William Gladstone, Chancellor of the Exchequer, made an unauthorized speech stating that the South would succeed in their separation from the North. The government disavowed this opinion with a speech from the Home Secretary, Sir George Cornwell, repudiating Gladstone and stating the government was not contemplating a change of policy. Britain remained officially neutral, sitting on the fence.

The reality that Europe was not going to become involved in the conflict was beginning to penetrate on the home front and in February of 1862 Eliza Stiles's sister Mary Anne writes to her:

> I am so glad that General Lee is in Savannah. I know that all human efforts will be made to save our homes and after that, if the enemies succeed in destroying us ... I trust that all I love will escape before the worst comes ... England treats us so badly, I did not think she would be so selfish, she is evidently determined not to help in any way unless we make ourselves independent ... it seems that

England and France do not mean to help us until we have helped ourselves, so as to be able to do without them—we will not thank them for such unwilling services.[4]

In many quarters there is beginning to be real animosity expressed against England, because despite the oft-quoted belief that England favored the South, Queen Victoria's official neutrality edict contradicted this view, no matter what contrary opinion was emanating from Confederate sympathizers in Liverpool.

Fall of Fort Pulaski—Savannah 1862

Even before Andrew Low returned to his family Savannah began to feel the impact of an impending hardening and worsening of their precarious position. The Union Navy had boats in the Savannah River below Fort Pulaski, and maneuvered to cut off communications between the city and the fort, but not before Commodore Tattnall, with his motley Mosquito Fleet, succeeded in getting a six months' supply of provisions to the garrison.

In February the Union boats gained an entrance through Wall's Cut into the Savannah River above Fort Pulaski, thus isolating the fortress. General A. R. Lawton, in command in Savannah at this time, instituted immediate measures to strengthen Savannah's various defenses, and, in a communication to the City Council, gave assurances that he would defend Savannah "to the last extremity." The federal forces, however, made no move against the city at that time. As the year advanced the austerity imposed on Savannah grew steadily worse.

A few months before the Lows were reunited, Major General David Hunter took command of the Union Department of the South. He was an uncle by marriage of Eleanor Kinzie Gordon, mother of Juliette Gordon, future daughter-in-law of Andrew Low. His premier position in the Union Army and conqueror of Fort Pulaski must have made life in Savannah increasingly difficult for Nellie Gordon, who also had brothers fighting on the Union side, while her husband was a Confederate officer. Major General David Hunter signed the order to commence the bombardment of Fort Pulaski, then under the command of a twenty-four-year-old Savannahian Confederate officer, Colonel Charles H. Olmstead of the 1st Georgia Volunteer Regiment. Olmstead has left a lengthy personal memoir for posterity.[5]

On April 10, 1862, the Federals opened fire upon Fort Pulaski, and in spite of the strong defense maintained by the garrison, the enemy's superior new rifled cannons did great damage to the casements and the walls, shells were dropping close by the powder magazine, and by April 11 the walls had been severely breached and it was obvious the situation was hopeless. Colonel Olmstead, fearing a disastrous explosion, decided the only course of action would be to surrender the fort to General Hunter, commanding the besieging forces.

The white flag of surrender was flown, and the cease-fire took effect. The capitulation came after thirty-two hours, and took the entire city by surprise. The defenders, including Colonel Olmstead, were shipped north to prison camps and Savannah was now unprotected. This reversal caused great anxiety and alarm for it was thought that the enemy would surely follow up this victory by an early attack on the city.

In a most controversial move two days after the fall of Fort Pulaski, General Hunter issued an order freeing all the slaves on Cockspur Island. On May 9 he extended the order to include all slaves in Georgia, Florida, and South Carolina.[6] Abolitionists cheered but his troops objected; Lincoln, understanding the political hazards of such a move, quickly revoked the order—the time was not yet ripe. Hunter also began recruiting a regiment of black troops, the 1st South Carolina; it would later form the nucleus of the famous 33rd Infantry. Known contemptuously as the "Nigger Ginral" Hunter's actions led to an execution order for his death being posted by the Confederate authorities. In Savannah Nellie Gordon was shunned by some.

A week after the fall of Fort Pulaski the Confederate government passed the Conscription Act, authorizing a military draft. This meant that Georgian state troops were now obligated to national service for the Confederacy. This did not go down too well as many "Rebs" were fighting for States Rights and to protect their lifestyle as much as for the Confederacy, and took great pride in their volunteer status. There was by no means only one reason for patriotism on either side in the conflict.

Colonel Charles Olmstead writes in his *Memoirs* that Andrew Low sent them a draft on Liverpool for 300 pounds—about $3,000—for their use in prison on Governor's Island at Fort Columbus, while Low was himself still incarcerated in Fort Warren. For Andrew Low the news of the fall of Fort Pulaski, and the cutting of all Savannah's arterial lifelines for trade, would have been a serious setback. The blow was severe and the necessity to return to see what could be salvaged even more urgent. Cotton was desperately needed in the mills of northern England, and cotton was decomposing in the fields and moldering in the warehouses of the South. Savannah was isolated from the world to all intents and purposes, and Low was rotting in exile. For a man of action the situation would have been intolerable.

The blockade along the coast became increasingly stringent, and the river was useless as an artery of trade. Commodities of all kinds were at a premium; the necessities of life brought fabulous prices, and the salt famine, daily becoming more acute, caused grave concern. Substitutes for coffee and sugar were largely used, and the consumption of other ordinary staples, such as bacon and flour, was of necessity sharply reduced; but notwithstanding the pressure of bitter privation, and the uncertainty and apprehension uppermost in the thoughts of the people, Savannahians, from the tone of the letters left for our education, remained defiant.

Countdown to Tragedy

In the middle of a steamy summer in wartime Savannah on June 13, 1862, Mary Cowper Stiles Low's beloved grandmother, Eliza McQueen Mackay, matriarch of the family, widow of Robert Mackay, devoutly Christian, moved on to her Maker. In May, Mary Low had written to her husband that her grandmother longed to lay eyes on him one more time; if he passed through Savannah on his way to Etowah Cliffs she might have got her wish. As she lay ill and feeble in her home of many years at 75 Broughton Street, nursed by her unmarried daughters Kate and Sarah, she would have been told of the arrival of her youngest granddaughter, Jessie.

During this period Captain Eddie Stiles wrote frequently to his mother, Mary Ann Stiles.[7] His letters written from the battlefield reveal many details of the increasingly difficult conditions. They are a good indication of what life was like for these young men in the arena, sons of the social elite, farmers, and sharecroppers alike. They are not only dying in battle—they are dying in droves of illness. The anguish of losing a child is rarely assuaged by the rightness or wrongness of war or the manner of his death. War is an equal opportunity employer and a family affair.

> Goldsboro, April 4th, 62. Dear Mother. We are having dreadful times here, so much sickness, men are dying every day. Yesterday, Shirley, who came a short time since to my company, started home with his brother's body who died the night before of pneumonia.... I did not believe men could be so selfish and indifferent as they have been in our regiment, two thirds of them would not wait on the sick if they were not made to do it, they would let them lay and suffer for want of anything. I have to make them relieve each other sitting up or they would leave it all for one or two to do. There is a great deal of pneumonia in the camp and I am afraid a great many more will die ... we have been without medicine.

A month or so later he wrote again to his mother:

> I am glad you can look so calmly at the coming battle, and if my letters are of any comfort to you, you must be comforted.... I don't feel any weakness myself in regard to the battle, I don't feel at all as

> though I were going to get hurt, but of course I place no reliance on my feelings, as that I think would be foolishness when there is so much danger, but it makes me have more confidence.

One letter in particular touched my heart as it graphically expresses the occasional bouts of camaraderie felt by these young men—one side wearing the blue, and one wearing the gray—both ripped out of the daily fabric of their lives. It illustrates how hungry the men in the field were for news of home. Captain Eddie Stiles was in the 16th Georgia Regiment, General Cobb's brigade, somewhere "near Richmond" on June 24, 1862, and wrote to his mother, enclosing a soiled newspaper:

> Dear Mother. The Yankees stand out in the open field within three or four hundred yards of us on one end of the line I was commanding. I waved a paper to them and they waved one back. I then sent a man out half way who put the paper on a bush and returned. The Yankee went and got it and left one in its place. I tried again this morning but they would not exchange, I suppose they had been ordered not to have anything to do with us. Yesterday there was pretty heavy skirmishing on our right and last night they evidently expected an attack and were very much alarmed.

In the same letter he tells his mother that "Uncle Joe" (the Reverend J. C. Stiles) had just come and told him about the death of his grandmother.

A scant two weeks later on her plantation at Clarksville, on June 26, Mary Anne Mackay Stiles, widow of Benjamin Stiles, sister of Eliza Stiles, mother of Eddie Stiles, died suddenly. For the men on the battlefields, in the prison camps, incapable of helping their family's burden, grief at the deaths of their mothers and sisters, wives in childbirth, and newborn children they would never see, would have been an added burden of impotence.

Nine months later Captain Eddie Stiles met and married a girl he barely knew, survived for two more years, and then died in battle at Guard Hill, Virginia on the August 16, 1864. He was twenty-eight years old.[8]

Henry Stiles, Jr.'s War—Fredericksburg

Every family in the South suffered the loss of a son, a husband, a father, a grandfather, a grandson; for some all the men either died on the battlefield or returned so grievously wounded an entire generation was lost. The Stiles family was no different.

Colonel Stiles's regiment had been sent to Virginia after the retreat at Hilton Head the previous November serving under General Stonewall

Captain W. Henry Stiles, Jr., Mary Low's brother, in 1862.
Later that year he suffered a serious abdominal wound
at Fredericksburg. *Courtesy Hugh Stiles Golson.*

Jackson through several campaigns. His son Henry was a captain in his father's regiment and was wounded through the thigh at Manassas after narrowly escaping being taken prisoner, a state he may not have survived. Conditions in the prison camps for both sides, Union and Confederate, were utterly abysmal. There was no Geneva Convention in effect governing the treatment of prisoners. Colonel Stiles at that time was also sick and had gone to Etowah Cliffs to recuperate. Hearing of his son's wound, he was determined to go to Virginia to bring him back. Eliza recounts the episode: "They had a terrible journey in a freight car filled with wounded and dying men and no comforts at all. When Grandfather recovered he returned to the Army and Henry stayed at home some months and went on again."

From the advantage of a century of hindsight trying to reconstruct both the chain of events and the mood and tenor of the times, one of the more baffling aspects of combatants' movements is how loose and mutable it all seemed. The men often appeared to come and go as they pleased, returning home to help with the planting with not a great deal of discipline or oversight involved. To a neutral observer the independent and volunteer nature, at least of the Confederate army, appears overriding. Captain Henry Stiles writes to his father, who had returned to his regiment in Virginia, from Etowah Cliffs on November 10, 1862: "I would really have gone on at the expiration of my furlough but I was so anxious to gather in our corn crop and determine how much we could sell. I also sow our wheat, which I have nearly finished; we have had but one rain since I have been home. I have never seen such a dry time. I am very anxious to get on to you. Mr. Low is here for a short visit."

Captain Henry Stiles returned to his regiment, and their next moment of fear came at the Battle of Fredericksburg, one of the most examined battles of the conflict. Historian Shelby Foote in his epic narrative says "Fredericksburg, the nearest to the nation's capital, was the largest in numbers engaged, if not in bloodshed—as the grandest as a spectacle, in which respect it equaled, if indeed did not outdo, any other major conflict of the war." [9]

Colonel William Henry Stiles writes to his wife from "near Fredericksburg," December 15, 1862:[10]

> The enemy broke through our lines just in front of us. General Early's brigade had to give way when we were ordered to advance and we made a noble charge & drove the enemy in utter confusion, but alas, although it was glorious it was a most fatal charge. Our son Henry led his company most gallantly & was shot down. I rushed up to him in a few minutes. The noble hearted boy could only think of me & not of himself, all he said and repeated constantly was "lay down Father, do lay down, or you will surely be killed". I told him, "No, my Son I will not be killed, but if I should be there was no better spot to fall than by the side of my gallant son." The ball which struck him penetrated the body about the abdomen, it did not touch the vitals, the stomach or entrails, but cut as the surgeons say, the lining membranes of the stomach. It passed through his body and lodged in his arm, just lodging in the skin on the opposite side, from which it was easily cut out, with the immense roll of wadding composed of parts of his overcoat ... it was just below the elbow & no bone broken or injured. The wound is of course, a very severe one, but the

> surgeons do not think it very dangerous. He suffers at times a great deal, especially when he coughs or moves the stomach in any way. How I escaped everybody says is a miracle.

The first part, written on the battlefield, gives a fairly optimistic assessment of the situation, and he goes on at great length enumerating all the friends and neighbors from Cass County that had either been killed or wounded in the battle, but then William Henry appears to become quite worried:

> I had just written this far in the field & on my return this evening I find Henry not so well having had quite a high fever today. I was a little depressed but sending for both doctors & begged them to communicate to me plainly if there was anything alarming in the change, they both assured me there was nothing unfavorable in the fever, that it was but the natural affect of the wound. That he would require nothing now but good nursing. Under these circumstances you or Eliza [Henry's wife], or both, better come on. Henry tells me he had written to Eliza today not to think of coming, therefore I see no alternative but for you to come. Mr. Low would be willing to accompany you. Yrs aff. W. H. Stiles.

For Eliza Stiles, writing in her diary, it was not the spectacle or the glory of battle that impressed, but it was the near loss of her oldest son Henry. Five months after returning to Etowah Cliffs in north Georgia, still on parole, Andrew Low accompanied his mother-in-law north. She writes to her grand daughter Katie: "Mr. Low went with me through East Tennessee, and your Mamma helped me pack my trunk. I took in a bottle of Brandy, which was very scarce, some wheat bread and biscuits, some preserves and arrowroot and a sponge cake, a little loafsugar, rags and any little comforts, which we then thought perfect luxuries."

Eliza Stiles and Andrew Low traveled north to Richmond, Virginia:

> We were detained 24 hours at the dirtiest house I was ever in at Dalton where the smallpox was raging, and I saw crowds of our men going to the surgeon to be vaccinated; then I saw a dead man carried through the streets on a stretcher without any covering, but his clothes. I was in an agony of mind about my son not knowing whether he was dead or alive, and this detention was very aggravating. When we went to the depot in the middle of the night to continue our journey, we could scarcely get to the cars without treading on soldiers who were lying on the ground so close together that it was difficult to pass among them. It was a Regiment of tired soldiers come for transportation to some other place and these poor crea-

tures we met all along the route, but with such a good and cheerful and hopeful spirit that it did one's heart good to talk to them. They were willing to endure all for their country.

It was Christmas morning when Eliza and Andrew Low finally arrived in Richmond to find her other son Robert and Henry's wife Eliza already there, having traveled up from Savannah by another route. They passed a miserable Christmas Day trying to arrange for Henry to be brought to Richmond as soon as he could be moved. They were fortunate to find a Savannah physician, Dr. Read, working there in a hospital as well as William Henry's brother, the Reverend J. C. Stiles. The Reverend Stiles enjoyed the sobriquet of being Stonewall Jackson's private chaplain. He was well known on the battlefields of Virginia for preaching to masses of soldiers from the back of his buckboard. With true Southern hospitality people rallied around, and Henry was taken to a friend's house to be nursed. That was Eliza's last entry, but Eddy's sister Sidney Stiles Elliott[11] continued the story for Katie Low:

> Taking up the account where your Grandmother stopped I will add that the party reached the house on the battlefield and found Henry still alive, but he could not be moved from there for many weeks. The wound was across the chest, from right to left, and the ball lodged in the left arm. That he was not killed instantly must have been because he exhaled his breath for the ball passed literally a hairs-breadth from the heart. When he fell some of his men laid him on his blanket, and tried to carry him off the field, but after two were shot he lay upon the ground until the battle was done, and was then taken to this house. Everyone was kind to them, even their old friend General Robert E Lee, busy as he was, went to see them and sent daily to see how Henry was, for there was little hope of life there. After weeks of good nursing by his wife and Mother, he was moved to Richmond, and as soon as he could endure the long journey, he was taken to Savannah. As the wound in his chest healed he had more and more trouble with the wound in his left arm, which had not been thought much of as no bones were broken, but on examination they found a large portion of his toothbrush in the fleshy part of the arm, and the bristles caused the irritation. The brush had been in his vest pocket when he was shot, and the ball had taken it into his arm.

After recuperating at Etowah Cliffs, Henry returned to his command and fought with Stonewall Jackson's Corps to the bitter end. Reverend Stiles's son, Robert A. Stiles, penned *Four Years under Marse Robert* in 1912 and memorialized many of the family stories of this period. All over the

South today the archives, libraries, and private collections contain many personal accounts of the terrible human toll of that fratricidal conflict.

Line in the Sand—Emancipation Proclamation

Throughout the struggle there was much confusion in the minds of foreigners and Americans alike as to why the war was being fought. Was it to retain the union of the nation or against slavery? Lincoln's own statement was that the war was being fought not to free the slaves, but to save the Union. He wrote this in his now famous letter to Horace Greeley in August 1862, but one month later, in September 1862, Lincoln issued the Emancipation Proclamation to take effect January 1, 1863. He proclaimed "slavery must die that the nation should live."[12]

This injunction caused great bitterness throughout the South and deepened the determination of the Confederate States to wrest a victory from the desperate struggle. The Savannah newspaper printed in its opinion pages: "With this edict, the War, in the eyes of Southerners, took on the complexion of a crusade on the part of the northerners—A crusade for the liberation of three million of Negroes, barbarians, and their enfranchisement as citizens. It will be known in all history as the most wicked, atrocious annals of civilization."

In Britain the Proclamation was received as might be expected—upper classes against, lower for. The eternal struggle for freedom of all oppressed people everywhere held true; to many working-class people the struggle for freedom from chattel slavery by black Americans was not that much different from their own struggle from economic slavery.

The effect rippled over the ocean, and voting rights were soon to come to working class Britons. The efforts of Gladstone of the Exchequer, later on Prime Minister, resulted in the 1867 Second Reform Bill, which gave the vote to ordinary householders in the towns, including nearly all the cotton workers. Thus the same storm that had brought emancipation to the black workers in the white flowering cotton fields of the South also brought the vote to white cotton workers in the grimy black soot streaked streets of Britain's industrial cities.

Matters got so bad in Britain that the fabric of society started to unravel, and rioting broke out in several districts. Every riot in the cotton belt had similar features. There was a sense of injustice articulated by born leaders of the masses, those always capable of either maintaining order or creating a disturbance. The mob follows mob rule. The war dragged on, and Britain belatedly realized that it must look elsewhere than America for other major sources of raw materials. India, Egypt, Turkey, and Greece emerged as new suppliers as well as new markets for manufactured goods. The door had also slammed on American emigration, always a safety valve, particularly for the Irish thronging the streets of Liverpool, and the government began to look toward forced migration of unemployed workers to Australia.

Death and Life Goes On

1863 was to prove as much an *annus horriblis* for the entire Low and extended Stiles family as 1849 had been for Andrew Low and his first family. It commenced on December 31, 1862, at Etowah Cliffs when Cousin Leila Habersham gave birth to her fourth child, a boy she named Frederic Augustus after his father. She writes to her husband in Savannah:

> His birth was quite unexpected at the time—the Dr did not arrive in time and my cousin Mary Low was the only one in the room with me when the child was born ... when they brought the little baby to my bedside and told me he was dead, I could not believe the sad truth.... I took the little baby in my arms and wept as only Mothers weep over their dead infants and when the morning of the New Year dawned, the light fell on his little hands folded in the icy calmness of death.

During her convalescence Mary Low stayed with her: "My cousin Mary Low was devoted to me during my sickness, bringing her knitting and spending the day in my darkened room, reading German hymns to me and sympathizing with me in every way, she having lost two little ones herself."

The Union forces continued to hold Fort Pulaski, and Savannah remained inactive as a port. Shipping was at a standstill, and the city suffered more and more from the scarcity of commodities caused largely by the bottling up of the river. Prices soared. Profiteers multiplied. Indignant citizens gave expression through the medium of the daily newspaper to their mounting anger created by the increasing army of speculators and extortionists. The price of cotton was stratospherical. In spite of these pressing hardships, the sacrifices made, and the heartaches suffered, a goodly portion of the citizens of Savannah found time to indulge in a variety of pleasures. The theater afforded many such entertainments throughout the year, and the old favorite performers, "The Queen Sisters," were repeatedly noted as playing here in both comedy and melodrama. The "Thespian Family—a purely Southern Dramatic Company" had an extensive repertoire and found favor with Savannah theatregoers.

One person who was not about to forget he had a country—two, in fact, as well as a large family to support—was Andrew Low. The paper reports that the usual annual business elections took place,

> On Jan 7. Re-elected Directors of Central Railroad and Banking Company. Andrew Low and J. Cunningham, R. R. Cuyler elected

> President. March 10, 1862. The Great Southern Insurance Company was chartered by the Georgia Legislature, December 20, 1861. Books will be opened in Savannah, Columbus, Augusta, Macon, and Atlanta. Commissioners in Savannah: Robert Habersham. Charles Green, Andrew Low, and John Anderson.

Business had to go on because one day the war would be over. The merchants of Savannah would be ready come hell first or high water.

Utilizing information taken from the Messrs A. Low & Company's circular titled *The Cotton Trade of Savannah,* on April 16, 1863, the *Times* of London portrayed a bleaker prognosis:

> Neither in Savannah nor Charleston is there any stock of Sea Island or Upland Cotton in store of any consequence. Since the war began, both places have been menaced and all the Sea Island, which has been sold, has been sent to the interior depots and villages, or any place out of reach of the enemy. Many of the planters have sold their crops, and still hold them on their plantations for the purchaser. There is now very little on sale, and a large proportion is held for investment of surplus capital and by the speculators for the end of the war ... after making deductions for parcels running the blockade and captures by the enemy the stock of Sea Island is estimated to be about 36,000 bales ... even when peace is obtained, and should agricultural industry return to its normal condition, it will be years before the quantity produced prior to the war can be obtained.[13]

Worry over his son Henry's wound, his own age and his deteriorating conditions took a toll on William Henry. On June 15 Colonel Stiles wrote from Richmond to James Seddons, Confederate secretary of war, asking to be relieved of command due to ill health. One of the rumors that persist is that Andrew Low had loaned him a great deal of money to keep his plantation in Etowah Cliffs afloat. This was not the idle request of a soldier distressed with war. William Henry Stiles by then was housing a large extended family under the roof of a crumbling unworkable plantation. There were the Low grandchildren, the wives and families of sons Henry and Bob, as well as the African servants and hands and their families. He had multiple financial responsibilities, and with his own health failing he asked for his release and his request was granted. During his entire war career, William Stiles had continued his lifelong habit of writing letters complaining to his superiors about a multitude of perceived and real insults to his status as colonel of a volunteer regiment. It is quite possible that the authorities of the Confederate Army were glad to be rid of him. Although brave, he had not been a particularly effective commander.

Mary Low's Death, June 1863

Mary Low had been reported as being extremely concerned over the well-being of their slaves, and her mother, Eliza Stiles, wrote her husband on February 3, 1863, that her daughter had been vaccinating the plantation children against a smallpox epidemic.

> Mary Low took two youngest children, and Maria and Anina (a Mackay slave) into Cartersville last evening to leave at 8 this morning for Savannah to spend a month. Katie and Mary both very croupy last night . . . the smallpox is in our neighborhood, and our Negroes are not allowed to go over the river off of our land. Mary vaccinated 67 of them the day before she left. She had done all the children and young people before then, so I trust we shall escape.[14]

Fred Habersham wrote to his wife Leila: "Carrie [sister in law] arrived safely this morning. Percy and I met her at the depot. Willie Low was sick on the journey. Mary and baby Jessie well. Mr. Low met them at Marlow."[15]

Two months later Eliza writes to her husband from Savannah indicating that her daughter had returned to Etowah Cliffs from that February visit, but had decided to return to her home and husband: "March 30th, 1863. Savannah: I came down with Mary and her children last Thursday and spent a few weeks with my Sisters. I had a dreadful cold when I left. . . . Mr. Low is delighted to have his family back again and says they should not go away in a hurry again."[16]

We have proof that Mary Low stayed on in Savannah from Leila Habersham's writings in her memoir. She says that she had been in north Georgia for eighteen months at Summerland and needing company traveled to Savannah on April 15, 1863, where she visited her many friends, including dining with Mary Low on Monday, May 4. The very next day Leila Habersham received the terrible news that her beloved husband Fred had been killed in battle, at Fredericksburg in Virginia. A letter from a fellow officer, Captain Fraser, gives the barebones of a tragedy that was becoming a daily occurrence for families all over the South and the North: "It is my painful duty to inform you of the death of your gallant cousin F. A. Habersham. He was killed on Sunday the 3 while fighting his gun against terrible numbers of the enemy who were charging our works. Fred was a noble brave fellow & in losing him I have lost a friend and tried officer."[17]

During these terrible times the strength derived from people's Christian faith is reflected in the words of Sister Carrie's fiancé, Robert Elliott:

> Would that the firmness which Christianity imparts might be with me to steer me aright under this unexpected calamity. But as

> deeply as I feel it, cheerfully would I suffer ten times the sorrow could I but whisper one word of consolation to the hearts that I know are bleeding in your midst today. But He who sends this terrible stroke can alone administer the relief for which we so long. He can only bind up the wounded heart and pour in the oil of divine consolation, and may He in his mercy be with us all, for otherwise we are without help, locked in the anguish of mortal sorrow.[18]

Mary Low proved once again to be a rock upon which her friends and family could lean. When Leila Habersham learned that Fred's body was to be returned, she asked Mary to write to her brother, Henry Stiles, who was still recuperating at Etowah Cliffs, to disinter the body of the baby buried at Summerland, so the father could be laid to rest with the son he had never seen. Fred Habersham's remains were brought to Savannah on the afternoon of Saturday, May 16. The funeral in Laurel Grove Cemetery was held the next day with full military honors, attended by a throng of citizens.

None of the notices show any suggestion whether Mary Low attended the funeral of Fred Habersham, and she is not mentioned at all in any of the many letters from Habersham family during the next four weeks. Hints are that maybe she was pregnant again, although no written proof has come to light, and due to the delicacy of the subject, it would not be a matter that would be discussed lightly. There remains some mystery still over the details of her condition and sudden death.

Unlike the carefree days of summer for much of the world, the months of June and July were the most hazardous of the year for Savannahians. The first news of the suddenness of her illness is to be found recorded in a letter published in *A Savannah Family,* dated June 16, 1863, from Bishop Stephen Elliott.[19] Exactly one month after the funeral he writes to Fred's mother, Mrs. Susan Habersham, from Savannah commenting how pleasant it was to think "the brave fellow had his Bible harnessed to him when he fell." Then the letter delivers another shock: "I fear Mrs. Mackay's family is about to receive another severe blow. I have just returned from seeing Mary Low & find her very, very ill, her mother not with her, & should her disease prove fatal, not likely to be. How full of death the world is now."

There is an indication in Cousin Josephine Clay Habersham's memoir *Ebb Tide,* where she says that Mary Low was at White Bluff recently, which must have been between early February and the middle of May before the death of Fred Habersham dampened everyone's spirits. At that time she was obviously in good health. She wrote on June 17, 1863: "Poor, sweet, pretty Mary Low died this morning! In the bloom of life! I remember her out here, not long ago, so bright and gay and independent, fishing

Mary Low's bedroom, where she died in 1863 in blockaded Savannah. *Courtesy The National Society of The Colonial Dames of America in the State of Georgia.*

and swimming every day. So young! . . . Poor Mary Low! I think of her constantly. So young and bright and gay! How sudden."

A large part of the difficulty in reconstructing the details of events so long ago lies in the imprecise manner in which people conveyed information, and the interpretation needs to be viewed through the prism of what was being said obliquely, and what was being conveyed directly. Therefore in this case the question is—What is the interpretation of "disease"? The onset must have been sudden otherwise undoubtedly there would surely be some indication in the copious correspondence from Eliza Stiles or the spinster aunts that her daughter was unwell or sick.

In the hot and humid days of a Savannah summer, particularly under wartime conditions, disease was rampant and typhoid particularly so; it also would have been extremely risky and dangerous to be exposed to smallpox, although Eliza Stiles insists that none of their Negroes had contracted the disease. Therefore, despite the death notice signed by Dr. J. J. Waring that reads "1863, 17th or 18th of June, Mary Cowper Stiles Low died; cause of death puerperal fever," it is quite possible that she was suddenly stricken with the disease of typhoid fever as a contributing factor; certainly the death notices throughout those few weeks of June 1863 list typhoid as the cause of many deaths. There was also yellow fever in the town, a normal occurrence in mid-summer.

Mary Low had given birth to Jessie exactly one year before. She had suffered a great many traumas during that and the previous year. Especially the arrest of her husband necessitated additional reserves of strength while alone during that pregnancy. Worry over her father's illness and her brother's wounding twice; the death of her cousin Leila's baby in her presence; the death of her cousin's husband Fred in battle, and subsequent reinternment of their dead baby, all wore her down. Even writing about the troubles and strains lined up like bottles on a wall is enough to give me heart palpitations from the safe distance of a century and a half. Taking into consideration the fact that Andrew Low had returned to her after more than six months of separation, it is possible she could have become pregnant three months after giving birth. But the mystery remains, and it is impossible to prove whether she was pregnant with a full-term child. Had she just recently conceived again and had a miscarriage resulting in infection? This, ironically, was also the cause of death of Andrew's first wife, Sarah, with an almost full-term infant requiring surgical removal.

Puerperal fever, according to Sally McMillen's monograph on the causes of death in childbirth in the antebellum South, was "a fever developing after childbirth and caused by infection ... often spread by medical attendants who assisted at successive deliveries ... it was the most feared of the epidemic illnesses associated with childbirth and rare among middle and upper class southern women."[20]

Andrew Low had access to the best medical attention the town could provide, and he also had, for the times, as modern and sanitary conditions in the home as possible. They even had a bathing room and running water. One rumor that has endured is that the fever may have resulted from an ectopic pregnancy, but it is not even certain that condition was recognized by the medical profession of the time. Another anomaly is the source of the footnote in the book *A Savannah Family* that "she and her child died"—but there was no mention of a child on the death certificate, the death announcement, or the grave.[21]

Therefore, the mystery persists regarding the exact circumstances surrounding her death. All we have to go on in empirical fact is that puerperal fever is listed on her death card, which does not make medical sense unless she gave birth, and Bishop Elliott's reference to the potential fatal nature of her "disease"!

In any event, for us it is an academic exercise—for Andrew Low it was an almost mortal blow. For the second time Andrew Low had to place a death notice, stark and brief, in the newspaper. It reads: "1863: June 18. The friends and acquaintances of Mr. and Mrs. Andrew Low are invited to attend the funeral of the latter, from Christ Church, this afternoon at 5 o'clock."

Andrew Low buried his second wife in the plot of ground under the oaks in Laurel Grove Cemetery in the company of his first wife, Sarah, and his first son, Andrew, Jr. Mary Low was thirty years, seven months, and two days old. Eliza Stiles returned with her son-in-law and her grandchildren to the empty and echoing house on Lafayette Square.

17

When the Ball Is Over, 1863–1867

AFTER MARY'S DEATH ELIZA MACKAY STILES MOVED INTO THE house on Lafayette Square in Savannah to take care of her daughter's children and to attempt to maintain an air of normalcy in their lives. Their grandfather, William Henry Stiles, had resigned his commission in the Confederate Army due to ill health shortly after the death of his only daughter. He, too, was struggling to maintain some degree of normalcy at their north Georgia plantation, Etowah Cliffs. By now Cass County had been renamed Bartow County in honor of Colonel Francis Bartow of the 8th Georgia Regiment, Savannah-born hero of the Battle of Manassas who had been killed on July 20, 1861, at the Battle of Bull Run. This was also a Southern slap at General Lewis Cass of Michigan, the county's original namesake, who opposed secession.

Plantation owners, including the Stileses, utilized the practice of hiring their Negroes out to do work for the Confederate Army. Their labor was essential because able-bodied males of all classes were away fighting, and the reality was that white slave-owners in the South reaped the benefit of the labor of black slaves even under wartime conditions. Some of the Stiles Negroes were hired out to a saltpeter company making gunpowder for the Rebels.

During the fall of 1863, William Henry attempted to make the neglected plantation profitable again, and "succeeded in selling enough cotton at 55 cents a pound to realize $24,422." He immediately spent $20,000 of it purchasing land near Dawson, Terrell County, in southwest Georgia, about fifty miles from the Alabama border, lying outside the projected route of the enemy's inevitable advance.[1]

On Christmas Eve 1863 Stiles wrote to his son Henry, now back with his regiment, stating his decision to close up Etowah, store the furniture, and move to Terrell County. He writes complaining that "troops are in the area, the Negroes are a problem and how difficult life is in a war ravaged land." Christmas brought a welcome gift for the bereaved Stiles family when Henry's wife, Eliza Clifford Gordon, gave birth to a daughter. Grandmother Eliza writes a poignant letter on December 28 to her son about his having named his new daughter after Mary, telling him he was blessed—"the dying prayers of your angel sister for you have been answered."[2]

By the beginning of January 1864, William Henry is writing to Eliza in Savannah complaining about an imbecile overseer and the difficulties of trying to get the people and stock ready to move to Terrell County. This was a dangerous and complicated maneuver under the circumscribed conditions: roads clogged with advancing and retreating soldiers, refugees, freed men, women, and runaways. One letter includes the names of sixty-eight Stiles slaves he is transporting. On arrival he immediately commences to clear the fields and erect buildings for the farm, and sends as much produce as he can to Savannah to help feed the family. Eliza is unwell; she is worried constantly with two sons still in the thick of the fighting, appears to be quarrelling with Mr. Low, and bemoans the fact that he is "mad" at her. Things are falling apart for everyone and the center is not holding.

In 1864 General William Tecumseh Sherman of Ohio assumed command of the Military Division of the Mississippi. He replaced General Ulysses S. Grant, who had been promoted and given command of all U.S. armies. Sherman immediately returned to Nashville and began planning his invasion of Georgia to coincide with General Grant's massive onslaught aimed at destroying Robert E. Lee's Army of the Potomac.

The correspondence at this period shows their increasingly fragile state of mind as Sherman takes command. Rumors of the Yankee advance and overstated atrocities run rampant through the streets of Savannah, like mercury escaping from a broken thermometer. The almost daily lifeline of letters to each other during this period represents an atypical mind-set of their class of Southerner during this capsule snapshot in time. Mundane chatter about "their people" and how William Henry had to put them on the train himself—he treats them like children incapable of taking care of themselves—is indicative of an inability to see the Africans any differently than they ever have: property, along with the cattle, goats, and horses, moving them a logistical problem to be solved. His language is not abusive, he is not cruel, he does not refer to them as inferior—he just does not view them as capable human beings.

During all this turmoil and hard toil, William Henry still finds time to continue his letter-writing campaign to whichever authority he feels had caused him discomfort at that particular moment. In March of 1864 Colonel Stiles wrote letters to Seddons, the Confederate Secretary of War, complaining of injustices done to him. He seems oblivious to danger around him and obsessed with his own affairs. He still has sufficient influence, however, to always receive a response. But by now Eliza seems to be mad at him too, saying he "cannot let go of anything" in regard to a letter he wrote to the War Department.

Their letters continue to paint a portrait of life that has become severely limited, especially when contrasted with the life they had been leading a mere decade before—the highest level of diplomatic existence in the elegant ambience of old Europe. Eliza is quarrelling with Andrew Low[3]—constantly complains about privations of life in Savannah, "held very cheap these days," but also sadly fusses over the death of a Negro servant McGill. William Henry responds that McGill was "a most civil and excellent Negro and I don't know how the family will be able to get along without him." He also talks about his cows being poisoned on the farm, and that one of the female slaves he has sent to Savannah wants her freedom; he petulantly states that he has no spare money and needs to be reimbursed for her passage. "I will certainly sell her if she deceives me for she had fair warning . . . and if she does not pay . . . I will sell her as soon as I come to Savannah. I do not know if it would do to tell her this or she might run away to go to the Yankees."

The impression given is that the farm Africans are annoyingly ungrateful and deceitful and do not know how well off they are; in contrast there is genuine affection for their house servants, most of which have been with them all their lives. By the end of April he is back at Etowah Cliffs, where he seems almost cheerful about the "excellent crops and thriving orchards" he found there, and tells his wife it is his obligation to go off to Dalton to look for a runaway "boy."

> I expect to go up to Dalton tomorrow in search of Paul, but I fear there will be little probability of finding him in over 60,000 men scattered and lying over ten miles square. An officer I conversed with yesterday told me that there were an immense number of Negroes among the troops up there, as an order paper came down recently that allowed them to have black cooks . . . all I can do is to try and ferret him out.

It is quite extraordinary in the midst of the mayhem the degree of effort they expend to try to find their runaways or have the slaves they consider stolen returned to them. The war is not going well at all and in May, Henry Stiles, Jr., who is now back in the thick of the battle with Gordon's Brigade in Virginia, writes that conditions are dreadful:

> I have never seen anything like the mud in my life, and the poor horses have had nothing to eat for five days, because no corn could

> be gotten, and there is no grass, or anything for them to pick at, besides that the horses are harnessed up all the time. I do wish the fight were over, for both man and beast are broken down and worn out. We have suffered very heavily on our side, but the enemy more so. . . . Grant will never get to Richmond though he has already cost us the lives of a great many good men and will doubtless cause us to lose a great many more. I have not heard anything of Eddy and the other Stiles boys since the heavy fight the other day. . . . I hope this fight will be the last we will have then the war will gradually die out.

Sherman's Advance

By the spring General William T. Sherman had assembled an army of 100,000 men in and around Chattanooga, Tennessee, and was on the move. His plan was to follow the railroad east to the sea. He was in command of three armies: the Army of the Ohio, the Army of the Cumberland, and his old Army of the Tennessee. Opposing him was Joseph E. Johnston's 60,000–man of the Army of Tennessee. In May 1864 the federal army entered Georgia and commenced its march upon Atlanta, its first objective. As the Union army advanced it pushed the retreating Confederates ever closer to Atlanta. The fighting around that section was fierce throughout the summer, characterized by skirmishes and raids. Many accounts were given in the newspapers of "Stoneman the Beast," a Union general, who, with his band of raiders, inflicted terrible depredations upon the countryside, accompanied always, according to the Southern press, by "fiendish brutalities and ravishment of women," many of whom were living unprotected on their farms and rural plantations. Fear was palpable.

On May 16 William Henry writes to his son Robert that "the enemy is advancing" and he may have to abandon Etowah Cliffs. He begs them to "send someone up to come and fetch his Aunt's Negroes as things are very uncertain—the sooner the better," and two days later to Eliza warning that the Yanks are coming. Johnston's army has had to fall back. During this tense and terrible time, they still write to each other almost every day as they have most of their lives.

Sherman's army crossed the Etowah River at Stilesboro, a small community named for Stiles, until he reached a position south of the Etowah River and dug in at Cassville. On May 21 a letter from John Smith to Cousin Sarah Mackay from nearby Roswell, writes, "God is on their side despite the fact that the Yanks are near." Nothing, including God, could stop the Yankee army, and Stiles with his remaining slaves left Etowah Cliffs only days before the arrival of Sherman's forces, burying many of his family's valuable possessions that he could not carry in their headlong flight. After the war, many of these valuables were dug up and reclaimed; and unlike many other fine homes, which were burned to the ground, Etowah Cliffs suffered relatively little damage through the Union army occupation.

By July 7 Eliza writes to William Henry, now safely in Terrell County, "that the enemy has reached Marietta and destroyed Roswell," where the Bulloch family lived, not far from Etowah Cliffs in north Georgia, and that "Mr. Low is anxious." The Bulloch family is a microcosm of the fratricidal bonds that were ripped asunder during this terrible time. Mittie Bulloch Roosevelt spent the war years in New York mothering the future President of the United States, her son Theodore Roosevelt, Jr. Many members of her family and friends suffered the deprivations and terrors of Sherman's progress, or at least endured the desolation caused when a massive army marches through, living off the land.

The sadness and hope inherent in this correspondence lies in the remarkable aspect that they are so ordinary in the face of the ghastly times they were living in—sketches of a people desperately trying to hold on to the reins of the humdrum details of running a farm and living a life with enemy troops camped on their doorsteps; their "people" behaving disrespectfully and running away—a world disappearing, like an ancient photograph fades from sight.

This entire sequence of letters during 1864 is unprecedented to me on a personal level. It shows the gradual disintegration of a life-style, yet also shows courage and fortitude in the face of almost unbearable sorrow and loss. The letters are completely filled with the details of everyday life—one in particular that sticks in my mind is when William Henry spoke of having a "bowl of strawberries from the garden for breakfast," and neighbor John Smith wrote to Sarah Mackay of wanting some old pieces of tortoise shell to "make her a thread winder so he could think of his cousin's fingers handling it in the winding of thread." The minutiae of needing to remember what life was like before the storm broke over their heads are as poignant as they are predictable.

Spinster Aunt Sarah Mackay appears to be the recipient of many letters from cousins and friends, and is the family chronicler. She was not married and had no family of her own to deal with, so she was the keeper of the flame of story, laboriously copying letters by hand and passing them on to family members, the only way information could be disseminated.

Sherman Enters Atlanta

On September 1 Atlanta fell to Sherman's army. Within two weeks hundreds of Union prisoners were transferred from the notorious prison camp in Andersonville to Savannah and Charleston. On September 12 Eliza writes that: "4,000 Yankee prisoners from Andersonville are in

Savannah and more gone to Charleston because we have neither the accommodation nor guards sufficient for them." From *A Present for Mr. Lincoln*, "the burden of handling prisoners was a terrible one for an already overburdened city. . . . I was shocked to see the pitiable condition of the prisoners. They were dirty and half clad and altogether the most squalid gathering of humanity it has ever been my lot to look upon."

Around the enclosure the writer observed there was "a large number of respectably dressed women, some of whom were throwing bread to the Yankees."

Sherman entered Atlanta and was given a tumultuous welcome by the overjoyed African element, suddenly rising to a plane of equality with the white citizens remaining in the city. The Savannah *Daily Morning News* of Sept 12 gave an account of a grand ball, attended by General Sherman and his staff. "The Negro woman was feted and toasted and monopolized the entire crew of Yankees and some of the sympathizers who have affiliated." Some time later Sherman issued orders for the evacuation of the city by the populace, many of whom found refuge in Savannah. On November 15 Sherman had the torch applied to the "Gate City of the South" and started on his famous "scorched earth" march to the sea, cutting a swathe of destruction, forty miles wide and three hundred miles long, as he progressed like a biblical scourge.

When criticized for his tactics, Sherman is credited with saying that he was not only fighting a hostile army but a hostile people, and that they must be made to feel the hard hand of war. When the news reached the seat of the government at Milledgeville that Sherman was closing in, the people were thrown into a panic. Governor Brown, whose first thought was to save the official papers, found it impossible in the general confusion to get help for this purpose in the ordinary way. He hurried to the penitentiary and made a patriotic speech to the convicts, promising them freedom and persuaded them to aid the militia in evacuating the Capitol. The result was they saved the most valuable records.

Savannah was itself experiencing a great deal of sickness, and Andrew Low was losing a ton of money in England. Cotton was extremely scarce and promised to become even scarcer as conditions prohibited planting or picking crops already planted. There was little labor left to pick it, and the roads were clogged with caravans of refugee Negroes fleeing toward freedom.

On November 8, 1864, Abraham Lincoln was reelected President, and he chose as his running mate Senator Andrew Johnson of Tennessee. Johnson was selected as Vice President to reward Southern Unionists and extend their influence into the South to assist in Reconstruction after the war.

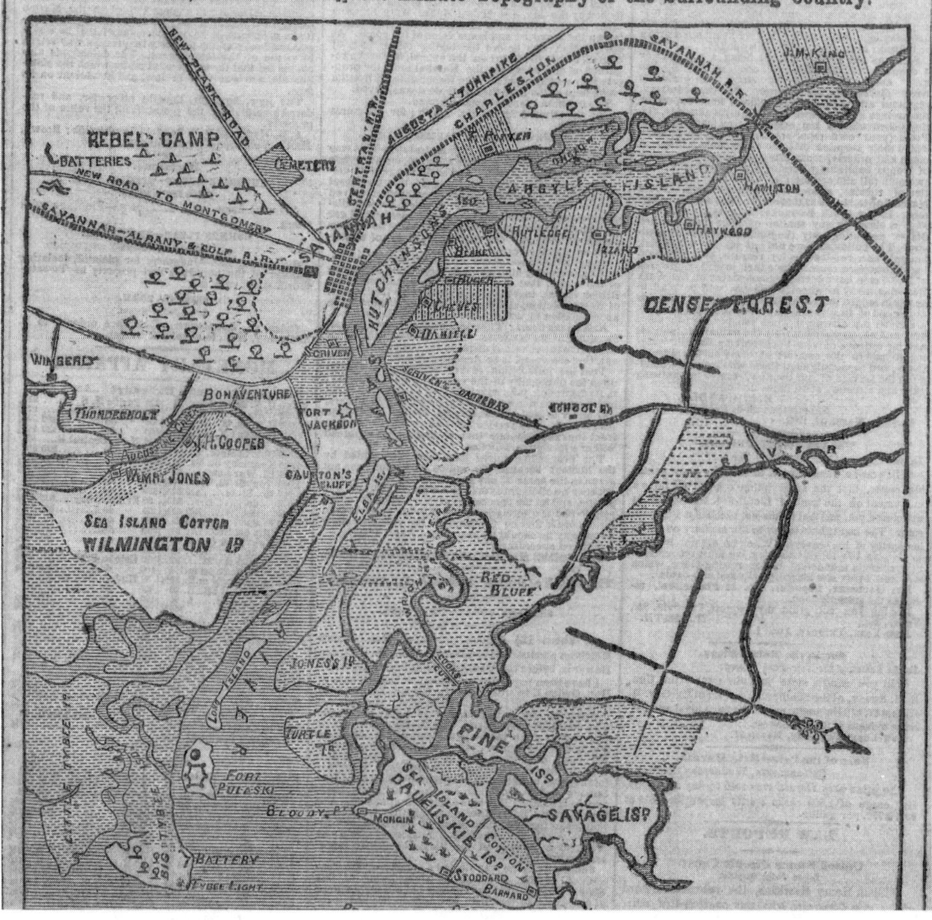

"Scene of Gen. Sherman's Operations," wartime map from the *New York Times,* shows the difficulty in defending or invading the coastal city. *Courtesy Hugh Stiles Golson.*

Savannah Falls—A Present for Mr. Lincoln!

As the year waned Confederate money rapidly depreciated in value, and the Savannah *Daily Morning News* expressed deep concern over the fact that "the market men and traders around the market were refusing Georgia Treasury notes of this year's issue." Conditions grew steadily worse in every area—commerce practically moribund, and many people were reduced to destitution. The need for recruits was so urgent that boys not even grown to manhood and men past military age were being summoned to fill the depleted ranks of Georgia Guard. So desperate had the situation become for the Confederacy that the question of making it legal to fill the ranks of the Southern army with black soldiers, as was being practiced in the Union army, giving them an unfair advantage in the minds of some, was being threshed over throughout the South and was much discussed in Georgia. Many diehard Southerners were opposed to such a measure and expressed the fervent hope that such a proposal would never be considered. On December 10 Sherman's army reached the outskirts of Savannah.

In spite of the generally upset conditions Savannahians, for the greater part of the year, had carried on in a more or less normal fashion, but as Sherman made his way southward, drawing closer and closer, a feverish excitement gripped the citizenry. Upon the call of Mayor Arnold frantic preparations were made to augment the defense of the city.

General William Hardee, in command of Savannah with only 10,000 troops, realized the futility of making a stand against Sherman's army of 60,000. He and his army quietly left the city during the night of December 20 and crossed the river on pontoon bridges into South Carolina, cutting the bridges loose behind them. Lieutenant Robert Mackay Stiles was one of the engineers who constructed the temporary bridges, and he evacuated with Hardee's army. Commodore Josiah Tattnall destroyed the Confederate ships and naval property assembled at Savannah; he blew up the ironclad ship *Savannah* on the South Carolina shore and then joined General Hardee's retreating columns.

The city was now defenseless and spiraled down into a chaos of looting and lawlessness. Mayor Arnold and the aldermen met the emergency in a truly praiseworthy manner, or at the least in a truly pragmatic Savannah style. They sallied forth to the enemy's camp, a short distance from the city, and reported to Brigadier General John W. Geary that the Confederate army had withdrawn from Savannah, and asked that protection be given to the people and property of the city. General Geary signified that he would comply with this request, and on December 21 he sent a brigade under the command of Colonel Barnum to occupy the city, which act the colonel accomplished with marked discipline. A military government was superimposed upon the city and order was maintained.

On December 21, 1864, General Sherman and his soldiers marched into Savannah. The federal hero-general took Savannah without a shot fired—and his first act was to send a telegram to President Lincoln saying: "I beg to present you as a Christmas gift the City of Savannah with 150 heavy guns & plenty of ammunition & also about 25,000 bales of cotton."

The first memory of cousin Caroline Couper Lovell in her memoir *Light of Other Days* states: "From the east comes pouring a sea of blue-coated soldiers, shouting, leaping, and brandishing their muskets. Mother told me afterwards how the loose women of the town rushed out in the streets to welcome the Yankees, kissing and embracing them, and dancing in an abandon of joy." More importantly, the Union Army restored law and order and cleaned the streets of filth and numerous dead animals.

In the many letters written by the general during his occupation of Savannah, he frequently refers to the comfortable conditions in which he is housed. General Sherman's billet was Charles Green's magnificent mansion on Madison Square—the prevailing wisdom was that Green offered his hospitality hoping to retain the captured 38,500 bales of cotton Sherman commandeered. One source states it was worth 25 million dollars, and whether or not that was the aggregate amount of all warehoused cotton in Savannah, all on Green's account, or some of it the property of the Andrew Low Company, in which he was still legally a partner, has never been confirmed.[4] After the war, both Charles Green and Andrew Low petitioned the victorious United States government for restitution of their cotton.

Because of the destruction of so much original material during those years, few original documents remain. One that does is the remnant of a diary written by a young girl.

Fanny Cohen was the daughter of Octavus Cohen, who was a close friend and business associate of Andrew Low, a lawyer and the postmaster of Savannah under the Pierce and Buchanan administrations. His home was where the present Lafayette Cooperative Apartments stand next door to the Andrew Low Museum and House in Savannah. Her diary covers the period between the day General Sherman's troops entered the city and January 3, 1865.[5] She mentions that "Mr. Low, our neighbor, brought a Yankee to see Father on business," and goes on to say that all through the meeting her father was afraid she would compromise them with her hatred of the Yankees. The men appeared to be engaged in business as usual! The women were defiant as usual! It is essentially an interesting insight of women having to do things like darn socks that they have never done before in their lives. They always had black slaves to literally do everything for them.

Caroline Lovell recalls her first memories of the occupation: "The Yankees established themselves in Savannah, their soldiers stationed in the Barracks on Bull Street in the heart of the city. The Union flag hung across the pavement in front of the archway, and, when in passing Aunt Sarah stepped out in the street to avoid it, she was seized by two soldiers, pulled back to the pavement, and forced to walk beneath it."

For a spinster woman from an elite secessionist family, this would have constituted unbearable humiliation and excruciating manners.

General Sherman visited with Eleanor Gordon to deliver letters from her brother, a Union colonel and one of Sherman's friends, at her house on Bull Street; and he played with the children, Eleanor and Juliette. Eleanor's father, John Kinzie, and two of her brothers were in the Union Army, another was in the U.S. Navy. This visit did not please her husband, Willie Gordon, when he heard about it at the front, and no doubt the good ladies of Savannah gossiped accordingly, with some of them cutting her dead in the street.

January 2, 1865, General Sherman writes to Secretary Stanton about the disposition of cotton and a petition on behalf of Edmund Molyneaux, a British merchant in Liverpool and Savannah, regarding indemnification for his confiscated cotton. Sherman refused, and makes it quite clear that no Englishman, especially those who had paid for arms and ammunition against the Union, would get any preferential treatment. He wrote that cotton was a prize of war and was one of the major reasons the war was fought. Stanton had previously instructed that all claims for cotton by British claimants were to be ignored.

Instead, Molyneaux's house on Bull Street was commandeered as headquarters for General O. O. Howard, to be vandalized by Union soldiers and the wine cellar drunk dry. Yankee officers were billeted in most of Savannah's homes, including Andrew Low's.

Secretary of War Stanton came to Savannah to talk to Sherman about his perceived negativity toward and treatment of blacks, especially concerning the drowning of hundreds of camp-following slaves at Ebenezer Creek and his refusal to enlist them as soldiers. Sherman was well known in his belief that blacks were not ready for service, and that to use them as soldiers was to encourage white Northerners to be lazy. He certainly did not believe in equality for blacks. It was partly because of his attitude that the now famous "forty acres and a mule" promise came into effect. In essence freed slaves were to be offered land on the coastal islands of Georgia, Florida, and South Carolina. Special Order # 15, January 11, 1865, set aside the barrier islands from Charleston south to the St. John's River to thirty miles inland. The order stipulated that no white persons could live in these areas set aside for the use of former slaves, who would, however, still be subject to military authority.

In Savannah Stanton held a meeting with leaders of the African community, led by Garrison Frazier, a freed sixty-seven-year-old Baptist preacher, to discuss the meaning of the Emancipation Proclamation. The meetings were held in Charles Green's house, and then Stanton spoke with an assemblage of several hundred Africans in the Second African Baptist Church on Greene Square.[6]

January 22, 1865, General Sherman left the city to cross the Savannah River and resume his march north into South Carolina, leaving Savannah unburned and practically untouched. On February 18 Union forces entered Charleston, including the black 54th Massachusetts Infantry singing "John Brown's Body."

Sherman's army forged its juggernaut advance north on its way to conquer the Confederate Army at Richmond. The war was taking a heavy toll in men and money, in both the South and North, and while in the South the business of merchants, bankers, and cotton factors was at a virtual standstill; the impact was equally heavy on Northern commerce as raw materials were being used for the war effort and not for trade. Suffering as well as profiteering continued to be an equal opportunity employer.

When Liverpool Was Dixie

Because of the destruction of much archival material and libraries during the Civil War, there is a dearth of details in Savannah on matters unfolding abroad, but the same does not hold true in Liverpool. An intriguing account of the activities of Confederate agents operating in Liverpool can be read in "The Diplomats that Sunk a Fleet," published by the U.S. National Archives and Records Administration.[7] This essay retells the details regarding the role played by Commander James Dunwoody Bulloch in the realm of Confederate ship acquisitions. Because we have no Isaac Low & Company records to draw on after Andrew Low's sojourn in federal prison, it is impossible to ascertain whether the firm or the principals continued to be as heavily involved as they had been in the matter of the *Fingal*.[8]

In Liverpool the continued need for cotton dominated the activities of merchants and factors until the ceasefire in 1865. There was conflicting opinion in the streets and dockyards of Liverpool regarding the building of warships in Birkenhead destined for the Southern cause because of increased employment for Liverpudlians. Meanwhile odd functions continued to be held promoting Liverpool's open support for the Southern side. One of the strangest was a Grand Southern Bazaar, held at St. George's Hall, Lime Street, Liverpool, in October 1864, which raised over $100,000 in five days for the Confederate Prisoners Relief Fund. The advertisement for the bizarre bazaar states: "the suffering of the Southern prisoners of war in sickness, wounds, and deprivation of every comfort of life: the multitudes of widows to whom nothing remains, and of orphans unable to help themselves, form an amount of woe which some who are blessed here with an abundance and peace have felt a desire to alleviate."

The patronesses of the Confederate Bazaar included a long list of marchionesses, countesses, baronesses, ladies, and just plain Mrs's. Mrs. James Bulloch manned the stall for Georgia, and Liverpool-born Mrs. Prioleau, the stall for South Carolina. The treasurer and presumable dispenser of funds was Charles Prioleau of the firm Fraser, Trenholm, Confederate bankers and blockade-runners. Unfortunately permission to visit federal prison camps to dispense the funds "to alleviate the suffering of Southern prisoners" was refused by Secretary of State William Seward, and it is unknown what eventually happened to the money. Seven months later, the war was over.[9]

The last Confederate flag was lowered in Liverpool on November 6, 1865, when the CSS *Shenandoah*, captained by Lieutenant Waddell, arrived in the Mersey. He lowered the flag, and his ship was ultimately turned over to the victorious Union authorities.[10]

The Center Cannot Hold

There was turmoil and bewilderment, and through it all Eliza Stiles struggled valiantly to keep it together, torn between conflicting needs. In a letter dated Savannah, March 2, 1865, to her husband who is back in Terrell County, she writes:

> With General Lee at our head and with the blessing of the Almighty we shall not be made slaves to these wretches, they think they are so liberal giving us food they stole from our plantations... perhaps they give mine to the Negroes—poor deluded creatures—with all their suffering they consider themselves in their 7th Heaven, freedmen and lazyness is back in form... many die daily in Savannah, smallpox is taking them.

Eliza Stiles and her son-in-law frequently had disagreements during the previous year, and she had sometimes made insinuations about his fondness for drink:

> Mr. Low had a bad fall one evening on the pavement and hurt his shoulder badly so that he could not raise his left arm for nearly 2 weeks. He got rheumatism in the same arm and we felt very anxious for a while feeling he might never recover the use of it again, but he is slowly getting over it—I think entirely, he has lost a great deal of flesh, the Doctor reduced him so much—he is very kind and much more calm than when you were here and for weeks after the new army came, he was always excited then, now he is as in former days, and my life in consequence is much more agreeable. Indeed altogether a different thing.

On April 2, pragmatic as he had been all his life, Andrew Low, having financial troubles in both England and Savannah, finally took an oath of allegiance to the United States. One week later General Lee surrendered the Army of Northern Virginia to Union General Grant.[11]

Abraham Lincoln's Assassination, April 14, 1865

The surrender of the Army of Virginia sounded the death knell of the Confederacy. This event, which occasioned gloom throughout the region, ushered in another war for the soul of the South and the body and spirit of the Blackman. But before that could happen another event of momentous import changed history perhaps even more than the war itself.

Celebrating the end of the most deadly and expensive war in terms of lives lost, property devastated, soul-destroying fratricidal war in America's brief and stormy existence, the gods took one more victim, the penultimate irony, the instigator himself. While maybe not the last man to die, this death had the most serious ramifications. On April 14, while attending the theater in Washington, D.C., President Abraham Lincoln was assassinated. The circumstances surrounding President Lincoln's tragic death and, subsequently, the arrest and trial of those implicated with actor John Wilkes Booth, the assassin, furnished much copy for the press and conspiracy theorists. There was a current belief in the North that Jefferson Davis, president of the Confederacy, had headed the conspiracy to assassinate Lincoln, and his name was repeatedly vilified in this connection in Northern papers.

Perhaps the ultimate irony, the father of John Wilkes Booth, Lincoln's assassin, was Junius Brutus Booth, a Shakespearean actor who frequently played the Theatre Royal in Liverpool.

In Savannah, as in most Southern cities the populace rallied.

> On April 21, pursuant to the call of Mayor Arnold, a large assemblage of the citizens of Savannah met at the Exchange today to give expression to their sentiments in relation to the assassination of Abraham Lincoln. The meeting was too large to be accommodated and removed to Johnson Square. A Committee was selected to draft resolutions expressive of regret. The Committee included Andrew Low, Charles Green, Robert Habersham, and others.

On April 26, 1865, General Joseph E. Johnston surrendered the Confederate Army of the Tennessee to General Sherman. The war between North and South was over, the war for emancipation just begun.

Trying to Put Humpty Together Again

Despite the removal of a certain amount of constant worry caused by the cessation of actual hostilities, the future was far from secure or obvious. The level of tension appears not to have decreased in the Low household and Eliza complained about Andrew's rudeness to her and "his wretched afternoon habits"—she wrote her son Henry: "If Mr. Low would only quit taking whiskey, things would work smooth. Poor man, it is such a dreadful failing, but I now don't trust anything said after dinner as I know he don't mean it, and he has put much more in my power lately in the home." [5 June 1865].

Andrew Low proceeded to put his own broken pieces together again, and left for New York and Liverpool to seek the means to do so. In June 1865 a governess, Miss Mary McCord, had been hired to help their grandmother with Andrew Low's children. A cousin, John Mackay Elliott, writes in his autobiography: "That summer I helped my Aunt Eliza Stiles and guarded the house where she and a governess cared for her grandchildren while their wealthy father Andrew Low was away. Their mother had died and, Savannah being in turmoil, I often prowled around the house at night."

He states that Tom the butler "entered the house with a key unknown to him"—inferring that Tom slept in the servants quarters and not in the main house, and it is recorded that as friend and confidante Tom Milledge was completely trusted by Andrew Low. Eliza writes to her own "dear children" telling them that having Miss McCord makes her life that much easier, and that Mr. Low is planning on bringing his two daughters out from England.[12]

Nevertheless, the situation is becoming problematical for Eliza Stiles. She is finding life in postwar Savannah increasingly hard to comprehend or even tolerate. In July 1865 Henry Stiles, Jr., returned with his wife and family to Etowah Cliffs, and Robert and his wife and family joined them shortly after. William Henry and Eliza planned to join them as soon as they had sold the plantation in Terrell and made satisfactory arrangements for former slaves. They are determined to rebuild, but plan on using only white labor from now on. William writes on July 1, 1865:

> Henry goes up with his family next week to take up his permanent abode in Cass, I shall remain here to take charge of the place and Negroes as they cannot be abandoned in these times—I expect to follow with the greater portion of the Negroes (if I can sell this place with all of them) in the fall. Henry says almost all the Negroes who left their masters last year in Cass have returned being heartily sick of freedom....

Colonel Stiles refused to leave Terrell to go to Savannah in case he had to come into contact with the Yankees. In the same letter he writes:

> You might think it more proper that I come to you but I have no disposition to come in contact with the Yankees. I used to be, as you know, very amiable in my youth, but now at 56 years I regret to say

that time and the experiences of the last few months have reduced me to a state in which so long as it exists I will never boast or even claim amiability again. I have not taken the oath of "Amity" as they call it, nor will I until I am absolutely compelled to . . . they may take all the property I possess—they may take my life but they can never obtain from me a supplication for pardon when I have committed no offense.[13]

William Henry is still, unquestionably, an unrepentant secessionist, which he remained to the end, judging by correspondence and a speech he gave begging the Confederacy not to give up. He wanted neither of Lincoln's alternatives, "submission or subjugation."[14]

Eliza confirms in a letter to her children in Etowah Cliffs that Andrew Low's only son was a delicate child, frequently ill with fever and coughs; the intimation is that he was also quite spoiled. The two older girls, Katie and Mary, were doing well with their learning, but both Willie and the baby Jessie were constantly ill, their health threatened and aggravated by the excessive heat of a Savannah summer and the Yankee occupation. She, too, has advice for Henry in how to deal with recalcitrant labor.

August 20th, 1865. If I were Henry I would make no contract with the Negroes for another year for the laws from the Freedman Bureau work very much against us and in favor of the blacks, its all a scheme to make us hire them and pay them monthly and if we fail our land will be sold to pay the blacks, which is just what the Yanks want if we hire Negroes—plenty of white labor will come later—we can take on Negroes again when they have tried freedom a while and found it is a poor thing in all but name. I would rather keep my land idle and do anything to make money, work for the Yankees or any one else.

It is probable the situation was exacerbated at Lafayette Square because it appears as though the only person Andrew Low really trusted was Tom, the butler. It is in this letter that we first hear a reference to coachman and butler Tom as having a wife and baby. Eliza writes about the servants:

I understand Mr. Low is very uneasy at the idea of leaving the children and says he will do anything in the world to keep me, I don't know how it will end, he writes to me very kindly and begs me to make a list of all that is wanted in the house, upstairs and downstairs. Celia [Anderson—one of "free" mulattos listed in the 1860 census] has taken everything from the lower story and left only bare walls. The new cook does pretty well and Tom has his wife & child

> here now, a baby 5 weeks old—but so far she has done nothing for me—Grace [Taylor, also one of the free mulattos servants named in the 1860 Census] comes daily and does nothing, she is so weak, she says—I keep all the keys and give out things but Tom buys the marketing according to his pleasure.[15]

In the fall, Andrew Low returned to Savannah, bringing his two daughters by his first wife, to help with the children of Mary Cowper. Eliza informs William Henry that "Mr. Low is more optimistic about the future," and she talks about the girls, her step grandchildren, Hattie and Amy. Her own optimism does not last long; she has terrible neuralgia in her face, a long-standing condition.

She is becoming increasingly worried about the parlous state of William Henry's health and writes that she fears that "wretched Terrell will be the death of him." He writes to Eliza complaining about a Negro, Dolly, running away and going to the Provost Marshall complaining that he ordered her off the property, which he claims is an outright falsehood: "The trouble with my Negroes has just commenced and I have no doubt will continue to increase until we get rid of them. They are obviously changing in character every day. They are unwilling to work although they are to be paid"

His tone is very testy and illuminating about life in immediate postwar reconstruction Georgia, and shows their inability to comprehend either the new rules or the new relationship. These letters give a clear indication of the impasse people found themselves in as they saw what they considered former property become paid servants with servants rights, concurrent with the curtailment by law of their own employers' rights.

For months William Henry had been in declining health. He was fixated on his antagonism toward the victorious Northern military and politicians—many of whom were his friends and associates in another life, a life that had seen North and South in unity. This must have taken an even more serious toll on his constitution and psyche than those who had lived exclusively in one or other regions of the country. William Stiles was Northern educated, Washington savvy, European skilled, at home in the halls of political power as in the fields of the rural South. He felt his personal betrayal was total.

Early in November a letter from his overseer came to eldest son Henry at Etowah Cliffs, saying his father is quite unwell with "dropsy of the chest." The warning bells are sounding. Eliza writes back that despite the arrival of his daughters, Amy and Hattie, "Mr. Low is hitting the brandy bottle." Eliza is homesick, worried, and desperately insecure.

In early December Henry, Jr., writes to Mr. Bryan, prospective purchaser of the Terrell County property, saying his father is in bad health and is going to Savannah to be with his wife, who needs to stay there to look after the children. They are not destined to have much time together.

December 20, 1865, Aunt Sarah writes to Henry that William Henry is getting worse. He died the same day—his death occurred exactly one year after Sherman's triumphal march into the city he loved so well. It would have been next to impossible for William Henry Stiles to ever reconcile to the loss of the life he had lived to the full. His funeral was conducted December 21 from Christ Church, and he was buried in the Mackay Lot in Laurel Grove Cemetery in Savannah, ironically on land his family had once owned. His grave is marked with the simple inscription "A Statesman, A Soldier, and an Humble Christian." This marker was later installed by his dutiful grandson, Willie Low.

The one who suffered most by his death was his much-loved wife and lifelong partner, Eliza Mackay Stiles, but she still had the responsibility of taking care of her own beloved daughter's children. True to her nature, she was not one to turn her back on her familial obligations.

The purpose expressed throughout the writing and research of this hybrid document—part reconstruction, part speculation—is not to condemn or to condone, rather to correct the record and try to speak to the truth of decisions taken by people who lived in a different place and at a different time. It is not a memoir because I have no memories of that place or time, but as with all families some of the members are more appealing than others. During the two years following the death of Mary Cowper Stiles and the conclusion of the combat phase of a brutal fratricidal war, the character of Eliza Mackay Stiles shines through as a real heroine. The dynamic of her relationship with her son-in-law Andrew Low, and his with her, must be accepted through the prism of their personal anguish and the reality of a situation over which they had little control. The same must be accepted for the views expressed as she and her husband saw their lives disintegrate with uncomprehending bitterness.

The postwar struggles of a people trying to remake their land into a more equitable nation were simultaneously unjust and just, as is inevitable when there are winners and losers embedded in wrenching change. If William Henry and Eliza had the opportunity to experience the pitiless transition together, then they may have been able to come to a more philosophical acceptance of the different reality they faced. If there were available records and personal narratives from their former slaves, then it might be possible to better comprehend the fear, loathing, and love on both sides. But it was not different: it is as it was. In the words of an ancient Persian poet: "The moving finger writes and having writ moves on. Nor all thy piety nor wit, shall lure it back to cancel half a line, nor all thy tears wipe out a word of it."[16]

Picking Up the Pieces

Grandmother Eliza spent her time at Etowah Cliffs and Savannah with her children and grandchildren. The remaining maiden Mackay aunts, Kate and Sarah, still lived in the family home on Broughton Street and helped in both households. Andrew Low was now the patriarch and the sole support of a sea of females, except for his only son William, born in 1860, now inevitably a spoiled six-year-old. The daughters ranged in age from Amy, a beauty of twenty of marriageable age; Hattie, eighteen and ripe for a good marriage; Katie aged eleven, a serious and thoughtful little girl; Mary aged seven; to baby Jessie, now a three-year-old toddler. This was a houseful, a handful, and a worry for a doting father determined to give his children the best. Savannah was seething: streets filled with soldiers, prostitutes, carpetbaggers, and scalawags, freed blacks dressed in finery, walking the sidewalks and riding in carriages. It was teeming and dangerous.

A most revealing letter was written in the winter of 1866, shortly after William Henry's death, by a cousin, Mary Elliott, widow of Robert Habersham Elliott. The recipient was Eliza Stiles, wife of Henry Stiles, Jr., at Etowah Cliffs. This letter indicates that already the green-eyed serpent of envy had commenced to sour the sweetness of family relations. In England, Hattie and Amy had spent much of their childhood at boarding schools learning to be proper young English ladies. To our twenty-first-century sensibilities the practice of sending one's children to boarding school at a very young age appears barbaric. It was, in fact, a most normal and regular occurrence, and much of the literature of the nineteenth century reflected the habit of upper and middle class British colonials sending their sons and daughters back to England away from the rigors and hardships of imperial existence. Mary Elliott writes:

> Amy keeps the house [meaning Lafayette Square] and is pleased with the power but both of them find it lamentably dull here, and I am not surprised, brought up as they have been I think it a very hard case for them to live here. I like Hatty, but Amy is supercilious and Mr. Low is constantly making foolish speeches about not allowing his daughters to associate with people here etc. which of course are repeated and exaggerated and it irritates those people who really have a pedigree which the Lows cannot boast of. They cannot endure their Hunter relations and speak of their old Granny and wonder how long she can last in a most disrespectful manner.[17].

The letter goes on in a distinctly catty vein:

> Mr. Low had provided them with handsome clothes but they wear them badly, velvet jackets are their plainest garments and you know

how ill fine clothes look when worn to breakfast and at all times. Soiled cuffs and gloves for visiting and ruched poplins for the promenade. I was quite tired of their lavender poplins, which they wear all the time and the most enormous train hoops I ever saw. They are very ungrateful and speak such funny funny English. I catch myself all the time wanting to laugh at or imitate them.

Under the circumstances of the privations and perceived humiliations Savannah ladies were laboring under—being forced to make preserves to sell to the Yankee occupiers to put food on their own tables—it is perhaps understandable that envy of cousins with many more obvious options would be the order of the day. It is also fully understandable that Andrew Low would see no future for his family in immediate postwar Savannah.

Postwar Reconstruction

For the merchants matters had commenced to improve. Savannah's surrender to General Sherman had been a most revealing episode embodying the pragmatic nature of the people who managed her welfare. At the end of hostilities Georgia was in a deplorable state; the war had brought ruin to thousands of her people and she had suffered widespread destruction of all kinds, including hundreds of miles of railroads. Industry was greatly demoralized, but the men in charge of commerce were not the kind to sit around weeping and wailing and gnashing their teeth—at least not in public. Andrew Low was amongst those practical persons, and during the year he had set about reorganizing, rebuilding, and reconstructing his own life.

In his official report on his campaign in Georgia (1865) General Sherman stated: "I estimate the damage done to the state of Georgia at one hundred million dollars—twenty million of which is insured to our advantage, the remainder being simply waste and destruction." Upon the close of the war the entire state had been brought under military rule, and federal officers were stationed in every city to enforce the restrictions placed upon the people. Georgians were soon to witness former slaves in high places and Negro soldiers in the ranks of the federal military organizations stationed in the state to enforce martial law. A curfew law was established in Savannah, and people coming into and leaving the city were required to show their military passes. Early in the year, "what to do with the defeated insurrectionists states" had become a provocative question in Washington, and the whole South was nervously watching developments in Congress bearing upon this issue.

By 1866 rampant radicalism was all but destroying the Union. Although the hostilities officially ceased in April of 1865, the status of the conquered states had not yet been determined. It seems the government had not thought that far ahead—what to do when the war was won! The question as to whether the seceded states were in the Union or not was still being hotly debated in Washington, and there were those who were determined to wreak malevolent vengeance upon the South. Some in Congress advocated treating the vanquished Confederate States as so many territories, with abridged political rights, their goal to establish Negro dominance in the South and to impose permanent military rule upon the Southern states. Lincoln's Tennessean Vice-President, now President Johnson, was staunchly opposed to the radicalism in Congress. He had a different philosophy and wished to deal himself with the "insurrectionary" states and to "reconstruct" them on what he considered a more equitable basis, which included returning confiscated land to its previous owners and appointing former secessionist leaders to powerful local state positions.

In opposition to this point of view, the Radicals in Washington, led by Thaddeus Stevens of Pennsylvania and Charles Sumner of Massachusetts, pushed through a series of laws designed to protect and expand the rights of freed slaves. Southern states were compelled to dissolve the all-white governments elected and start again, to write state constitutions that guaranteed the rights of all their citizens, including the right to vote. The government sent in federal troops to impose the laws on reluctant constituencies. It was obvious that the peace would be as contentious as the war.

Before the year was out Georgia was obliged to execute a new state constitution in conformity with the tenets laid down by the federal government. This was required of all seceded states as a pre-requisite to reinstatement in the Union. This instrument legally abolished slavery in Georgia, which in essence was already an accomplished fact. As a result of the war, Georgia had lost her slaves valued at $3,000,000,000. By the freeing of the Negroes, her whole economic system, as with all the slave-holding states, had been overturned. Georgians were immediately concerned with an urgent labor problem growing out of the new status of the black and what many of them viewed as his "irresponsibility consequent upon his unaccustomed freedom."

Their response was to promote immigration. Societies were organized for the purpose of encouraging emigrants from Ireland and Sweden and other European countries, which, in effect, relieved the dearth of laborers in Savannah and Georgia in general, by an influx of white immigrants anxious to receive the promised benefits of a worker shortage.

The war was over and Northeastern industrialists were intent on reconstructing the nation to their own benefit. Andrew Low proved during his imprisonment that he still had valuable and extensive connections in the New York/Boston/Philadelphia axis, and would not have been sitting on his hands during this active early period of reconstruction. Arthur Link in *The American Epoch* writes, "the business classes had executed a bloodless revolution. They had ... wrested control of the political institutions from an agrarian majority, and changed the character, but not the forms, of representative government in the United States." With the absence of any input from Southern states, the Northeast set out to make colonial dependencies of the conquered South.

President Johnson finally issued his long-delayed Peace Proclamation, which, in effect, lifted certain hampering limitations from the Southern states, thereby stimulating commerce. Georgia particularly benefited from this loosening of restrictions. The rehabilitation of her transportation system, so terribly disrupted during the war, was begun. The Atlantic and Gulf Railroad was promptly put in order, and the Central Railroad was re-laid "at the rate of a mile a day." Also, the work of removing the gunboats and other vessels sunk during the war by the Confederate authorities to obstruct the channel below the city, was embarked on with dispatch for the purpose of facilitating river traffic. In anticipation of increasingly large cotton and lumber shipments through Savannah, several steamship lines were established between the city and Northern ports.

Of more interest locally was the question of whether the city was to have her first street railways. True to form as an innovator, one of the investors and movers of this form of transportation was Andrew Low, despite much opposition by vociferous objectors that found expression in the newspapers. In line with his lifelong understanding that transportation is the key to progress, he once more shows he fully comprehends the new world he now inhabits. May 1867:

> The undersigned Commissioners, having accepted from the City the Charter of 'The Savannah Street Railway Company' will open its books for subscription at the Exchange Long Room from 10.a.m. to 1. p.m. on the 20th of this month and will keep them open for ten days thereafter, during hours named above. Shares $50:00 each; ten percent must be paid at time of subscription. Andrew Low, Edward Padelford, Henry Brigham, Jacob Waldburg, John Stoddard, John L. Villalonga, Frederick W. Sims.

In November 1867 Savannahians witnessed Negro voters at the polls for the first time. In an editorial the local Savannah newspaper depicted the event as a burlesque, and stated: "As an election, the affair lacked one essential element—opposition. The Negroes had it all their own way, and, though they have had a taste of that invaluable privilege the right of suffrage, they have yet to learn what an election is. So far, then the forced Negro suffrage in the South is a nullity."

One antidote to the increased threat of a black power base was the formation of white supremacist groups. The best known was the Ku Klux Klan, which came into being at this time. It had its origins in Tennessee and was at first a social club, but its members soon discovered that the fearsome regalia resembling white-sheeted medieval inquisitionists that they wore on their nocturnal depredations terrified the black population. This secret order then spread rapidly over the South. Its actions turned to what they called "corrective measures against emboldened blacks and scalawags wherever they showed a disposition to dominate local affairs," measures that included shooting, lynching, and cross burning. Around Savannah this function was reserved to the rifle-and-gun clubs. During the previous two years, "Black Codes" of differing degrees of draconian severity were imposed in every Southern state governing permissible conduct by the emancipated African. Because slavery had been abolished this did not mean that local power structures believed that blacks were ready for or deserving of equality with whites.

Removal to Leamington Spa

Considering the turbulence caused by the uncertainty of reconstruction, it is now that Andrew Low made the decision to remove his entire family from Savannah. He would certainly have seen the writing on his particular wall and fully understood that with five daughters to marry off and one son to educate as heir to his own still substantial fortune. Finding his daughters suitable husbands would be far more likely in England than in the impoverished South, where an entire generation of the cream of Southern manhood lay "moldering in the grave."

The records show that Andrew Low removed his entire family to Leamington Spa, in the County of Warwickshire, in September 1867. Life for the two older Low girls began again in a more familiar setting, and the four younger children were brought up as English gentry in what their father viewed as a more suitable milieu. The Savannah records never reflected this reality, and it certainly accounts for emotions vocalized later on by relatives. The conventional wisdom had always had it that the Low family moved to England almost a decade later. This earlier move creates a completely different viewpoint of how Mary Cowper Stiles Low's children formed their characters and what their determining influences were in childhood and influenced subsequent marriages.

It was no wonder that the envy expressed by the cousins left in Savannah festered. The Low girls were swanning it around with the elite of England while in the South conditions were still deplorable. The girls lived with governesses and tutors in the upper-class spa town of Leamington, patronized by royalty, while in Bartow County and Savannah the Stiles

Andrew Low's children, ca. 1868: Hattie, Jessie, Mary, Katie, Willie, and Amy. *Courtesy The National Society of The Colonial Dames of America in the State of Georgia.*

families suffered through the hardships of Reconstruction and what they considered the intolerable attitudes of the Yankee carpetbaggers and upwardly mobile blacks.

Life at Etowah Cliffs—Death of Eliza Stiles

During their lifetime William Henry and Eliza Stiles, through good times and bad, when apart had written to each other regularly, sometimes on a daily basis. After he died one of the few firsthand accounts, albeit from hindsight memory of a small child, is the memoir of granddaughter Caroline Cowper Stiles Lovell, who writes that her grandmother had been incapacitated for some time before her death: "In spite of her powerful character Grandma Stiles was not much more than a shade to me. Her bedroom at the Cliffs was the delightful southeastern room downstairs . . . there were twin beds placed near enough for Grandmother and Grandfather to hold hands. . . . Grandmother was an invalid in her last years."

Her Low grandchildren had moved to England. Robert and Henry were

Andrew Low, ca. 1870. *Courtesy The National Society of The Colonial Dames of America in the State of Georgia.*

trying to keep the family plantation afloat. The life had gone out of Eliza and in December 20, 1867, on the same anniversary as the fall of Savannah in 1864 and the death of William in 1865, Eliza Mackay Stiles died in her much-loved Etowah Cliffs, and was buried without her husband under the magnolia tree on the edge of her garden. Her grave, despite the many losses during the war, was only the second one in the family graveyard.

Caroline writes about her grandmother's death: "I saw her lying on the couch beside the window. Her head was lifted, her high nose profile clearly out against the light, and her face as white as the handkerchief bound under her chin." She was fifty-eight years old.

The federal military authority continued until August 3, 1868, when it was announced that "the military authority, known as the Reconstruction Acts, hereby terminates in the State of Georgia, and everything appertaining to government of said State is transferred to the proper civil officers." Thus Georgia became again, nominally at least, a sovereign state and two years after that, in 1870, Georgia was readmitted to the Union.

Part VI

Savannah–Leamington, 1867–1932

18

The English Squire, 1867–1883

By 1867 Andrew Low had firmly established his family in upper-crust Victorian England, living in rented mansions as was the norm. During the next decade he continued to conduct a more limited business on both continents—retaining his Savannah directorships as an American businessman, maintaining his Liverpool factorage business, and living the life of an English squire.[1] Before Andrew Low dissolved his primary Savannah affairs, he forgave the debt owed by the estate of William Henry Stiles in favor of his sons, Henry and Robert, an act of compassion that is documented in correspondence in the Stiles family collections. This clearly showed that he retained a sense of moral allegiance to the family of his wife, Mary Cowper Stiles.

Leamington Spa

Lamintone, meaning a farm, on the River Leam first appears in the public record almost a millennium ago when it was listed in the Domesday Book published in 1086, an account of the England of those times packed to bursting with facts about eleventh-century England and its inhabitants. By the time Andrew Low made the decision to relocate his family, Leamington was one of the recognized Regency and Victorian spa towns, like Cheltenham, Bath, and Brighton, that was entitled to call itself "Royal" for the patronage of the royal entourage.

The fashion for taking the spa waters goes back in England to the early 1600's. Leamington prospered because of the first recorded benefit in 1491 of the mineral salts spring at Leamington Priors that fed the waters from its location in north Warwickshire. The original spring lay on property owned by the Earl of Aylesford, and the first well house was built over the spring in 1804. Eventually seven saline springs were discovered; in 1814 a pump room was erected to produce the waters for public use; and by 1860, when the owner of the baths decided to sell the building and grounds for building plots, a Royal Leamington Spa Pump Room Association was formed. Today the grounds are gorgeous manicured public gardens right across from the Pump Room, now a heavily patronized center for tourist information and local studies, and a public library.

Success of the baths drew visitors in abundance and accounted for the proliferation of everything from boardinghouse up to fully furnished grand mansions. This invasion led to a wide variety of entertainment to keep the visitors content, ranging from traveling players to pleasure gardens, theaters, gaming rooms, libraries, picture galleries, concerts, and for the well-to-do and aristocracy a series of fancy balls both charity and private. One would imagine one needed to take a certain amount of care in deciding where to be seen and where not to be seen for maximum exposure. Many Americans appeared to both have visited and lived there, including the famed American author Nathaniel Hawthorne, who stayed there for a time in the 1850's and wrote extensively of its genteel pleasures saying, "such a Paradise as the English only know how to make out of any given flat piece of land."[2]

William Makepeace Thackeray, an acquaintance of Andrew Low's, is reported—in one of the books sold now to tourists—to have stayed there.[3] Thackeray is best known for his satirical and moralistic studies of upper and middle class England, and it is quite possible that originally it was from Thackeray that Andrew learned of the social suitability of Leamington Spa as a safe haven for his family of daughters. Certainly a familiarity with such heroines as Becky Sharp in his well-favored novel *Vanity Fair* would have been as good a guide as any to the pitfalls and traps inherent in the manners, mores, and morals of British society.

Another reason for living in Leamington by the latter third of the nineteenth century was the increasing ease of rail transportation built in the 1840's. Competition from seaside resorts and continental spas gradually drained the transient population away and increased the reputation of Leamington as a fashionable residential town. Here many socially acceptable former colonial civil servants along with naval and army officers came to retire, attracted by the plentiful supply of maids, cooks, and butlers and large houses now cheap to buy or rent. Leamington Spa was a favorite vacation spot for Americans supportive of the Confederate cause during the Civil War, including Mr. and Mrs. Thomas Gholson, some of Hugh Stiles Golson's relatives.[4]

The town continued to grow and New Town, which included fashionable Clarendon Square at the north end of the Parade, became the center. The result was that a number of people of influence sought either to build or to reside there in fine mansions with stables for horses and coaches and ample room for servants. The local newspaper, *The Warwickshire*

Observer and Beck's List of Visitors, lists their comings and goings under the heading "Nobility, Gentry and Clergy."

The Lows first appear in these pages in the September 26, 1867, edition, residing at 31 Clarendon Square. This was a smaller townhouse running along the top end of the square. A year later they moved to a much larger house on the side of the park at 42 Clarendon Square, details of which were listed when it came on the market following their move around the corner to Beauchamp Hall in 1884.[5] These substantial town homes lining the sides of elegant squares are still spectacular, but now broken up into more manageable spaces for modern realities, and the comparison to Savannah's equally elegant layout is inescapable. As the town continued to grow, many churches grew alongside. It is to be expected that the Lows would have attended the Episcopal Chapel, Christ Church, erected in 1825, which stood at the north end of the Parade in Beauchamp Square, adjacent to where they lived in Clarendon Square.[6]

There were of course problems that affect all growing towns, such as sewage, but nothing compared with the conditions in Savannah, Georgia. Leamington was an infinitely healthier and safer location to bring up five daughters than postwar Savannah, embroiled in the throes of a brutal reconstruction period; and it seems even the schools were excellent although the 1871 Census indicates the presence of a governess in the Low household. It is quite probable that following the marriages of the two eldest sisters the younger girls would all have attended boarding schools.[7]

Royalty continued to honor Leamington with its presence throughout the nineteenth century. An examination of the attendance at hunt balls, charity balls, and meets of the Warwickshire hounds clearly indicates the presence in the neighborhood of an impressive selection of potential suitors ranging from earls and baronets all the way down to more humble captains and majors in acceptable regiments such as the Grenadier Guards, or lieutenants in the Royal Navy. Many of these men had good solid English names going back generations, often younger sons with breeding but lacking the wherewithal to support a lifestyle in which they had been raised. If his major motivation was to secure good marriages for his five daughters, who it certainly would be known had prospects as heiresses in their own right, Andrew Low made an excellent choice; the field was both crowded and respectable despite the fact that they were Americans.

Social Mores and Manners

The complex code of conduct of society during the Victorian and Edwardian eras was a thicket of unwritten taboos and prescriptions that provided fertile fields for purveyors of etiquette manuals, romance novelists, and satirists, and to fully appreciate the pecking order could take decades.

Even Prince Albert of Saxe-Coburg, Queen Victoria's beloved German consort, was never totally accepted in British Society—not because of his pedigree, but because he was a foreigner. British aristocracy and landed gentry were pastoral people, not to be confused with the bucolic or rural. They were emotionally involved with their land and their stately homes, even though an impartial observer could be excused for supposing that they gave the impression of being more attached to their horses and dogs than to their children. New titles did not impress the county set; it was family history that counted, but money certainly oiled the wheels of acceptance and it did not matter much if the money came as dollars derived from commerce.

By the time the Lows arrived, Warwickshire had become a hub for an assemblage of hangers-on around royalty, especially those who ran with a fast set that swirled around Edward, the Prince of Wales, and the heir to the throne. Since the death of his father Prince Albert from typhoid fever in 1861, Queen Victoria had been prostrate with grief, unfairly laying some of the blame on her eldest son and allowing him few responsibilities of state. Consequently, despite his happy marriage to Princess Alexandra of Denmark, his energies soon turned toward debauchery and over-indulgence, a lifetime obsession with rich food, horses, and frequent indiscretions with married women and actresses.

Leamington was close enough to London, and yet far enough away so that reckless behavior could be overlooked, an ideal place for a royal personage to meet his mistress, married perhaps to a close friend, at a stately home shooting or weekend party. A major scandal in Warwickshire embroiled the royal personage when in 1869 Sir Charles Mordaunt, owner of nearby Walton Hall in Wellesbourne, filed a petition of divorce against Harriett Moncreiffe, his young wife, citing two of the Prince's close companions. She, however, confessed to having had sexual relations with the Prince of Wales himself, an act that signed her certificate of excommunication from respectable society. It did not really matter much what one did as long as one never admitted to indiscretion. Telling tales was to court social ostracism, and for washing one's dirty linen in public, the punishment was banishment.[8]

January 18, 1868, the *Royal Leamington Spa Courier* publishes a detailed account of the Warneford Hospital Charity Ball. "Miss Low" was one of the attendees. This ball was the must-attend event of the winter social scene, and this Miss Low would have been the eldest daughter Amy, enjoying her first season out and about in Leamington Society. The ball was held under the patronage of the Right Hon. Lord and Lady Leigh,[9] Right Hon. The Earl and Countess of Warwick, the Right Hon. The Earl and Countess of Aylesford, the Right Hon. Lord and Lady Willoughby de

Broke, Sir Charles Mordaunt, Bart. M.P. and Lady Mordaunt—the crème de la crème of Warwickshire aristocracy. The Lows had been in residence about four months, and from that time on at most society events the two eldest Misses Low, daughters of Sarah Cecil Hunter Low, are shown in attendance.

Population censuses are one way of tracing individuals whereabouts on a specific day at a specific time although if a person happens not to be actually in the home when the census taker details the information he or she will not appear. The 1871 Leamington Census shows residing at 42 Clarendon Square: "Harriet Low, age 22, head of family; Catherine Low, age fifteen, scholar; Mary Low, age twelve, scholar; William Low, brother, age ten, scholar; Jessie, age eight, scholar."

They are all listed as Americans, which of course they were by birth. In addition there is an Anne A. Blake listed as governess, Mary McCain as nurse domestic; Eliza Hemmitt, cook; Caroline Parsons, parlor maid; Amelia Jiffs, housemaid; Mary Arum, kitchen maid; and James Arnsley, butler. All the domestic help are from nearby towns or counties and all would be English, except for the nurse who was from either Ireland or Scotland.[10]

Andrew Low is not in residence, and an examination of the Savannah 1870 Census shows him present in his own home. This census taken during a period of considerable turmoil was the first official one following the end of both the Civil War and the Emancipation Proclamation, and would have been the first time that former slaves would have been actually named, instead of being listed merely by age, gender, and racial classification. There were no official records naming slaves prior to emancipation. In some instances, names and relationships can be traced through cemetery records, plantation ledgers, and family papers. The effort to clarify the status of Andrew Low's former slaves and servants remains imprecise as neither Tom nor Mosianna Milledge is recorded as resident at Abercorn Street at that time.[11]

The reason Amy Low is not listed in the English census is simple. By 1871 Andrew Low's decision to remove his family to England paid off when his eldest daughter made an excellent marriage to a royal naval officer on a career fast track. The Savannah, London, and Liverpool newspapers announced the match in the society pages as was normal: one of them, the *Liverpool Mercury*, on July 21, 1871, announced: "Married on June 22nd, at St. James Church, Piccadilly, London, by the Rev. Robinson Duckworth, MA, chaplain in ordinary to the Queen, Lieut. Harry Tremenheere Grenfell, RN. Youngest son of late Admiral John Pascoe Grenfell, to Amy, eldest daughter of Andrew Low, Esq. of Savannah."

The Duckworth name had been linked to that of the Low merchant

Mosianna and Tom Milledge, ca. 1880. Tom was purchased by Andrew Low & Company from slave trader Wylly Woodbridge. He became Andrew Low's butler and caretaker of the Lafayette Square property. Mosianna cooked for Willie and Daisy Low in Savannah and abroad. She invested her income by building rental property in the Beach Institute neighborhood. *Courtesy The National Society of The Colonial Dames of America in the State of Georgia.*

enterprise for many years in Liverpool, and that connection could have been the point of confluence. Two years later his second daughter, Hattie, also married well, to an army officer. That marriage also took place in fashionable St. James Church in Piccadilly, London, officiated by the Queen's chaplain. That notice read:

> 1873, August 2nd:—Married at St. James' Church, Piccadilly, by the Rev. Robinson Duckworth, M.A. Vicar of St. Mark's, St. John's Wood, assisted by Rev. Charles C. Wood, Rector of Broxholme, Lin-

> coln, George Coke Robertson of Nottinghamshire and Broxholme, Lincolnshire, Major 17th Lancers, Harriet Anne, second daughter of Andrew Low, Esq., of Savannah, Georgia, USA.

Later on, a Savannah diary reveals that Major Robertson had an income of ten thousand pounds annually, a not inconsiderable sum for the times, as well as a respectable country estate comprising Widmerpool Hall in Nottinghamshire, and a village of seven farms and about thirty cottages.[12] The older Low girls had arrived in English society.

The four children of Mary Cowper were essentially brought up as English gentry from their earliest formative years, and there is no record that their father ever became a naturalized American citizen—although he did take the mandatory oath of allegiance to the United States following the end of the Civil War. They were probably also legally British despite having an American mother and having been born in America. Whether they were viewed as American in society in England is unclear, although that remained the Savannah conventional wisdom, but probable as the appellation would have brought more social cachet than their origins as the offspring of a Scottish-born Liverpool merchant.

Andrew Low's only son and presumptive heir, Willie, still a very small child at the death of his mother in 1863, viewed his elder half-sister, Amy, more as his mother than his sister. He was educated at the proper English public school establishments for a gentleman, an education that left him singularly well equipped to run with the horses and hunt with the hounds of late Victorian early Edwardian society, gentry and nobility alike, but not much else.

As the census shows him being tutored at home in 1871, it is likely that he went to the prep school Winchester following Amy's marriage. Winchester College, founded by William of Wykeham in 1382, serves as the model for the great public schools of England.[13] As he apparently never served an apprenticeship such as his father had in the Andrew Low Company, either he was not given an opportunity to achieve the skills required to navigate the river of commerce or his father did not consider commerce his destiny or vocation.

The fact that Andrew Low chose to live in the county of Warwickshire instead of the mercantile centers of the north is revealing. Liverpool had always been known as a commercial center where a merchant factor could become a gentleman by virtue of success, while adjacent Manchester was renowned as a thriving industrial center where its spinning and weaving textile mill owners were considered rougher men who worked with their hands. In Victorian England, although immensely profitable, neither significant industrial hub had the kind of social cachet that the shires of Warwickshire, Gloucestershire, Oxfordshire, and Northamptonshire boasted. Here was where the landed gentry had their country estates, mostly rented homes for the outlanders, while maintaining town houses in the fashionable quarters of St. James, Eaton, Grosvenor, and Sloane squares in London.

Low's friend and coconspirator, James Dunwoody Bulloch, was still residing in Liverpool, having been refused reentry to the United States after the war. This was because of his notorious success building ships in Liverpool shipyards despite Britain's supposed neutrality, running the Yankee blockade, and destroying Union shipping. In 1873 the United States government demanded that the British government should pay compensation for the damage caused by these Confederate warships.

This was known as the *Alabama* claim for the ship dubbed by her hull number #290 by Thomas Dudley, the U.S. Consul in Liverpool—she was actually named *Enrica*. In her Bulloch slipped down the River Mersey from Laird's Birkenhead shipyard on July 29, 1862 under the collective noses of England and America's secret agents and sailed for the Azores, where she was met by two Confederate supply ships, commissioned, and renamed the *Alabama*. The CSS *Alabama* would go on to sink more U.S. merchant ships than any other warship before or since. She, together with the *Florida* and *Shenandoah*, had accounted for half the total number of Union vessels captured or destroyed. The result was that the British wound up paying over three million pounds in compensation for allowing the Confederate government to build and purchase the ships in English ports.[14]

Today the original dry dock where the *Alabama* was built is preserved by order of English Heritage and remains part of the strange phenomena whereby Britain lays claim to the American Civil War as a "very British affair." This claim partially rests on the preponderance of people of British descent that fought on both sides, wearing both the gray and the blue, and interest in the war remains almost as strong in Britain today as it does in America. Many a family can lay claim to have made the ultimate sacrifice of one of their own forebears.[15] Part of today's myth for those who continue to preserve the memory of "When Liverpool Was Dixie," is that James Dunwoody Bulloch lies in a foreign field, forgotten by most of his countrymen, but honored by enthusiasts of Civil War history. The name of the house his descendants lived in was "Roswell," and Bulloch's grave is in Smithdown Road Cemetery, Toxteth; Liverpool is a shrine to these aficionados.

Back to Business

Two of Andrew Low's first moves were to sever his partnership association with Charles Green and rebuild his wharves on the Savannah waterfront. The year after he removed his family to the watering holes of uppercrust society in rural England, he reshuffled his business partnerships, completing the task he had testified to in his testimony to get out of incarceration. After severing his official partnership with Charles Green, he took in as partner a former Confederate Army officer, Lieutenant James D. Hopkins. The company continued to operate as commission agents in both Savannah and Liverpool. His former partner was also rearranging his own transatlantic commerce by taking in as partners his own nephew and son, Josiah Green Low, Charles Green, Jr., of Savannah, and Alfred Dobell of Liverpool.[16]

Low continued to maintain his Savannah residence, in his frequent absences leaving the house on Lafayette Square in charge of the butler, Thomas Milledge.

Caroline Lovell, author of *Light of Other Days*, says that every year the Stiles children were taken to visit Mr. Andrew Low. She says that "the old man came back to Savannah every winter to attend to his affairs and must have had a dreary time alone in his big house."

She writes:

> Mr. Low had been very kind and generous to our family, and Aunt Kate and he were good friends . . . no house in the world will ever seem to me to be as grand as the Low's house. . . . We would be herded into the dining room at the back of the hall, where Uncle Low, like an old bear in his den, would be seated in semi-darkness, reading his paper beside the fire. He was a stout old gentleman, with light eyes, and a full reddish beard, and his voice was like a growl.

It is possible that the portrait painted when he was a slim handsome young man would have been hanging over the fireplace along with that of his beautiful wife, Mary Cowper, just as they hang today. Caroline Lovell's account gives an indication of the close relationship that always existed between Andrew Low and his former slave, the butler Tom Milledge: "Old Tom, Mr. Low's butler, who was as black as coal, was once taken to England by his master, and there he had a trying experience. He all but died of the cold, but what he minded much more was the constant quarrelling of the white maids for the honor of 'walking out' on his arm!"

Caroline was daughter of Robert Stiles, who was married to Margaret Wylly Couper. Her uncle, Henry Stiles, Jr., was married to Eliza Clifford Gordon. The memoirs recount that the Gordon grandchildren "lived a much more luxurious life than we did." After the war the two families lived together at Etowah Cliffs, perhaps with some degree of discomfort because by 1872 Robert had built a home for his own family nearby. He named it Malbone after their famous relative, the well-known miniature painter Edward Malbone, who was cousin to patriarch Robert Mackay.

Robert E. Lee Visits Andrew Low for the Last Time

In 1870 General Lee and his daughter Agnes stayed with Andrew Low. Since his West Point days he had been maybe suitor, but certainly friend, of Eliza Mackay Stiles and was very fond of her children. Accounts say he first stayed at the home of Alexander Lawton at the corner of York and Lincoln, but moved to Andrew Low's home for peace and quiet. General Lee, in a letter published in *Recollections and Letters of General Robert E. Lee* by his son Captain Robert E. Lee, writes to his wife on April 2:

> Yesterday, several gentlemen from Savannah met the train in which we came from Augusta—General Lawton, Mr. Andrew Lowe (sic), Mr. Hodgson etc. I found they had arranged amongst themselves about my sojourn, so I yielded at once, and after depositing Agnes at General Lawton's, I came off to Mr. Lowe's, where I am now domiciled. His house is partly dismantled and he is keeping house alone, so I have a very quiet time.

The daily newspaper announced on Tuesday, April 5, 1870:

> Our visitor—Yesterday morning it was rumored that our distinguished guest, General Robert E. Lee, would receive visitors from 12 p.m. to 3 o'clock p.m. at the residence of Andrew Low, Esq. on Lafayette Square, corner of Abercorn and Charlton Street. As soon as the fact was known, a large number of ladies and gentlemen, among the latter nearly all of our prominent citizens and several ex-officers of the federal army, who have made Savannah their home, repaired to the palatial residence of Mr. Low, to pay their respects to the most distinguished General of the latter half of the nineteenth century. General Lee received his numerous visitors in the parlor, each being introduced by General A. R. Lawton. The General received them with a cordial grasp of the hand and a kind "I am glad to see you."

The following day another posting in the Savannah *Daily News* gives a remarkable insight into the mind-set of the day when the mayor and the aldermen of Savannah paid their respects:

> The peculiar position which the Southern people occupy in the body politic forbade any open demonstration of respect and honor to the illustrious visitor, and his known feelings in reference to any outward demonstration of respect and veneration for an illustrious name, has prevented any general token in way of ceremony. . . . After an exchange of compliments, varied by a few pleasant remarks, in which were recalled the memories of past trials, and many thoughts and prayers, and a "God Bless you" the delegation took their leave.

> There was no politics, no reference to the past, excepting only as they allied themselves to the character and services of the distinguished patriot.[17]

There is an indication that General Lee was in declining health by then; and on April 12, accompanied by Andrew Low, he went by steamboat to Cumberland Island to visit his father's grave, and then went on to Florida, returning on April 25 to Savannah before returning to Virginia.[18] He writes:

> Mr. Andrew Lowe [sic] was so kind as to go with us the whole way, thinking Agnes and I were unable to take care of ourselves . . . we have returned to our old quarters, Agnes to the Lawton's and I to Lowe s. We shall remain here a week.

Six months later, the revered Southern Civil War hero was dead. The notice in the Savannah newspaper read: "General Robert E. Lee. Died, October 12, 1870. Born January 19th, 1807." He was honored in Savannah by Christ Church as a "communicant." His widow, Mary Custis Lee, writes in a letter to Aunt Kate Mackay in Savannah that Andrew Low had been extremely kind to the Lee family and mentions that Low had given Robert E. Lee photographs of all his family during the visit which was his last.

> I was much interested in the beautiful photographs which Mr. Low gave to the General of all his children, especially of dear Mary. Who could ever have thought that one so endowed with thoughts and activity should so soon have been called away. I heard through my friend Annie Leigh of your visit to them in Leamington. Remember me to Mr. Low of whose kindness and hospitality both Agnes and her father spoke frequently.[19]

Another link was severed.

Andrew Low Gets His Cotton Back

There were many loose ends caused by the war that had to be cleared up, and it speaks to the character of Andrew Low that he showed himself fully prepared to fight for his rights and good name even if the amounts involved were relatively minor and the plaintiff was infinitely more powerful with awesome punitive powers. In 1871 the case of the *United States* v. *Andrew Low and Charles Green* came to the attention of the public; the brief read: "The United States seeks to recover $1,360:54 amount of duties on goods stored with customs officials and for which each defendant gave bond on December 1, 1860." The defendants produced the cancelled bond, showing that the goods were withdrawn and the duties paid on August 30, 1861.

They claimed with some legal audacity that on August 30, 1861, there was no United States government in Savannah. At the time the goods were delivered to the defendants, Low and Green, they were in the possession of the Confederate States. If the duties had not been paid they would have been sold. The United States only resumed their authority over the customhouse about December 22, 1864. The execution of the bond is not denied, but the government's position was that the obligation of the bond assumed by its makers meant that they owed duties to the United States, that this obligation had not yet been met, and nothing but their payments could discharge the bond. The amount of the duties, $1,360.54, were to be paid in gold with interest from December 22, 1864, the date when the United States received possession of port and customhouse, to be paid in currency. The courts did not buy the argument and the government lost that round. On December 4 the verdict came down for the defendants Charles Green and Andrew Low.

Cotton was still King! The war was fought over cotton and so it seems was the peace going to be.The *Savannah Morning News*, May 27, 1873::

> Washington, the court of claims has rendered the following judgments for cotton seized by General Sherman's forces at the time of the capture of Savannah, and sold by the United States. In favor of William Battersby $87,014; In favor of William Battersby & Andrew Low, $3,940: in favor of William Battersby and Octavus Cohen, $7, 881; in favor of William Battersby executor of Thomas Metcalf, $485,242; the latter being the largest single judgment ever rendered by the Court of Claims. Battersby is an alien subject of Great Britain, who has resided thirty years in Savannah; the other parties are citizens of Georgia. The cotton claim of William Miller, another British subject, was dismissed on the grounds that the cotton for which he sued was purchased by him outside of the Union lines, and in violation of the regulations then in force.

Judgment was rendered for $155,534 in favor of Charles Green of Savannah, who is a subject of Great Britain. The main question in this case was whether an alien domiciled during the rebellion within the insurrectionary states could be guilty of the crime of treason against the United States. The court of claims, following a decision of the United States Supreme Court at the last term, decides this question affirmatively, but also holds the same decision that aliens guilty of treason by failing to observe their obligations of qualified allegiance were included in and pardoned by the President's amnesty proclamation.

It appears the former partners in crime were home free! Business was changing, and in keeping with the uncanny ability the Andrew Low Company in all its incarnations had demonstrated in keeping abreast of current times, the firm moved into new territory once again. A notice in the Savannah newspaper informs us that:

> 1872, January 1st, The steamship "Darien", the pioneer of a line of passenger and freight ships which from this date will make direct trips to and from Savannah and Liverpool, was cleared yesterday by Messrs Andrew Low & Co for Liverpool. We expect much of the southern travel which heretofore went to Europe via Northern ports will be re-directed to this line.

Liverpool was still the major gateway in Great Britain for immigration to America; and Liverpool's trade directory, *Gore's Advertiser*, listed in its annual events calendar that "in 1872 the month of March saw 14,874 people emigrate, carried in 58 ships." Passenger travel was a lucrative business carrying thousands of Irish to rebuild postwar America, competing for the labor of four million freed blacks in the North and in the South. This heritage is evident in Savannah's annual St. Patrick's Day mayhem.

On July 29, 1872, Edward Anderson, another friend of longstanding, now mayor of Savannah, writes in his diary of a riot caused by a few Negroes using seats on a streetcar reserved for whites. Andrew Low had been one of the original subscribers to the much opposed streetcar company.[20]

Andrew Low, now sixty years old, ended a three-quarter-century tradition. On September 2, 1872, the Savannah newspaper announced to the world: "Andrew Low and Co partnership dissolved and new company formed to be known as Hopkins and Wood. John D. Hopkins, Andrew Low, Savannah; and James Torrance Wood, John Wood, Liverpool, England. Andrew Low having retired from Isaac, Low & Co in Liverpool announced the conditions in which Low put up $100,000 in gold as capital."

Three years later that partnership also dissolved on account of the death of the senior partner, John D. Hopkins, and continued under a new name. Two years after that, Andrew Low finally shut up shop in Liverpool. The ball was finally over, the last waltz played. The dancers went home.

That is the record of the wind-down of Isaac Low & Company, with offices in Liverpool, New York, and various manifestations of the Andrew Low Company in Savannah. Liverpool's *Gore's Advertiser* had carried the existence of the Isaac Low Company in its pages every year and every edition from 1819, more than seventy-five years. The 1877 issue carried the last entry of Isaac Low & Company in Liverpool, still at the Apsley Building, 4 Oldhall Street, near the Cotton Exchange. Keeping his directorships in Savannah, Andrew Low retired to live the life of an English squire.

Another mystery was finally cleared up when in the *Savannah Morning News*, May 26, 1876, announced: "Captain John Low, formerly of Savannah, died at Griffin, Ga. on the 24th inst, in the 93rd year of his age. His friends and acquaintances are respectfully invited to attend the funeral services at Laurel Grove Cemetery, at 8.0. clock this (Friday) morning."

This was John Low, British alien and river pilot prominent in the period of the War of 1812, and no relation to either Andrew Lows. The age given would make him born in 1783, and that is where the information probably came from in the "Who's Who" in *Children of Pride* that for many years caused the confusion about who Andrew Low's father was—an error that still appears to be inscribed in the fragmented story of Savannah's past.

Further Tragedy and Turmoil

In 1874 the Stiles family suffered another terminal blow. Robert Mackay Stiles was killed in a freak buggy accident in Cartersville when his conveyance struck a large rock on the country road returning to Malbone after a day spent celebrating with friends in town. He was thrown out, struck his head, and never recovered consciousness. He died of concussion of the brain a few hours later. He was only thirty-eight years old and left a grieving widow and eight children. His death was an unsustainable blow to his loving Aunt Sarah, and she went into a decline from which she had no strength to recover and died the following year.[21] Caroline Lovell writes: "Aunt Sarah had been failing ever since father's death, and when the next winter came, Aunt Kate and herself went down to Savannah alone, and there Aunt Sarah died in her garret room and was buried in the family lot in Laurel Grove Cemetery."

That winter Andrew Low deemed it appropriate to bring his daughters Katie and Mary to Savannah for a visit. They had finished school in London, and he decided to bring them over to see their American relatives. In her book written from memory, Cousin Caroline Lovell recalls their visit to Etowah Cliffs in Bartow County.[22] This description represents the best, in fact the only, physical description of the girls at this age. It also depicts vividly the submerged sense of envy regarding their obvious wealth and freedom. The family of Andrew Low was not suffering the deprivations of the post–Civil War South; they were attending expensive schools, patronizing exclusive dressmakers, and being presented to Queen Victoria at court. This envy only seems to have increased in Savannah chronicles as the years progressed.

> Katie was small, with a trim figure, a pretty piquant face, dark eyes and hair, and the most brilliant color we had ever seen. Mary was tall and graceful, with irregular features, amber eyes, a lovely mouth, with the enchanting smile that now and then appears in the Stiles family, and you felt at once her unusual personal charm. ... Everything they said, everything they did, everything they wore interested us deeply. We had never seen such beautiful underclothes

Mary Cowper Low's children, ca. 1874, when they visited Savannah. Left to right, Willie, Mary, Katie, and Jessie. *Courtesy The National Society of The Colonial Dames of America in the State of Georgia.*

> before, or sheer lacy nightgowns, or dozens of different kinds of boots and slippers . . . I had never had but one pair of shoes at a time in my life! The girls brought up their own port and claret, and to my surprise drank tumblers of it at dinner, which perhaps helped them enjoy our simple fare. . . . While the girls did not wear evening dresses at night, they always dressed in pretty gowns, which to our amazement, were put on by their maid, a nice cheerful white girl. She was called by her surname. Katie had already come out in London society and Mary was to come out the following June, and to be presented at court. She pinned a tablecloth to her dress as a train and showed us how she would approach Queen Victoria, making a deep curtsey, kiss her hand and back gracefully out of her presence.

When the Low girls left, they sent a trunk full of clothes for the Stiles children and from then on often visited in the winter times. Caroline wistfully recalls how exciting it was to hear of hunt balls, of theaters and operas, and of travels on the Continent and how to them still struggling in postwar Georgia the Low girls appeared to be rolling in wealth, wealth which she admits they shared generously with their cousins. Caroline always retained deep feelings of affection for her Low cousins and writes:

> Never, in spite of all the many sorrows that have come to them, as they come to all, have they forgotten their American cousins, or ceased to care for them. Dear Katie, most wonderful of all, whose entire life was spent in unselfish service for others; lovely, sweet, charming Mary; and later on, Willie and Jessie, so handsome and attractive; they came into our lives at a time when we felt the glamour of romance, and in memory they will always remain young and beautiful, loving and generous.

Tragedy struck again at the Stiles family, as recorded in Caroline Lovell's memoir. Once again, Henry Stiles is almost mortally wounded.

> Baltimore was a ferocious Jersey bull, of whom everybody but Uncle Henry was afraid of. Told that the bull had broken out of his pen and was eating a pile of shucked corn in the lot, Uncle Henry went down and found a number of the renters on the outside of the fence, none of them daring to go in and drive the animal away. Uncle Henry walked into the lot, and struck the bull on the flank with his hand, ordering it off. The animal turned away sullenly, then, as Uncle Henry walked back to the gate, swung around, lowered his head, and rushing at him, tossed him in the air, then, as he fell, gored him savagely in the thigh . . . the wound in the leg had to be sewn up. . . . it is quite a deep gash, and the main artery came within a hair's breadth of being cut.

Sadly, this time he was not so lucky. It was thought that the wound caused the terrible internal injury sustained during the war to reopen. His strength still sapped by this war trauma, he had not the stamina to survive a second deep wound, and died a violent death while in his prime, at the age of forty-five. The gods of war claimed the eldest Stiles son.[23] As for Baltimore, he was sold in exile to Texas, where he was blinded.

Henry's dreadful end caused further tragedy, and the only surviving member of Robert and Eliza McQueen Mackay's extensive family fell into a decline. Aunt Kate began to fail, dying of pneumonia three weeks later.[24] She was buried in Laurel Grove Cemetery next to her beloved sister, Sarah, who ironically had died shortly after the tragic death of her other nephew, Henry's brother Robert Stiles.

In 1877 reconstruction was over, but not without a last historical lurch. In the hotly contested presidential election results of 1876 between Re-

Willie dressed for a costume ball, and in his Hussars uniform, 1880's. *Courtesy The National Society of The Colonial Dames of America in the State of Georgia.*

publican Rutherford B. Hayes and Democrat Samuel J. Tilden, a bitter battle over wrongly counted or uncounted votes threatened to split the nation once again—"Tilden or War" became the rallying cry in many Democratic newspapers. In a compromise agreement Rutherford Hayes became President of the United States on March 4, 1877—the Republicans won! As promised, one of Hayes's first acts was to order federal troops out of Southern cities, and former rebels all over the South triumphantly reclaimed the statehouses in their respective capitals. It was the final betrayal for the black man, and many things went back to the way they had been before the war, except now the slave was ostensibly a freedman, remaining hostage only to economic bondage, a lesser kind of equality.

Taking Care of Family

In 1879 Andrew Low wrote his will in Leamington. He left his daughters stocks and bonds and the bulk of his vast fortune to his son William.[25] An interesting social and legal aspect is that the rights of women in Victorian England, in a country ruled by a woman, were tenuous at best. Men basically had total power over their wives and daughters, and presumably sisters. The first British Marriage and Divorce Act was passed in 1857

A studio portrait of Willie, 1880's. *Courtesy The National Society of The Colonial Dames of America in the State of Georgia.*

giving women some rights, but the stigma attached was so powerful that most society women steered clear of claiming any legal rights in the event of a divorce. Andrew Low's will had been written before the Female Matrimonial Property Act came into force in 1889 in England. Prior to that the wife's property belonged to her husband, and indeed she was also his property. It seems as though Andrew Low was fully cognizant of that potentiality and ensured that his daughters would control their own money, although he made Harriet Robertson and Amy Grenfell's husbands his executors, along with his own lawyers in Savannah.

Andrew Low had lavished everything money could buy on his children and certainly appeared to have done his best to protect his daughters' future financial security against exploitation. Unfortunately he did not appear to have had the same perspicacity with his son. Willie Low had attended the best schools. After graduating from his prep school at Winchester, he had gone on to attend Brasenose College at Oxford University, where he appears to have had something less than a stellar career. He is reported to have found time to belong to the college's two dining clubs, the Octagon and the prestigious Phoenix Common Room (the oldest dining club in the university) to which he was elected in 1880. He is also listed as a member of Vincent's Club, the university club for sportsmen, although he does not appear to have gained any sporting honors. The alumni records show him matriculating on January 22, 1880, aged nineteen. He was being trained as an English gentleman to run with the hounds, raise racehorses, and to gamble and drink with the best society had to offer.[26] The one thing he did not appear to be trained for was to follow in the commercial footsteps of his father.

Jessie Low, aged eighteen, and Katie accompanied their father with a white maid for his annual winter visit to Savannah in November 1880. She left a detailed account of the trip in her journal. They sailed from Liverpool on the *Britannic*, via New York (which she loathed), and arrived on November 30 at eight o'clock in the morning. We pick up her description:

> We expected to find Tom there but he was not so we waited about an hour and he never turned up, we were beginning to think he was ill or something, so Papa sent a man up in a carriage. I could not have stayed there much longer without being sick as the whole wharf was covered with guano and the smell was something awful.... This is a queer place, the roads are simply awful, up to your boot tops in sand, & the pavements all ups and downs, the crossings are boards thrown across the street. The squares are very pretty though, such nice trees about. I did not remember our house one bit. I was very disappointed in the garden as I imagined it much bigger; the camellia trees in the back garden are lovely though and full blossom at present. We found Tom outside all right, he had been down to the wharf at 7.o. clock, but they told him the ship would not be in until the afternoon. While we were at breakfast Col. Anderson came in to see how we were . . . then Cousin Leila and Meta called. I do not remember anyone here, we went down to see Aunt Elliott in the afternoon and to see Mrs. Anderson in the evening.
>
> Wednesday, Dec. 1st. Katie and I spent the whole morning making the drawing room look respectable; it looked very like an old lodging house when we came. Mosianna had put on all the old antimacassars and bows they had had when we were out before, it does not look half bad now we have covered all the marble tables and stuck our frames and things around. The house is rather decayed but not half so bad as I expected and I was agreeably surprised in the piano, to be sure it is not lovely but not half bad on the whole. I have been waking the old thing up since I have to be here he has been asleep for so long. Tom would not have another man to help him. We have got

> a black housemaid named Susan, a very nice girl indeed. I thought I should not like black servants but I do, they seem, I mean the servants here a very nice class of Negroes. . . . We have meals at such unearthly times here, breakfast at 9, dinner at 3, & supper at 7, the food is very good indeed, much better than England but somehow I never feel hungry at those hours. Tom is always coming up to me and saying 'Miss Jessie, you tell me what you like to eat and I get it,' he is a nice old chap, but is beginning to look old though.[27]

Their arrival started a social whirl as everyone in Savannah it seems wanted to meet the Low sisters, and it was during this first visit that Jessie became good friends with the Gordon girls, especially Daisy and Mabel. Andrew Low gave his daughter Katie a Bible for Christmas. It is inscribed "Katie, with Papa's best love, Christmas, 1880. The Lord Help Thee and Keep Thee. Numbers V1.24." This Bible is now part of the collection of Low memorabilia at the Andrew Low Museum. Sadly, the usual New Years celebration was marred by the sudden devastating death of seventeen-year-old Alice Gordon, Daisy's sister, who had been taken ill while away at school in New York.

Jessie and Katie paid a visit to their cousins at Etowah, and she remarks that she preferred life in the country, doing what she loved to do, riding and shooting, just like her mother before her. Jessie had a sharp eye for details of life in the South in the years following reconstruction, which on the surface had returned to normal, and she appeared to be much happier than back home in Leamington. They sailed for England on March 26, 1881, aboard the White Star Line Steamship *Germanic*, C. W. Kennedy, Commander, sister ship to the *Britannic* they had come over on three months earlier. A passenger list of that trip is tucked into the pages of her diary. By the time she left Savannah, she and Daisy Gordon had become firm friends, and it is then that they determined that Daisy should make a reciprocal visit to Leamington in the near future.

Amy and her little boy Bruce,[28] although they frequently resided at their London house on ultrafashionable Grosvenor Street, are regularly at home in Leamington, as her husband, who they all call "Harrie," is often away at sea in the Royal Navy. Hattie and her husband, George Robertson, who is now a member of the yeomanry, the English version of the American volunteer militia, habitually come to stay. Hattie complains about being so poor they will have to leave Widmerpool, their country house in Nottinghamshire, but Jessie remarks that she still entertains as much as always. Katie and Mary are living at home and Willie is away at Oxford. Despite Jessie's complaints that she never does anything, their lives are filled with dressmakers, shopping, theater, visits from young men, teas,

Admiral Sir Harry Tremenheere Grenfell and Amy Low, Lady Grenfell, ca. 1880. *Courtesy The National Society of The Colonial Dames of America in the State of Georgia.*

dinners, parties and balls, hunting and riding around the county in their pony traps—activities in which all the girls are proficient. They have packs of dogs and stables of horses. All in all, this was a typical life for the county gentry, with the addition of occasional visits to the children in the charity wards of the local hospital and ministering to the poor!

In August of 1881 the family goes for a summer seaside holiday to Folkestone. It is Willie's twenty-first birthday, which seems to pass without much fanfare except for a daily game of tennis. In September, Amy goes up to Scotland, and that October Willie is due to sit for his exams and goes off to a tutor to cram. At the end of November Jessie writes in her diary: "Papa sailed for New York on the new Cunard ship, George and Hattie came here for the dog show. We met Willie there and he came home with us. He has been very ill lately and was not able to go up for his exams, it was his last try, they won't let him try again, although illness prevented him from going up." This is the first indication that Willie's application to his studies was not up to scratch.

Hattie Low (Mrs. George Coke Robertson) of Widmerpool Hall, ca. 1880. *Courtesy The National Society of The Colonial Dames of America in the State of Georgia.*

In 1881 on December 23 the Savannah newspaper announces: "Mr. Andrew Low Esq. was painfully, but not seriously, injured on his return trip from Liverpool to New York. The seas were running very high, a gale was blowing when he was thrown from his chair. He was on his way to Savannah, but will be forced to stay in New York for a few days."

That short announcement evokes the image of a man who refuses to give up or in to either age or infirmity. Despite his bad fall at the age of sixty-nine, he certainly was not going without a fight and his mental acuity did not appear to be impaired in the least.

On December 26, 1881, Jessie's last entry for the year reads: "Heard poor Papa had an accident going out, fell and hurt himself badly on board ship, layed up in New York with nurse. Jan 2nd, Will came back just in time to get ready to start, left for Liverpool Jan 4th, sailed today, Jan 6th in the 'Britannic' for New York."

Equipped for business or not, Willie Low was the heir apparent and was needed to assist his father. Unfortunately there are no more diaries for four years, so the entire story of Willie and Daisy's courtship and his relationship with his father in the last years is still only available through the Gordon letters, other memoirs, and biographies, although some hints can be gleaned from Jessie's memories in the two daily diaries she keeps for 1886 and 1887.

Andrew Low's Last Stand

The story of the proxy fight for the Central Railroad is a fascinating piece of Georgia history and shows clearly Andrew Low's lifelong character, ability, and desire to fight for his sense of rights and wrongs.

Andrew Low was one of the original subscribers to stock for the construction of the Central Railroad in the mid 1830's and a few years later the Central Railroad Bank. In 1844 Andrew Low, Jr., was elected director of Central Railroad and Banking Company, a position to which he was re-elected for almost forty years.[29] After a lifetime of service on the board of directors he retired; and in 1882 four new directors were elected, including E. P. Alexander of Louisville, a former Confederate general.[30]

The election of General Alexander started an internal fight, as it appears that it was his intention to issue income bonds based on earnings of the Ocean Steamship Company, a subsidiary of the Railroad Company. The opposing stockholders viewed the election of Alexander as a raid. The current president of the railroad, Colonel William Wadley, resigned as president of the Ocean Steamship Company. Immediately an injunction was filed against the directors of the Central Railroad. Wadley originally came to Georgia to construct Fort Pulaski, and early on entered into the service of the Central Railroad as an engineer and rose to become its president. At this point, the fight was between the Alexander faction and the Wadley faction, with Andrew Low out of the picture.

Then fate stepped in, when on August 11, 1882, William M. Wadley died suddenly in Saratoga. The death of Colonel Wadley threw a spanner in the works, as his death opened up the question of the lease of the Georgia Railroad. The railroad was leased to Colonel Wadley, and his interest in the case was transferred to the Central, Louisville, and Nashville Railroad. The board claimed that the death of Colonel Wadley in no way affected the case and its question would be settled in the U. S. Supreme Court.

Hoping to take advantage of the situation, a special election was held, and General Alexander was named president of Central Railroad in place of the late lamented Colonel Wadley. Captain W. G. Raoul remained as vice-president. Andrew Low's name was published as having been elected as a new director, nominated by General Alexander. Two months later Captain Raoul resigned to run at the head of the ticket against General Alexander at the next general election in January 1883.

The catalyst for this impending fight for control focused on a letter written by Andrew Low's friend William W. Gordon, Jr., and Alexander published a response in the Savannah paper on December 18, 1882:

> In your paper this morning I find a letter from Capt. W. W. Gordon, in which Mr. Andrew Low is made to complain in a long cable

> message that his name was published without his authority in the list of directors printed with last annual report of this company—the simple fact which relieves the Board from any imputation of fault is that no intimation that Mr. Low had declined, or would decline the position, ever reached the Board or myself until after the annual report had been published. No one is better aware of this fact than Capt. Gordon himself is. His letter is the first, the last and the only communication, personal or official, direct or indirect, which has been received by myself or the board from Mr. Low or any of his family.

And that, as is said, put the fox in the hen house! The controversy continued to rage over the Christmas season in the pages of Savannah newspapers.

It seems that the new president was no friend of Andrew Low's. In a power play to install his own cronies, Alexander had voted against Low a year before, persuading his friends not to vote for him either, although he had been considered one of the most valued directors of the Central Railroad for forty years. This may indicate that Andrew Low's retirement from the board had not been entirely voluntary. Now, with the death of Wadley, General Alexander wanted Low back as a director, had printed his name in the annual report without his authority, and Andrew Low was most upset! And he was saying so with great vigor. He was not about to be used as a pawn in anyone's chess game.

The proxy fight was the talk of the town and on January 1, 1883, the paper clarifies matters somewhat by printing: "The excitement over the contest for directors of the Central Railroad, which ran very high on Saturday, subsided somewhat yesterday. The controversy appeared to center on a block of stock owned by E. H. Green. It appears as though Andrew Low has thrown his hat into the opposition party led by W. G. Raoul."[31]

The next day it was all over, and on January 2 the paper trumpeted:

> . . . after the most exciting contest ever known in the history of Southern railroads elections yesterday resulted in the choice of a Board of Directors favorable to the elevation of Captain W. G. Raoul to the Presidency of that great corporation, whose lines traverse the entire state and extend far beyond its limits. . . . The new board, with the exception of Judge Gresham of Macon and Mr. E. H. Green of New York is composed entirely of citizens of Savannah, which will be of some advantage in this city.

Whether Andrew Low threw the weight of his still considerable influence into the fray on a personal level remains pure speculation. Certainly he appears to have used William Gordon as his surrogate to express his position in the public arena, and it is indisputable that it was the group he favored who won.

This must have been a great triumph for him personally, and an indication that he was still a fighter for his own interests. It is a provable fact that he held a great deal of stock in the railroad company in trust for his daughters' portion of his estate, so it was also them he was fighting for. He would have been seventy-one years old now, and not in the best of health. Shortly after, he suffered a minor stroke, and was being cared for by his daughters, confined to his home in Leamington.

The coda to the story was that on October 8, 1883, it was announced that under the new management: "A combination has been formed between the Western and Atlantic and Central Railroads in Georgia. It is a contract that strengthens the Central and keeps under its control the only outlet to the West for Georgia railroads."

That same year Georgia celebrated its 150th birthday with Savannah serving as host city and Superintendent Bryan published *Savannah, Georgia's Chief Seaport—A Brief Sketch of Savannah's Commerce*, a pamphlet that recaps the story of the S.S. *Savannah* as well, and in essence is also a recap of the influence of the Andrew Low Company throughout the nineteenth century.

19

Exit the Buck, 1882–1886

By the end of the nineteenth century on the surface little remained in the South to remind people of the destruction wrought in the bitter fighting that had taken place. Businesses, homes, railroads, farms, churches—all rebuilt. Cotton, tobacco, sugarcane, and rice flourished in once stripped and burned fields. Institutional slavery was a thing of the past, and the eleven states of the former Confederacy had been reinstated as full members of the Union.

For white Southerners it was business as usual. For the four million freed slaves, whose lives, future, and freedom was supposedly at the heart of this fratricidal conflict, not all benefited. The years after reconstruction had seen a steady erosion of black voting rights. To many white Southerners black suffrage was a threat to their vision of a peaceful compliant society, They utilized as many innovative strategies as state legislators could come up with to halt and even turn back the tide. Such devices included grandfather clauses, poll taxes, and literacy tests, all designed to disqualify the African freedman. It would be a full century from the end of the Civil War before legal equality finally came.[1]

In Liverpool James Dunwoody Bulloch, who had remained after the war, had become something of a local hero. John Low, officer on the C.S.S. *Alabama* had retired from the sea, gone into the marine insurance business, married again, and had four children. John Low's first-born son by a first marriage in Savannah had immigrated to New Zealand.[2]

In London, Leamington, and Savannah the Low children lived the same kind of life dubbed "high cotton" as their grandparents and parents had lived prior to the war.

The Lows and the Gordons

Juliette "Daisy" Gordon, daughter of Eleanor "Nellie" Gordon and William Washington Gordon , Jr., of Savannah, reconnected with the Low

Daisy Gordon enjoys the fad of the Japanese aesthetic, ca. 1880. *Courtesy The National Society of The Colonial Dames of America in the State of Georgia.*

family in the summer of 1882 on her first European tour when she visited them at their residence at 42 Clarendon Square, Leamington. Daisy wrote to her mother describing this visit. She is not very gracious about Andrew, to whom she appears to have developed quite an aversion. Andrew Low is rumored to have had a minor stroke on his return to England, possibly triggered by his fall in December 1881. His only son had begun a pattern of making occasional visits to America in his father's place, presumably to oversee various business concerns, a practice that continued until his death, and seems to somewhat contradict the wisdom that Andrew Low had no confidence in his son.

The Low and Gordon offspring were related through their Uncle Henry Stiles's marriage to Eliza Clifford Gordon. The Lows had left Savannah in 1867, when Willie and Daisy were both extremely young, and it has never been verified exactly when they first met again as young people, although it could have been in any number of places. Daisy was in school in New York, studying painting at Mesdames Charbonniers, at the time Willie came over after his father's injury earlier in the year. She also tells her mother that the Low sisters had shown her around the high spots of London. Willie was already known as a "young man around town," so it is quite logical he would have escorted them in these excursions. It is inconceivable that she would not have spent a considerable amount of time in his company. From Leamington she writes to her mother "you don't know how I long to see you at times. I am glad you and Papa are not like other parents I could mention, Andrew among them."

Reading between those lines one can see in hindsight that it was on that first visit that she and Willie fell in love, or at least she with him, that Andrew and his only son were not on the best of terms, and her feeling toward "the old man" was already colored by her growing infatuation for Willie. She, inexplicably, considering her open and confiding nature, does not mention him at all to her parents. Photos and descriptions show him at that age resembling a slim, elegant blonde Greek god, and it is easy to see how an impressionable young girl could be smitten.

The year after her European tour Daisy wrote to her mother, who was away, that Willie had arrived in Savannah. He would have been twenty-three years old then and brought a fox terrier sent as a present from Jessie and Mary Low. Dogs appear in all the photographs ever taken of any of the Lows *en famille*, and in a later one at Beauchamp Hall a vixen, a female fox, is with the pack. Her explanation of Willie's presence was that "old Low was too ill or (cranky) to come over."

On December 8, 1883, an advertisement appeared in the Leamington Courier of the sale of 42 Clarendon Square, stating that it had been the residence of Andrew Low Esq. for the past fifteen years: "To Be Let, Furnished or Unfurnished, or to be Sold—The above named commodious Family Residence, with its spacious Reception Rooms and complete and convenient arrangements, is one of the most commodious and comfortable Mansions in the Royal Spa. Price of the Freehold, 1,500 pounds. Rent, Furnished 250 pounds per annum, Unfurnished 110 pounds per annum.

That year the Low family moved around the corner, to an even larger, grander, and more commodious mansion of gray granite stone named Beauchamp Hall, on Beauchamp Avenue.[3]

Beauchamp Hall, Leamington, Andrew Low's residence, after 1883. *Courtesy The National Society of The Colonial Dames of America in the State of Georgia.*

By 1884, Daisy had returned for a second trip to Europe. She found Andrew Low depleted in health and spirits. In a letter to Nellie she wrote:

> Mr. Low seems feeble; he wept when he saw me because he took me for you. He considers himself a dying man, although the doctors say he may and probably will live for twenty years. He is a great care for the girls and I am sorry for them, though they are happy and comfortable in this lovely house . . . they are tied at home like prisoners by old Andrew's illness, the only way they can have any change is by asking their friends to see them.

There is no way of knowing whether she was being secretive because she knew that her father would not approve, as the matter had already been discussed in Savannah, and she had specifically promised her parents before she went abroad that she would not lose her head over Willie.[4]

> He does not know I am coming to Europe, for I have not written to inform him, so there is little likelihood of my seeing him, even if I visit his sisters, for he is never at home. There will be no such friendship between us as you mention even if we do meet. His education and disposition both make him seem younger than I am.

It appears even then the young man had acquired a reputation for being a playboy, dependent on his father for his support. It is doubtful that his more extreme behavior and expensive tastes would have been supported or tolerated by his father, who although ill, still strictly controlled the household purse strings.

The following year an incident occurs that speaks clearly to Daisy's often willful nature. She is in Savannah looking after her father while her mother was in New Jersey attending the birth of her daughter Eleanor's first baby. Daisy went to a doctor with an earache for which she insisted on being treated with silver nitrate, exactly the wrong treatment because it was an abscess that then burst through the eardrum. The accident left her deaf in that ear. Willie Low was in Savannah and came to visit, another opportunity for them to get to know each other.

We are fortunate to have another personal word portrait of Willie Low in that time frame from his cousin Caroline, who in the fall of 1884 had married Tod Lovell and moved to live with her in-laws at Rosedale, a cotton plantation on Palmyra Island in the Mississippi River. In an unpublished manuscript, "Bend of the River," she writes:

> In February of that first year I received a letter from my cousin Willie Low, who had come over from England to see his relatives in Georgia. He wrote from Savannah to say that he would like to come to see me on his way to Mardi Gras in New Orleans. I had met him the year before when he came over on his first visit, and he and I were devoted to each other. He was as generous as he was lovable, and he had sent me for a wedding present, a splendid traveling bag made of alligator skin, and fitted in ivory, and on every one of the toilet articles the name "Caro" was engraved. When I received his letter, Tod and I consulted the family, and with their consent, I wrote him to come.... Willie Low was very handsome at this time, a perfect blonde with crispy waving yellow hair, and English complexion, gray eyes and classic features. He was in the first flush of his youth, had just left Oxford, getting through by the skin of his teeth, and was thoroughly enjoying his freedom. He showed me a sachel full of the bills he had made at college, and they amounted to six thousand pounds. He had not yet shown them to his father.

Dear Willie! If he had only been as limited in means as his American cousins, he might have had a happy life.

The biography of Daisy Low written by her niece, Daisy Lawrence, recounts a letter written by Daisy's mother Nellie:

> Eleanor says that Willie Low wanted desperately to learn to become a business man, and went to some friends of his father in London, saying he wanted to come in and learn the business from the ground up. They said that business was fluctuating and it would take him years to learn—and in his situation, there was no point to

Portrait of Jessie, Mary, and Katie Low, after 1880. *Photo courtesy The National Society of The Colonial Dames of America in the State of Georgia.*

it. They advised him to get his father to buy him a farm, but Willie made it clear that he wanted to earn his own living.

Nellie's letter also says that Willie wanted to tell his father about himself and Daisy to gain his consent to their marriage, but Daisy would not let him. She may have been afraid Andrew would deny her beau's request for her hand, and Willie might have wished to support himself because he had come to the same conclusion. They were all wrong.

It seems that Willie was not as "inconstant" as the Gordon parents thought him to be. Gathering courage from Savannah, he wrote to his father of his wish to marry Daisy Gordon. He asked for an income or settlement that would allow him to support a wife. He also wrote to her father, Willie Gordon, and in a very revealing line says: "I must confess that there is little to expect from my Father, as he thinks me nothing more than a good-for-nothing boy, and even if we have to wait a long time we are willing to do so."

When Willie Low did not hear from his father, William Gordon wrote to Andrew Low telling him of the letter he had received from his son.

> I cannot consent to this if you object, but he seems earnest about it and I write to ask your views about it . . . as Willie has no means of his own and no profession from which to derive an income, it will

be impossible for him to marry without knowing definitely upon what he can count for support. My own means are not sufficient to ensure any amount worthwhile considering, to my daughters after marriage.

Jessie introduces the question of her brother's courtship of Daisy Gordon on January 8, 1886:

> Last night a letter came from Willie saying that he had spoken to Mr. Gordon about marrying Daisy and that he had agreed on two conditions, viz that he would settle down and live within his income and that they should live for six months of the year in Savannah. He said that Mr. G was writing to Papa and his letter came by the same post. I have been worrying so much about it all ever since Willie's last letter came, as Papa was so cross and when he was told, refused to give an answer. I had such a long talk with him one day about it, he began by being furious with me but I stuck to my point and at last he joined it and we parted most amicably in each other's arms. I told him that I thought it would be the turning point in Willie's life and that he seemed so much in earnest, it will give him something to live for instead of idling away his life. I would rather he married Daisy than anyone and I am devoted to her, she is a real good sort and will, I think, keep him straight as she is not one to stand any nonsense. The only part of it I shall hate is their living out there part of the year. He won't like always missing the hunting, but sufficient the day the evil thereof. And all I want is for them to be thoroughly happy. I have known all along that they were fond of each other.

Andrew was in poor health with a nurse in constant attendance, so rather than upset him at night they waited until the following day to give him William Washington Gordon's letter.

> Well, in fear and trembling we took the letter to Papa this morning, thinking he would be furious but he took it very calmly and was most amiable. He said that he would give his consent & that if they were both in the same mind after a year they might marry & that he would give Willie the Savannah property for an income, which I think is most generous of him as it represents three thousand pounds a year. I don't think the others care very much about it, as none of them were as fond of Daisy as I was. Amy says he ought to have married an English girl.

Allaying all their fears, already incapacitated physically but unimpaired mentally, Andrew Low had his eldest daughter, Amy Grenfell, write back agreeing to an income amounting to fifteen thousand dollars a year and blessing the union. In a letter written in April 1886, Daisy writes to her brother Bill telling him that she and Willie had been in love for four years, and good as engaged for nearly two, which is a certain confession that they had formed their attachment on her first trip to Europe. Interestingly enough, on hearing the news of the impending match some of the Gordon relatives expressed the same kind of disapproval as the Stiles-Mackay relatives had for Andrew Low's marriage to Mary Cowper Stiles some thirty years before.[5]

Andrew Low's Decline

Andrew Low insists he is worse—the doctors say he is not. He sleeps all day and never goes out. There are constant rows between the sisters and everyone is getting on each other's nerves. Amy's only son, Bruce, had died two years earlier, and she has become most dictatorial, appearing put out over Willie's impending engagement and worried that her husband has not received his expected promotion. Mary is deeply unhappy, and Jessie thoroughly discontented with her life. She is corresponding during this period with Hugh Graham, who is working on a ranch out in Alberta, Canada; and when Willie is home, he frequently brings young male friends to dinner, including a Frank Green, who is later to play a key role in our story. At the end of January her diary says:

> A rather dreadful thing happened this afternoon, Papa had not been at all well all day, he went to lie down in the front drawing room this afternoon and when Katie went in there about four o'clock she found him lying on the floor, he had slipped off the sofa and had not been able to pick himself up again. He was in a great state of mind, refused to speak and went to bed after tea. He is always so cross when he is ill and won't speak a word to us ... he is so restless he won't keep quiet a minute but is too weak to walk about much. He gets so frightened about himself it is difficult to manage him.

That night he had another stroke and his condition worsened, making communication even more difficult. On February 15 a letter comes for Andrew Low from Willie in Savannah, saying he has sailed and will be home in a few days, and Jessie hopes that "things will smooth down a bit when he comes." When Willie arrives home on February 21, it is with the sad news that "old Tom" had died twelve hours after he left Savannah.

Death of Thomas Milledge

The Savannah newspaper devoted a considerable amount of column inches to his passing in its February 8, 1886, edition:

> Thomas A. Milledge, an aged colored man died of Dropsy yesterday at the residence of Mr. Andrew Low at Abercorn and Charlton Streets. Milledge was for many years the tried and trusted servant in the family of Mr. Low. His funeral will take place this afternoon, and will be attended by Eureka Lodge No 1 of colored Freemasons, and also the Forest City Light Infantry.[6]

Lifetime slave, servant, and finally trusted friend, Andrew Low left him $300 per annum in his will for his lifetime, but he did not live to enjoy it. Since August 20 is given as date for Milledge's birth, it is possible that he was given the same date as Andrew Low's christening, since as a former slave, sold several times, it is quite likely that the actual date of his birth was unrecorded.

Andrew Low Moves Offstage

The summer heat arrived with Andrew's health deteriorating daily. On June 1 Jessie writes to her trusted diary:

> It is no good trying to blind oneself to the fact that he is seriously ill. I find it so hard to realize and it seemed to come over me tonight in such a wave that perhaps he is dying; I can't bear to think of it. Oh God, what shall we do without him, he keeps us all together and we should be like a ship that had lost her helm. I am devoted to Papa although I never show it and I think how awful it must be for him to think we none of us care for him, but we do. I wonder if he thinks of dying and is frightened.

Along with her fear for her father, her dreams of living happily ever after with her beloved brother and soon-to-be sister-in-law have melted like the winter frost.

> I feel Willie hates me, so my ideas about living with him and Daisy will never come off, of course he is very young, but he does make me feel so cross, the life he leads, never thinks of paying his bills etc. I hope he will turn over a new leaf when he marries.

Despite his father's worsening condition at the end of June, Willie goes up to London to attend the Derby, one of Britain's premier racing events enthusiastically patronized by Edward, the Prince of Wales, and not to be missed for any reason by anyone in the social orbit. Two days later Jessie tells her journal:

> Our troubles and illnesses never seem to end. Willie came back from London tonight with a broken arm, put his elbow out bear fighting (wrestling) after dinner at the Army Navy Club, after the

The last image of Andrew Low, with Katie, at conservatory, Beauchamp Hall. Mr. Low suffered from advanced gout and found relief at Dr. Jefferson's spa down the hill. *Courtesy The National Society of The Colonial Dames of America in the State of Georgia.*

> Derby. It will be a six weeks job, as if we had not enough ill people already. We have not been without now for three years. Amy was talking today about if anything happens to Papa what we should all do, she says go abroad and we would have to go with her. I don't know what would become of me. I don't seem able to fit in with any of my people, none of them like me. I should like to go in for doing some kind of work but I am afraid I am not fitted for it. I am not strong enough for hospital nursing and am not fitted for the sisterhood.

By June 20 it has been necessary to bring in another nurse, causing another family row by angering Katie, who feels it is their duty to take care of Andrew themselves. By then he had become almost unmanageable, requiring twenty-four-hour nursing. Walton, his valet, cared for him in the daytime, but could not stay up day and night. Andrew's considerable weight made it impossible to handle him alone. On the 22nd, Willie and Harry Grenfell went up to London for the *levee* (dance) and to have his dislocated arm rubbed. She writes:

> He does not seem to understand anything now or know in the least what he is doing. We all had a long talk and agreed that he really was becoming imbecile. We don't know what we are to do as he will not be able to sign checks and we only have a certain amount of money in the bank here, and when that is gone we cannot draw on the London bank without his signature. Amy also thought he ought to be made to do a codicil to the will before he gets worse, but I doubt now his ever being able to do either.

Without the male guidance they had been used to, the sisters seem to be growing increasingly distraught and Jessie wonders aloud that she thinks Willie should come home. On the morning of June 26 the doctors said that Andrew was very much worse and had not two days to live. They telegraphed Willie, Harry Grenfell, and George Robertson in London to come immediately, which they did that evening.

Andrew Low breathed his last at noon on Sunday, all his children and sons-in law around his bedside. Jessie writes:

> He died very peacefully, just seemed to sleep his life away, he sighed and then it was all over. He did not suffer at all . . . he looked so calm, peaceful and happy; one knew that he was at 'Rest.' I prayed so hard to God all Saturday night and Sunday morning that he should go quietly and that Mother and Brucie should meet him. I wonder if they did, he had such a smile on his face, he had not had for years, I think they must have.

His death certificate shows cause of death as "Diabetes." His son-in-law Harry Grenfell reported date of death as June 27, 1886, a month before his seventy-fourth birthday, his occupation listed as "Gentleman."[7]

Reading the Will

The death notice in the Leamington Courier was very short, just the standard obituary. He was originally buried at Lillington, near Leamington, where Amy's only son, Bruce Grenfell, was also buried. The family had always known that it was his wish to be buried in Savannah, to lie with his wives and other children, but it was not possible to take him over immediately because it was prohibited to ship dead bodies in the summer because of deterioration occasioned by the heat. He was buried temporarily in a lead-lined coffin in a vault in the country churchyard. After the funeral the will was read, and Jessie gives us a first hand account:

> Only Katie and Amy went in to hear it, I think it is dreadful that these things have to be done so and money matters discussed. Pascoe Grenfell, Harrie [Grenfell], and George [Robertson] are executors. Papa left much more than I thought he had, indeed I never had an idea what he did have or how it was settled. He left us girls 60,000 [pounds] each and all the rest to Willie, with the exception of a few legacies and charities in America.[8] He left 750,000 altogether, Pascoe said he never saw a man's affairs arranged better or money so well invested. We girls were to have the safest investments, they were to be chosen by the Trustees, so Pascoe has done it. Willie made it up to 70,000 each as it was always Papa's wish that we should have 10,000 more each and he always intended to have a codicil to his will, but he put it off, but he told Willie & Harrie & George about it. It is kind of Bill to do it for us, though of course it was Papa's wish he was not bound to carry it out. All our money is in railways in America & will bring us in over 2,000 a year, so if we all live together we ought to live very comfortably. Willie will have £16,000 a year after the first year but the succession duty is simply enormous, I had no idea of it before. Willie will have to pay £21,000 to the crown the first year, which of course will leave him nothing. . . . Papa was always such an honorable and just man, all his life never owed a penny. I hope we shall all follow his example; there is no reason why we should not do so for we will have plenty to live on. Willie seems so young to be the head of the family and our guardian. I hope his responsibility will make him older and wiser, and that when he marries Daisy he will settle down quietly and be happy with her.

Andrew Low's will was long and left the bulk of his estate, including his property in Savannah, to his son William Mackay Low . In Savannah he left his affairs in the hands of "my friend" and Harvard-educated lawyer Alexander Lawton, the same General Lawton who was in charge of Savannah's defenses during the Civil War, and to Thomas Mayhew Cunningham, also a lawyer.[9]

In addition, he specified that each daughter should receive the income from the trusts set up to administer her legacies and be paid "for her sole and separate use independently of her husband." He covered the contingency of any of them still being minors at the time of his death by appointing Amy Grenfell and Harriet Ann Robertson, assisted by his cousin Lieutenant General Alexander Low. C. B., to perform the duties of guardians of their persons. In return for this duty he willed his cousin one thousand pounds. In fact, none of his children were minors at the time of his death, Jessie the youngest being twenty-four years old and Willie twenty-six.

He left his affairs in the hands of his sons-in-law, Harry Tremenheere Grenfell (who was eventually knighted on attaining the rank of admiral in the Royal Navy), George Coke Robertson, and to his friend Pascoe Du Pre Grenfell of Eaton Square, London. All these men were top drawer in both nations and must have had close relationships with the family and certainly felt they owed this obligation to Andrew Low.

The *Times* of London listed a brief obituary—the Savannah newspaper a longer one. The sentence that seemed to sum up Savannah's attitude toward Andrew Low most positively was: "He was a man of strict business integrity and would tolerate no person or principle in which he did not have the fullest confidence. He was a gentleman of benevolence and was always ready to extend a helping hand to the unfortunate."

The actual terms of his charitable legacies in Savannah were extensive.[10] After the Will was published the Savannah newspaper wrote another article marveling at the "immense estate" left by Andrew Low, with the estate in Georgia estimated at $150,000 and his personal estate in England at in excess of 600,000 pounds—over three million dollars and in those days, truly immense. Jessie's detailed description seems to indicate it was even higher.[11]

In the immediate emotional aftermath of his father's death, Willie's proposition was that they should all stay on at Beauchamp Hall, but the impracticality of such an arrangement soon became evident in view of his imminent marriage. Daisy would not wish to start her new life as Mrs. Willie Low, in a new country, in the daily company of her husband's three youngest sisters, and part-time company of the two older sisters and their husbands. It appears that it was Amy who advanced the decision to look for a country home nearby for them all. She appeared to have considerable anxiety that she would be excluded from their future plans.

It was decided that Amy would stay in England to look for a suitable home. Katie, Mary, and Jessie would go abroad to take the waters at a spa, while Willie went to New York on estate business. They would then all return to Leamington to pack up the house. Willie would return his father to Savannah for reburial, and the three younger girls would go to Savannah for the wedding, which had been radically advanced, and stay through the winter. Their major worry was what to do with all the dogs.

Their last task before they temporarily went their separate ways was to endow a bed in the name of Andrew Low at the Warneford Hospital. The day before Willie left for America, he had one duty to perform: Jessie writes on July 20, in London: "Willie took us to see the diamonds he has bought for Daisy, such lovely ones, a huge crescent with huge stones . . .

then there is a very fine star that can be either part of the crescent or not."

While in London the sisters visited with their great-aunt, Mai Le Coulter, sister of General Alexander Low. Jessie becomes extremely upset when her aunt insists on talking about their inheritance, and warning them against fortune hunters seeking to marry them for their money.

Jessie describes letters she has received from America commenting on her father: "Nellie Gordon wrote a very nice letter saying how she knew how kind he was, although he was rough on the outside, and how straight forward and honest he had always been and how he hated anything that was not quite straight in business."

It becomes obvious in these pages how different Willie and Andrew were in temperament, and easy to see how there could have been friction between them. While the girls were all in London preparing to go abroad, a bombshell was dropped. In Jessie's words:

> Heard from Hattie this morning saying George had heard from a lawyer in Scotland to say Papa had a sister alive, a maiden lady, Miss Mary Low, we never knew of her existence before, it was so funny Papa never mentioning his family to us at all. I think he must have quarreled with them though he seems to have allowed them a good deal.

This diary entry verifies finally the conventional wisdom in Savannah that Andrew Low's executors knew nothing of his origins or family in Scotland until after his death. It is also absolute proof that he did not leave his two oldest daughters with his family following the death of Sarah Hunter. At long last, another mystery is cleared up although motive and meaning is still unclear.

Two years later, Andrew Low's last surviving close relative died.[12] Mary Low, his older sister who never married, was still residing in the gray granite home on Pearse Street, Brechin, where he had spent his formative years learning the trade of merchant on the local level. She is buried in the graveyard of Brechin Cathedral with their parents and other siblings. Jessie Low Graham's diary has provided proof that the members of his family knew that he came from Brechin partly because of the fact that his sister's name is added to the handsome table monument that still stands.

Andrew Low Returns to His Wives and Children

Andrew Low's son did not waste much time starting to dissipate that "immense fortune." In August Willie Low arrived in New York on estate business and promptly received unfavorable publicity when a New York newspaper printed that he had bet a huge amount on the outcome of a polo match.[13] Juliette was in Cooperstown visiting friends and Willie rushed up to explain the situation, which, according to her reaction, he appeared to be able to do to her satisfaction. The adverse publicity had blown to Savannah on the winds that all scandal rides, and in order to assuage the anxiety she knew her father would be feeling at the news of his worst fears that his future son in law was a profligate gambler, reckless, and unreliable. She wrote to her father saying: "Willie and I are no longer at odds. If you see a lot of rubbish in the papers about his having bet heavily on the polo match, you must not believe it. He said he had laid one big wager for the team, on commission, not for himself. It is untrue that Willie bet $50,000 to $25,000 as the New York *World* said."

Willie was still her golden boy. People in Savannah were not so charitable, and talk started up once again of how excessive and unstable he was, with some threatening to boycott the wedding which was planned for December. The Gordons would have considered such a rejection a social disaster.

Willie returned to England to honor his father's wishes. In Savannah it was reported in the *Morning News* of Saturday, November 13, 1886, that Andrew Low safely reached his last resting place:

> The remains of the late Andrew Low were brought to Savannah Thursday night on the steamer Chatahoochee. Yesterday morning undertaker W. D. Dixon and a representative of the family had the casket containing the body removed to Laurel Grove Cemetery and placed in the family vault there. The remains were sealed in a lead casket, which was encased by a rich oaken casket. In the afternoon about twenty carriages, containing friends and relatives of the family were driven out to the cemetery. Rev. Thomas Boone, of Christ Church, read the burial service. The flag on the Chatham Armory and the flags on the Ocean Steamship Company's vessels were at half-mast.

And again, on November 19, 1886:

> The St. Andrew's Society is called upon to lament the death of one of its oldest and most respected members—the late Andrew Low—who departed this life at Leamington, England, on the 27th day of June last, in his 74th year of his age. Mr. Low was born in Scotland in 1818 and came to Savannah when a youth. He soon developed marked business ability, which associated with the highest mercantile integrity; ultimately placed him at the head of the prominent house, which long bore his name and augmented under his influence. He joined the St. Andrew's Society in 1831 at the age of 18. After having amassed a fortune he moved with his family to

Jessie, Katie, and Mary Low with ten dogs and a fox at Beauchamp Hall. The Lows were known for their multiple dogs which accompanied them everywhere. The vixen is to the far left, oblivious to the camera. *Courtesy The National Society of The Colonial Dames of America in the State of Georgia.*

> England, but made frequent visits here, which he always held in affectionate remembrance as the cherished spot where he was married, where his children were born, and where he achieved success. Many of its charities, he remembered in his will and his mortal remains have found their last resting place in its soil. A copy of these resolutions will be sent to his family. The committee drafting them were George A. Mercer, Jas. Stewart and William Rogers.[14]

Today he rests in Lot 521 in Laurel Grove with his two wives, infant son, and a premature baby, the handsome white marble monument chosen by his children standing guard for eternity. His butler, Thomas Milledge, is buried in the same cemetery, but in the black section.[15] Scottish born, Savannah merchant and factor, Liverpool cotton tycoon, and finally English squire, Andrew Low is laid to rest with the women he loved the most. A tribute to a man whose life saw great triumph, wrenching tragedy, and a lifelong loyalty to those he loved and with whom he conducted business.

Preparations for the Nuptials

Katie, Mary, and Jessie had sailed for Savannah on November 11, 1886, to finally bury their father and see their only brother married. Willie had met his sisters in New York, where after a few days shopping they went on to

Studio portrait of Mary, Katie, Willie, and Jessie, ca. 1886. *Courtesy The National Society of The Colonial Dames of America in the State of Georgia.*

Baltimore to choose the monument for Andrew Low. Jessie writes: "We decided on a large cross 11 feet high in three steps and a marble coping with pillars at each corner, the lot is 28 ft square and we have to put something around and the man advised us not to have railings as they wear so badly in that climate. I think it will look very handsome."

Alterations on the house on Lafayette Square had already begun in preparation for its next incarnation under a new master and mistress. Jessie writes:

> It seemed so funny coming back to the old house again but it all looked so different. They have taken every bit of furniture that was

Daisy and her bridesmaids. The bride is in the center, Katie Low is seated to the left, Jessie is standing at the far left, and Mary is seated, second from right. *Courtesy The National Society of The Colonial Dames of America in the State of Georgia.*

> here away and got all new. Daisy chose it all. It is all very grand but I don't think at all suitable to this climate. The curtains and chairs all red plush ... the bedrooms upstairs are all very grandly furnished. Mary and I have the front room which is all done up in grand inlaid work which is fearfully difficult to keep clean.... Daisy's is all inlaid Chippendale and Katie's is carved oak, and they have furnished the little middle room.... We miss old Tom awfully, he always saw to everything. Mosianna seems quite useless and either can't or won't work so we must engage someone to help us with the housework. We have got the same old cook and a new manservant called James ... then there is Tommie, Tom's son, who is a very smart funny boy ... we engaged a white housemaid to help Mosianna as she does simply nothing. She used to be with the Gordon's and left them to be married, she has a child about 16 months old that she brings with her.

The house and grounds are bustling with workmen all over the place adding a new story to the building at the bottom of the gardens, which is filled with packing crates as the new furniture arrives daily.

The Fairy Tale Wedding

The wedding was reported in the Savannah newspapers: "A very pretty wedding took place at Christ Church at noon yesterday. The bride was Miss Juliette Gordon, daughter of the Hon. W.W. Gordon and the groom

Daisy's wedding party in the garden of the Gordon House, 1886. Willie is standing in the middle, with Daisy seated in front of him. Nellie Gordon stands to her daughter's left. *Photo courtesy The National Society of The Colonial Dames of America in the State of Georgia.*

was Mr. William Mackay Low of New York, son of the late Andrew Low. The Rt. Rev. Bishop Beckwith, assisted by Rev. Thomas Boone, performed the ceremony."[16]

Jessie Low was one of the bridesmaids and her version was a bit racier:

> December 21st. Daisy's and Willie's wedding day, a glorious one in point of weather. Poor Bill was beginning to be in rather a funk and besides was not very well. We girls dressed directly after breakfast, Mary and Katie's dresses looked very well, and the bridesmaids much better than I expected. Mary Couper [sic] and I started down to the Gordon's house at 11.30 to pick up the other bridesmaids and our flowers. We found them dressing all over the house. I went up to Daisy's room and helped her dress. She looked awfully well, better than I have ever seen her before, she did her hair on top of her head, which suited her and had a bright pretty color. ... Katie arranged her veil and it was pinned on with the diamonds Willie gave her and the crescent in front of her dress, and she wore the diamond bracelets we gave her ... it is so hard losing Willie, as I don't know a man is ever the same to his sisters after he is married. When he came to the part where it says, "Those whom God joins together let no man

The Low sisters visited their aunt Eliza Gordon Stiles at Etowah Cliffs, February 1886. The group is posed at the base of the cliff, on the river bank. Mrs. Stiles is seated, center. Jessie is seated at far right, Mary is to the rear, right, and Katie sits front and center, holding the anxious dog. *Courtesy Hugh Stiles Golson.*

> put asunder" it was grand, he paused a long time before he went on. Willie spoke out so well and he did look so handsome. I felt so proud of him. Daisy spoke out well too and looked up in Willie's face all the time, she certainly is devoted to him and I do hope they will be happy together.

Unfortunately even that happy time was marred with the clouds of later tragedy. Ironically, it was at the wedding that a grain of the rice for good luck lodged in Daisy's good ear and she basically went almost totally deaf and spent her honeymoon on St. Catherine's Island ill and in pain—a bad omen!

The next year in his father's place William Mackay Low was elected director of Savannah Light & Gas; and one year after that, Alexander R. Lawton and Thomas Cunningham, the executors of the will of Andrew Low, filed a final account and received letters of admission.

Exit the Buck

So the long saga of the century-long mercantile company at the Sign of the Buck's Head began to segue into a story of scandal-ridden Edwardian England, a weak son of a strong father, and daughters marrying well.

This story has taken us through a broad sweep of canvas from the migration of Scots to colonial Georgia, the Jacobite Rebellion of 1745, American Revolution of 1776, the sacking and burning of the French privateer *La Vengeance* in 1811, the War of 1812 between America and Britain, the Industrial Revolution in Europe, the rise of cotton and mercantilism in the South and Liverpool, the Indian Wars against the Seminoles in Florida in the 1830's, the expulsion of the Cherokee nation in the 1840's, and the espionage treason story of 1861. This story spans from the abolition of slavery contributing to the fall of the South after the War Between the States, to the heyday of the British Empire under Queen Victoria in the 1880's and the Edwardian Era led by her dissolute son, Edward, Prince of Wales. This story is told through the tangential and direct influence of one extended family linking two continents, the Low family. This was a long journey.

The irony is that Andrew Low's decision to remove his family from the horrors and chaos of postwar reconstruction in the South had propelled his son into the decadence of an era that was perhaps the most permissive in English society. Had he remained in Savannah, had his son been raised in the merchant countinghouses of Bay Street instead of one of the best public schools in England, things might have been different. The name of the House of Low may have been as prominent in the twentieth century as it was in the nineteenth. This is the fascinating game of the "what ifs" of history.

20

The Children's Legacy, 1886–1932

THE IMMENSE FORTUNE HIS FATHER LEFT TO WILLIAM MACKAY LOW allowed him to play the role of country squire and gentleman-about-town to the hilt; and according to contemporary accounts, he was an extremely generous host who held his own in the highest circles. The years between his father's death and his own death nineteen years later were almost an aberration in British history, with two diametrically opposed rivers of acceptable behavior running side by side, or one under the other, known and tacitly condoned.

The surface one was a rigid, morally restricted regime imposed by Queen Victoria, whose grief at the loss of her beloved consort Prince Albert in 1861 left her emotionally bereft and stunted; the other was the dissolute sensual world of her jaded eldest son, Edward, Prince of Wales. When he became King Edward VII, it followed forty years of being refused any real responsibilities his rank entitled him.

In no other milieu would Willie Low's particular attributes of wealth, sporting prowess, extreme personal charm, and good looks have allowed the same entrée into this society. Despite the surface glitter it remained rigid and conformist to a social code stratified in birth, position, and an unwritten law of conduct that only the British truly understood then or now.

The Victorian Age and the Edwardian Age ran concurrently, but with polar opposites of acceptability and accountability. Above all there were utterly different codes of behavior for men and women: within the latter category, unmarried women and married women.

By the time Willie blazed onto the scene, fueled by his infusion of money, the fast set was in its heyday. This state of dual societies had existed for twenty-five years, already well established as was the acceptance of Americans into the close-knit cadre of the prince's friends, providing of course that they were well heeled or well bred enough to have married into the upper classes of England. Beauty was a vital asset, brains a distinct disadvantage, and money an absolute necessity.

In this universe, which Willie Low occupied as a minor star orbiting around the innermost sun of the Prince of Wales, horses occupied a central position. On the stage of this dilettante life fox hunting in the winter and horse racing in the spring dictated the calendar; autumn grouse shooting on Scotland's wild and boggy moors came in a close second. Sandwiched between all these activities was the strenuous three-month London season starting in April, with a break for sailing at the Cowes week-long regatta in the Isle of Wight in July, before heading north in August for rest and recreation in the Scottish Highlands, followed by partridge and pheasant shooting overlapping the foxhunting.

All this hard work was book-ended by house parties where husbands slept with their mistresses, often other men's wives, while in turn those wives' husbands were attending separate house parties in the next county practicing the same pursuits. The practice gave a whole new meaning to "male tail," the passing on of ancestral names and land to the eldest son. As long as the lady provided the noble name with an heir, a spare, and some marriageable daughters, it mattered little whom the younger children resembled.

The Victorian Age and the Edwardian Age were perhaps simultaneously the most rigid and dissolute in England's long history. Such became Willie Low's life, and it could never have existed without the nucleus of his father and great-uncle's fortune.

The Fairy Kingdom

Following their fairy-tale wedding and their nightmare honeymoon due to Daisy's ear infection, the semiofficial sanctioned biography, *Lady From Savannah,* in the chapter titled appropriately "Fairy Kingdom," gives a romantic account of the early months of Willie and Daisy's marriage.[1] Tom Milledge's widow, Mosianna, was cooking for them in the newly renovated and expanded mansion on Lafayette Square, and they were giving memorable dinner parties, the focal point of Savannah society.[2]

Willie and Daisy, who had returned from their week's honeymoon on St. Catherine's Island, went up to Atlanta to see a special doctor as her ear was hurting her a good deal. The doctor found that a grain of rice had got in it and caused a serious inflammation that made her even deafer than she had been before.

Immediately after New Years, the Low girls went on an extended trip finishing up in Florida. In January they attended the wedding of Cousin Bessie Stiles to Alfred E. Mills in Brunswick, as did Caroline Lovell.[3] Following the wedding she visited Savannah and gives us another insightful peek into Willie's state of mind immediately after his marriage. Caroline writes in her unpublished manuscript:

> Daisy Gordon had just been married in Savannah and his three sisters had come from England for the wedding, and came down to Brunswick for Bessie's. Their father had recently died and they were in deep mourning, and I remember how beautiful the three of them—Katie, Mary and Jessie—looked in their elaborate black evening gowns, covered with jet . . .
>
> While I was there [Savannah] Willie Low took me for a drive on the Thunderbolt Road, which runs out from the city to the salt marshes south of it. "I'm not going to make a fool of myself, Caro," Willie said, "and throw my money away. And what's more I'm not going to lead an idle life. I intend to work. There'll be shooting in the spring and summer." Perhaps racing was to be a part of it, for the ambition of Willie Low's life was to improve the breed of racehorses in England. Many years later, I saw his stable of forty hunters and racers, at Wellesbourne, his place in Warwickshire.[4]

On February 24, 1887, they all sailed for Liverpool on the *Britannic*, the same ship they had sailed over on three months before. The sisters all had the same cabins they had on the way out. Daisy had a large one leading out of the girls' shared cabin while Willie had the captain's cabin on deck, which they all used as sitting room. The ship made a record run across the Atlantic despite storms, but unfortunately, the day before they arrived at Queenstown in Ireland Daisy became quite ill. Jessie writes:

> Daisy got very seedy the day before we got there, not sea sick, we could not find out what it really was for a long time. She cried and said she was in agony and would not tell us where it was and would keep on doing the most imprudent things. She really had a chill from not wearing enough clothes and it turned into wind chill, the doctor said, as whenever she took peppermint or anything like that, she felt better, but it was some time before we found this out. We did everything we could for her. I think she imagined she had internal inflammation and sometimes thought she was going to die. Poor little thing, I really feel sorry for her, she has never been ill in her life or seen anyone ill so knows absolutely nothing about sickness and imagines all sorts of things. We have all been brought up in such a stoical way to see and bear so much pain and say nothing, that it seems funny to see people give way entirely as she does. She is so obstinate and would not do anything the Dr told her and would do the most silly things, she wanted something different the whole time

> and never took it when it came and cried the whole time. She has been so fearfully spoilt at home, to make a sort of baby and have her mother fetching and caring for her, that she expects every one else to do the same. Of course, we didn't mind it a bit but she will find every one else won't see it in the same light and it is a poor lookout if she can't stand more than that amount of pain. Of course she was most uncomfortable as we had put mustard poultice all over her stomach to bring the pain out, and gave her a strong dose of castor oil.

So, with that distinctly unsympathetic note from her sister-in-law and no word as to how her husband dealt with her illness, Daisy walked through the door of her magical kingdom.

Daisy's Debut as a Married Woman

On arrival Willie and Daisy went immediately to Leamington, and the girls moved into their new rented home, Launde Abbey, to be met by an "avalanche of dogs," Amy looking very well, and Harry hobbling about on a cane.[5] He had been very ill himself from an old bullet wound that had gone bad. The house was very large, an old Elizabethan manor house, set in a park that is now a Christian retreat, with extensive stables, gardens, and a chapel. Unfortunately, Amy, who seems to be calling the shots, does not care for it at all, despite the fact that it was her choice, and is anxious to take a house in London for three months and is already talking about leaving.

A week or so after Jessie had settled in, Willie sent a telegram saying he had to go to London on business and didn't wish to leave Daisy alone, asking someone to go to watch over her. Jessie went, finding Daisy most unwell. In fact, it turned out that Daisy was sicker than had been suspected, with a possible internal abscess. Jessie writes:

> I found her still in bed, and at first I tried to make her rouse herself a bit more and get up, but it was no good, so I left off trying. I thought she was very cross and peeved, but I soon learnt to make allowances for her, poor little thing, it is awfully hard on her being so seedy, and coming to a strange place away from all her people. She went straight to bed when she arrived and has been there ever since, and has not even seen the house yet. Poor little thing, I am afraid it must be very lonely for her and I am afraid Willie does not give her much of his society. I thought Haines (the doctor in Leamington) was keeping her too low only on slops and too much in bed, but when she did get up, she could not stay more than a few minutes. She has got so dreadfully weak and still has these bad attacks of wind. Haines thinks the abscess is still going on discharging inside her. Poor thing, I am afraid she has not got a very good constitution.

Equestrian oil of Willie Low by James Linwood Palmer, early 1890's. At the time of his divorce, Willie owned fifty racehorses. *Painting courtesy The National Society of The Colonial Dames of America in the State of Georgia.*

> It is a bad beginning for them and very disappointing, as of course, Willie wanted to take her about to know all his friends and go to all the race meetings. Willie did not come home until Saturday.

Racing was another focal point for dissonance. Daisy worked herself up into a state about Willie riding in the race meetings, and thought he would be killed. This attitude could not have improved their harmony as one of Willie's first acts when he inherited was to purchase a stable of racehorses, and the sporting life almost immediately became the engine of his existence.

There has always been some confusion about Willie Low's nationality, whether he was an American in England or an Englishman in America or even both, and his birth certificate in Newport, Rhode Island, August 3, 1860, shows his father's place of birth as Savannah, Georgia, which we know to be erroneous. He was, however, unquestionably born in America

Willie Low, ca. 1890. *Courtesy The National Society of The Colonial Dames of America in the State of Georgia.*

and that presumably conferred American citizenship on him. There has never been any proof found of his father taking out naturalization papers, although his great-uncle Andrew Low most definitely did. Neither is there any record of Willie Low in the Warwickshire electoral registers drawn up for voting purposes, so the inference is that he never actually took out British citizenship, and was not qualified to vote. That did not prevent him from joining the yeomanry.

These details present a rather different aspect of Willie and Daisy Low's early months of marriage, and shed some light on the nature of their relationship in the context of later events. The entire family went up to London in the month of May, including Mrs. Gordon, who had come over for a visit, going out frequently to social events, including one attended by the prince and princess, which would have referred to the Prince of Wales and Princess Alexandra. The diary states they then made a lightning quick trip to America before returning to attend the festivities in England. 1887, the year of the Golden Jubilee of their venerated Queen Victoria, was celebrated with great pomp and circumstance as an opportunity for Britain's man-in-the-street to commemorate their imperial heritage, accentuating a people's common bonds and common aims. The vivid proceedings served as a reminder of the power of Britain's position in the world at that moment. The mood of the nation was soon to change, and the Jubilee marked the climax of an extraordinary age. They attended the final tribute. The naval review took place at Spithead, the waters between the great naval port of Portsmouth and the Isle of Wight known as "the roads." The Lows watched the might of Britain pass before their eyes on a private yacht, with Amy and her husband Admiral Grenfell; this was a heady beginning for a Savannah girl despite her superficial sophistication. Unfortunately Jessie's earlier diaries come to an abrupt halt at this point, and we have to rely on records and letters in the Gordon Collection concerning Daisy and Willie's subsequent movements.

The Next Generation—Tragedy Strikes Mary Low

The unmarried Low daughters had been positioned extremely well by their father's will, and the knowledge of their inheritance would certainly have been well known in their social set. They were ripe fruit for the plucking, and it did not take long for one fortune hunter to expose himself. It was 1887, during the pre-Christmas festivities, and a family party had gathered to share the occasion in Leamington. Mary Low was celebrating her recent engagement to thirty-one-year-old John Francis Green, a major in the 5th Dragoon Guards, and popular adjutant of the Yeomanry Cavalry, in which Willie Low was a captain. In the late nineteenth century, Willie, as the titular male of the family and his sister's guardian, should automatically have assumed the task of vetting the field of suitors for Mary's hand. In this case, it would appear from the facts that he may have been the one who introduced them. Major Frank Green was a frequent visitor at Beauchamp Hall even before Andrew Low's death, often standing in for Willie as the Misses Lows's escort to county balls.

The major kept rooms at nearby fashionable Clarendon Hotel when he was on duty in Warwickshire, and he had come down to visit the Lows, perhaps to discuss plans for the wedding or maybe Mary's dowry. Major Green was the son of Mr. Thomas Green, a respected barrister-at-law of the Inner Temple in London, who resided in nearby Badley, Northamptonshire. Frank Green, in all probability, had no more prospects than his military pay. The marriage was to have taken place in London on January 18, and no doubt, the happy couple was discussing their nuptials when a fatal knock came at the door.

Mary Low leaning on pedestal in 1888, passing through New York on her way home. *Courtesy The National Society of The Colonial Dames of America in the State of Georgia.*

Arthur Powell, butler at Beauchamp Hall, testified at the inquest that it was ten in the morning when a lady arrived in a cab. She first asked if Mr. Low was in, and when told he was not, she asked if Miss Mary Low was in residence. When the answer came in the affirmative, she enquired if Major Green was also there. She then made a request to see Mary Low, and was told that the family had not yet come down for breakfast. The butler allowed the lady to wait in the drawing room, asked her name which she refused to give, and went to fetch Major Green. The major immediately told the butler, without asking the lady's name, to tell her to go back to her hotel and wait there for him. The butler testified that as she was passing though the hall on the way out, she stopped and said, "You may say it is the Major's wife."

The caller was a tall handsome woman of about fifty years of age named Mrs. Rayner, and it transpired that she and the major had had a nine-year intimate relationship, which he had broken off to marry Mary Low. This was not agreeable to the lady, and on a whim, she had taken a train to Leamington to confront the major with his infidelity or perfidy. She testified that in September Major Green had gone up to Scotland, and had written to say he had become affianced to someone else. The reckless major, however, had neglected to indicate to Mary Low and presumably her brother that he was otherwise engaged. Following a confrontation in his rooms at the Clarendon Hotel with his former mistress, Major Green literally blew his head off with one of the shotguns he kept in a cabinet in his apartment. He perhaps meant to place the muzzle in his mouth, but in his hysteria missed and blew the left side of his face quite off. The verdict of the inquest was suicide while temporarily insane.[6] The jury donated their fee to charity.

Since she did not attend the inquest, which seemed more concerned with preserving the major's honor than Mrs. Rayner's reputation, it is not recorded how Mary Low learned of the terrible conclusion to her wedding plans.

The Savannah newspaper report of the incident tells that when Major Green was informed by the butler of the lady's arrival in the Lows' drawing room: "Immediately Mr. Green seemed very much 'confused and dismayed' and after sending word by the butler for the lady to meet him at the Clarendon Hotel 'turning to his entertainers, the Major said that the lady was the widow of a brother officer, who had fallen in the Ashantee war, and was constantly bothering him about business matters.'"

The last words the major are said to have uttered were that he was reckless and intended to kill himself. At least, that was one word he kept, and whether in the world of complicated Victorian morality that fatal act satisfactorily preserved his honor is for arbiters of social justice to determine. As for Mary's reaction, suffering such extreme humiliation would have broken any young woman's heart.

The mythology that passed down through descendants has it that my grandmother, Mary Low, was a sad and depressed person. From the distance of the future that is hard to believe and, after her marriage several years later, the many photos that remain show her to be a beautiful woman, a gentle, loving, and solicitous mother. Several ledgers of household accounts that have survived prove her competence as keeper of a large country home necessitating a multitude of servants for the stables, gardens, household, and nursery. Sadly she died the year before I was born, and all I know is that my own father adored her, and she left his eldest son, born just before she died, a substantial legacy of her own money from her Low inheritance.

Marriage for Jessie Low

As would have been the custom, Willie Low took a ten-year lease on a house named Lude and a grouse moor near Blair Atholl in the Scottish Highlands, owned by the Duke of Atholl. The Low sisters frequently joined their brother and sister-in-law during the shooting season. These events also served as informal marriage marts where suitable admirers could be examined at leisure. It was here that youngest sister Jessie met up again with her future husband, Hugh Graham. She had been corresponding with him for several years while he was ranching in Alberta, Canada, even before Andrew Low died.[7] There are photographs of shooting parties at Lude, which Mary Low is also in, and it is believed that her future husband, David Charles Guthrie, owner of an estate called Craigie near Dundee, also rented in the vicinity.

It would be interesting to know whether the Low children knew that seventy-five miles to the east of where they feasted and feted that their father was born in the ancient market town of Fettercairn, and had learned the trade of merchant in neighboring Brechin, at which he had become enormously successful, and made the money that allowed them to cavort with the nobility. If they knew, they might have speculated that had he not been so successful, they might have been the servants to those they now socialized with. In the social climate of the times, with its absurd snobbishness, there would have been absolutely no profit in revealing or dwelling on their father's more humble Scottish origins. None of their visitors' books emphasized their Americaness, but in fact the opposite. They had all reinvented themselves as English with no mention of Scottish pride by now. In fact, a slight sneering tone always surfaces in reference to Americans, a fairly typical English attitude that still prevails. It is the love-hate between Britain and America that is the basis of its "special relationship."

Jessie Low just prior to her marriage. *Courtesy The National Society of The Colonial Dames of America in the State of Georgia.*

Hugh Graham's mother was Jane Hermione, one of the daughters of the Duke of Somerset, and his father was Sir Fredrick Graham of Netherby on the Scottish border, near Gretna Green. According to family legend they were all cattle thieves and ruffians! Hugh was the second son and therefore had no expectation of inheriting title or land. He did, however, have the right connections: there were four peerages in his family. Jessie was an heiress and the planned alliance would have been satisfactory to all.

The guest list at her sparkling London society wedding was liberally sprinkled with titled relatives of the groom.[8] She married well as her husband had ancestors going back to Scottish Montroses of the seventh century. But it was also a classic match. Jessie had the money and Hugh Graham had the cachet. The youngest of Andrew Low's daughters by Mary Cowper Stiles Low was the first to marry; she was also the one who knew her mother the least—only a year old when her mother died. It is apparent from both her diaries and letters that Jessie was obsessed with money and

The Lows entertain houseguests at Lude, their leased Scottish hunting lodge, 1887. Left to right: Alfred Grenfell, unknown, Mary Low, Daisy, Frank Dugdale, Willie, Jessie, Jack Maxwell with the fish, and Katie. Daisy is the only one standing and seems out of the mix. *Courtesy The National Society of The Colonial Dames of America in the State of Georgia.*

its management. In a collection of letters from her to her mother-in-law, Lady Jane Hermione Graham, regarding her household expenditures, she begs for advice as to how she could cut down, a necessity she was most concerned with. Another Graham relative suggests that giving the servants skimmed milk would help cut down on household expenses.

Ronnie, their first child, was born in 1891. They lived first near Oxford at Bucknell Manor. Their second child, Alistair, was also born at Bucknell Manor as was their daughter Sibyl. There was another daughter, Mary, who died during World War I while nursing in Leamington—it is said of a broken heart due to the death of her fiancé in the war. The Grahams then rented a huge pile called Offchurch Bury near Leamington, belonging to Lord Aylesford, Warwickshire nobility, and ultimately moved to Barford, near Leamington.

The gentry in those days usually rented fully furnished, as opposed to owning their lavish country houses, and the Bucknell Manor visitors' book shows a slice of Edwardian upper-class country life bearing a distinct resemblance to the Robert Altman film *Gosford Park*. The book shows that mostly visitors were family and American relatives, over for the hunting and shooting. They bought an English style of living with their

American cotton money, all seeking upward mobility, living the life of English landed gentry. To be fair, this attitude was not put on to be worn like a cloak. It was inherent in the system.

Wellesbourne House—The Smart Set

By 1890, Willie had finally found the home he wanted, Wellesbourne House in the village of Wellesbourne, near Warwick. The original house was built in 1819 as a small hunting box as the village commenced to become a social center for Warwickshire gentry hunting with the North Warwickshire hounds.[9] It was gradually expanded during a succession of owners until it was bought by Willie Low, who proceeded to remodel and expand the house to hold extensive house parties attended by local nobility and occasional royalty. Elegant stables housed his famous selection of racehorses and hunters; and later on, a motor house held Wellesbourne's first motor car, AC 59, a 20 horsepower 19 cwt Golton.[10] The description of the house listed by the estate following his death reads:

> A valuable freehold country mansion surrounded by magnificently timbered parklands of about 55 acres, conveniently divided into paddocks, and used as an excellent stud farm. The house, surrounded by beautifully laid out grounds and walks, contains entrance halls, four reception rooms, 20 bedrooms, bathroom, ample domestic offices and lighted throughout by electric light. It has stabling for 40 horses, Carriage houses, grooms rooms, gardeners, stud grooms, and laundry houses, a most efficient electric supply, extensive range of greenhouses, motor garage and chauffeur's residence and numerous outbuildings.[11]

A house indeed fit to entertain a prince and his attendant courtiers. It was a typical Edwardian life for a young man with good connections and unlimited wealth. Andrew Low had done extremely well for his children, financially at any rate, and his daughters married as well as any of the contemporary American women who crossed the threshold into British high society, such as Jennie Churchill.[12] She was formerly Jennie Jerome from Brooklyn Heights, and had moved into the upper strata of English aristocracy by marrying politician and diplomat Lord Randolph Churchill, the second son of the Duke of Marlborough. Jennie Jerome's place in the history books was assured as the mother of famous Renaissance man—politician, historian, soldier, and painter—Sir Winston Churchill[13] There was, in fact, a considerable contingent of Americans living in the neighborhood. At least half a dozen had put down roots within six or seven miles of Wellesbourne House, including at one point Marshall Field, who had rented another big house in the village, Wellesbourne Hall.[14]

Daisy was presented at court to Queen Victoria, her sponsor the Marchioness of Hertford. The Wellesbourne visitors' book, now on display at the Juliette Gordon Low Birthplace in Savannah, is a veritable Who's Who of the well known and in some cases notorious names of the excesses of the Edwardian era.[15] Daisy's biography recounts that Willie had never introduced Daisy to the Prince of Wales until the Prince spied her at the Warwickshire Yeomanry Ball and demanded to meet her, saying he "didn't know she existed although he had known Willie for years." Husbands were understandably reluctant to introduce their wives to the royal heir to the throne, as the *droit de seigneur* of medieval times appeared to thrive in Edwardian England. Daisy later presided over a luncheon for the Prince at Wellesbourne House that is described in detail in her biography from her mother's letters.

Not long after moving into their elegant and comfortable Warwickshire home, Daisy had had to give up hunting for health reasons and was unable to share in some of the more physical sporting activities that Willy lived for. Her deafness contributed to her occasional difficulties at social events, as she could not always hear the nuances in conversation at the dinner table. It was now that she channeled much of her energy into learning the art of blacksmithing and other creative pursuits. It has long been repeated that Daisy herself beat out the iron gates for Gordonston Park,[16] but their massive size questions that possibility. They now hang in the garden of her birthplace in Savannah. Daisy remained very close to her family from Savannah, and in 1891 her parents and Sister Mabel visited her. It was at the Albemarle Hotel in London that Mabel met Rowland Leigh, son of Baron Leigh, Lord Lt. of Warwickshire of Stoneleigh Abbey, who she later married.

Mary Low Marries

Then tragedy struck again! Hattie Low Robertson died in 1891 at Widmerpool Hall, near Nottingham, her husband's home. Hattie, Andrew Low's second daughter by Sarah Hunter, is buried on the grounds in the chapel. It is said that her husband, George Coke Robertson, in the true tradition of Victorian romance novels, loved her so much and was so distraught by her death that he refused to allow her room to ever be changed. They had no children.

A few months later Mary Low married David Charles Guthrie of Craigie at Wellesbourne House, Warwickshire, on November 21, 1891. Mary Low's wedding was a far more somber affair than her younger sisters or her sister-in-law's in Savannah.[17]

Charlie Guthrie's father was James Alexander Guthrie, former Director of the Bank of England. His mother, Ellinor Stirling, was the daugh-

David Charles Guthrie, husband of Mary Low, ca. 1885. *Courtesy The National Society of The Colonial Dames of America in the State of Georgia.*

ter of Sir James Stirling, first governor of Western Australia. After her husband's death she remarried an Arbuthnott and moved to Surrey, England.[18] One of Charlie's sisters, Violet, married the Honorable James Montagu Stuart-Wortley and lived on the south coast in a cavernous house on the edge of the cliffs called Highcliffe Castle.[19] The Guthrie family traced their ancestry back to Scotland in the twelfth century, many of them serving in high positions in the households of the kings and queens of Scotland. One irony is that Guthrie Castle, in the hamlet of Guthrie in Angus, lay a mere ten miles from Brechin, where Andrew Low spent his youth; and the Guthrie Chalmers Company, the merchant banking

Mary Low Guthrie reading, after her marriage in 1888. *Courtesy The National Society of The Colonial Dames of America in the State of Georgia.*

company that D. C. Guthrie derived his income from, was founded in 1800, by Patrick Chalmers of Aldbar in Brechin. Mary Low's marriage brought the circle to completion.

Photographs of Mary Low Guthrie of the period show a tall, beautiful woman with lovely hair and a frequently pensive expression. In her young life she had already experienced much sadness. She and her husband lived all their lives in a large country home, East Haddon Hall, in the pretty village of East Haddon in Northamptonshire. A neighboring estate, Althorpe, was the home of the Earl Spencer, father of Diana, Princess of Wales. Charlie and Mary Guthrie had four children—Carolus, who died very young, James Alexander, known as Hamish (my own father), and two daughters, Christian and Margaret. In 1906 D. C. Guthrie wrote a family history for private publication called *The Guthrie Family,* which sheds a great deal of light on Scottish history and the Guthrie family story. My grandfather died at the end of the First World War in 1918, and my grandmother in 1932, a year before I was born. And thereby hangs yet another tale!

Mary was perhaps the most sensitive of the Low girls, wounded by her mother's death, shattered by a fiancé's scandalous suicide, saddened by her own eldest son's death as a child. She was a loving mother, a good housekeeper, and she certainly spoiled her eldest son Hamish. When her husband died they were married for less than twenty years.

Katie Low—The Suffragette

Katie was the eldest of Mary Cowper's daughters and for her entire life appeared to be the responsible one. She never married, but her name has been recorded for posterity through her involvement with philanthropy. During the nineteenth century poverty was endemic in many working class areas of major cities in England. It was the custom for socially minded individuals to associate themselves with good works. In this the era of women's suffrage there is no record that Katie Low ever chained herself to a railing like some, but she certainly contributed a great deal of her time and money to various women's organizations.

Her principal philanthropy was associated with a school she had attended known as the Francis Holland School, where she served as treasurer for the United Girls School Mission (USGM) for fifteen years until her death in 1923. In her memory, a settlement house was built in Battersea known to this day as the Katherine Low Settlement House.[20] Settlements were meant to be places where people could come to live in a community, bring skills, and care to benefit it. Katie Low would be proud to be associated with the work that the community center has done and continues to do in her name. Katie Low lived at 106 Park Street, London, and used to rent a country house every year for the hunting season.

All the Low girls were keen horsewomen, especially Amy and Katie, and adored riding to hounds. Katie was always the children's favorite maiden aunt. She was independent and savvy, a go-getter, a businesswoman, a caregiver, a suffragette (maybe), a champion of the underdog, and the keeper of the family's reputation and name (witness the diaries of her grandmother she painstakingly had transcribed). She was careful to protect her sisters' and brother's reputations (although that must have been a thankless task in Willie's case). Her character, perhaps, stems from having known her mother Mary Cowper the longest and best, and being made recipient of her Grandmother Eliza's stories.

Daisy's Fairy Tale Crumbles

The fairy-tale existence of the mistress of Wellesbourne House began to fray around the edges; cracks began to mar the smooth surface of a social life the envy of many of her friends across the ocean. William Low was spending more and more time abroad with his male cronies, rarely taking his wife with him. His energy was directed almost solely at racing, and he had developed a minor reputation with his successes.[21] Her letters, although rarely complaining, contain indications that they were drifting apart. Around this time Juliette Low had an "illness"—the description in her biography indicates that it could have been "female complications," possibly resulting from a miscarriage. Certainly there is no proof at all of that except that later sister Mabel mentioned it, but it could account for the further estrangement of Willie and Daisy. Willie was an extremely heavy drinker even for the excesses of the times. He remained on good terms with Daisy's parents, and in 1893 loaned William Washington Gordon $100,000. Gordon mortgaged his Savannah wharves as collateral. He paid it back in full by January 1, 1894. In 1893 Eleanor Kinzie Gordon founded the Georgia chapter of the Colonial Dames of America, two years after the national organization was founded. She was elected the Georgia chapter's first president.

There are signs that perhaps the master of Wellesbourne House was not averse to doing favors for his friend the Prince of Wales, and on the occasion of a huge party—a *bal poudre*—for the new Earl and Countess of Warwick, George and Alice Keppel stayed at Wellesbourne House. George was the younger son of the Earl of Albemarle, and his wife Alice Keppel later became notorious as mistress to the then Prince of Wales, and remained his favorite until his death as King Edward VII. Willie Low certainly had the ear of royalty and of the aristocracy. The question remains as to how much the permissive behavior of this set may have widened the rift between Willie and Daisy.

In *The Warwickshire Scandal* Lady Elizabeth Hamilton writes:

> The Prince also visited the Lows at Wellesbourne House which stood on the very margin of Sir Charles's Walton estate. The American Willie Low was a member of the Prince's set, sharing his interest

> in horses, gambling, and the ladies. His attractive wife Juliette, from Savannah, Georgia, would entertain the Prince to dinner cooked by her coloured cook Mosianna Milledge and by the ever-popular Rosa Lewis who came along with her bevy of pretty helpers. The Prince was always happy to dine anywhere if he knew Rosa Lewis would be there and the Lows tickled his palate with unfamiliar delicacies such as sweet potatoes, waffles and peach-fed hams all imported from America. The Countess of Warwick would come too, lending Juliette a red carpet to put down in the Prince's honour. The Prince was no doubt amused to think of his friend Willie bidding fair to oust Sir. Charles Mordaunt from his traditional position in local society. Willie Low was an excellent shot, leased a top class grouse moor from the Duke of Atholl, and out hunting was always seen to be up with the leaders.[22]

There is absolutely no doubt that Willie Low was no parvenu and was completely accepted in Edwardian society.

One element that set their entertainment apart was the reputation of their cook, Mosianna Milledge. She became renowned in Edwardian England for her incomparable Southern cooking, and was a character and a personage in her own right. Mosianna was noted for teaching her special brand of exotic cuisine to the fabled society cook Rosa Lewis, cook and courtesan to royalty.[23] Mosianna was also unique for the times, as she owned property in Savannah, supposedly purchased in 1894 at 513 East Gaston Street.[24] Lord Warwick, one of the more illustrious members of the social set the Low's moved in, as the legend goes, unable to pronounce or more likely remember her name, called her "Mozambique" and she called him "My Gawd."[25]

Willie plays a rather prominent role in Daphne Fielding's *The Duchess of Jermyn Street,*[26] about the life and times of the notorious Rosa Lewis, cook and proprietor of the famous Cavendish Hotel on Jermyn Street in London. Willie Low and Rosa Lewis were great friends, and there are rumors that their relationship extended beyond the bounds of friendship. She also proved to be a good friend of Daisy's and stood by her in her later travails.

It was dashing Willie Low who aroused Excelsior's (her husband) jealousy more than any of the other swells, for Rosa was always dropping his name, speaking of him with exaggerated admiration, as she recalled the lavishness of his entertaining, the delicacies of his table and cellar, his ability to bring down brace after brace of pheasants with his quick left and right as well as charm any other bird off a tree with his risqué jokes and high spirits.

A rather more frank tittle-tattle is expounded when Mrs. Fielding writes about Rosa Lewis' reputed love affairs, which she conducted with the utmost discretion.

> I have reason to believe that that Rosa was in love with William Low, who in his heyday must have been a most attractive man ... rich roistering Willie was her Southern beau, and he flitted in and out of the Cavendish scene laden with gifts of peach fed hams, sweet corn, molasses and Southern comfort ... at Warwick races, he kept open house in the club room and Rosa had the difficult task of providing lunches for an unknown number of guests. She was less worried by this problem, however, than the by the ardour of her employer, who was a connoisseur not only of four footed fillies but also of the two footed variety, and was as adept in the boudoir as the field of sport. But it was not so much these aptitudes of his that worried her as the presence in the background of his wife.[27]

In 1895 Daisy and Mabel visit Egypt without her husband; this marked the start of Daisy's friendships with several high-ranking British military men. She was beginning to live her own life. When the lease expired on Lude, Willie rented another grouse moor at Meallmore in Inverness, way north in the Highlands where the original Mackay family came from. The Earl of Warwick wrote in his own memoirs about the hospitality Willie provided on his shoots. Sir Charles Mordaunt of Walton Hall near Wellesbourne House also had a lodge nearby and had a shoot at Cawdor Castle—all of this recounted in Elizabeth Hamilton's *Warwickshire Scandal.*

In the plethora of memoirs and biographies written about the hedonistic life of Edwardian England Willie Low is mentioned with surprising frequency. One of his great friends was the Earl of Warwick, who in his memoirs, *Memories of Sixty Years,* wrote.[28]

> When I recall the number of old friends who have gone before, I think of them with little regret—Moriendum est omnibus. One of the best and dearest I ever had was Willie Low, who lived and died at Wellesbourne, near Warwick. He inherited a lot of money, and was very generous. He was fond of pigeon shoots, and used to hold them in a big meadow behind the house, a marquee, with a big brazier of coal, being erected on the ground and well stocked with all manner of good things.

The earl describes in detail a memorable trip taken with Willie to indulge in big-game fishing in Florida via Savannah, where they enjoyed the Southern hospitality of General and Mrs. Gordon. From the British perspective of their social class both Jessie's diaries and the earl's memoirs

Daisy Low and her sister Mabel Gordon at Wadi Halfa, Sudan, 1895. Daisy's apparent sadness reflects the state of her marriage. *Courtesy The National Society of The Colonial Dames of America in the State of Georgia.*

present a rather positive portrait of the relationship in Savannah between black and white at the end of the nineteenth century. Jessie writes poetically of the enthusiastic celebration of Emancipation Day, when former Negro soldiers dressed up in their blue uniforms and plumed hats paraded in the streets. She and her cousins frequently attended African churches to listen to the music, and they used to indulge in after-dinner impromptu drawing room concerts in what they termed "Negro sing-alongs." The earl's description of life in post-reconstruction Savannah is even more munificent:

> Almost half the population is black, and as far as I can see, the best kind of black. Although slavery is, of course, a thing of the past, all the old families seem to have retained their black servants, and the friendliest relations exist between the whites and the Negroes. . . . At night after dinner, we would go into the garden, where there would be a company of Negroes with beautiful voices engaged to sing to us the old songs of the plantations. I am not musical, but I never had enough of those songs. The Southern melodies, for the most part in a minor key, have a haunting beauty of their own that would be impressive anywhere, but by night, in the beautiful gardens of the old time Southern town, they had an indescribable quality. It was not only the four Europeans they appealed to: the passers-by would gather at the garden gates and the street would be crowded

> with listeners. It was a picture of a world familiar only in books that these Negro singers conjured up, and they gave me memories which I value to this hour, and take a pleasure in setting down here.

Another source corroborates the information we have that Willie Low was an extremely generous individual.[29]

> Mr. Low, like other gentlemen of substance at the time, was involved in charitable works, giving, for example, 100 cwt of coal to the poor in winter. An extract from the vestry Order Book of May 19th 1897 runs: "This day William Mackay Lowe, Esquire, authorized G. H. Granville to commemorate Her Majesty the Queen's Diamond Jubilee on the completion of the 60th year of Her Majesty's reign on June 22nd 1897 by entertaining and feeding the whole of the adult population, men and women of Wellesbourne, Mountford and Hastings, the expense of which he, William Mackay Lowe has volunteered to bear. Seven hundred and sixty-six persons were fed, including the sick who were unable to attend, messengers being sent to their houses with the food." For this number of people it was considered necessary to provide 6 rounds of beef (370 lbs), 10 sirloins (200 lbs), 8 hams (130 lbs), 12 legs of mutton (96 lbs) as well as 10 fillets of veal, 100 4 lb loaves of bread and 28 lbs of cheese, 6 barrels of beer 150 bottles of ginger beer, 100 lbs of plum pudding, not forgetting salt and mustard, 'salad if possible', tea sugar, milk, cake and buns, so it seems that Mr. Low must have had to foot a fairly heavy bill! Afterwards the food and ale left over was distributed to sixty families in the neighbourhood.

From the time Daisy became mistress of the manor, sister Mabel spent time every year with her as Willie began to wander more and more. Rowland Leigh was still courting Mabel and they are finally allowed to marry. William Gordon, her father, had refused the match until then, and conventional wisdom is that it was because of the way Willie Low treated Daisy that had given him a poor opinion of Englishmen. Daisy tells her brother Arthur in a letter, "I see so little of Billow I feel there is no human affection for me except in this family."

In the United States President McKinley promoted William Washington Gordon to brigadier general, representing Georgia when the Spanish-American War broke out. The entire Gordon family went with Gordon to Miami, where Daisy soon joined them to work with the wounded in the hospital. Whether this action was one Daisy truly believed her duty to perform or whether it was one way out of what had become an intolerable situation is not clear.

The Wicked Witch Appears in the Mirror

Then the story of what appeared to be a disintegrating marriage that could perhaps have been patched up, or at the least plastered over like so many of that era, took another twist. The classic femme fatale arrived on the scene. While on holiday it is believed that Willie met the woman who was to become the nemesis of the Low and Gordon families—the dreaded Mrs. Anna Bateman.

In a monograph written by Jane Davidson[30] she states that it was 1898, and that it was her grandmother Jessie Graham who had introduced them! Jessie had lost her little boy Ronnie, aged nine, and Willie had taken her to Wales to recuperate from her grief; it was while staying in a hotel there that he met Mrs. Bateman. Mabel Gordon Leigh, writing many years later, thought they met in 1895. Two local historians of the Wellesbourne scene, Peter and Rosalind Bolton, maintain that the records provide some clues regarding the intimate nature of their friendship.[31] He writes that the names reported, presumably in the social columns of the local newspaper that documented the gentry's comings and goings on, included a big party at Wellesbourne House in January 1901—the Earl of Warwick, Lady St. Oswald, Miss Campbell, Mrs. Leigh, Hon. Mrs. Bateman, and Lord Dungarvon amongst the attendees.[32] So obviously Willie's behavior, considered outrageous by his family and Daisy's supporters, did not impact at all on his social standing.

In England an era was about to come to an end. On January 22, 1901, in the eighty-third year of her age, and the sixty-fourth year of her reign, Queen Victoria, her children around her bedside, the portrait of her beloved consort Prince Albert over her bedpost, died in her summer home Osborne House in the Isle of Wight. The Victorian Age was over. The rakish Prince of Wales became King Edward VII. At the time of his accession Edward was in his sixtieth year, with a well-deserved reputation as a *bon vivant* and a womanizer more interested in the corridors of country houses than the corridors of power.

The Pot Boils Over

Back in Britain on August 21, 1901, Daisy writes to Mabel from Meallmore, the shooting lodge in Scotland, that Willie, who has been "taking the cure at Nauheim," had returned, looked well, and that "Mrs. Bateman comes Friday." It is obvious that she knew about the existence of Mrs. Bateman at that time. Then everything in her world collapsed. Hard on its heels another letter arrived begging Mabel to come to her. Mrs. Bateman had moved in and taken over, was giving orders to the servants, and Daisy had been relegated to another wing. Willie was being poisonously rude to

Daisy. The family rallied to her aid. Katie Low arrived posthaste, and Daisy and Mabel left. In October of 1901 Daisy returned to Wellesbourne to pack and leave for Savannah. William Gordon met Willie in Paris, where he stated he did not want a divorce, apologized for his behavior, and asked for time to break off the affair with Anna Bateman.

In February, Daisy was still waiting to hear from Willie and return to Wellesbourne. Her husband had neither written nor sent her money. Four months later Willie Low wrote to Daisy saying Wellesbourne was shut up, and he had gone to Scotland to Meallmore. He asked her consent to live apart, but still does not appear to have asked for a divorce. William Gordon wrote to him requesting that he make a settlement on his wife through the hands of his brothers-in-law George Robertson and Harry Grenfell. Daisy wrote to Willie agreeing to the separation. Most of their friends and all his family at this point appear to be very much on Daisy's side, horrified at their brother's actions.

Unpredictable as ever, by now Willie refused to give her a settlement unless she agreed to a divorce; he wished to marry Mrs. Bateman, but insisted she not be named as corespondent in the case. Daisy finally breaks down and agrees to initiate a divorce, but this was England, and divorce was not that easy with tremendous stigma attached to the woman, and Willie seemed determined to protect his mistress rather than his wife.

The entire episode written by niece Daisy Gordon Lawrence is quite candid, reflecting the official Gordon perspective of events. It is a common story of a dissolute man, naive wife, and a fortune-hunting woman. Willie still refused to allow Mrs. Bateman to be named as corespondent—stalemate! The letters that have recently come into the possession of the Andrew Low House from the estate of Jane Davidson, mostly from Katie Low and Jessie Graham's estates, and currently restricted, shed quite a bit of light on the attitudes of the various players in this drama. During this time, Daisy spent a lot of time in Rosa Lewis' hotel on Jermyn Street.

Willie Low was drinking himself to death, and Katie was afraid his brain was affected. Letters in the estate files show the degree of concern, and how Katie and the other members of the Low family tried to get him treated, even committed. Daisy finally agreed to Willie's terms, and in the summer of 1904 she signed the divorce petition. Willie offered a settlement of 2,500 pounds a year with collateral from 10,000 shares he had invested in Guthrie-Chalmers, D.C. Guthrie's trading company. Inevitably his drinking became uncontrollable, he became mentally ill, and had to be hospitalized.

A Harley Street doctor, Charles Beevor, in an opinion dated October 12, 1904, says that he had examined Mr. Low in consultation with Dr. Oldmeadow, and found him to be suffering from a brain disease he called

"General Paralysis." He further stated he had almost completely lost his speech due to a form of "epilephiform attack," and that he also certainly was mentally incapacitated—symptoms that sound suspiciously like delirium tremens. He suggests giving power of attorney to a relative. Willie could not have been totally incapacitated because he categorically refused to give away his power; he did, however, agree to sign a codicil allowing his family some protections. The entire family were united by now, and extremely concerned about not only their brother's mental capabilities, but also their own future.

Rebounding, he made a remarkable recovery, was released, and returned to Wellesbourne under the care of his sisters, Katie and Amy, where they all spent Christmas. Willie wanted to invite Mrs. Bateman, and when they refused, he had a violent fit of temper and ordered them all to leave. Vindictively he then instructed his lawyer Mr. Gasquet to cut off Daisy's allowance. Jessie injudiciously entered the fray and wrote to Daisy saying that she knew that Willie had gone to a hotel with an innocent woman, presumably for evidence for the divorce and to prove his infidelity, and Daisy only wanted his money. Mabel Leigh wrote that Jessie acted out of spite.[33] Daisy immediately stopped divorce proceedings. Willie was furious with his sister and wrote to Daisy asking for things to proceed. They met one more time in London, where Daisy had rented a house, and he once more begged her to give him a divorce without naming Mrs. Bateman. She refused. Letters between Mabel Leigh, Katie Low, and Daisy's mother Nellie seem to indicate that at the end even Daisy was feeling great grief at the depths Willie had sunk, but hoped that his relationship with Mrs. Bateman would bring him happiness.

The negotiations became irrelevant when on June 8, 1905, William Mackay Low died at age forty-five, from an "epilephiform attack" at Ruthin Castle, Ruthin, County of Denbigh, North Wales, one of the family seats of the Cornwallis West family. A letter to Nellie from Mabel in the Gordon family collection describes both the death and the funeral:

> Dearest little Mamma: I sent you Katie's letter, I enclose her telegraph. It seems she stopped George Robertson telegraphing D as she thought I had better break it to her, and they each thought the other had wired— Mrs. Lewis [Rosa of the Cavendish Hotel] sent me a wire to her from one of the servants saying Willie was dead—He died at Ruthin Castle, a place near Chester, Mrs. Bateman had taken. He went for a motor drive in the afternoon and seemed a little tired. He was all right at dinner but went to bed early saying he felt rather tired. Baker who had gone back to him gave him his medicine, he said he felt better and Baker went across the room, heard

> Willie stumble, and just got back to him as he fell—he never regained consciousness but was very violent and died 1:35 am on June 8. Katie was spared seeing that woman, but she (Mrs. B) had made Willie sign a paper saying in case of illness, or death, all directions were to be given by her—I went down to Widmerpool where Daisy was staying with May Egerton, told Daisy and brought her home. Everyone has been most kind, not only Daisy's friends, but Willie's have written D saying they know how she will feel it, and how glad she must be that she was always so good to him. If he had died two years ago, noone would have realized what a tool he had become in that woman's hands; but I think that everyone now realizes how she entirely dictated and ruled him—Anyhow, now the fighting will be with her, which is one comfort. Daisy is splendid as she always is in every crisis. Of course, Rowley and I will go to the funeral with her—anyway now the nightmare of divorce has gone forever, and that is like having a heavy stone gone . . . devotedly, Mab.[34]

His obituary reads:

> Sportsmen generally will regret the death of Mr. W. M. Low. . . . The deceased gentleman had been for nearly twenty years a prominent owner and breeder of racehorses . . . important races won by Mr. Low were the Cesarewitch with St Brie in 1896, the Champagne Stakes at Doncaster with Mark For'ard in 1898 and the Derby Gold Cup with Littleton in 1903, Elopement carried his colors second to Diamond Jubilee in the St. Leger of 1900.

Willie Low was buried in the Chapel at Widmerpool Hall near Nottingham.[35] Mrs. Bateman chose the funeral site and legend has it she placed a bundle of love letters on his breast before the coffin was closed, with a note saying "Sleep well, beloved!" Daisy and the Low sisters all attended.

After the funeral Mr. Gasquet, Willie's business agent, read the will; perhaps prudently Daisy decided discretion was the better part of valor and was not present. Willie Low's last will and testament appoints as executors his brothers-in-law, Harry Grenfell and George Coke Robertson. He leaves fifty thousand of his preference shares in Guthrie Chalmers to his trustees instructing them to pay the interest income to his wife, Juliette Magill Low, during her widowhood, until either her death or remarriage, whichever came first, after which (should she die or remarry) the income from her trust should be divided equally between his sisters Jessie Graham, Mary Guthrie, and Amy Grenfell. He leaves 10,000 of his Guthrie Chalmers preference shares outright to his sister Katie Low. He leaves the whole of his freehold property at Wellesbourne, including all furniture and household effects, to his half sister Amy Grenfell.

Then came the kicker:

> I give all the rest of my preference shares and the whole of my ordinary shares in Guthrie Chalmers, and all the residue of my real and personal estate of what nature whatsoever (including all of my property in the United States of America) . . . unto Anna Bateman of the Manor House, Morley, in the county of Derby, widow.

This Will is dated December 8, 1902.

In a codicil dated two years later, Willie rescinds the terms of his original will giving Daisy the income from 50,000 shares of Guthrie Chalmers stock on the grounds that he had made a settlement of 2,500 pounds a year upon her, in substitution for, not in addition to, the life interest in the trust. He also stipulated that the settlement sum should not be taken out of his property at Wellesbourne House—which he has still left to Amy Grenfell—but instructed that it should be taken out of his general estate.

With that codicil, he had left his wife a meager annual settlement, had cut his sisters Mary Guthrie and Jessie Graham out altogether, unmarried Katie had an outright gift of 10,000 shares in Guthrie Chalmers, Amy had the valuable property Wellesbourne House, and all its household effects—his mistress Anna Bateman got everything else.

To add to the consternation felt on the reading of this extraordinary document, it was already known that the firm of Guthrie Chalmers, in which he had much of his money invested, was on somewhat shaky financial ground.[36]

Let the Games Begin

As could be expected all hell broke loose. Daisy refused to accept the terms and contested the will![37] Anna Bateman wrote to Harry Grenfell, one of Willie's two executors, to say she would not back down. The battle was on![38]

The power struggle that ensued was intense, exhaustive, and bitter. Not only between Anna Bateman, the mistress, and Daisy Low, the scorned wife, but all the sisters as well. Items squabbled over included the sale of Willie's prize orchid collection. Amy claimed that the sale would allow for the dispensation of more than half the gardeners at Wellesbourne, which would save a considerable amount of money. The agent, Gasquet, had arranged for the sale of the extensive wine cellar and cigar collection by Christie's auction house, keeping back the wines Lady Grenfell wanted.

An opinion of one of the magistrates examined in great detail the interpretation of "household contents" left to Amy Grenfell in Willie's original will—the opinion decided that horses, motorcars, and carriages did not, especially the car left at Ruthin Castle, count as household items. Wines, brandy, port, cigars, and silver cups did qualify providing they actually resided at Wellesbourne House. The stallions at stud at Kineton did not! Orchids and plants would qualify. Animals and stock could not, especially the dogs! Gasquet personally took two bulldogs home with him so they would not fall victim to the bickering. A myriad Solomons busily went to work to chop up the booty.

In a letter to Admiral Grenfell Charles Gasquet expresses concern over the possibility of a court battle:

> I hope that matters may be amicably adjusted, but as you know where ladies are concerned, it is nearly impossible to say when they will be governed by reason and not by sentiment. In confidence, I do not think that anyone would have the least chance of upsetting the Will. Mrs. Low has not alleged mental incapacity and looking at the Will as a whole, it is a perfectly reasonable one in view of the fact that Mrs. Low had taken divorce proceedings against her husband, and that he had hoped when they were terminated, to marry Mrs. Bateman.

These letters from Katie and Jessie's estates are quite combustible. Gasquet writes to Amy "as for Mrs. Low, I cannot think she will be so insane as to refuse to compromise. She must know that twenty minutes in the witness box would destroy her case." He also reassures her that neither she nor her sisters will ever have to communicate with Mrs. Bateman.

Writing to Harry Grenfell, on duty in Valletta, Malta, Gasquet cuts straight to the chase, warning of the dangers and pitfalls of a prolonged struggle and the benefits of a settlement:

> As to the general question, the two defendants now stand in this position. Mrs. Bateman was willing, and authorized me to make proposals of a settlement upon the terms of her paying Mrs. Low 40,000 in cash, 7,000 the value of the American real estate and 25,000 pounds in Guthrie Chalmers & Co. Ltd. This would have constituted in my opinion a satisfactory settlement. But Mrs. Low absolutely rejected these proposals. What more she wants, I cannot think, as there is no larger liquid sum, and the validity of her deed of settlement appears to be open to doubt. Recently, however Sir George Lewis has told me that she was open to reduce her terms. It has been a difficult task to screw these parties up on the terms, but I feel sure that it is, as I always told you, simply a question of settlement. The case will never come into court. Neither Mrs. Bateman

> nor Mrs. Low could possibly afford to let it go to trial. Directly terms are actually agreed, I will send you a telegram 'all satisfactory' by which you will know that the matter has been finally adjusted. Mrs. Bateman is continuing her 'rest cure' in the South of France and Mrs. Low wishes to go to America, so that I hope the telegram will not be long before it is dispatched to you.

By April 1906 the American estate was added to the tussle for the spoils of war, and poor George Coke Robertson was left the sole surviving executor of William Mackay Low's contested estate. Right in the middle of this muddle Vice Admiral Sir Harry T. Grenfell died, less than a year after he was knighted in that year's Birthday Honours. Andrew Low's eldest daughter had achieved the ultimate English accolade, entitled to be called Lady Grenfell.[39]

Wellesbourne House was advertised in the *Times* of London on July 14, 1906, to be put up for auction by "John Margetts and Sons, at the Mart, Token-house Yard. London. E. C. on Tuesday, the 17th day of July 1906 at 2.0' clock precisely." Newspaper clippings at the time of Amy Grenfell's death list her as residing at Wellesbourne House, which would indicate that the house was not sold that day at auction, but that many of the contents were sold to raise the cash to disburse the settlements. Amy Grenfell died in 1917. She is also buried at Widmerpool Hall in Nottinghamshire with her sister and half brother.

Willie Low blazed a brief trail like a comet touching the lives of many during an extraordinary era in British society. Like Icarus he flew too close to the sun, and also like Icarus, refused to heed the example of his father Daedalus, and burned out in the heat generated by his excesses.

Daisy Picks Up the Pieces

Daisy's travails were not yet over, and in 1906 she was informed that the shares of Guthrie Chalmers she was being urged to accept as part of her settlement were practically worthless.

Daisy fought the will vigorously, on behalf of her sisters-in-law as well as her herself, and finally Anna Bateman agreed to pay Mary and Jessie the same amount as Amy and Katy. Daisy received 40,000 pounds in discharge of her annuity, and 50,000 in Guthrie Chalmers stock. She also received all of Willie's Savannah holdings, including the house on Lafayette Square, built by her father-in-law, Andrew Low. Conventional wisdom has it that the reason Mrs. Bateman gave that up was that under American law Willie was deemed to have died intestate because his will had only two signatures instead of the three witnesses required, hence all his property and investments in America reverted to his widow.

Juliette Gordon Low, still living in London, with courage and indomitable will picked up the pieces of her shattered world. During 1911 she met the British hero of Mafeking, Baden Powell, in Scotland, where he had formed the Boy Scouts. That summer, impressed with his work and perhaps with the man himself, she formed a corps of Girl Guides to teach the girls nursing, childcare, and how to tie knots. Later that year Baden Powell and Daisy sailed together for America on the *Arcadian*. On board was a young woman named Olave Soames. Daisy left the ship in Jamaica, and before the ship reached New York Baden Powell was engaged to Miss Soames.[40] The engagement was kept a secret for a year; Daisy only knew about it just before the marriage. Soon after, she started the Girl Scouts of America movement in Savannah.

David Charles Guthrie died in 1918 and Hugh Graham in 1925, leaving the two youngest Low women, Mary and Jessie, widows. Katie Low died a few years later, having never married.

According to family lore, Mrs. Bateman was a widow with a large fortune when she met Willie and never needed his money. Mrs. Bateman remarried in 1913 to a man young enough to be her son, a Commander Russell Lister-Kaye, Royal Navy. His grandfather was a baronet, his grandmother the daughter of an earl, and he became gentleman usher to King George VI in the years just before World War II. Lister-Kaye and Anna lived happily ever after. She eventually died in 1947; her husband, having married again, died in 1960, one hundred years after Willie's birth! Whether or not they benefited as much as has been imagined from Willie's windfall is debatable as the firm in which he had most of his investments, D.C. Guthrie's family firm, Guthrie Chalmers, drifted into bankruptcy in the 1930's and became defunct, its shares almost valueless.[41]

Juliette Gordon Low died in 1927 leaving the house and stables on Lafayette Square to brother William Washington Gordon III, who then sold the Andrew Low House to the Georgia Chapter of the Colonial Dames, with the Girl Scouts retaining the stables and servants quarters as their headquarters.

The End and the Beginning

It is ironic that diaries kept by professional writers and ordinary people alike are frequently the way in later years one is able to verify conflicting memories. Well-known English author Evelyn Waugh and Jessie Low Graham have this in common in terms of this biography, although it must be said that Evelyn Waugh is ruthlessly candid about his relationships while Jessie preferred to deal in banalities and insinuations. Reading between the lines it is possible to strike a balance between fact and fiction. It was because of Jessie's diaries that I was able to finally verify several

The Andrew Low House's carriage house and stable, ca. 1935. Daisy established the Girl Scout office in the rooms Tom Milledge once occupied. She willed the building to the Girl Scouts, and today GSUSA maintains the building as its First National Headquarters. *Courtesy The National Society of The Colonial Dames of America in the State of Georgia.*

uncorroborated elements of this story. The first was contained in a piece of loose paper given to me by Jessie's granddaughter, in her grandmother's handwriting. It listed details of a gravestone found in a churchyard in Brechin, Scotland, that proved to be the resting place of Andrew Low's father, mother, and siblings.[42] Evelyn Waugh writes extensively in his published diaries details of his close friendship with Jessie Graham's son, Alistair, who had already been linked to Evelyn Waugh's knowledge of Willie Low's life through his input to Rosa Lewis' biography: "She showed a similar solicitude to Alistair Graham, the nephew of her old admirer Willie Low. In those days he was a wild young man, and she took him under her wing and into her heart."[43]

The closeness of their relationship described in the introduction to Waugh's diaries by his editor Michael Davie, as one that was "enlivened by his friendship with Alistair Graham." This friendship supplied material for two of Waugh's best-known comic novels, *Decline and Fall* and *Vile Bodies*, part of which he wrote in an attic room at Barford, where Jessie Graham lived.[44]

On Bank Holiday, August 3, 1926, Jessie, Alistair, and Evelyn Waugh set off for a driving trip to Scotland, staying en route in Carlisle with her late husband Hugh Graham's eldest brother, Sir Richard Graham. They went on to Netherby, the Graham's ancestral home, then to Edinburgh and further north. It was possible that it was on this trip that Jessie paid a visit to the cathedral at Brechin, although the visit is not mentioned in Waugh's diaries. They were certainly in the vicinity. On the return trip Waugh recounts:

> Mrs. G was in a towering rage all the time from York to Barford, and was intolerably rude to Alistair, who provoked her, and to me, who did not. Arrived at Barford she proceeded to attack me violently for being consistently rude to her all through the expedition. It ended with my resolving heartily never to visit her again.

This was a threat he did not carry out although there are no more mentions of the Grahams in his diary after 1927.

Of passing interest is a reference to Daisy Lowe [sic] staying at Barford in the summer of 1925, "quarrelling incessantly with Mrs. G" and Jessie falling into a rage when she discovered that Alistair was covering Waugh's overdraft at the bank. She immediately took off to visit Mary Low Guthrie at East Haddon who was "living in solitary splendour with a bevy of superannuated old retainers." It is here that he mentions my own father, Hamish Guthrie, who was visiting his mother with his second wife, Stella.

Mary Low Guthrie died 29 July 1832, and is buried in East Haddon churchyard.

Journey's End

Historical research always involves a form of necromancy. Digging in the dirt, revealing secrets, exposing lies. It is also a form of therapy, a catharsis of the past, allowing the living to commune with the dead. Many cultures dig up their ancestors in annual ceremonies, propping them up in their shrouds to join in the festivities of the alive before gently, caringly, and reverentially laying them again to rest until its time to join the party once more.

One month after her sister Mary Low Guthrie died, Jessie Low Graham wrote to her relatives in Savannah. Caroline Couper Lovell gathered these family letters into an unpublished memoir called *Tannie's Journal.*

> My Dearest Cousins: This letter is for all of you. I have been wanting to write all winter but have been very poorly indeed. Life is too lonely for words.... The young people have no use at all for the old. One sees that on all sides. Now about dear Mary. One can not wish her back to the "existence" she has lived for past two years. She got

Captain James Alexander "Hamish" Guthrie and Elaine Brigstocke Guthrie with their two children, David and Jennifer, at Tredington Manor, Warwickshire, 1933. *Courtesy Jennifer Guthrie Ryan.*

queer fancies, took no interest in anything outside and slept most of the time. Her girls went over week ends, but they, like all modern young people, bored with illness and old age. I got over always about once a week, in spite of being so ill myself [sic] but she never seemed to want to see anyone. I saw her four days before she died, and she knew both Alie [Jessie's son] and me, and talked for a half an hour, then relapsed into semi-consciousness, and was quite unconscious for two days before she died. She had two nurses. I went over twice after and for funeral. I don't know anything about how she has left things, except Christian [eldest daughter] is to have East Haddon, not divided, but I have been told nothing, except she left Margie 200 lbs. I am glad of that. The girls did not let Hamish [James Alexander Guthrie, her only surviving son] know till she was dead. He got back in time for the funeral. I did not see him to speak to. He sat in front of me at church, and then went off and saw no one. It was very quiet. She asked for no one to go except near relations. I tried to get

> Hamish to come and see me next day, but he went straight back to Minorca, where he left the girl and child, and is to marry her now. I shall miss Mary more than I can say!!! She is my last, and I myself, the last of my race. I have also outlived nearly all my friends and generation over here, and my life is too empty and lonesome for words. I don't want to go on living. I fear this is a gloomy letter, but I am very down and out, and now have to make all arrangements for my death. I had set all my affairs in order, when I thought I was going to have an operation before. Now I have to see to everything again, and my maid leaves me today. I have been so good to her when she was ill, nursed her, sent her to hospital, and waited 8 weeks for her. Now she leaves me just as I need some one. I hate strangers round me. It's useless asking Syb to write how I am. She has not done one thing for me since I have been laid up. She seems to have no natural affection except for her children. Everyone else can go to the wall.
>
> Well good bye dear cousins. I long to join the dear ones on the other side, and Death has no terrors for me. I am tired of Life. Thank Caro for her letter. Love from Jessie

The "girl and the child" my father was to marry when the divorce from his second wife came through were my own mother and brother; mimicking his own grandfather, he too was twenty years older than his young wife, Elaine.

Jessie Graham died May 13, 1934, at Barford, and is also buried in the small graveyard of the lovely old church at East Haddon.

On one of those soft melancholy November days in England when the rain is not falling as much as permeating the skin, misting the hair, and soaking the clothes, I stood in the ancient mossy graveyard of the East Haddon church. My attention is focused on a short line of gray and orange lichen-covered gravestones marking the last resting place of some of the characters I had come to know so well in my journey of the past seven years. These were the bones of my own family—the Guthrie's—including my grandmother, Mary, and my grandfather, David Charles. I had never been to East Haddon Hall before, which is no longer owned by the family, for reasons that will need to await explanation for the writing of the sequel to this biography. Suffice it to say that on account of dissension in the next generation of children my father was not laid to rest in the graveyard of his childhood home.

I have traveled very far in both time and miles in my journey to meet my ancestors, and on that day I was very sad because ten days before my only full blood brother, David Charles Guthrie, had died suddenly in my presence. He was "the child" of Jessie's letter.

My quest for the essentials was over, and all that was needed now was to endeavor to put complex relationships in perspective while striving to continue walking my own truth, and still do honor and justice to every single soul who played a central or peripheral role in the drama of the forebearers' lives. This is that attempt. I trust the ancestors—mine and all the others—will feel I have risen to the challenge.

The motto of the Guthrie family is Latin: *Sto Pro Veritate.* I have always taken that to contain the essential meaning "I Am the Truth." That is my purpose in writing this account of the triumphs and tragedies of the roots and branches of the House of Low. Today I am at peace. I have done my best and that is all anyone can ever do. Truth and fact are not necessarily the same thing. Fact is interpretation of what the writer perceives as the truth. Truth is interpretation of what the reader defines as the facts.

The past has gone, the present lives in the now, and the future awaits. It is time to move on.

Epilogue

America's fascination with the preservation of social history has spawned a cottage-industry interest in ancestry. The advent of the internet has seen an explosion of on-line sources where distant cousins correspond with even more distant cousins, creating massive trees with deep roots and myriad branches. An interesting misinterpretation or rather competition lies in the disdain academic historians feel for their "family history" brethren in terms of methodology and importance. In fact, both disciplines complement each other, and an examination of marriage alliances is every bit as important as the mergers of businesses. Continuity and memory depends on the interest of family members in both safeguarding and protecting their ancestors stories. In Savannah the Lows disappeared because there was no one left to carry the flame of family history.

The main emphasis of this project has been to correct the record as far as is humanly possible, surrounding the lives of both Andrew Lows. Books are regularly published replete with erroneous facts about the Lows culled from various secondary published sources based on faulty premises. Many of these contemporary books focus on sources available in Savannah and other Georgia archives, and repeat the conventional wisdom without corrections. Few have explored the role of the British-American merchants who tended to dominate the commercial scene—logically as cotton was the lifeline passing through the ports of Savannah and Liverpool, the end for marketing the raw material to feed Britain's exploding textile industry.

Much confusion exists concerning the multiple Andrew and John Lows and their relationships to each other, or not, as the case may be. The factual information is readily available in a multitude of special collections, particularly those at the Georgia Historical Society in Savannah, the Barnsley Papers at Emory and Duke universities, the Scarbrough

Papers at the Georgia Department of Archives, the Kollock Letters, the Mackay-Stiles Papers at the University of North Carolina, many collections at all campuses of University of Georgia and on *ad infinitum*. There are also the extensive records of the Scottish Church, Old Parish Records registering births, marriages, and deaths going back centuries. Liverpool is a veritable goldmine of records and archives starting with the Liverpool Records Archives, the University of Liverpool, the Maritime Museum, and a multiplicity of historians and experts in all fields from cotton to the Civil War. Liverpool has devoted enormous resources to recording its colorful history. And then there is Scotland with incomparable records in their official and unofficial repositories, especially the Scottish Record Archives in Edinburgh, the Mitchell Library in Glasgow, and various Aberdeen archives.

Neither the Low Company nor Low family in either Savannah or Liverpool has its own special collection—other than the extensive group of Andrew Low, Sr.'s letters in the Hutchison-Dawson Papers at the Georgia Historical Society. The fact there was no one to carry the torch for the Lows means that they were passed over as history started to emerge as Savannah's most prolific legacy feeding the tourist boom. No one reconstructed the progress of the Andrew Low Company from 1800, their activities in Liverpool, or the antecedents of the Low family in Scotland from many available primary source and genealogical records, for either dissertations or histories of Savannah's merchant elite. That error has also been corrected. The exhaustive and extensive research notes for this project, spanning a seven-year period, will be deposited in an archive and made available to anyone interested in the period of time and the subject matter . . . warts and all!

Andrew Low and the Sign of the Buck attempts to right these wrongs, correct the record, and tell a ripping good yarn in the bargain. How well we have succeeded must wait for history to decide.

Jennifer Guthrie Ryan
Hugh Stiles Golson

Family Tree

The Low Family

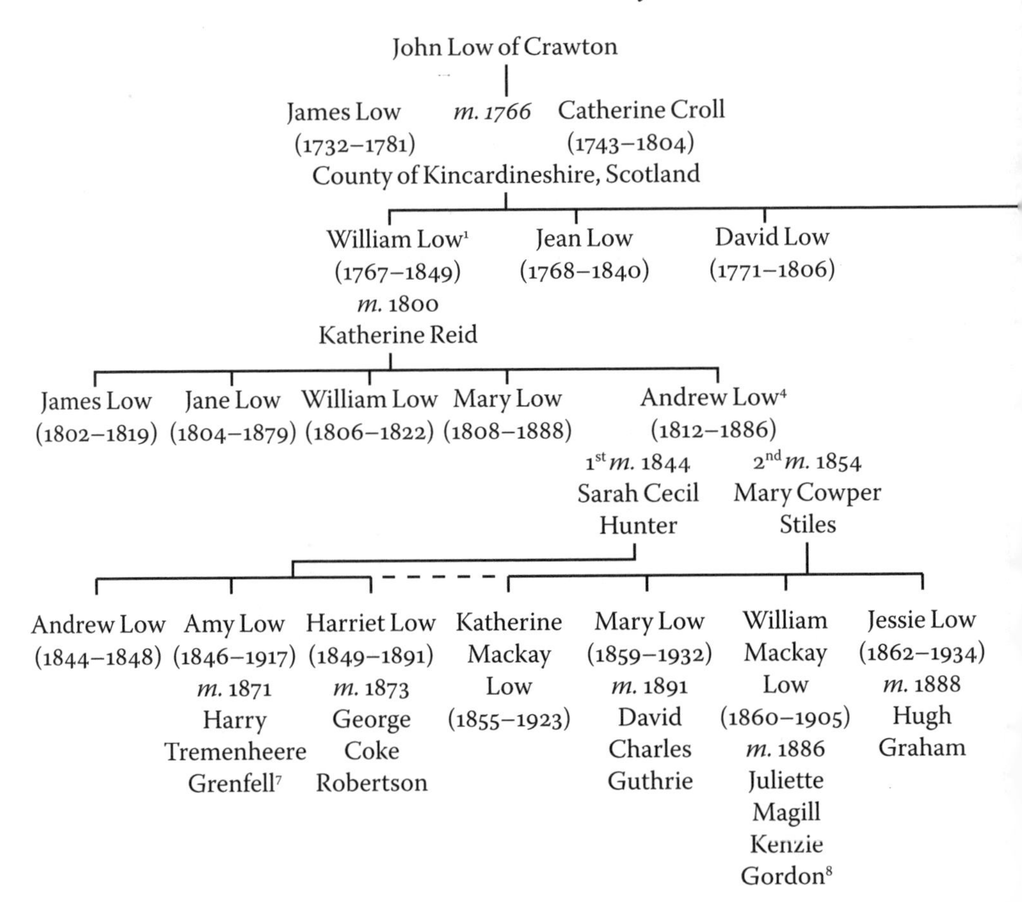

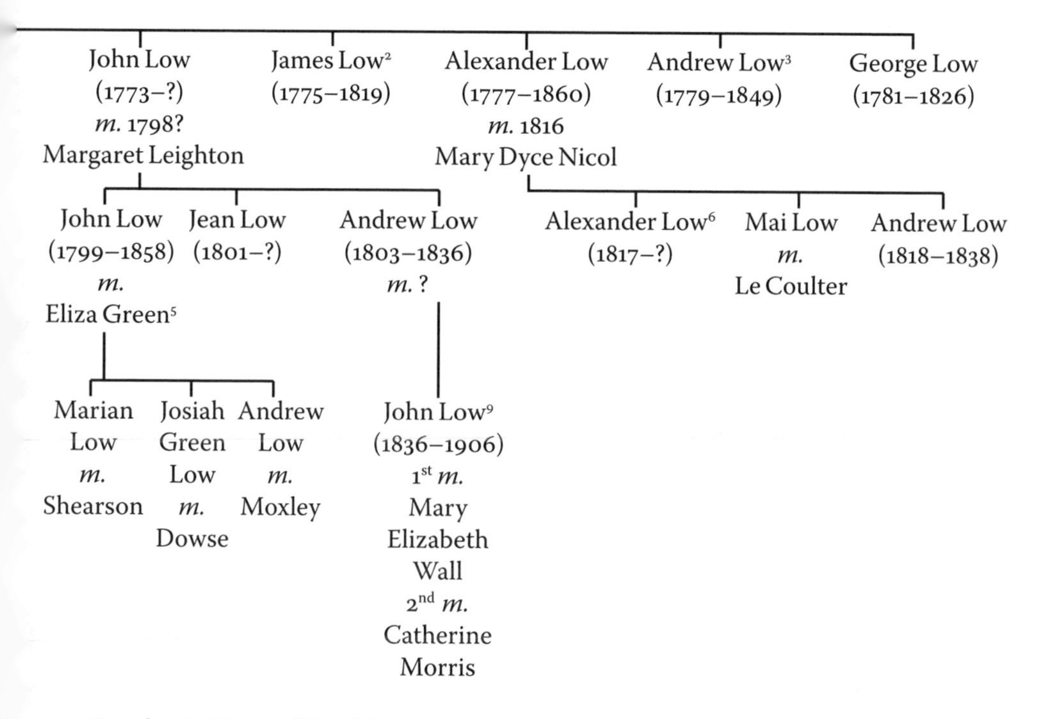

1. Burgher in Town of Brechin
2. Master of *Georgia*
3. Immigrated to Savannah 1800; joined by brothers Alexander and George; founded Andrew Low Company, The Sign of the Buck
4. Immigrated to Savannah 1829, joined A. Low Company; inherited company in 1849
5. Sister of Charles Green, partner of Andrew Low (b. 1812)
6. Lieutenant General, British Army
7. Admiral, Royal Navy; knighted upon attaining rank
8. Founder of Girl Scouts of America
9. Officer on Confederate ships *Fingal* and *Alabama*; descendants in New Zealand and Tasmania

Notes

Part I: Scotland to America, 1600–1800

Chapter 1: Genesis: Scotland and Georgia, 1730–1782, *pages 3–15*

1. The *Declaration of Arbroath Abbey* is an excellent example of Medieval Latin prose, author unknown, dated Apr. 6, 1320. One of Scotland's most prized possessions, as important to the Scottish people as the *Declaration of Independence* is to Americans.

2. Prior to that there is a record of another James Low born to James Low in Crawton in 1699; this certainly could be our James Low's father and grandfather. Another entry of a John Low born to John Low, Oct. 2, 1689, in Lumgair—a nearby croft or hamlet—takes the family even further back. Low is an exceptionally familiar name in the northeast region of Scotland. The significance is that it proves a presence of this particular Low family as tenants in the fishing and farming hamlet of Crawton as far back as 1699.

3. Dr. Charles McLean, architect and historian at Dundee University in Scotland, steered me to the discovery of one of the most important pieces of proof in the records: RHP 41, a 1780 Survey Plat including Crawton, located in West Register House, Edinburgh, Scotland.

4. T. C. Smout, *A History of the Scottish People, 1560–1830*. This text lays out a clear explanation of the Protestant Reformation of the church in Scotland. The early chapters, especially the one called "The Course of the Protestant Reformation," are an excellent source.

5. Following World War II, Home Rule for Scotland became a staple discussion for both Labour and Conservative governments of Great Britain. Modernization was a key component of the New Labour Party under Prime Minister Tony Blair, and when elected to power in 1997 devolution was one of the first items of their agenda. In Nov. 1998 the Westminster Parliament passed the Scotland Act, and the first elections to the Scottish

Parliament since the 1707 Acts of Union took place in May 1999. A contemporary account containing many of the original documents that influenced the original act sheds much light on the three-hundred-year- old argument. P. H. Scott, *The Union of Scotland and England* (1979).

6. A BBC publication by Christopher Lee titled *This Sceptred Isle, 55 BC–1901* gives the general reader an excellent access to the mysteries of British royal dynasties, battles, and beheadings.

7. George, 10th Earl Marischal, a former colonel in Her Majesty's Guard, who had a reputation as a military genius, and held a grudge against King George I on account of his dismissal from the service in 1714, supported the cause of the Old Pretender. In Dec. 1715 James Stuart landed in Peterhead near Aberdeen and proceeded to Fetteresso Castle in Kincardine, owned by his friend, the Earl Marischal. There, in the presence of the Earl of Mar and other noblemen, the Earl Marischal proclaimed him King James VIII of Great Britain. Archibald Watt, *Highways and Byways Around Stonehaven.*

8. An entry and sketch of an ancient gravestone was recorded in the *Pre-1855 Monumental Inscriptions for Kincardineshire* listed in Page 240 Kineff/Catterline (13b) entry as: "8. FS [flat stone] Jas. Low tent in Crawton d 12. 11. 1781, aged 49." The balance of inscription is also further proof, since the coincidence of two Low families having the same information is astronomical: "wife Cath Croal d. 19. 3. 1804 aged 58, children, David 28.9.1806 age 35, Jas d at sea on passage from Savanna 29. 7. 1819 aged 44, George d at sea on passage from Savanna 2.1826, aged 45, Jean d. Stonehaven 29.5. 1840, aged 72."

9. The origins of the Scottish Episcopal Church stem from the decision in 1690 to impose a full Presbyterian settlement on the national Church of Scotland, meaning government by elders instead of an episcopacy or government by bishops. More than half the established clergy in Scotland loyal to the Catholic faith of the Stuart kings refused to accept this stricture and remained Episcopal, for which they were frequently persecuted. Overwhelmingly support for the Jacobite cause of returning the Stuart dynasty to the throne came from the northeastern regions, including Angus, Aberdeen, Banff, Forfar, and Kincardine. The Lows allegiance to their Marischal landowners would in all probability have made them Episcopalian in belief.

10. Smout, *A History of the Scottish People.* A fermetoune was a settlement or hamlet scattered around a central farm with a tenant, collectively operated using plough horses or oxen for cultivation as well as the communal labor of his subtenants, servants, and seasonal workers. The local laird or nobility would own the land itself, to which the occupants paid rent in various forms, although tenants could also own some portions.

11. It is now generally agreed that Oglethorpe's town plan is derived from Pietro di Giacomo Cataneo's plan for an ideal city, published in Venice in 1567. Not only was the text available to Oglethorpe, but also his service to Prince Eugene, Duke of Savoy, took him to towns built on Cataneo's design.

12. Anthony W. Parker, *Scottish Highlanders in Colonial Georgia: The Recruitment, Emigration, and Settlement in Darien, 1735–1748* (Athens: University of Georgia Press, 1997). The Highland Scots who settled the town of Darien, Georgia, in the eighteenth century were fleeing a Scotland where the traditional dominance of the Highland clan system was in decline. The Trustees of the Georgia colony successfully recruited these soldier-settlers in 1736, many of them from the Inverness area, to help defend Oglethorpe's embryo colony against the Spanish.

13. *Colonial Records of Georgia*, Georgia Historical Society Archives, Savannah.

14. Sir Keith Thomas, "James Edward Oglethorpe: Sometime Gentleman Commoner of Corpus," included in John C. Inscoe, *James Edward Oglethorpe—New Perspectives on His Life and Legacy* (1997). The book of essays is dedicated to the memory of renowned Colonial Georgia scholar Phinizy Spalding (1930–1994), author of *Oglethorpe in America* (University of Georgia Press, 1984).

15. There had been three unsuccessful uprisings before the "Forty-Five" in 1708, 1715, and 1719. The Old Pretender was still living in exile in France when his son, the popular and glamorous Prince Charles Edward, mounted an audacious invasion of Great Britain. At first he, the Scottish clans, and a handful of French troops were successful and crossed the border to march on London, but their triumph was fleeting, and they were forced to retreat back to Scotland. In Apr. 1746, on a bleak Scottish moor near Inverness, named Culloden, the Crown army routed the rebels in a massacre—killing a thousand Scots in less than half an hour. The prince fled back to France, but his supporters paid a heavy price for their loyalty, many of them executed by beheading or hanging. About 1,150 were transported to the Americas. Draconian laws were passed against the Episcopalians, and the bagpipes and wearing of the kilt banned. That was the end of aspirations for a Stuart restoration and has imbued the figure of Bonnie Prince Charlie with legendary proportions.

16. An interesting postmortem on Oglethorpe's military career and his relationship with the Duke of Cumberland is found in Dr. Edward J. Cashin's recent monograph, *Glimpses of Oglethorpe in Boswell's Life of Johnson* (*Georgia Historical Quarterly* 83, no. 3 [Fall 2004], pp. 398–495).

17. *Index to English Crown Grants in Georgia, 1755–1775*. In 1970, when the Georgia state attorney general determined that all marshland in Georgia belonged to the state, this "paramount title" became extremely

important, and many individuals began trying to trace their titles back to these English Crown grants. The documentation was held in the Office of the Surveyor General in Atlanta's State Archives. Pat Bryant was in administrative control of Georgia's original land records. She and her assistant, Marion R. Hemperly, were literally swamped with requests for detailed information concerning the more than five thousand grants to Georgia land which were issued by the English Crown. In all, nine substantial paperbound offset-printed volumes appeared out of the offices of the Surveyor General during the period 1972–74. The first volume, edited by Pat Bryant, was devoted to Georgia's coastal islands and appeared in Feb. 1972. Subsequent volumes were published (two edited by Bryant and six by Hemperly) and a table explaining the historical transition of Georgia's civil divisions from districts to parishes and finally to counties.

18. Several new histories of Savannah delineate this period. See Walter J. Fraser, Jr., *Savannah in the Old South* (University of Georgia Press, 2003) and H. Ronald Freeman, *Savannah Under Siege* (Freeport Publishing, 2002).

19. Edward J. Cashin's *Beloved Bethesda* (Mercer University Press, 2001) goes into rich detail about Habersham and Clay. For genealogy, see J. G. B. Bulloch, *A History and Genealogy of Habersham, Adams, Clay, Stiles, and Other Related Families* (Columbia, S.C: R. L. Bryan, 1901).

20. In the 1930's as part of the depression-era federal Works Progress Administration, the Savannah Writers Project segment of the Federal Writer's Project produced a series of essays on the legendary Savannah River Plantations, a culture based on rice. Beginning in 1938 the *Georgia Historical Quarterly* began to publish these essays, and in 1947 the Georgia Historical Society collected them in one volume titled *Savannah River Plantations,* edited by Mary Granger.

21. In 1892 Sidney Stiles Elliot, godmother to Katie Low, sent her a packet of family papers and told her, "Did you know that you had French blood in your veins? Joseph Clay's wife was Anne de Legardere, her family were Huguenots who left France at the time of the Revocation of the Edict of Nantes and settled in Ireland, she came to this country with her father, traveling for his health when she met Joseph Clay and married him—her only brother was a linguist, he died in India in the employ of the East India Company, he was unmarried so that name is extinct as well as Malbone, Mackay and McQueen." Wm. H. Stiles Collection, 1747–1892, Emory University, Atlanta.

22. For extensive coverage of the Stiles family, see Henry Reed Stiles, *The Stiles Family In America* (Jersey City: Doan & Pilson, 1895). To understand the interconnected families of Bermuda, see Henry C. Wilkinson, *Bermuda From Sail to Steam,* 2 vols. (London: Oxford University Press, 1973).

23. Samuel Stiles is buried on Green Island, about fifteen miles from Savannah in the family burying ground. Photos of the site were made by photographer William Wilson prior to 1892. Sidney Stiles Elliott writes: "The Stiles were originally English & moved to Bermuda about 1632 having received a grant of land from the English Govt, they came (Samuel Stiles and 2 of his brothers) to this country about 1760. Green Island came into his possession about the end of the Revolutionary War ... we go to the island for a short time every year." Wm. H. Stiles Collection #22. Box no. 1, item 1, 1747–1892. Emory University, Atlanta.

24. Mackay and Stiles Family Papers, 1743–1975, located at the Wilson Library, University of North Carolina, Chapel Hill, contain primary source journals, letters, and other documentation of these two Southern families. Eliza McQueen Mackay, mother of Mary Cowper Stiles, was the granddaughter of John Smith, a prominent South Carolina planter, and the daughter of John McQueen (1751–1807) of Georgia and East Florida. Her aunt, Mary Smith, married Basil Cowper, who removed his family to Jamaica at a plantation named Barron Hill after the American Revolution. The Cowpers had two daughters, Mary Anne (1776–1856) and Margaret (born 1777), who married John McQueen, Jr. (1773–1822). The Cowper family is not to be confused with the Couper family, the daughter of James Hamilton Couper (1794–1866), who married Robert Mackay Stiles (1836–1874), brother of Mary Cowper Stiles, and son of Eliza Mackay and William Henry Stiles. More information is also to be found in *The Letters of Don Juan McQueen to His Family* and *The Letters of Robert Mackay to His Wife,* both edited by Walter C. Hartridge.

Chapter 2: Birth of the Buck: Scotland, 1766–1781, *pages 16–23*

1. Murray, *The York Building Company—A Chapter in Scotch History* (Glasgow, 1883).

2. The University of Edinburgh on behalf of a consortium set up by the Scottish Confederation of Universities has made the original volumes of the Statistical Accounts available to the general public on-line.

3. Keay, *The Honorable Company: A History of the British East India Company* (1991). "The Honorable Company," or "The Grandest Society of Merchants In The Universe" as the British East India Company was known during the heydays of its illustrious history, was an exclusive monopolistic consortium of English merchants formed to ply the East Indies spice trade in competition with the Dutch. Over two hundred years it grew from a loose association of Elizabethan tradesmen into a powerful commercial enterprise that came to control half the world's trade, and as a political enterprise, it administered an empire. A tenth of the British exchequer derived from customs receipts, and its armed forces exceeded

that of most sovereign states. Without it there could have been no British India and no British Empire. Scots played a major role in the powerful company, in both its armies and its merchant trade following the Acts of Union of 1707.

4. Smout, *A History of the Scottish People, 1560–1830.* Robert Burns's great-grandfather, who died in 1743, lies in the graveyard at Glenbervie, a few miles south of Catterline and Crawton in Kincardine. The great poet Robert Burns (1759–1796) is considered by Scots as equal in stature to Shakespeare, the Bard of England. His works are still celebrated all over Scotland, and the world where Scots congregate on his birthday of Jan. 25, as well as on St. Andrew's Day. His poems expressed the spirit of Scottish nationalism through the expressiveness of his songs, satire, and poems in the Scottish language that was still spoken in the ferme-tounes and hamlets of rural Scotland in the lifetime of the young Low brothers.

Chapter 3: The Widow's Mite, 1781–1800, *pages 24–34*

1. Watt, *Highways and Byways Round Stonehaven.* The gravestone in Catterline lists David Low, second son of James and Catherine Croll, as being "Feuar of Arduthie." In 1795 Robert Barclay purchased the estate of Links of Arduthie, a waste ground then, later the site that became the New Town of Stonehaven. To encourage settlers Barclay offered feus in perpetuity, each one comprising an eighth of an acre, thereby planning and laying down the foundations of the town, and lived to see it become a prosperous community. This is a positive indication that the Low family had access to funding around the same period of time that Andrew Low, Sr., emigrated to America.

2. *Annals of Fordoun* (1740): "Sir John Arbuthnott is now the laird of Fordoun, his father possessed the lands and the barony of Cairntoun alias Fordoun, upon which stood the large farm called Pittengarden." Sir John also owned land in the parish of Kinneff, adjacent to Catterline. This working farm, which survives to this day, was then a substantial ferme-toune about ten miles from Crawton. In 1742 William Low, a subtenant on the farm, married Elizabeth Nicol; they had children George, James, David, John, Alexander, William, and Isobel. The coincidence of the same names is a clue that William Low may have been either a brother or uncle of James Low of Crawton, and it is feasible that following his death Catherine Croll could have called on one of them to manage her own farm. Another coincidence is that several generations later D. C. Guthrie's mother, Ellinor Stirling, after the death of her husband, James Alexander Guthrie, married an Arbuthnott. D. C. Guthrie married Mary Low, daughter of Andrew Low, Jr. They are my grandparents.

3. Cameron, *The History of Fettercairn.* Archibald Cowie Cameron, A.M., L.L.D., was the schoolmaster of Fettercairn. His history was written in 1882 and published in 1899 by John Menzies in Edinburgh.

4. James Anderson, *Black Book of Kincardineshire.* Anderson lived in Stonehaven and this text was published by William Johnston, Barclay Street, in Stonehaven during the latter 1700's. It has been extensively used as a reference for seventeenth-century Scottish social studies, and is very useful in terms of a contemporary account, personified in the inscription by Dryden: "All things are full of horror and affright." There are copies of this fascinating book in many Scottish libraries.

5. David Dobson, author of dozens of books on emigration from Scotland to America, is arguably the world's foremost authority on the subject of eighteenth- and nineteenth-century migration, including a six-volume series on *Directory of Scottish Settlers in North America, 1625–1825.* The records in Dobson's books are culled from a wealth of sources. Family and estate papers, testamentary and probate records, burgh muniments, registers of sasines, registers of deeds, Sheriff's Courts records, Courts of Sessions and High Court of Justiciary records, port and customs records, contemporary diaries and journals, contemporary newspapers and magazines, professional and university records, Privy Council and Colonial records, records of the Episcopalian and Presbyterian churches, monumental inscriptions, the various passenger lists and emigration lists that survive—and that list is only the tip of the iceberg of the information he has scoured. Dobson has left no stone unturned to provide posterity with as accurate a record as he can of our ancestors' movements. He was born in Carnoustie, Scotland, in 1940, and educated at the Dundee Institute of Technology, the Dundee College of Education, and the University of St. Andrew's.

6. David D. Black, *History of Brechin to 1864.* The story of the hanging of Andrew Low is contained in this book by the town clerk of Brechin. Angus Archives in Montrose contain the original handwritten manuscripts and transcripts of the trial. Andrew Low was convicted of stealing on Sept. 22, 1784, and was hanged in 1785. The judge in the affair was Patrick Chalmers of Aldbar; the Chalmers and Guthrie family later formed the Guthrie, Chalmers Company.

7. In 1688 parliaments of both Scotland and England agreed to joint sovereignty by the Dutch William of Orange, married to Catholic Stuart King James's daughter Mary. James went into exile and the nation remained Protestant. This was the "Glorious Revolution" and guaranteed that the nations would remain Protestant.

8. During the decades leading to the first convening of Scotland's Parliament in 1999 since 1707, a veritable cottage industry erupted amongst

experts and historians, reexamining Scotland's turbulent and frequently controversial history and exploring Scottish identity past and present. One of the best to emerge is T. M. Devine, *The Scottish Nation—A History, 1700–2000* (University of Aberdeen, 1999).

9. Thomas Paine was born in Thetford, England, in 1737. He had little schooling, and worked at a number of jobs before being influenced by Benjamin Franklin to emigrate to America in 1774. In 1776 he began to write and publish his "American Crisis" series of thirteen pamphlets, and published the influential *Common Sense*, which established him not only as a truly revolutionary thinker, but also as the American Revolution's fiercest political theorist. In 1787 Paine returned to Europe, where he became involved in revolutionary politics. His largest and most influential work was the 1791 *Rights of Man*. To be expected, his work branded him as a radical and he was persecuted both in England and in France, where he fled before the French Revolution, and finally back in America, where he died in New York in 1809, poor, ill, and despised for his extremism and atheism. His works since have become a bible as a must-read defense of those who believe in the essence of democratic beliefs. *The Thomas Paine Reader* (1987), edited by Michael Foot and Isaac Kramnick, is an excellent place to start reading his ideas, especially *The Age of Reason*, a notoriously fierce attack on traditional Christianity.

10. T. C. Smout, *A History of the Scottish People, 1560–1830*.

PART II: SAVANNAH AND SCOTLAND, 1800–1829

Chapter 4: The Sign of the Buck: Savannah, 1800–1811, *pages 37–50*

1. Coll # 5125SP-10 (1804–1852) Book A: Chatham County Superior Court—Aliens declared to become citizens and those admitted to citizenship. In Naturalization Index of Superior Court of Chatham there is no record of Andrew Low, Sr., being naturalized or actual swearing in.

2. Mary Granger, ed., *Savannah River Plantations* (Savannah Writer's Project, 1947), 55–92.

3. There are many comprehensive books written by scholars and writers of popular history on Henri Christophe and leaders of the Haitian Revolution. One useful overview by Eric Williams, prime minister of Trinidad and Tobago from independence in 1962 to his death in 1981, is *From Columbus to Castro—The History of the Caribbean*. Another that mentions his service at the siege of Savannah is a biography by Hubert Cole, *Christophe, King of Haiti* (Eyre & Spottiswoode, 1967).

4. The first newspaper in Georgia, the *Georgia Gazette*, was published in Savannah in 1763. The Georgia Historical Society contains an extensive collection of subsequent newspapers published in Savannah and other

regions of Georgia on microfilm. There is also an extensive indexing system, giving easy access to subject matter from early colonial days to the present. These newspapers contain a wealth of colorful detail on life in Savannah, the state, and the world.

5. John Masefield, "Cargoes," in Harriet Monroe, ed., *The New Poetry: An Anthology* (1917).

6. Professor Devine confirmed that the reference to this practice could be contained in the collection called the Spiers Bowman Papers, at the Mitchell Library, Glasgow.

7. Joseph F. Waring, *Cerveau's Savannah* (Georgia Historical Society, 1973).

8. Gibbons left the city for river trade in New York harbor and became the principal in the U. S. Supreme Court case of *Gibbons* v. *Ogden,* which reaffirmed the federal power over interstate commerce.

9. *History of Fettercairn,* small locally produced tourist-oriented history of the region in Fettercairn Public Library.

10. "George Low"—article by Marion Hemperly, in *Georgia Historical Quarterly* 51, no. 4 (Dec. 1967), 454, about the naturalization of Isaac and Low.

11. June 1, 1808. Deed Book. 2-B, 268–9. Andrew Low, Sr., purchased two Negro girls, aged 18 and 14, from Mrs. Teresa Pine—listed in Abstract Genealogy File, Georgia Historical Society.

12. James Hunter, *A Dance Called America: The Scottish Highlands, the United States and Canada.* (Edinburgh: Mainstream Publishing Company, 1994).

13. Reference to Deed Book June 25, 1810, Book; 2-E, 4094. The tax digests of 1830 and 1831 list Lots 1 and 13 Frederick Tything, Derby Ward, as belonging to Low, Taylor & Co. The 1830 digest lists Andrew Low & Co. as owning two slaves, one saddle horse, and merchandise. Following Andrew Low, Sr's death in 1849, Lot 1 Frederick Tything, Derby Ward, is listed in the tax digests as the property of Andrew Low, Jr.

14. Genealogical Committee, *Marriages of Chatham County, Georgia Vol. 1* (Georgia Historical Society, 1993), p. 147.

15. A. E. Sholes, *Chronological History of Savannah* (Savannah: Morning News Print, 1900), p. 68.

16. Genealogical Committee, *Register of Deaths in Savannah, Georgia Vol. 11* (Georgia Historical Society, 1984).

17. Granger, *Savannah River Plantations.*

18. *World Almanac 2001.* In 1808 the U.S. Congress outlawed the importation of slaves. This did not stop the trade, and between 1808 and 1860 250,000 slaves were illegally imported.

19. Waring, pp. 13–14.

Chapter 5: The War of 1812: England and America, 1812–1818, *pages 51–61*

1. Stouf's map, "Plan of the City and Harbor of Savannah," 1818, and McKinnon & Wright's map, "Plan of the City of Savannah," 1820.

2. Sholes, p. 65

3. Waring, pp. 27–29

4. For a detailed account of the Jefferson administration and the prelude to the War of 1812, see Dumas Malone, *Jefferson the President—Second Term* (Boston: Little, Brown and Company, 1974).

5. There are several published and unpublished accounts of this brawl that turned into an international incident, among them are Hugh S. Golson, *The Privateer Riots of 1811: The Merchants of Savannah Provoke Napoleon's France* (Savannah, 2004); and Clifford L. Egan, "Fracas in Savannah: National Exasperation in Microcosm, 1811," in *Georgia Historical Quarterly,* 54, no. 1 (Spring 1970), pp. 79–86. Newspaper accounts include "Burning of the French Privateers," in *Columbian Museum and Advertiser,* Monday, Nov. 18, 1811; and the *Republican and Savannah Evening Ledger,* Saturday, Nov. 16, 1811.

6. Fortunately, the *Columbian Museum and Advertiser* copy at the Georgia Historical Society, though extremely fragile, is legible and gives lots more gory details of the encounter.

7. *Columbian Museum and Savannah Advertiser,* Thursday, Jan. 2, 1812. The newspapers were filled with alibis and excuses for just about everyone involved.

8. Andrew Low's birth certificate reference is to be found in the Fettercairn Old Parish Registers.

9. The words to *The Star Spangled Banner* were written by lawyer Francis Scott Key of Georgetown, Maryland, during the bombardment of Fort McHenry, Baltimore, Sept. 13–14, 1814. During the event, Key wrote the stanza on the back of an envelope and the next day completed the poem. The original copy remained in the family for 93 years until in 1907 it was sold to Henry Walters of Baltimore. In 1934 it was bought at auction by the Walters Art Gallery, Baltimore, for $26,400. In 1953 it was sold for the same price to the Maryland Historical Society. *World Almanac 2000,* p. 472.

10. Kenneth Scott, ed., *British Aliens in the United States during the War of 1812.*

11. Descendants Gary and Carol Todd of Austin, Texas, have proved that the John Low, River Pilot, recorded as being a British Alien during the 1812 War, was the same John Low who owned steamships and was harbor master in Savannah in the 1840's. In addition, he was married to and divorced from Lavinia Low circa 1846. He also is the John Low who is listed as living and dying in Griffin, Georgia, in 1876. He was not Andrew Low, Jr.'s father.

Chapter 6: The Burgher's Son: Scotland to Liverpool, 1812–1818, *pages 62–69*

1. The claim that Andrew Low, Jr.'s father is "John Low, born 1783, died 1876" appears in the Who's Who in the Biographical Appendix of the original publication of *Children of Pride: A True Story of Georgia and the Civil War* by Robert Manson Myers (Yale University Press, 1972).

2. The John Low listed as Andrew Low's father was probably mistaken for the John Low who was resident in Savannah in 1818, working as a "River Pilot" and married to (and divorced from) Lavinia Low. This is also the same John Low mentioned in the records in Savannah as a "British Alien" during the War of 1812, and who died in 1876. Through other descendants' research he has proved to be no relation.

3. At the Church of Latter Day Saints Family History Library in Salt Lake City I discovered what I believe to be the origin of the entry in the International Genealogical Index online that states erroneously "John Low is the father of Andrew Low, born 1813." On checking Film # 1553814, where the "Patron Submission Form" is recorded, it told me that my great-grandfather, Andrew Low, and the John Low the document named as his father after their deaths had their names submitted to the Church of Latter Day Saints, for Temple Work. This means that the church has had them baptized, endowed, and inducted for eternal redemption and protection. Essentially in the belief system of the Church of Latter Day Saints, Temple Work goes way back to the work done by Christ in the Temple in Jerusalem, and is a direct command from God. I was told that only relatives could submit names to the church for Temple Work, although that is a rule that is not strictly adhered to. It seems to be the case with the Andrew Low–John Low patron submission. It is probable that someone submitted the information in the Who's Who on Andrew Low, listed in Robert Manson Myers book *Children of Pride* of the letters of the Reverend Charles Jones Colcock, and may also be the one who submitted the names to the Temple in Boise, Idaho, for this work. Although which submission came first is still a mystery. *The Holy Temple* by Boyd Packer claims that the work of redemption through adoption is mandated by the tenets of the Church—in this context "adoption" refers to the relatives of all lineages in order to be "sealed to the parents" and that genealogical work is to be considered Temple Work. This is the absolute reason that when using the IGI one needs to be extremely careful about accepting the accuracy and veracity of the information, and it is always necessary before making any claim of relatedness that the Original Parish Records be checked. The information contained in patron submission forms can come from anyone anywhere.

4. My cousin Jane Davidson, granddaughter of Jessie Graham, youngest daughter of Andrew Low and Mary Cowper Stiles, had done a degree of

research on the lineage of our ancestors; and her notes have been of considerable assistance in rectifying the wrong information that has been published, enabling verification of the facts. Jane Davidson died in South Africa before the work could be completed.

5. Birth registration Dunnottar Parish Church of Scotland Old Parish register reads: "1767. James Low, Tenant in Crawton, had a son baptized called William. Witnesses, Frances Milne in Cowieswell and George Croll in Pollburn, Parish of Laurencekirk."

6. Parish of Fettercairn, County of Kincardine Old Parish Registers, 1812: LOW: William Low and his wife Catherine Ried [*sic*] at Forewoodside had a son born July 20th and baptized 20th August named Andrew. There is *no* record of an Andrew Low born to John Low in *1813* in any OPR in the Church of Scotland. The IGI Index Batch & Source: Ba: C112574. So: 993313: Andrew Low M. Father: William Low. Mother: Catherine Ried: c: 20 Aug 1812, Fettercairn, Kincardine, Scotland.

7. The certificate of record can be found in Scottish Record Office, General Register House, Edinburgh.

8. Eric Foner, Preface to *Reconstruction.*

9. Hugh Thomas, *The Slave Trade.* The British Parliament passed an Act in 1807, stating that no new ships should be employed in the slave trade. The belief expressed by William Wilberforce was that if the slave trade was abolished American plantation owners would take better care of their slaves in order to increase them by procreation instead of purchase. The bill passed Feb. 23 by 283 to 16 votes, received royal assent on Mar. 25. The trade was to be illegal after May 1, 1807. Of course it was impossible to enforce and the slave trade continued albeit illegally. In fact it flourished.

10. George Chandler, *The Merchant Venturers.*

11. Later became wife of William Henry Stiles and mother of Mary Cowper Stiles, Andrew Low, Jr.'s second wife.

12. A fascinating journal in the Southern Historical Collection at the University of North Carolina written by Robert Mackay during this period on one of his transatlantic voyages describes in detail the wealth of knowledge a merchant needed to know.

13. Oct. 5, 1816, Robert Mackay died in New York City, buried in Trinity churchyard, leaving the plantation "Grange" to Eliza Mackay, his widow. She kept the plantation until Sept. 1832, when she sold the Grange to William Washington Gordon, lawyer, soldier, and industrialist, also grandfather of Juliette Gordon (see Granger, *Savannah River Plantations,* "Colerain Plantation"). There is some indication that Mackay may have owned the ship *Georgia,* which later shows up with James Low as part owner as well as Andrew Low. The widow Eliza McQueen Mackay continued to

live at 75 Broughton Street, between Abercorn and Lincoln streets. She also continued to run Sedgebank after her son John died in 1848, with her son Robert helping her. After Robert Mackay, Sr.'s death the ledgers in the Southern Collection continue in her writing. The ledgers provide a remarkable insight into the relationship of antebellum plantation owners with their slaves, many of whom they considered family. The Southern Historical Collection also contains papers of the Anderson, Barnsley, Screven, William Page families, and businesses. It is probably the most researched collection of extant papers in the study of antebellum life in the South.

14. Norman Douglas Nicol, *History of Nicol Family,* Shavertown, Pa. Alexander Low married Mary Nicol of Fetteresso in Kincardineshire in 1816. Her brother was James Dyce Nicol, who later married Catherine Loyd of Manchester banking Loyd's and became MP for Kincardineshire; and her cousin, William Nicol, was a well-known Bombay merchant who married her sister in 1822. Mary Nicol Low died 1867 at Norwood, Bath, England. Alexander died Mar. 25, 1860; both buried at Bath. Walter C. Hartridge's genealogical charts at the Georgia Historical Society, Savannah, link the Nicoll, Anderson, and Cunningham families. Sarah Anderson was related to the Mackay-McQueen family—so there were very early connections in both Scotland and Savannah.

15. According to Jane Davidson's research notes, the farm Criggie near St. Cyrus, Kincardineshire, was owned by a family called Scott until 1797, but Alexander Low gave his address as Criggie when he married Mary Nicol in 1816. A family named Forsyth-Grant now owns the property. St. Cyrus is the modern name for the village. Previously it was named Ecclesgreig. Mrs. Davidson claims that Forsyth-Grant gave her information that links the Low family through the marriage of Jessie Low to Hugh Graham. She states that the land belonged to Graham of Morphie. John Graham of Morphie was the third son of Sir David Graham of Old Montrose, and he was seated at Morphie in 1370—Gilbert Graham had a charter from King Robert III of Scotland in 1398. Robert Graham of Morphie was heavily in debt on the estate circa 1696, and he had to sell nearly all his lands. The debtor Robert married the eldest sister of John Graham of Claverhouse, "Bonny Dundee." Viscount Dundee was killed at the battle of Killiecrankie. He was constable of Dundee. All the Grahams, including the Netherby Grahams (her family connection), are directly descended from the previously mentioned Sir David Graham of Montrose. The dukedom took the name from Montrose; their castle was originally in Kincardineshire also, but was destroyed during the civil war. On account of Jane Davidson's death none of the above has been verified. It does, however, locate the families in the same geographical location of Scotland for centuries.

16. *Gore's Advertiser*, Liverpool Records Office. By 1816, William Low(e) has moved to 13 Vincent Street, St. James, Liverpool, the area where later Andrew Low was to live. It is now that the names of other characters in the story start to show up. The categories in the trade directory include cotton brokers, and in Liverpool a Hugh Duckworth shows up at 2 Rumford Street, the location of the later Civil War offices of Charles Prioleau. Godfrey Barnsley has offices at 1 Oldhall Street, right near the cotton exchange, and the category of "merchants" has grown hugely, but includes yet no Lows, Greens, or Isaacs.

17. Records at Angus Archives, Montrose, Scotland, and Brechin Public Library, reference section.

18. David Black, The *History of Brechin 1864*. The original market day was Sunday, but this was changed later as Scots believed that Sunday was no day for commerce. The High Street contained the gabled merchants' houses of the early eighteenth century, a type once common in Scottish burghs. The merchants lived above the shops and had warehouses above and workshops at the rear. Many of the merchants were linen factors and the town had many handloom weavers. Another account in the pamphlet *Angus Heritage Trails* states: "Brechin is a small burgh whose origins date back 1000 years. It was the Cathedral town of the pre-reformation diocese of Brechin. The burgh developed from the 12th century when the bishop granted permission to hold a weekly market. King Robert I, renewing the Bishop's right to hold a market on Sunday's, granted a charter in 1321. After the Reformation the burgh gradually acquired the rights and privileges of a royal burgh. In 1641, it was formally accorded this status in a royal charter granted by King Charles I. The burgh grew up beyond the Cathedral precincts in that area that now comprises Church Street and the High Street. It is the birthplace of Dr. Thomas Guthrie who founded the Ragged Schools of Edinburgh."

19. David Charles Guthrie and the Honorable Mrs. Stuart Wortley, *The Guthrie Family* (1906). My grandfather and his sister compiled this family history. It traces the lineage of the Guthries back to the eleventh century. It is also an account of the founding of the Guthrie Chalmers Company and includes account books of the *Britannia* in a collective trading adventure. It was reprinted by the Guthrie clan in America in recent years. Violet Stuart Wortley also wrote several biographical accounts of the family, and they have been collected by Mike Allen, curator of Highcliffe Castle.

20. David Charles Guthrie, born at Craigie, June 30, 1778, died at Portland Place. His eldest son was David Charles Guthrie of Craigie, born July 25, 1861, christened at Craigie. M.P. for S. Northants, High Sheriff, 1905. Married Mary Low, daughter of Andrew Low of Savannah.

Chapter 7: King Cotton: Great Britain–USA, 1815–1829, *pages 70–85*

1. Walter C. Hartridge, ed., *Robert Mackay's Letters to His Wife,* in the section of Letters titled "From England" he mentions "Robert Isaac—a Scottish born merchant of Savannah and Liverpool, was a member of the important firm of Andrew Low & Company." He states that at the time of Robert Mackay's visit there "the African trade" was the pride of Liverpool.

2. William Wilberforce (1759–1833) is arguably the best known of British abolitionists. Attaining a seat in Parliament for Hull in Yorkshire at age twenty-one, a sudden conversion to evangelical Christianity led him to approach politics from a position of strict Christian morality. He was influenced by the Reverend John Newton, slave trader turned evangelist, who authored the hymn "Amazing Grace." The interpretation of Christian morality for him, unlike a majority of his fellow evangelicals, meant embracing abolition of the slave trade, influenced by Prime Minister William Pitt the Younger, a staunch supporter of abolition. The Abolition Act, making the trade in slaves illegal in British ships, passed in 1807. It continued and remained a reality in British colonies for another quarter of a century. The Emancipation Act of 1833 was read into law in the House of Commons on July 26. Wilberforce lived to see his life's work accomplished. He died three days later on July 29, 1833. It would be another thirty years before American slaves were to receive their own emancipation.

3. A BBC television series and accompanying illustrated book, *The Rise and Fall of King Cotton,* by Anthony Burton, details the symbiotic relationship between slavery in the Southern states of America and the exploitation of the working poor and especially children in the textile mills of northern industrial England.

4. The British still claim that the first transatlantic ship to cross was the *Royal William* in 1833, and the first regular steam packet from Liverpool to America was started by Cunard in 1840.

5. Details of S.S. *Savannah* are culled from pages of contemporary New York, Savannah, and Liverpool papers. See also "An Address by Alexander R. Lawton: Transportation, Railroads, and Canals," in *Georgia Historical Quarterly* 111, no. 1 (June 1919). A scale model of the S.S. *Savannah* can be seen at the Ships of the Sea Maritime Museum, 41 Martin Luther King Boulevard, Savannah. The museum was a gift from Mills. B. Lane and is located in the mansion on West Broad Street originally built by architect William Jay for William Scarbrough.

6. The Act to Incorporate the Savannah Steamship Company was approved by the Georgia State Legislature Dec. 19, 1818. The corporators were: William Scarborough, A. B. Fannin, J. P. McKinne, Samuel Howard,

Charles Howard, John Haslett, Moses Rodgers, A. S. Bullock, John Bogue, Andrew Low & Co., Robert Isaac, I. Minis, S.C. Dunning, J. P. Henry, John Speakman, Robert Mitchell, R & J Habersham. James S. Bullock, Gideon Pott, W. S. Gillett, and Samuel Yates, all of Savannah. The directors were William Scarbrough, Robert Isaac, S. C. Dunning, James S. Bullock, and Joseph Habersham. The capital stock was $50,000.

7. See Malcolm Bell, Jr.'s *Savannah Ahoy* (Savannah: Pigeonhole Press, 1959).

8. The restored mansion is now the Museum of the Ships of the Sea owned by the late Mills Lane, who in a plaque inside the museum publicly credited Godfrey Barnsley, Scarbrough's son-in-law, with bailing Scarbrough out in the 1830's.

9. The Temporary Deed of William Scarbrough to Robert Isaacs is held in the collection of Scarbrough Papers at the State Department of Archives and History, Atlanta, as is his Last Will and Testament.

10. "Inventory of the Property Belonging to the Estate of James Low," Records of Chatham County, Georgia Historical Society, Savannah.

11. The notice in the newspaper on Nov. 11, 1819, in *Shipping News* states: "Ship Georgia from Liverpool: Friday morning the 12th November, 1819: Port of Savannah Arrived Ship GEORGIA, Varnum, Liverpool, 50 days, to A. Low & Co, owners, with an assorted cargo of seasonable goods, to Wm Taylor, James Dickson and Co., A. Low & Co, Wm Gibson: Passengers: Col. Harden and family; R. Isaac, Wm Gibson. 3 in steerage."

12. The lazaretto was built on the west end of Tybee Island through an act passed by Governor Wright, June 15, 1767. It was to be a two-story house of tabby brick forty feet by twenty with walls twelve feet high. Downstairs there were two rooms, upstairs one. A keeper's house having a brick chimney was to be built nearby.

13. Dr. William Waring, "Report to City Council, 1821," Georgia Historical Society, Savannah.

14. Old Parish Registers for St. Nicholas Parish in Aberdeen in Family History Centre, King Street, Aberdeen, Scotland. The staff and volunteer members of the Aberdeen Family History Centre are unsurpassed in their knowledge, their courtesy, and passion for the subject of Scotland's family history. They also have a large collection of books, many of them written by their own members; the organization numbers over 11,000 members all over the world.

15. Robert Hutchison was related by marriage to the Bulloch family of Savannah and Roswell. He was James Dunwoody Bulloch's uncle and James Stephens Bulloch's brother-in-law. James Bulloch was Martha (Mittie) Bulloch's father. Thus, it all stayed in the close-knit community of commerce linked by marriages.

PART III: SAVANNAH–LIVERPOOL, 1829–1841

Chapter 8: The Merchant Price, 1829–1836, *pages 89–96*

1. The two-mile marker for White Bluff Road still stands under an oak at Bull and Henry streets. The "mile and half house" would be approximately in the athletic fields of Forsyth Park today.

2. This correspondence can be examined in the #2226 Hutchison-Dawson Collection at the Georgia Historical Society. The author has transcribed many of the handwritten letters (in Andrew Low's small but easily read handwriting) and deposited the transcripts in the collection. They are a priceless source for details of the mercantile trade and go a long way toward returning the Andrew Low Company to their rightful place as one of the prominent international mercantile companies of the nineteenth century.

3. The listing for the *British King* in Liverpool's Maritime Museum, Lloyd's Register, shows she is a brig of 239 tons, built in 1825, in Sunderland, Scotland, although she is not listed as being owned by a John Low. The registration for the ship *Robert Isaac*, also built in Sunderland in 1825, is listed as being owned by Low and Company.

4. Susan Mays, *Interpretive Report,* National Society of the Colonial Dames of America in Georgia, owners of the Andrew Low House and Museum in the State of Georgia. Commissioned for informational purposes for the docents.

5. Andrew Low, Sr.'s will in Archives of Andrew Low House and Museum contains the clearest indication that the Low family remained in touch and close, at least until the death of Uncle Andrew in 1849.

Chapter 9: The Indian Affair: Florida, 1836, *pages 97–107*

1. Jeremy Paxman, *Friends In High Places—Who Runs Britain?* (Penguin Books, 1991). See the chapter "Stand Uneasy."

2. According to Kenneth Coleman's *History of Georgia,* "the militia was of particular importance to such an exposed colony, as Georgia had only a few regular troops stationed there since the departure of Oglethorpe and his Scottish regiment from Fort Frederica."

3. George Pratt Insh, *Scottish Colonial Schemes—1620–1686.* (Glasgow: Maclehose, Jackson & Co., 1922).

4. There are varying spellings of Yemasee. Charles Hudson uses Yamasee; the *Columbia Encyclopedia* uses both Yemasee and Yamasee: Google search turns up Yemasee! We shall use Yemasee and compromise with apologies to the purists if it is wrong.

5. Charles Hudson, *The Southeastern Indians* (Knoxville: University of Tennessee Press, 1976).

6. John Ehle, *Trail of Tears: The Rise and Fall of the Cherokee Nation* (Random House, 1988).

7. Andrew Jackson, seventh President of the United States, Democratic-Republican, later a Republican, was born on the border of North and South Carolina in 1767. He defeated John Quincy Adams in the 1828 election, carrying both the South and the West, and served from 1829 to 1837. "Let the people rule" was his slogan.

8. Gordon Smith, *History of the Georgia Militia, Vol. I.* In Smith's meticulously researched four-volume publication on the Georgia Militia, in the chapter on the Second Seminole War (1835–1843), partly because Lieutenant William Elon Basinger of Dade's command was from Savannah, the news of the slaughter caused an outpouring of grief and a patriotic fervor in the city.

Chapter 10: Passing the Baton, Savannah to Liverpool, 1836–1841, *pages 108–115*

1. The portrait has been returned to the Andrew Low House by purchase from Christopher Davidson of Kenya, son of Jane Davidson, the granddaughter of Jessie Low Graham.

2. "Liverpool 24th Jul 1837. Per Buchanan & Denniston, New York per Gen Washington."

3. In 1839 Lucy Isaac has her residence at 1 Mount Vernon Road, Edge Hill, a respected suburb. The 1839 Liverpool's *Gore's Advertiser* shows Andrew Low of Isaac Low & Co residing at 6 Hardy Street, nearer to the city center. Several later inserts show that her son Robert Isaac, Jr., also boarded at the same address on Hardy Street, as did a Sarah Reid, the family name of Andrew, Jr.'s mother, Katherine Reid Low. This street runs parallel to Nelson Street, now the center of Chinatown, just down the hill from Rodney Street, in what is now Mount Pleasant, near the Anglican Cathedral. This was an affluent part of town. Isaac Low & Co has their offices at 8 Oldhall Street, adjacent to the old Cotton Exchange during this period.

4. On Feb. 26, 1841, in Savannah at a meeting of subscribers to the inauguration ball of the newly elected President Harrison, Andrew Low, Jr., appears as one of the Managers.

5. The will of Andrew Low, Sr., is in the archives of the Andrew Low House & Museum.

6. Mr. W. W. Law, a noted Savannah historian, in the oral portion of one of his tours of Laurel Grove South in 1995 referred to "Tom Anderson Milledge, lived in A. Low's carriage house, and was a member of the Second African Baptist Church." This is the only reference we know of to the middle name of Anderson, but it could have significance, as the name of

one of the Stiles-Low lifetime servants was a mulatto woman named Celia Anderson. The Anderson and Mackay families were related by marriage to the Lows.

Part IV: Savannah, 1844–1860

Chapter 11: The Crown Prince: Savannah, 1844–1849, *pages 119–134*

1. Historian Walter C. Hartridge's genealogical research gives the lineage of John Hunter as an officer in the British Army and a native of County Donegal, Ireland, who came to Savannah about 1795 with his sisters Isabella and Lydia, to join their brother William Hunter, a Savannah merchant, and half sisters to James and Alexander Hunter, also Savannah merchants. If this is true almost definitely, the Hunters would have had to be Scottish born, those America called Scotch-Irish fleeing to Ireland as a way station, either as part of the Catholic persecution of Protestants by the Stuarts, or as Protestant Cromwellians, in the conquest of Ireland by the British. If they remained Episcopalian Stuart sympathizers hailing from Kincardine in northeast Scotland, they had family connections to the Lows, and certainly in Savannah the Hunters and Lows supported each other and both Episcopalian and Presbyterian churches. These lines of demarcation become extremely blurry when removed by continents from local persecution.

2. *Savannah Morning News,* Apr. 3, 1809: "Married on the 30th ult. By the Rev. Dr. Kollock, Mr. Alexander Hunter, Merchant, to Miss Harriet Bellinger, both of this city." The same issue noted that Harriett Bellinger had a letter waiting at the Post Office.

3. The Bellinger family was an old and prominent one in South Carolina history. Edmund Bellinger, who immigrated to South Carolina about 1688 and was created a Landgrave, was born in England, county of Westmoreland. The files indicate that Captain Sir Edmund Bellinger was given his original land grant as a reward for piracy on the high seas. He had four sons and four daughters by his wife Elizabeth Cartwright, the two eldest born in England, the rest in Carolina. *The Aldridge Compendium of Genealogy: First Families of America* states that Captain Sir Edmund Bellinger of Northumberland settled on James Island, South Carolina, married Sarah Cartwright. Sarah and Elizabeth were also the names of the two Hunter sisters, daughters of Harriet Bellinger and Alexander Hunter.

Other interesting historical odds and ends; they appear to have lived in Stono, the site of the first slave rebellion; the name Elliott features prominently in their marriages, as does a relationship to Charles Pinckney—this would bring them all into the highest degree of colonial aristocracy, original land grant holders. Another branch of the Bellinger family came from the Rhine, were part of a sect called Palatines who fled to England thence to America to escape religious persecution. A William Bellinger seems to have been a planter from St. Bartholomew's Parish in South Carolina through receipts from the widow Bellinger for the sale of slaves, dated 1741. The name of Mr. J. G. Bullock of Savannah shows up in letters trying to trace his ancestry back to the first Edmund Bellinger of the late 1600's. One letter dated 1893 says that they are listed in Burke's Peerage, the bible of British nobility. One member of the Bellinger family seems to have married into the Telfair family. Elizabeth Bellinger, born Nov. 8, 1751, married Mar. 21, 1769, William Telfair of Savannah. Their country seat, "Belfair," is a gated community near Bluffton, S.C.

4. As part of the estate of Jane Davidson, passed to her son Christopher Davidson in Kenya and South Africa, was a lovely miniature, purportedly to be that of Sarah Low and one of her children. It is now one of the prized exhibits in the Andrew Low Museum.

5. This diary is archived in the extensive Southern Historical Collection at the University of North Carolina, as is the Mackay-Stiles Collection. The diary is much used by scholars and researchers as an extraordinary glimpse into the nineteenth-century lives of planters, merchants, and politicians in the antebellum South, a period of time in American civilization that has been defined as pre–Civil War society based on Southern nationalism, slavery, and a plantation aristocracy.

6. The church stood on Drayton Street, now the parking lot south of Parker's Market; Brown Ward stretches from Whitaker to the burial ground at Abercorn, so Andrew and Sarah's Perry Street house was probably east of Drayton.

7. There is a handwritten marriage settlement available for transcription in the Andrew Low House Archives, but it is extremely difficult to read and decipher.

8. Purchase of Lot 13 and 14 on Lafayette Ward—Inferior Court of Chatham, $3,000. Deed. Chatham County, 3E258-259

9. *The Register of Deaths in Savannah, Georgia, Vol. VI* (1989), p. 27.

10. In the legal notices of Chatham County Sheriff's Sales on Thursday morning, Nov. 30, 1848, appeared the following notice: "On the first Tuesday if December next, before the Court House in the City of Savannah, between the legal hours of sale, will be sold, All that Wharf Lot situate, lying and being in the city of Savannah, and known and distinguished in the plan of the said city by the Number (2) Two, East of Bull Street and Lincoln Street and bounded East by a lot late Peter Kean's, West by a Lot owned by the estate of the late Robert Isaac, and North by the Savannah River. Levied on by virtue of a Fi. Fa. founded on foreclosure of Mortgage, issued out of the Superior Court of Chatham County in favor of Lucy Isaac and

Robert Bruce Isaac vs. Margaret Scott, Executrix of Robert Scott. Signed. Elisha Wylly, Sheriff." Andrew Low, according to the deed in Chatham County Records, purchased the lot. See also John M. Cooper's "Map of the City of Savannah" (1856).

11. Collection #2226 Hutchison-Dawson at the Georgia Historical Society contains two poignant documents sent by Robert Hutchinson to his own wife, Mary, who was also in the latter stages of pregnancy. The first letter, dated May 11, referred to the illness of Mrs. Low, who had miscarried and had to be delivered of a dead infant by surgical assistance. The second letter is dated nine days later on May 20 and speaks of Sarah Hunter Low's death that same day. Robert Hutchison was at that time married to his second wife, Mary Caskie, who was the sister of the first wife of James D. Bulloch.

12. Sally Gregory McMillen, *Motherhood in the Old South* (Louisiana State University Press, 1990). This monograph details the hazards of childbirth and infant mortality in the antebellum South.

13. Andrew Low, Sr., was still listed as living at 6 Hardy Street, Liverpool, and it is probable that if incapacitated during the last few months of his life he was taken care of by friends. There were not the same facilities then such as nursing homes or retirement homes. Today 20 Nelson Street is still the same as it was then except that in a frequently renovated Liverpool it is now adjacent to the huge dragon-shaped Oriental arch leading into the garish Chinatown District. One can still look up at the second floor windows and in the mind's eye see the room where Uncle Andrew Low would have died. No burial record has been located in either Liverpool or Scotland, and it is unknown whether his body was buried there or returned to his native land.

14. The source for this information is David H. Galloway, *Directory of the City of Savannah for the Year 1849. The Register of Deaths,* in the entries for Andrew Low's son Andrew's death in 1848 and for Sarah Low's death in 1849, lists their address at the time of death as Perry Street in Brown Ward. Perry Street in Brown Ward borders the southside of Chippewa Square and extends across Drayton Street. Bancroft indicates in his 1848 directory (page 18) that Jasper Ward (Madison Square) had a 1–1/2-acre parade near the United States Barracks. The same directory lists the offices of the Andrew Low & Company at 58 Bay Street.

15. The old jail building stood on Macon Street between Drayton and Abercorn. According to Low House historian Alice Daily, there may have been structures pertaining to the operation of the old jail on site where the Low house now stands. The old jail was torn down in 1845. *The Interpretive Report* at the present museum contains many details of the construction of the Andrew Low House, including the fact that the contractor was

in all probability Matthew Lufburrow, a local master builder, with whom John Norris is known to have worked. In 2003 architects discovered a fourteen-foot-deep well lined with gray bricks under the house. One theory is that as the house was one of the first in Savannah to have indoor plumbing, and the well sits below its second floor bathing room, it may have been used for drainage. It is still unknown when exactly the indoor plumbing was put in.

16. Detailed description of the Andrew Low House appears in Mary Lane Morrison's *John S. Norris—Architect in Savannah, 1846–1860* (Savannah: Beehive Press, 1980).

17. The 1850 Census records that Andrew Low gave a value to his business and property of $75,000. U.S. Department of Commerce, Bureau of the Census, Georgia, 1850 no. 1657. Schedule 11-Slaves, 148. Georgia Historical Society Microfilm M432–89. Additional research on Andrew Low's slaves can be found in Appendix 2 of Susan Mays's *Interpretive Report.*

18. Historian Daily claims that at that time the carriage house was only one story high, a second story was added later, and there would have been no real room for living quarters for slaves. Most lived in small houses on streets on the east and west side of the city. Many of these small homes east of Price Street are being restored and selling for premium prices.

19. David J. Griffin, "Savannah's City Income Tax," in *Georgia Historical Quarterly*, vol. 50, no. 2 (June 1966); Charles H. Olmstead, *Savannah in the 40's.*

20. Charlotte and Emily Brontë were both sent away to school at a very young age. Charlotte later used the experience as motivation of characters in her most famous book, *Jane Eyre.* Two other children's classics, *The Little Princess* and *The Secret Garden,* by Frances Burnett Hodgson, also draw on the experiences of young children sent away to school.

21. See the Clarence letters in the Southern Historical Collection, Mackay-Stiles Papers. Most of them appear to be dated a decade or so later. Other letters from Eliza Mackay Stiles in later years also refer to "Mr. Low thinking of sending his daughter Katie to Mrs. Clarence."

22. One of the rumored theories that have been floating around based on a handwritten identification on the back of a 1956 photograph of Andrew Low and his daughters is that they may have located in the Isle of Wight, although there is absolutely no extant proof. The Isle of Wight was indeed a most popular vacation spot for the well-to-do in Victorian times, partly due to the fact that Queen Victoria spent a considerable amount of the summer at Osborne House with her consort Prince Albert and her brood of children. In addition, a highlight of the social season was the yacht regatta and races at Cowes, an absolute must to be seen at. But the

remoteness of the island, off the south coast of England, would have made it an unlikely place for Andrew Low to have chosen to send his two young daughters to school.

23. On Mar. 14, 1853, Thackeray arrived in Savannah to give a lecture at the Young Men's Literary Association at St. Andrews Hall. The building still stands at the southwest corner of Broughton and Jefferson streets. See a later letter written by Thackeray and the rosewood desk he wrote at on his several visits to the Low House in Savannah as part of the exhibits in the Andrew Low House and Museum. Source: William Makepeace Thackeray, "Letter to Unknown Correspondent, 14 February 1856." Colonial Dames Collection #965, Folder 131A. Georgia Historical Society.

24. A framed note from William Makepeace Thackeray dated Savannah, Mar. 19, 1853, is one of the exhibits in the Andrew Low House and Museum.

Chapter 12: High Cotton: Savannah, 1850–1860, *pages 135–153*

1. *The Letters of Robert Mackay to His Wife* compiles many of the details that describe the early lives of Mary Cowper Stiles's maternal grandmother and grandfather, Robert and Eliza Mackay, in their own voices. The originals of the letters come from the collection presented in 1936 to the Colonial Dames Society by Mrs. Franklin B. Screven and her cousin Miss Phoebe Elliott. Mrs. Screven's mission had been to assemble and collect scraps of letters still in the possession of family and to make them available for research by writers and scholars interested in the social history of the South. With this goal in mind, she presented the majority of these private records to the Southern Historical Collection of the University of North Carolina at Chapel Hill and others to the Colonial Dames Collection now housed in the Georgia Historical Society.

2. See Charles J. Johnson Jr., *Mary Telfair: The Life and Legacy of a Nineteenth-Century Woman* (Savannah: Frederic C. Beil, 2002).

3. The materials in the W. H. Stiles collection at Emory University contain some ambiguous penciled notes regarding Robert E. Lee's purported romance with Eliza Mackay. Hugh Golson believes that the emphasis on the connection may have been made by Frank Screven, son of Bessie Stiles (Elizabeth Mackay Stiles Mills Screven). Frank Screven printed a monograph in the 1950's on letters between Lee and the Mackays, which created the buzz about a romance.

4. Christopher Harwell, *William Henry Stiles: Georgia Gentleman-Politician.* Ph.D. dissertation, Emory University, 1959. Much of the material used in this dissertation was borrowed by Harwell from Robert and Susie Stiles at Malbone, and eventually wound up in the archives at Emory

University. Robert's father, William Henry Stiles III, died in 1944 and was the last occupant of Etowah Cliffs. Many of the papers belonged to his mother, Eliza Clifford Gordon Stiles. Etowah Cliffs then sat empty and derelict, and boxes of family material were discarded or moved for safer keeping.

5. The well-documented expulsion of the Cherokee nation from their lands in the eastern States, and relocation to western lands, mainly in Oklahoma, is beyond the scope of this biography. Amongst the many books written are John Ehle, *Trail of Tears: The Rise and Fall of the Cherokee Nation* (Random House); James Mooney, *History, Myths and Sacred Formulas of the Cherokees* (Historical Images: Asheville, N. C.); Grace Steele Woodward, *The Cherokees* (University of Oklahoma Press).

6. The period of William Henry Stiles's service to the federal government occurred during the presidency of John Tyler (1841–45). When Tyler succeeded William Henry Harrison, who died a month after he took office, Tyler was often referred to as "His Accidency." In 1845 James Knox Polk, Democrat and a former governor of Tennessee, was elected President and served only four years. He was succeeded by Zachary Taylor, who died after only sixteen months and was succeeded by Millard Fillmore (1850–53). These frequent presidencies coincided with William Stiles's attempts to regain a prominent position in the political arena leading up to the Civil War.

7. Barnsley, the English-born son of a cotton mill owner, had come to Savannah from Liverpool in 1824, at the age of eighteen, and prospered as a cotton broker with offices in both cities. He was involved with the Scarbrough family, marrying a daughter Julia, and they built a home in Cass County called "Woodlands," near Kingston. The carved *meridiennes* in the front parlor of the Andrew Low House and Museum are from Woodlands.

8. 1845—Jan. 11, House of Representatives, Washington, D.C.—W.H.S. to wife (Folder 71, 1811–1845—W.H.S. Papers), Southern Historical Collection, University of North Carolina.

9. Copies with transcripts of the Austrian diaries of Eliza Mackay Stiles are archived at the Robert Woodruff Library, Emory University, Atlanta.

10. Ledger is part of the Mackay-Stiles Papers at the Southern Historical Collection, University of North Carolina.

11. Sinai was the first of six generations to serve the Stiles-Mackays. The Kincaid family, her offspring, left Malbone for Chicago in the early 1930's.

12. There remain no records of reminiscences of Mackay-Stiles-Low slaves in the various collections scattered around the country to balance the account or provide a different perspective, a fact the authors regret.

Chapter 13: Lovely Manners: Savannah, 1854–1860, *pages 154–172*

1. The three other books in the Savannah Quartet by Eugenia Price are: *Savannah*; *To See Your Face Again*; and *Before The Darkness Falls*—all published by Random House.

2. Eugenia Price, *Stranger in Savannah*, Afterword, pp. 750–51. "The letter used by Natalie Browning Latimer in her effort to convince Eliza Anne Stiles that Mary Cowper should not be forced to marry Andrew Low contains the exact wording from a letter Mary Elizabeth Huger of South Carolina sent to the Mackay sisters in Savannah." It does not, unfortunately, give the date, year, or source of the original document. Hugh Stiles Golson says that Price promised to give him a copy of this letter, but never did. His recollection is that her research assistant found the letter in the Wilson Library, probably the Southern Historical Collection, Chapel Hill. Golson goes on to state that he is not sure exactly who Mary Elizabeth Huger was, but that she may have been Margaret Mackay Elliott's daughter Mary Stiles Elliott (1843–1919), who was wed to Joseph Alston Huger. This Mary Huger was Mary Cowper's first cousin. Another possibility is that she may have been Joseph Alston Huger's sister or close relative. According to Caroline Lovell, Mr. Pinckney Huger regularly stayed at the Mackay house.

3. This refers to material contained in a memoir written in the 1920's and 30's by Caroline Couper Stiles Lovell, born May 7, 1862, to Robert Mackay Stiles and Margaret Wylly Couper. The Mercer University Press, Macon, Georgia, published *The Light of Other Days,* with introductions by Hugh Stiles Golson and LeeAnn Whites in 1995.

4. *Light of Other Days,* p. 58.

5. This portrait of Mary Cowper Stiles, from the Caroline Lovell Collection, has been used as the cover of a book edited by Anna Habersham Wright Smith called *A Savannah Family, 1830–1901.* The contents of the book are papers from the Clermont Huger Lee Collection, written by Leila Elliott Habersham, taken in part from *A Sketch of the Life of Frederic Augustus Haberham.*

6. This reference to "the wealthiest man in Savannah" appears to originate with a lecture, "Andrew Low's House," delivered in Jan. 1966 by Walter Charlton Hartridge to the Georgia Historical Society: "The extent of the nephew's good fortune can be measured by the list of earnings which the Savannah town fathers compiled when they attempted to impose a municipal income tax on all citizens. Andrew Low, the younger was credited with the primary annual income of a quarter of a million dollars, the highest in town, second place being held by his partner, Charles Green (who was credited) with $80,000."

7. Southern Historical Collection, University of North Carolina.

8. Smith, *A Savannah Family, 1830-1901.*

9. David McCullough, *Morning on Horseback* (Simon and Schuster, 1981), in his notes for p. 47, Ch. 2, "Lady from the South," credits the source of this story to the reminiscences of Mrs. William Baker, formerly Evelyn King, one of the bridesmaids at the wedding. It was given in a 1920 interview to Peggy Mitchell, a young reporter from the *Atlanta Journal.* Later as Margaret Mitchell she wrote the all-time bestseller *Gone With the Wind.*

10. Malcolm Bell, Jr., *Major Butler's Legacy. Five Generations of a Slave-holding Family* (University of Georgia Press).

11. Robert Hutchison, partner and agent for Andrew Low, Sr., following the death of Robert Isaac, was the executor of the estate of Mittie's father, James Stephens Bulloch. The connections between the Bullochs and the Lows were close and complicated, and Hutchison was one of the links. Robert Hutchison was married first to Corinne Elliott, who was sister of Hester Elliott, James Stephens Bulloch's first wife, and mother of James Dunwoody Bulloch. Corinne Elliott Hutchison and their two children died in the wreck of the *Pulaski* in June 1837 (as did William Mackay's wife and children), but Robert Hutchison survived the wreck. Robert Hutchison's second marriage was to Mary Caskie, sister of Lizzie Caskie, who was the first wife of James D. Bulloch, thus making him Bulloch's brother-in-law. Robert and Mary had two daughters (one of whom she was pregnant with when Andrew Low, Jr.'s first wife, Sarah Hunter, died in 1849); one survived childhood and lived for a while in Liverpool with James D. Bulloch. There are letters from James Bulloch in the Hutchison-Dawson file at the Georgia Historical Society, which show a very caring side to his nature and consideration for his extended family. Hutchison's third wife was to a Caskie cousin, much younger than he was, but she, too, died young. Robert Hutchison died in Savannah in 1862, and a letter from Lucy Sorrel Elliott, now married to Daniel Stewart Elliott, to her mother-in-law, Martha Bulloch, saying how sad it was that he died all alone. There are rumors that Hutchison took Daniel Stewart Elliott to Europe following the duel in which he killed Tom Daniell. These family ties encompassed both commerce and family matters. They trusted their own. Source for this information is Penny McMillen, former volunteer at the Bulloch Hall museum in Roswell, Georgia.

12. David McCullough, *Mornings on Horseback,* p. 51: "According to family tradition, brother Dan [Daniel Stewart Elliott] also fell head over heels in love with one of the bridesmaids [Mittie's sister Anna, Mary Cooper Stiles, Evelyn King, and Julia Hand] who was already engaged to another and much older man, and who rode off leaving Dan broken-hearted. This romantic episode, it is further said, ended tragically in the

girl's unwilling marriage to the older man, to a duel and 'much else that was unfortunate.' But since the only known duel in Dan's stormy life, that with Tom Daniell, took place three years later and since Tom Daniell was both unmarried and Dan's own age, the story is open to a good deal of question—unless, of course, an entirely different duel was fought earlier and did not prove fatal, in which case there would be no record of its ever having occurred."

My own conclusion is that the Elliott-Daniell duel had nothing to do with whether Stewart Elliott was infatuated with Mary Cowper, or she with him. Certainly it had nothing to do with Andrew Low, which is a good thing, because if Stewart Elliott had killed my great-grandfather in a duel, for love of Mary Cowper, I would not be here to question the veracity of the gossip!

13. Gordon Burns Smith, in his *History of the Georgia Militia, 1783–1861*, vol. 4, gives a detailed account of the duel where Stewart Elliott kills Tom Daniell, taken from a previous account written by sometime Savannah mayor and prolific writer, Thomas Gamble, in 1931, and titled *Dan Elliott and Tom Daniell Dueled to Death Across the River.*

14. Another of those extraordinary six-degrees-of-separation coincidences that abound is the fact that back in colonial times, even before the foundation of the state of Georgia, Archibald Stobo, a Presbyterian minister from Glasgow, sailed with his wife and daughter Jean on the ill-fated expedition to found a Scottish Trading Company at Darien on the Panamanian isthmus in the late 1600's. A William Low and a Daniel Mackay were two other prominent members of that doomed attempt. The Stobos ended up fortuitously in South Carolina, and Jean Stobo married James Bulloch of Glasgow to found the Bulloch clan in the New World.

15. A letter from the daughter of Robert E. Lee indicates that Mary Cowper was content with her decision to marry Andrew Low: "Miss Mary Custis Lee to Mary Cowper Stiles Low," Arlington, May 18, 1854:

> Dear Mary: You must not think that I have been unmindful of you or your proceedings because I have not been earlier in expressions of interest & offers of congratulations, for such a condition would be a very erroneous one. I have often thought of you, & wished to write and tell you so, but various circumstances continually prevented the execution of my intentions, & for the last three months, stretched on my back on a sofa, with a lame foot which was kept elevated in the air on a raised board, anything like an epistolary communication with my absent friends has been impossible. And so "Miss Mary is going to be married" a most extraordinary determination truly, after our long night talks about the delight of old maidenhood! Really,

Miss Stiles, you are, as a cousin of mine always says, a very un-stable character. However, ladies are privileged to change their minds I believe, & I must not call you to account for exercising one of the few rights of our sex, even though poor I should be left like the last rose of summer, a respectable spinster, all my lovely companions, not faded, but gone. Dear Mary I wish you every happiness in the new position which you will now occupy, & wish I could have been present to witness the "wedding," but the stern fates render such a pleasure impossible, & I must submit to their decree as patiently as I can. In your last letter you spoke of a flying visit to the Point on your way to the embarkation. Now it is not fair that Papa should be the only one of the family favored with a sight of the "bride" & I would propose that she gives us at least one day at Old Arlington. Can she not? It is a compensation you owe me for rejecting my two brothers besides a cousin, Lawrence Butler, or two, Louis Marshall! And now I will trespass on your time & patience no longer but with sincerest well wishes and congratulations say good bye. Give much love to your dear mother & remember me to your father and brothers, also to my new cousin Mr. Low—he is a cousin, you know, for *my* papa is *your* uncle & married people count but *one*. Adieu! Marsilee Lee. I will not direct this note because I am not certain what your name will be at the time of its receipt.

Robert E. Lee assumed the position of Superintendent of the U. S. Military Academy at West Point in Sept. 1853.

16. Andrew Low was a member of the Board of Directors.

17. *Frederic Augustus Habersham* memoir written by Leila Elliott Habersham.

18. The purchase of the portrait of Mary Cowper Stiles Low resulted from negotiations by Hugh Stiles Golson as agent for the Friends of the Andrew Low House with Christopher R. Davidson. Christie's in Pretoria concluded negotiations, including the only portrait extant of Andrew Low, Jr., painted in 1836 in Savannah by George W. Conarroe (see chapter "Passing the Baton"). A number of other items were also purchased at that time, including the set of amethyst, circa 1815, originally belonging to Archduchess Maria Louisa, second wife of Napoleon I. The set was sold at the auction of her estate in Vienna in 1849 and purchased by William Henry Stiles for his wife, Eliza. These items had passed by inheritance to succeeding generations of the Stiles descendants, had gone to England, and then eventually wound up in South Africa after passing to Jane Davidson, who inherited from her uncle Alistair Graham, brother of Jane's mother, Sibyl Hickson, daughter of Jessie Graham, daughter of Mary Low.

These items are now on display at the Andrew Low House and Museum.

19. House originally had a parapet that remains visible in the attic. A second roof is over the original. Alice Daily, Andrew Low House historian.

20. Letter is part of Colonial Dames Collection #965, Folder 131A, at the Georgia Historical Society. In addition, a framed note and photograph of Thackeray is part of the exhibits in one of the bedrooms of the Andrew Low House and Museum.

21. Andrew Low purchased Lot #521 in Laurel Grove Cemetery on Mar. 9, 1858, and his first wife, Sarah Low, and Andrew III were reburied there on May 25, 1858. The Mackay family lot #486 lies directly behind the Low lot. In it lie Eliza Ann McQueen Mackay, 1862; Robert Mackay, Jr., her son, 1857; William Mackay, son, 1859; her unmarried daughters Sarah, 1876 and Catherine (Kate), 1879; her son-in-law William Henry Stiles, 1865. The patriarch Robert Mackay, who died on a business trip to New York in 1816, is buried in Trinity Church in New York City. The grave of Mary Low's child who died in 1856 is marked in garden tiles and hosts an old boxwood.

22. *Monumental Inscriptions of Angus*: Brechin Cathedral Kirk. Date of recording: Mar. 14, 1986. Name of recorder: Mrs. K. B. Smith.

23. Inventory of William Low, Merchant of Brechin Ref #: SC47/40/19: pp. 422–23: Inventory of Katherine Reid Low Ref #: SC47/40/24, pp. 562–63. The inventory of the furnishings, wearing apparel, other effects, and cash in the house were valued at fifty-three pounds and change, a lot less than a thousand dollars in the value of currency at the time. The granite stone house on Pearse Street was not included in the value of the estate although it obviously was owned outright by William Low, and Katherine Reid Low continued to live there after his death, as did her unmarried daughter Mary, as shown on her own death certificate in 1888. The widow's estate was a little higher than her husband's, but not by much.

24. The misspelling of Kincardineshire was probably the result of Georgia Historical committee working from handwritten census documents. It is from this 1860 Census of Chatham County, p. 224, that Andrew Low's place of birth is extrapolated in Susan Mays's "Interpretive Report" commissioned by the Andrew Low House. The 1813 date of birth given in that report, however, is an error. The rest of the 1860 Census reads: "Mary 27F, Savannah; Emma (Amy) 15F, Savannah; Harriet, 12F, Savannah; Catherine 5F, Cass Co; Mary, 1F, Savannah; Anderson, Celia (M) 37F, Savannah, Mulatto; Taylor, Grace, (M) 50F, Savannah. Schedule 11 also lists 3 other slaves, 2 Black males 42 and 39, and 1 Black Female, age 15." The Census lists mulattoes and black slaves separately.

25. The birth certificate issued by the State of Rhode Island lists name of the child as "William K. Low, Male, born August 3rd, 1860, on Trouro

Street. Father, Andrew Low, birthplace Savannah. Mother, Mary Stile, Savannah, Ga. Usual residence of Mother, Newport, Rhode Island. Filing Date: Feb. 13, 1861. Book 1, Pg 51." From the numerous mistakes contained in this official document for genealogical purposes, it is easy to see how errors creep into the conventional history of an individual. During his lifetime, in primary source letters, journals, and diaries written by family, he was always referred to as Willie and occasionally Bill. In the several secondary source books written mentioning his position in Edwardian society, he is also referred to by that diminutive, with that spelling. Only Daisy apparently called him Billow. William Mackay Low was used in his obituary.

26. Transcriptions of the papers of her three-times grandfather Godfrey Malbone by Mary Cowper Low have now become available to us as part of the heritage handed down by her children to their children and children's children and form part of the collection of Low material at the Andrew Low House and Museum.

27. According to *Light of Other Days* in later years, Andrew Low managed the money of both maiden aunts Kate and Sarah and did so successfully; they were able to send Eliza Stiles's grandsons to college in the 1870's during postwar reconstruction hardships.

28. General Alexander Low was the sole surviving son of Alexander Low, brother of Uncle Andrew Low and Mary Nicol. Their other son, Andrew, was killed aged nineteen by a runaway horse in a bizarre accident in Nice, France. There was also a sister, Mai Le Coulter, who was also "recognized" by the Lows after they moved to England, and she left them several family items.

29. A poignant parallel between the two men's lives lies in the fact that Charles Green lost several wives and small children, and married three times, the first to Catherine Jane Burroughs, who died in 1844, and left three sons: Benjamin 8, Charles 5, and infant Andrew; this was the same year Andrew Low married Sarah Hunter. In 1850, the year after Andrew Low had lost most of his family including his wife Sarah and small son, Charles Green married Lucinda Ireland Hunton of Prince William County, Virginia. This marriage linked the families of Mackall, Moxley, Sorrel, and Low. Charles Green's sister Eliza Green had married John Low, Andrew Low's cousin in Aberdeen. They had three children—Marion, Josiah Green, and the youngest, another Andrew—adding to the ongoing confusion regarding which Andrew Low was which. This youngest Andrew was born in Liverpool in 1839, and came to Virginia in the 1850's to run the farm at Vint Hill, Virginia, owned by his uncle Charles Green. Lucy Green died in 1866, probably in childbirth, and Green married again in 1869, to a woman thirty-two years his junior, Aminta Elizabeth Fisher, related to the Sorrel

family. By then his relationship with Andrew Low had ended in acrimony.

30. The house was not built with bracketed eaves. Originally a crenellated parapet wall hid a low-sloped roof. See Smith engraving of city, 1856.

31. Mary Morrison, *John S. Norris: Architect in Savannah, 1846–60* (Savannah: The Beehive Press, 1980). John Norris came to Savannah originally to build the Custom House. Born in New York State in 1804, Norris had made the typical progress from mason to architect. In 1839 he went to Wilmington, North Carolina, to supervise construction of St. James Episcopal Church, designed by Thomas U. Walter. As supervising architect, Norris was responsible for hiring laborers, overseeing the work, and purchasing materials and supplies. Norris designed and supervised construction of a Custom House at Wilmington, which led him to submit a design for Savannah's proposed Custom House in 1846. During the last decade before the Civil War, John Norris became the principal architect of Savannah, spending several months each year in Savannah and returning to his family in Brooklyn during the torrid summertime.

32. Martha Summerell, *Faithfully Yours, Charles Green: The Life and Times of a 19th Century Cotton Merchant.* This monograph contains snippets from letters Charles Green wrote during his incarceration in Fort Warren and adds details to the competitive nature of his relationship with Andrew Low. Copies of this document can be found through the St. John's Parish House Acquisition Board.

Part V: Savannah–Liverpool–Leamington, 1860–1872

Chapter 14: Our Peculiar Institution, 1858–1860, *pages 175–191*

1. *London Times*, Jan. 18, 1850.

2. Frances Anne Kemble, *Journal of a Residence on a Georgian Plantation in 1838–1839* (Athens: University of Georgia Press, 1984). Fanny Kemble's *Journal* covers a span of about fifteen weeks spent on her husband Pierce Butler's estate on Butler's Island and St. Simon's Island. Following her divorce in 1849, she considered publication to tell the truth about slavery as she saw it. The manuscript was circulated privately, but was not made available to the general public until the middle of the Civil War. Longman and Company published the London edition of the *Journal* in May 1863. The New York edition was issued by Harper and Brothers in July 1863.

3. D. J. Harris, *Liverpool and Merseyside Cotton Merchants, 1820–1850.* Harris claims that little is known about Liverpool cotton merchants on account of the dearth of records, but we are most fortunate that the group of cotton merchants featured in an essay by D. M. Williams includes the

firm of Isaac Low and Company, founded in 1819 as a sister company to Andrew Low and Company, Savannah.

4. Edmund Molyneaux's uncle, Thomas Molyneaux, was mayor of Liverpool in 1807, also a known slave trader, as were other members of the Molyneaux family. Duke University has a log of a slave ship, which called in at Savannah in the 1790's, Master, Charles Molyneaux. Thomas' descendants were partners of the Liverpool cotton broking firm of Molyneaux, Taylor & Co. Source: Nigel Watts, descendant.

5. "The Cotton Factorage System of the Southern States," in *American Historical Review* 20 (1915), pp. 557–65.

6. *World Almanac 2001*. p. 445.

7. Walter Edgar, *South Carolina: A History* (Columbia: University of South Carolina Press, 1998). The Second Great Awakening was a massive religious revival that swept the country in 1802, having a tremendous influence on Baptists, Methodists, and Presbyterians.

8. Copy of the Reverend Stiles's *The Voice of Our Fathers* is at the Georgia Historical Society, Savannah.

9. William L. Andrews and Henry Louis Gates, eds., *The Civitas Anthology of African American Slave Narratives* (Washington, D.C.: Civitas Counter Point, 1999).

10. Frederick Law Olmsted, *Cotton Kingdom: A Traveller's Observation on Cotton and Slavery in the American Slave States* (New York: Mason Brothers, 1861); David Cohn, *The Life and Times of King Cotton—America's Cotton Story*; Bertha S. Dodge, *Cotton, The Plant that Would Be King—British Cotton Story*.

11. E. N. Elliott, *Cotton Is King and Pro-Slavery Arguments, Comprising the Writings of Hammond, Harper, Christy, Stringfellow, Hodge, Bledsoe and Cartwright* (Augusta, Ga., 1860).

12. "Mill Children," *The Rise and Fall of King Cotton*, ch. 7. The excerpt is taken from *A Memoir of Robert Blincoe* by John Brown, published first in 1832, reprinted in 1977. Anthony Burton, British Broadcasting Corporation, 1984, companion to television series of same name, is the editor of the book.

13. Captain Ralph Semmes was later to become master of the famous CSS *Alabama* with John Low, young cousin of Andrew Low, serving under him.

Chapter 15: Recent Unpleasantness, 1860–1862, *pages 192–218*

1. Richard Brooke, *Liverpool As It Was* (Liverpool Record Office, 1853).

2. *When Liverpool Was Dixie*. Liverpool Records Office plus numerous online sites detailing the interest in the Civil War in Liverpool.

3. *Liverpool and the American Civil War*, Information Sheet No. 89, Liverpool Maritime Archives and Museum.

4. *The Annals of Liverpool, 1076–1880.* Altogether more than 600 blockade-runners violated the blockade some 8,000 times. They brought in over 600,000 small arms, 550,000 pairs of shoes, and large quantities of luxuries. They also took to Europe about 1,250,000 bales of cotton.

5. Sir Arthur Arnold, *The History of the Cotton Famine* (London, 1864). Arnold writes that "1860 was the 'annus mirabilis' of King Cotton." His flowery prose articulated a very real potential disaster.

6. In Liverpool a tremendous amount of information exists on Charles Prioleau and Fraser Trenholm & Co. of Charleston, elevating the man and the firm, merely because their records remain for study because of the diligence of the Liverpool Records Office and interest in Liverpool's history. *Civil War and the Confederacy,* Microfilm records, Liverpool Records Office.

7. Alexander A. Lawrence, *A Present for Mr. Lincoln,* p.82. The Union administration appeared to believe that Andrew Low also had something to do with the successful blockade-busting *Bermuda* that successfully escaped from Savannah with a cargo of eighteen-hundred bales of cotton just days before the arrival of the *Fingal.*

8. Henry Hotze returned to England and in May 1862 founded *The Index,* a newspaper with offices located on Bouverie Street, London. Copies of these papers have been reissued by Adam Matthew Publications, and are listed in the acquisitions of the Liverpool Record Office in the catalog *Civil War and the Confederacy* as *A Weekly Journal of Politics, Literature and News* "devoted to the exposition of the mutual interests, political and commercial, of Great Britain and the Confederate States of America." Other sources cite the newspaper as being the "Propaganda arm of the Confederates in Britain."

9. There has been almost as much wrong information published about the various John Lows as there has about the various Andrew Lows. John Low of the *Fingal* episode—I believe after extensive correspondence with descendants in Australia and New Zealand—was a cousin of Andrew Low and son of another Andrew Low, who in his turn was the youngest son of Uncle Andrew's brother, John Low. As recorded on John Low's marriage certificate to his second wife Catherine Morris in Liverpool in 1867, he lists "Father, Andrew Low, Gentleman." If that is still confusing, examine Uncle Andrew's Will, which names many of his surviving family. In any event, the young John Low went on to serve admirably in the Confederate Navy, serving under Captain Ralph Semmes on the CSS *Alabama.* See Stanley Hoole's *Four Years in the Confederate Navy*—do not, however, accept the genealogical information in the introduction as that is where the confusion commenced that he was Andrew Low's nephew. After the Civil War John Low returned to Liverpool and became prominent in the marine

insurance business. Source: a sheaf of obituaries at the Georgia Historical Society, Savannah. He is buried in Liverpool's Golbourne Cemetery and is an icon for Civil War history buffs. There is proof that John Low was married twice (first wife was Mary Elizabeth Wall, m. 1860) and had a first son named John (Jack), probably born 1860–62 in either Savannah or Virginia, although no birth certificate found for John (Jack), although he is recognized in John Low's Will. This son immigrated to New Zealand, his descendants have been traced, and I have conducted extensive correspondence with them. John Low also had four children by his second wife, and has descendants still living in Tasmania, Australia. I have also corresponded with the Sweetingham branch of the family, and we have together sorted out some of the facts that remained unclear.

10. This John Low, originally born in Aberdeen, had lived many years in Liverpool, where to compound the confusion his youngest son, also named Andrew, was born. The family of John and Eliza Low also lived in Virginia following the marriage of Charles Green to his second wife, Lucinda Hunton, who had a property in Prince William County purchased in 1855 by Charles Green from Mrs. A. E. Moxley, a house called "The Lawn" totaling 470 acres, a sizable estate near Gainesville. I believe that it was this John Low's brother Andrew, both sons of Uncle Andrew's brother John, who was the father of John Low of the *Alabama*. Although I cannot prove it conclusively, I believe that John Low (1773, brother of Andrew Low, Sr.) became a mariner, married a Margaret Leighton of Dunnottar. They had a son John, born 1799 in St. Nicholas, Aberdeen. This I believe was the John Low who became a partner in Low Taylor in Savannah, married Eliza Green, and was first cousin to Andrew Low, Jr.

11. "Sidney Stiles Elliott to Katie Low, (5-6-1892)," Wm. H. Stiles Collection, Series 1, Typescript (bound) 1747–1892, Robert Woodruff Library, Emory University. Mrs. Elliott states: "Regina S. Gray was a cousin your Grandfather Stiles with whom your Grandmother was most intimate, one of the Clay's married a Gray of Boston ... it was the Grays who helped your Mother during the war when your Father was taken prisoner and your Mother had such a hard time getting through the Yankee lines to get back to her children."

12. Montgomery Cumming, *Table of the Descendants of Joseph Clay* (1897). William Gray, Jr., of Boston was a grandson of Joseph Clay, Jr. He was Mary Low's second cousin.

13. Eliza Stiles, "Letter to My Grandchildren." Stiles Collection, Emory University. More information is available in this typescript for Civil War buffs.

14. "M. C. Elliott to her Sisters, 1-23-1862," Stiles Collection, Emory University.

15. *Official Records of the Civil War; Prisoners of War Series* 121, vol. 2, p. 1032.

16. "M. C. Low to her Husband, 5-16-1862." Mackay-Stiles Collection, University of North Carolina. This is the only letter extant in her own handwriting to her husband.

Chapter 16: Guns and Roses, 1862–1863, *pages 219–239*

1. Percival Elliott, born 1840, died in May 1865 in Lincoln Hospital, Washington, D.C., immediately following the end of the war.

2. Mary Ellison, *Support for Secession: Lancashire and the American Civil War,* University of Liverpool.

3. Norman Longmate, *The Hungry Mills* (London, 1978).

4. "Mary Ann Stiles to Eliza Stiles, Feb. 11 and Feb. 22, 1862." The widow of Benjamin Stiles writes her sister from her plantation "Barron Hill" in Clarkesville, Ga. Mackay-Stiles Collection, University of North Carolina.

5. Lilla Hawes, ed., "Memoirs of Charles Olmstead," *Georgia Historical Quarterly* 41. These memoirs continue in several volumes and contain the day-by-day experiences of the Civil War experiences of Colonel Charles Olmstead, starting with his command of Fort Pulaski in 1861 and continuing through his incarceration on Governor's Island, New York.

6. Alexander A. Lawrence, *A Present for Mr. Lincoln* (Ardivan Press, 1961), p. 71. Written by a native of Savannah, Lawrence was a prominent attorney, jurist, and historian. This book is one of the best researched and notated of the myriad books written about the Civil War focusing on Savannah's role in the conflict, admittedly from the perspective of the city and its people.

7. Captain Stiles was son of William Henry Stiles's brother Benjamin and Eliza Mackay Stiles's sister Mary Ann. Both of them were daughters of Eliza McQueen Mackay, the matriarch of the family.

8. Benjamin Edward Stiles (Eddie), captain, C.S.A. Born Apr. 24, 1836; married Mar. 24, 1863, Clelia Peronneau; died Aug. 16, 1864.

9. Shelby Foote, *The Civil War—A Narrative: Fredericksburg to Meridian* (Random House), p. 20.

10. William H. Stiles Collection, Emory University, box 1, folder 7.

11. Sidney Stiles was Eddy's sister. Born 1840; married first cousin William Henry Elliott, M.D., 1862; died 1925.

12. *World Almanac 2001*. Voting rights for ex-slaves were to be embodied in the Fifteenth Amendment to the Constitution passed some years later. "Amendment XV: The following amendment was proposed to the legislatures of the several States by the 40th Congress, 1869 and ratified Feb 8, 1870. 1: The right of citizens of the United States to vote shall not be denied or abridged by the United States or by any State on account of

race, color, or previous condition of servitude. 2: The Congress shall have the power to enforce this article by appropriate legislation." In fact, after a brief period when blacks did vote, it was not until 1964 that an omnibus civil rights bill cleared Congress July 2, signed that same day by President Lyndon B. Johnson, banned discrimination in voting, jobs, public accommodation etc. Not until a new Voting Rights Act signed by Congress on August 6, 1965, following the civil rights march led by the Rev. Martin Luther King, Jr. from Selma to Montgomery, Alabama to demand federal protection of black voting rights, did the promise of the Civil War become legal reality.

13. *Times of London* (Apr. 16, 1863).

14. Susan Mays, *Interpretive Report*, note 117: "Eliza Stiles to W. H. Stiles February 3, 1863," Mackay-Stiles-Wylly Papers, Georgia Historical Society.

15. *Frederic Augustus Habersham Memoir*, collection of Clermont Lee.

16. Mackay-Stiles Collection, University of North Carolina, Chapel Hill.

17. Unidentified newspaper report, "Lt. Frederic Habersham, of Read's Battery, Kershaw's Brigade, McLaws Division, was killed in one of the late engagements on the Rappahannock, near Fredericksburg."

18. *Habersham Memoir.*

19. *Habersham Memoir*. Bishop Elliot to Mrs. Susan Habersham, June 16, 1863, *Frederic Habersham Memoir*, pp. 189–90.

20. Susan Mays, notes 118, 120, and 121.

21. *A Savannah Family*, p. 190. "Mary Cowper Stiles and her new baby died the next day." Susan Mays also in her *Interpretive Report* states "the blow fell either on the 17th or 18th of June 1863 when Mary and her baby died." She cites as her source the *Register of Deaths in Savannah, Georgia*, but an examination of Mary Low's death card reveals no mention of a baby. The card reads: "Low, Mary. Lafayette Square 6/17 1863—Age: 30. Savannah, Puerperal Fever. Dr. J. J. Waring. Buried in Laurel Grove Cemetery. Lot 521. The biography of Juliette Low (Gladys Denny Schultz and Daisy Gordon Lawrence, *Lady From Savannah*) on p. 125 also states that Mary and her child died, but there are no footnotes to source their information either.

Chapter 17: When the Ball Is Over, 1863–1867, *pages 240–263*

1. Harwell, *William Henry Stiles: Georgia Gentleman—Politician*, Emory University.

2. Unless otherwise indicated the letters quoted and referred to in this section are from the Mackay-Stiles Papers in the Southern Historical Collection, University of North Carolina, Chapel Hill.

3. "Eliza Stiles to W. H. Siles, Folder 50, March 28th, 1864." Mackay-Stiles Collection, University of North Carolina. Mrs. Stiles writes "that Mr. Low has not been in her room since he left." This letter is important because it speaks to Andrew Low and Eliza's relationship as being extremely tense a year before Sherman took Savannah.

4. Lawrence, *A Present for Mr. Lincoln.* The version of events in this book primarily uses letters and original sources, which makes it valuable and posits a theory that the North was unhappy with England's construed pro-Southern attitude and expresses the sentiment voiced by General Sherman that after the war is over he fervently hopes that the South will join with the North and fight England.

5. Phillips-Myers Papers, University of North Carolina. Donated by Fanny Cohen's niece.

6. Whittington B. Johnson, *Black Savannah, 1788–1864* (University of Arkansas Press, 1996). The position of the African church in Savannah was prominent in Savannah from its very early inception, as was the relative status of slaves and free blacks. In the blurb on the book's back the publishers claim "Johnson maintains that, unlike New Orleans or Charleston, Savannah had a comparatively small population of free blacks, containing only a slim majority of mulattoes and a few large property owners and a group he called 'nominal' slaves, slaves in name only, who lived apart from their masters, seeking and finding their own employment. This had a profound impact on the emergence of a thriving black class structure, resulting in an autonomous black community in a key city in the Old South."

7. Kevin J. Foster, "The Diplomats Who Sank the Fleet—The Confederacy's Undelivered European Fleet and the Union Consular Service," in *U.S. National Archives & Records Administration Magazine* 33, no. 3 (Fall 2001).

8. *When Liverpool Was Dixie* is an admirable online site (www.csa-dixie.com/liverpool_dixie) maintained in Liverpool by Roy Rawlinson of Southport and is a veritable goldmine to be sifted for details of further Civil War history and the British connections.

9. John Bennett, article originally appeared in *Crossfire—The Magazine of the American Civil War Round Table,* no. 61 (Dec. 1999).

10. Liverpool historian and Civil War buff Bob Jones conducts remarkable tours of sites and situations known as the American Civil War Heritage Trail, relating to Liverpool's connection with the war, including James Bulloch's home on Wellington Street, Waterloo; his grave in Toxteth Cemetery; Charles Prioleau's magnificent mansion at 42 Abercrombie Square, now property of the University of Liverpool; and Captain John Low's grave in Golbourne Cemetery.

11. R. E. Lee, *Recollections of Robert E. Lee* (New York: Konecky & Konecky), p. 153. On Apr. 10, 1865, General Lee issued his last order to the Army of Northern Virginia: "After four years of arduous service, marked by unsurpassed courage and fortitude, the Army of Northern Virginia has been compelled to yield to overwhelming numbers and resources."

12. Alice Daily, historian, claims that in a letter dated Apr. 18, 1865, Eliza Stiles writes: "Mr. Low planning to go to England and talks of taking Katie [who would have been about ten years old] and leaving her at Miss Clarence's." Despite lack of verifiable proof, we have assumed that it probably was with Miss Clarence that Andrew Low had left his daughters Amy and Harriet in 1851 after the death of Sarah Hunter Low.

13. "W. H. Stiles to Eliza Stiles, July 1st, 1865." Mackay-Stiles Papers, University of North Carolina.

14. Harwell, *William Henry Stiles.*

15. "Eliza Stiles to W. H. Stiles, August 20, 1865." Mackay-Stiles Papers, University of North Carolina. This letter is the first time Tom's wife has been referenced, but neither child nor wife named. Tom is assumed to be the person named as purchased by Andrew Low and Co. from slave trader Wylly Woodbridge in 1844 for $398.92. The purchase is recorded in Chatham County records 1844-3B741. The assumption and conventional wisdom in the oral history of the Low family is that Mosianna Milledge, who later on came to the attention of the public as "Willie Low's Southern cook" in Edwardian England, was Tom Milledge's daughter. It is in this letter that Susan Mays references in *Appendix 2—Slaves/Servants Owned/ Employed by Andrew Low* of her *Interpretive Report for the Andrew Low House and Museum* that "this baby may be Mosianna Milledge, who later became the cook." This presumptive assumption that Mosianna was Tom Milledge's daughter has now been contested by a research report prepared in 2005 for the museum, commissioned by curator Tania Sammons and researched by student April Duffie attending Armstrong University. This report claims that Mosianna was Tom's wife and not his daughter.

16. *Rubaiyat of Omar Khayyam.* This is a translation of the eleventh-century Persian poet known in his time as a skilled mathematician. Edward FitzGerald translated the work anonymously in 1859 supplying the English-speaking world with an adaptation of Omar Khayyam's timeless poetry.

17. This letter is the third recorded indication in the archives of possible friction between Andrew Low and his Hunter in-laws; the first from Edward Anderson on the occasion of the marriage of Andrew and Sarah Cecil; the second in the letter from a Huger cousin regarding the marriage of Mary Cowper to Andrew and now this more direct allusion. This certainly could account for the reason he had sent his two daughters to England to be educated after their mother's death.

PART VI: SAVANNAH–LEAMINGTON, 1867–1932

Chapter 18: The English Squire, 1867–1883, *pages 267–291*

1. More details have become available to the record through recent acquisitions by the Andrew Low House of papers and letters obtained from the estate of Katie Low, the eldest daughter who never married and appears to have set herself up as the torchbearer of the family reputation of her father, sisters, and brother. There is also a set of five journals, written by the youngest daughter Jessie Low, dated 1880–1889. Unfortunately they have many gaps with nothing at all to cover 1882–1885. They do, however, furnish some corroboration of events that were suspected as well as personal details of several crucial events.

2. Nathaniel Hawthorne was also U.S. consul in Liverpool from 1853 to 1857, his offices in the Washington Building long demolished.

3. Jenny Long and Andrew Barber, *Graciously Pleased: Royal Leamington Spa—150 Years.*

4. www.americancivilwar.org.uk. There are many accounts of Civil War connections listed in the American Civil War Round Table (UK) magazine, *Crossfire.*

5. Beauchamp Hall, built probably circa 1863, was purchased by the Kingsley School in 1922 and is still operated as a school.

6. An original supposition now confirmed by Jessie Low's diaries. The entire family attended various churches, but Jessie, before her marriage, appeared to be drawn to the more romantic and missionary aspects of the church than the other sisters, often idly musing about not being suited by temperament to join the "sisterhood."

7. There is a later notation that Katie and Mary attended school in London, and Jessie's diary indicates out-of-town friendships with girls from school that she attended, probably in Eastbourne.

8. Elizabeth Hamilton, *The Warwickshire Scandal* (Norwich Michael Russell Publishing Ltd.) Here is a detailed account of the Mordaunt cause célèbre.

9. Lord Leigh was the Chief Lieutenant of Warwickshire. His son, Rowland Leigh, later married Mabel Gordon, Juliette Gordon Low's sister.

10. The handwriting on the 1871 British Census is difficult to read so these are approximations of their names, but it is obvious that they are all white. The American 1850 Census mentions eleven black servants-slaves and categorizes them by age and gender, but not by name. The American 1860 Census mentions two free females, members of the Low household, named Celia Anderson, mulatto, aged 37, and Grace Taylor, mulatto, aged 50. The Schedule 11 lists three more—two black males, ages 42 and 39;

and one black female, aged 15. Susan Mays's report in an appendix for the Andrew Low House and Museum gives a detailed breakdown of the Low family slaves in America.

11. The 1870 Savannah Census rolls examined at the public library by the authors shows "Andrew Lowe, 60 M W cotton merchant $100,000/100,000 England." Obviously Andrew Low had retained a great deal of his considerable wealth despite the deprivations of the war. Under the name of Lowe, it goes on to list Mary, a 55-year-old white female housekeeper, three teenage children, Agnes 18, Andrew 16, Janie 14, and John 24, a clerk in the store; plus an assortment of servants listed as mulattoes by the names of Gillin, Brown, and Munto. There is absolutely no mention of a Milledge in residence anywhere in the neighborhood. The only two Millege's (note another spelling) who show up in the non-indexed 1870 Census rolls are Margaret, aged 20, and William, 23, both servants at Aaron Champion's house. The overall picture of the Low household became even more confused. The first confirmation in a written record showing Tom and Mosianna as husband and wife is an application dated 9th Sept/69 for William Millidge; Father—Tom at Andrew Low's and Mother, Mosianna. Brother, Tommy (note spelling).

12. After the death of George Coke Robertson in 1924, the estate had to be sold. Widmerpool Hall is now occupied by of the Automobile Association in England. Most of the tenant farmers bought their farms, and the cottages have been turned into country homes for commuters.

13. Jeremy Paxman, *Friends in High Places* (Penguin Books, 1991). In England during the nineteenth century the term "public" when applied to schools meant in fact "private," and there were a mere handful of top-notch ones, such as Eton and Harrow, where the cream of Britain's aristocratic crop were schooled to become future prime ministers and generals.

14. It was on the CSS *Alabama* that Andrew Low's cousin, Captain John Low, would build his well-deserved reputation as a Confederate war hero.

15. Another website celebrating Britain's participation in America's Civil War is www.acws.co.uk.

16. Josiah Green Low was the eldest son of John Low and Eliza Green Low.

17. Source of quotes in memo from Anna Wright Smith to Andrew Low House and Museum on occasion of tour of house celebrating anniversary of General Lee's visit in first week of Apr. 1870. The same occasion was recalled in the *Savannah Morning News*, Apr. 1, 1926, in a lecture by A. R. Lawton, son of General Alexander Lawton.

18. Historian Walter C. Hartridge in a lecture to the Georgia Historical Society says that Lee wrote a letter to his family stating that "the Low

house was partially dismantled," although not given was the reason, which was that his family were already in residence in Leamington Spa and presumably they would have taken much of the furniture and household effects with them, although in her 1886 diary Jessie mentions that much of the "old furniture" had been stored in the Andrew Low Company office on the river.

19. Anna Habersham Wright Smith, ed., *A Savannah Family*, p. 267. Letter from Mary Custis Lee to Aunt Kate Mackay on the occasion of General Robert Lee's death in 1870.

20. This nineteenth-century riot presaged the twentieth-century riots prompted by Rosa Parks, who one hundred years later had finally had enough. Although the scene was not Savannah, but Montgomery, Alabama, Rosa Parks refused to either move to the back of the bus or give up her seat in the front for anyone. Following a citywide boycott, a federal court declared bus segregation ordinance unconstitutional.

21. Sarah Mackay, born Apr. 11, 1815, Savannah, Georgia. There are several published versions of her death as *A Savannah Family* tree states she died Mar. 7, 1876, in Virginia Springs, Virginia. Caroline Lovell's version, *Light of Other Days,* p. 116, buried in Laurel Grove and died in Savannah. Family Bible Records of Deaths lists Mar. 7, 1876, Sarah Mackay, aged 60 years.

22. Caroline Couper Lovell, *The Light of Other Days,* Chapter 12, "Transition."

23. William Henry Stiles, Jr., born 1834, Savannah, Ga.; died 19 Dec. 1878, Bartow Co., Georgia.

24. Catherine Mackay (Kate), born Aug. 7, 1811, Savannah; died Jan. 7, 1879, Bartow Co. (formerly Cass Co.) at Malbone.

25. Although William Mackay Low is the recorded birth name of Andrew and Mary Low's only son, he is always referred to in family letters, journals, and memoirs as "Willie," a practice that is followed in this biography, except where the name appears on legal documents.

26. The Royal Commission on Historical Manuscripts in London recorded in Foster's *Alumni Oxonienses* (reprint 1968) refers to William Mackay Low as matriculating at Brasenose College, Jan. 22, 1880, aged 19. Source: Letter to Colonial Dame Mrs. Katherine Simmons, Apr. 4,1995. Brasenose College Archivist, Mrs. Elizabeth Boardman, in a letter to Mrs. Simmons, May 23, 1995.

27. It is now in the 1880 Census that the relationship between Thomas Milledge and Mosianna Milledge is confirmed for the first time. The Census reads: "Milledge, Thomas, B, M, 53, Servant; Milledge Mosianna, B, F, 36, Servant; they are listed as having three children residing with them: William, aged 23; Thomas, aged 13 and Mary, aged 10." This is the final

proof that had been sought, and a copy is documented in April Duffie's research report. If the ages were correct, that would have Mosianna born 1844; Thomas, Sr., in 1827; the eldest son, William, 1857; Tommy, Jr., in 1867; and Mary in 1870. So despite the fact that the ages are off by several years it is logical to suppose that the baby mentioned in the 1865 letter from Eliza Stiles could have been Tommy. By the standards and principles adhered to in attempting to ascertain facts from extant records, this is not a totally satisfactory conclusion, but taking into account the sparseness of pre-emancipation records it must suffice. Unless descendants can be traced of the Milledge family, the mystery must remain half solved. The other document that corroborates this conclusion is an application by William Millidge (note different spelling of name) dated Sept 9/69, with an address at Drayton, and Charlton, aged 12 years. Father listed is Tom at Mr. Low's, Mother, Mosianna, and Brother Tom. The oddity on these records, which are believed to be the Freeman Bank records, is that the recorders still differentiate the color of a man's skin—and in the category of "Complexion," there are varying shades ranging from Light through Dark Brown to Black—William is listed as having a "Light" complexion. In any event, it is indisputable that the records show that in 1880 Thomas and Mosianna Milledge were recorded as man and wife on the Chatham County Census Records. The authors were unable to confirm the claim that this information is also contained in the 1860 and 1870 Censuses. Any other interpretation must be left to the experts in the examination and analysis of pre- and post-emancipation records, or the locating of Milledge descendants.

28. Bevill Bruce Grenfell, only son of Amy and Harry Grenfell, and at that time the only grandchild. He is mentioned in Andrew Low's Will, written before the boy died in 1884.

29. The other directors elected in 1844 were R. R. Cuyler, John W. Anderson, Asa Holt, Isaac Cohen, William Crabtree, Jr., Henry McAlpin, Matthew Hopkins, and William Durden.

30. The retiring directors were J. J. Gresham of Macon, Andrew Low, George Cornwell, and Jacob Rauers of Savannah. The new members were General E. P. Alexander of Louisville, C. H. Phinney of Augusta, Captain Robert Falligant, and Malcolm McLean of Savannah.

31. The Alexander party ticket was comprised of E. P. Alexander, E. C. Anderson, Robert Falligant, J. F. Gilmer, E. H. Green, A. L. Hartridge, Henry R. Jackson, M. McLean, George S. Owens. The Raoul party ticket was W. G. Raoul, E. C. Anderson (on both?), George Cornwell, Abram Minis, John W. Guerard, Andrew Low, J. Rauers, H. C. Comer (substituted for P. R. Pyne of New York),William Hunter, George J. Mills, W. W. Gordon.

Chapter 19: Exit the Buck, 1882–1886, *pages 292–312*

1. *World Almanac 2001,* p. 451. Omnibus Civil Rights bill cleared Congress July 2, 1964, signed the same day by President Lyndon Johnson, banning discrimination in voting, jobs, and public accommodation.

2. Descendants of the children by the second marriage of Captain John Low to Catherine Morris in 1867 in Liverpool live in Australia, and family genealogy has been confirmed with descendant-in-law Philip Sweetingham. The Sweetinghams recently donated the pennant of the CSS *Alabama,* passed down through the ensuing generations, to the museum in Mobile, Alabama. Descendant Lani Rimington of Auckland, New Zealand, has provided much proof of a previously unconfirmed first marriage of Captain John Low, wife now identified as Mary Elizabeth Wall, presumed to have been in Savannah circa 1862, but now known to be in Culpepper Courthouse, Va., and son from that union, John (Jack) Low.

3. The large building built in the mid-1860's became the Kingsley School in the early 1920's and remains so today.

4. Daisy's diaries and personal letters between her and Willie have all vanished, in all probability destroyed to protect her reputation. Letters from Juliette Gordon to her mother and sisters are part of the several collections of Gordon Family Papers in the Southern Historical Collection at the University of North Carolina and in the Georgia Historical Society in Savannah. Much material was used in *Lady From Savannah,* the semiofficial account of her life written by her niece Daisy Gordon Lawrence and Gladys Denny Schultz.

5. The details included in the letters in the exchanges regarding Willy Low's desire to marry Daisy Gordon come from *Lady From Savannah* and the recently acquired diaries of Jessie Low Graham.

6. *Savannah Morning News,* Feb. 8, 1886; Thomas Milledge's obituary appears on p. 8, "Death of an Old-Time Servant"; funeral notice, p. 2.

7. All the details of Andrew Low's death and subsequent events are taken verbatim from the untranscribed, unpublished diaries of Jessie Low Graham, youngest daughter of Andrew Low and Mary Cowper Stiles. These diaries are in the possession of Jessie's descendants. There are five handwritten journals that range from 1881 to 1886, with a four-year gap in the middle. They are an extraordinary account of life in America and Europe of the privileged class, and provide us with previously uncorroborated details of the family.

8. Generally, historians use the figure of a 1–10 value of nineteenth-century currency compared to twentieth-century currency.

9. Andrew Low's will and two codicils, the first raising the legacies to his daughters, the second leaving 25,000 pounds to his only grandchild,

Bevil Bruce Grenfell, is long and incredibly detailed and well organized. Probate was completed by three of the executors—Grenfell, Robertson, and Pascoe Du Pre Grenfell—on July 10, 1886. No mention is made of General Low's participation, so it can be assumed that he was unavailable to perform his duties at that time. Andrew Low's cousin General Alexander Low was the eldest son of Alexander Low (Uncle Andrew's brother) and Mary Nicol. Andrew Low's probate will was filed in 1886 at Preston, Lancashire, and published in directory in Liverpool Record Office. A copy of the will is to be found in the Andrew Low House and Museum's Archives.

10. "To the Union Society of Savannah, Five Thousand; to the Episcopalian Orphan Home of Savannah, Two Thousand Dollars; to the Widow Society of Savannah, One Thousand Dollars; to the Female Orphan Asylum of Savannah, One Thousand; to the Sisters of Mercy, located on the south side of Liberty for the Catholic Female Orphan Asylum under their charge, One Thousand Dollars."

11. The entry in Jessie's diary is the first indication that the amount of the girls' individual bequests may have been higher, as she says it was 60,000, and then indicates that Willie raises it to 70,000. The Will itself reads 40,000 pounds, and there is a codicil leaving a further 10,000 to each of the girls, so unless the value of the stocks was higher than Andrew Low had anticipated in 1879 when the Will was written, there is a discrepancy between the details of the Will and Jessie's account in her diary. In any event, it was a considerable legacy in the value of money in the late nineteenth century.

12. Sister Mary Low's death certificate found in Brechin Papers in Angus Archives, Montrose, Scotland.

13. *Lady From Savannah*, pp. 174–75.

14. Another error in the history archives. It was 1812 and he was seventeen years old.

15. No proof of Mosianna Milledge's burial location has been found, but there is some physical evidence that it may be in a concrete vault buried next to her husband, Thomas Milledge.

16. *Savannah Morning News*: "The chancel was beautifully decorated with evergreens and plants. Lohengrins wedding march was played. His best man Mr. Fred Habersham attended the groom. The bride's dress was white-corded silken train, trimmed with pointe lace; her sash was looped with an elegant crescent of diamonds. Her veil, which reached to the end of the train, was caught at the side with a diamond star, and she wore a handsome diamond shoulder ornament. She carried a bouquet of lilies of the valley. The eight bridesmaids were dressed in white silk short dresses in the English style, trimmed with tulle, and wore bonnets of the same

material. The ushers wore boutonnieres of lilies of the valley. Her father, W. W. Gordon, gave the bride in marriage. After the ceremony, a wedding breakfast was served. Mr. & Mrs. Low will reside in the Low residence on Lafayette Square, which the groom has elegantly fitted out."

Chapter 20: The Children's Legacy, 1886–1932, *pages 313–347*

1. The newly acquired diaries of Jessie Low Graham have added a considerable store of detailed first-hand knowledge to the material contained in the most widely read biography of Juliette Gordon Low, titled *Lady From Savannah,* written in 1958 by Gladys Denny Schultz and Daisy Gordon Lawrence, and published by J. B. Lippincott Company, Philadelphia and New York. The authors had access to a great number of diaries, letters, and other primary source material. The foreword to the book describes these sources as well as documenting the gaps that occur through the deliberate destruction of sensitive letters. Many of the letters of the Gordon family, especially Nellie Gordon, Daisy's mother, are located in two collections at the Savannah Georgia Historical Society and the Southern Historical Collection at the University of North Carolina. So, despite lack of either an Index or annotated footnotes or endnotes, it is possible to ascertain where the original source of much of the material is located. The author's claim that Daisy referred to her husband as "Billow," however in the diaries and letters from his own family he was always referred to as Willie, and occasionally Bill. The authors therefore use the Low family spelling throughout.

2. Another piece of confusing information has entered the conventional wisdom as recounted in Susan Mays's 1995 *Interpretive Plan Proposal for the Andrew Low House.* In Appendix 2 covering "Slaves/Servants Owned/Employed by Andrew Low and Family" she writes, "Tom's daughter, Mosianna, was part of the household staff in the Low's Savannah house by the 1880s". We have already proved through the 1880 Census that Mosianna was Tom's wife, now his widow. The *Proposal* continues: "Eleanor Kinzie Gordon writing to her daughter, Juliette, prior to her marriage to Willie Low writes: 'There is an excellent cook at the Lows, who was there all last winter. Why don't you keep her? Her mama is Jane.'" Mays makes the presumption that Mosianna is the person about whom Mrs. Gordon wrote. Jessie Low Graham's newly discovered 1886 Diary has refuted that assumption and refers to Mosianna in terms that suggest she is probably acting as housekeeper and that "we have got the same old cook." There is no other mention of Jane in letters from any other member of the Low or Stiles family. Further examination of the published and primary sources of references to Mosianna show only one reference in Daphne Fielding's

book *Duchess of Jermyn Street* as Willie Low's cook at Wellesbourne Park (p. 48). There are only two references to Mosianna Milledge in Juliette Low's biography *Lady From Savannah.* The first, Chapter XII, p. 179: "She [Daisy] had a large staff of servants, with Mosianna Milledge, daughter of the Tom Milledge whom Thackeray immortalized, presiding in the kitchen. Mosianna's cooking rivaled Liza Hendry's to the latter's acute discomfort and jealousy. The Low parties were delightful, but their dinner parties soon became famous." The second, p. 196: "On one of her visits home Daisy persuaded Mosianna Milledge, who had been her cook during the time she and Willy lived in the Low house after their marriage, to return to England with her." (The rest of the story tells about the Lord Warwick "My Gawd" legend). "Mosianna got too homesick for Georgia after a while and Daisy had to let her return." Susan Mays states in her appendix, "there are many references to Mosianna Milledge in *Lady From Savannah*." I only found the two listed here. It is logical to make the assumption that the legend of Mosianna being Tom's daughter originated with the biography rather than the *Interpretive Report.* Emphasis has been placed on recording the perceived origins of the errors that have crept into the record, because that is one of the primary purposes of this book, and not to criticize other authors. This is an attempt to correct the record or at least provide sufficient facts and rumors for others to continue to seek the truth.

3 This was Bessie Stiles's first marriage; her second was to Franklin Buchanan Screven.

4. Caroline Lovell, *Bend in the River.*

5. Jessie Low spells Harry Grenfell's name consistently as "Harrie" throughout her five diaries. The authors have used the same spelling when copied from Jessie's diaries; in other instances the name is spelled Harry. George Robertson and Hattie Low Robertson had a home in London on Grosvenor Street at the time so it would be unusual for them to have stayed in a hotel with Willie and Daisy.

6. Leamington *Courier,* 24 Dec. 1887. Details of inquest of Major Frank Green is reported verbatim.

7. Jessie Graham makes several mentions in her diaries about corresponding with Hugh Graham, who is in partnership with a Bill Cochran on a ranch near Edmonton, Alberta, Canada. He had attended farming college and gone out there to ranch. Jane Davidson in her research notes says that Jessie met Hugh Graham on the boat on one of her trips to America. On the journey over to Savannah for Willie's wedding she mentions meeting someone who knew Graham in Canada, so obviously she already knew him. Hugh Graham mentions in his own diaries that he stayed at Lude, the shooting lodge in Scotland in Sept. 1887 at Willie's invitation, so probably the marriage was arranged then.

8. A notice appears in Dec. 1, 1888, in the *Times* of London Court Circular, and the marriage took place on Nov. 24, 1888: "The marriage of Mr. Hugh Graham, second son of Lady Hermione Graham and the late Sir Frederick Graham, Bart of Netherby (near Scottish border), and grandson of Sir James Graham, the eminent statesman, with Miss Jessie Low, youngest daughter of Mr. Andrew Low, of Savannah, Georgia, USA, took place in St George's Church, Hanover Square, on Saturday afternoon."

9. An original photograph of Wellesbourne House exists, located in the Warwickshire County Museum.

10. Peter and Rosalind Bolton, *A Wellesbourne Guide*; personal letters between Peter Bolton and Mrs. Katherine Simmons, member of the Georgia Chapter of Colonial Dames while staying in England in 1995.

11. London *Times*, July 14, 1906. An advertisement listing the sale of "The Residence of the late W. M. Low, Esq."

12. Ralph G. Martin, *Jennie: The Life of Lady Randolph Churchill.*

13. Coincidently Ruthin Castle in North Wales, where Willie Low died, was one of the family seats of George Cornwallis West, who married Jennie Churchill following her husband's death.

14. Peter and Rosalind Bolton.

15. Anita Leslie, *Edwardians in Love* (London: Arrow Books Ltd., 1972).

16. Gordonston Park was created by Daisy Low and her brother out of the family farm on Skidaway Road in Savannah. Several years ago vandalism forced the neighborhood to donate the iron gates to the birthplace on Oglethorpe and Bull streets in Savannah, where they have been mounted on the wall in the garden.

17. The newspaper account states: "In a most quiet manner in the quiet village church of St. Peter's in Wellesbourne, the marriage of Miss Mary Low, daughter of the late Andrew Low, of Savannah, Georgia, U.S.A. to Mr. David Charles Guthrie, son of James Alexander Guthrie J.P. of Craigie Castle, took place on Saturday, at half an hour after noon. Owing to a recent bereavement suffered by the family of the bride, only the relatives of the two families were invited, and besides these, there were some 40 or 50 of the villagers present to witness the ceremony. The service which was partly choral, was conducted by the Hon. Rev. Canon Leigh, assisted by the Rev. Beresford Potter (vicar), and during the course the choir sang Psalm 128, and the hymn 'Thine For Ever God of Love' . . . the bride was given away by her brother, Mr. William Low, of Wellesbourne House, whence the marriage took place, and with whom for several years she and her sisters resided at Beauchamp Hall, Leamington, and they were well known to the inhabitants of the Royal Spa and to its neighbourhood. On the banns she was described as being of Woodhouse, Mansfield, Not-

tinghamshire and the bridegroom of the parish of St. George, Hanover Square, London."

18. David Charles Guthrie is descended from the Guthrie of Craigie branch of the Guthrie lineage. The family heritage can be found in *Burke's Landed Gentry.*

19. Violet Stuart Wortley wrote many biographical books on the Guthrie family that have been collected by Mike Allen, the curator of Highcliffe Castle.

20. Mary Guthrie's daughters, Margaret Martin, and Christian Scott Robson, according to their children, continued to make contributions to the Katherine Low Settlement House throughout their lives.

21. In addition to William Mackay Low's impressive collection of racehorses listed in his obituary in the Warwickshire papers, there was also a portrait of "Rightaway" ridden by jockey Mornington Canyon, which has disappeared. In addition, several other Lynwood Palmer horse paintings were commissioned; two of them, "Mares & Foals" and "Dark Bay," were both Willie's horses, but they too have vanished and were probably sold in South Africa. Another called "Boy Prince in His Stall," by J. Wright Barker, also went to South Africa and has probably been sold. Fortunately one painting has survived and is currently in pride of place in the Andrew Low House in Savannah. By James Lynwood Palmer, 1897, it is a study of William Low and hunter set in a Warwickshire landscape, oil on canvas. The painting is an ideal depiction of the best of who Willie Low was—master of Wellesbourne House and connoisseur of horses. Mrs. Joyce Guthrie, fourth wife and widow of Hamish Guthrie, sold the painting to the museum.

22. Lady Elizabeth Hamilton, *The Warwickshire Scandal.*

23. Daphne Fielding, *Duchess of Jermyn Street.* Chatty, a gossipy biography of Rosa Lewis, famed proprietor of the Cavendish Hotel on Jermyn Street, London, contains a great many errors, including saying that Willie Low is from South Carolina, so one cannot take it as being gospel truth. Katie Low deliberately redacted all mentions of Jermyn Street in letters, indicating that she did not wish the rumors about a possible relationship between her brother and the famed courtesan-cook to become public.

24. Mosianna Milledge herself turned out to be something of an entrepreneur. The Historic Savannah survey book of 1979 lists 513 East Gaston and 514 and 516 East Hartridge streets as built for Mosianna Milledge. There could have been others torn down before 1979. Since that time, 514–516 (a double house) has been razed by St. John Baptist Church for parking.

25. The confusion surrounding the relationship between Tom and Mosianna Milledge has been covered at length in previous notes, but

it is fully accepted that the conventional wisdom and oral history that has her, as Tom's daughter, is wrong, and that the 1880 Census confirms their marital status. There are still numerous details that do not exactly match, and the only extant photograph is one that appeared in Daphne Fielding's *The Duchess of Jermyn Street*, p. 100, identified as "Willie Low's Negro Servants." Unfortunately the book gives no credits for the source of the illustrations. In addition, Fielding imparts the following information on p. 48: "In his [Willie Low's] kitchen at Wellesbourne Park, Rosa [Lewis] made friends with his old colored cook, Mosianna, and Joe, the Negro butler, both of whom had been slaves to his father-in-law, General Gordon, before the Civil War." That statement is riddled with errors, so even the provenance of the photograph remains doubtful. Later that same photo was used in a Savannah newspaper article on Rosa Lewis' Southern cooking. It is true that Mosianna accompanied Daisy to England at one point after they occupied Wellesbourne Hall, but as Tom Milledge, her husband and Andrew Low's butler had died in 1886 it is unlikely he also accompanied them.

26. Daphne Fielding, *The Duchess of Jermyn Street: The Life and Times of Rosa Lewis of the Cavendish Hotel*, foreword by Evelyn Waugh. (London: Eyre & Spottiswoode, 1964). This book was turned into a television drama in England called *The Duchess of Duke Street* probably to protect people's reputations.

27. Although Daphne Fielding does not reveal the name of her confidential informant for this rather scurrilous account of Willie's peccadilloes, my guess would be that it was the notorious exposer of aristocratic English mores, Evelyn Waugh. In his foreword to the book he claims he was introduced to the Cavendish Hotel by Mr. Alistair Graham, the son of Willie Low's sister, Jessie Low Graham (of more later!), whose relationship with Evelyn Waugh may account for the frequent mention of his uncle in the book about Rosa Lewis' life and loves.

28. Earl of Warwick, *Memories of Sixty Years* (London, 1917).

29. Letter from Elizabeth Hamilton to Stephen Bohlin, curator of Juliette Gordon Birthplace, Savannah, Sept. 10, 1987.

30. Jane Davidson, oldest daughter of Sibyl Hickson, daughter of Jessie Low Graham, was an avid researcher of the Low and Stiles family history until her death in South Africa in 1999. Her research formed the basis of much of my own quest for verification, and the authors are grateful to her for the contribution her work has made to this project.

31. Peter Bolton to Katherine Simmons.

32. Stratford *Herald*, Jan. 11, 1901.

33. Letter from Mabel Gordon Leigh to her mother.

34. "Gordon Family Papers," Georgia Historical Society.

35. Widmerpool Hall is today the headquarters of the Automobile Association of the U.K.

36. Chalmers, Guthrie & Co., registered 1899, was a Scottish mercantile company founded around 1801, with branches in many Scottish merchant towns. The company was involved in many overseas adventures in Asia, South America, Africa, etc. The company owned ships, insurance, banking, and mercantile endeavors, with an address at 9 Idol Street, London, and Dundee, Scotland. Some of the documents of the original company can be found in D. C. Guthrie's self-published book, *The Guthrie Family* (1906). The windup of the company is recorded in *Register of Defunct Companies*, published by Macmillan.

37. The letters from the estates of Katy Low and Jessie Graham comprise a great deal of the correspondence during the divorce attempt, the fight over the will, the death, etc., and tend to illuminate the Low's side of the story; and they appear to be trying to protect Willie's reputation, or maybe their own! The Gordons portray the event as being "Daisy's tragedy," but, in essence, she emerged relatively intact, and it is her later achievements that have gone down to posterity, and Willie is only remembered as Daisy's dissolute husband! The authors of *Lady From Savannah* say that a package of letters, presumed to be Daisy's to her husband and Willie's to her, had never been found—probably destroyed, maybe by her brother Arthur Gordon to protect her reputation. Unfortunately no one is left to verify that particular piece of gossip.

38. A document filed in the Probate Divorce and Admiralty Court Division of His Majesty's High Court of Justice entitled *Robertson v. Low and Bateman,* dated Aug. 29, 1905, reads "touching and concerning the validity of the Will [of William Mackay Low] with a codicil thereto of the said deceased dated respectively the 8th day of December 1902 [original Will] and the 12th day of November 1904 [codicil]." The courts placed the entire estate under an administrator.

39. "Letter from Charles Gasquet," W. M. Low Estate Papers. Admiral Sir Harry Tremenheere Grenfell received his title in the 1905 Birthday Honours.

40. William Hillcourt with Olave Soames, Lady Baden Powell, *Biography of Baden Powell* (Heineman, 1964).

41. Jane Davidson, monograph on Willie Low. There are a great many errors of fact in this essay on Willie, but some fascinating details of speculation!

42. Jessie's granddaughter Kitty McDuff Duncan insists that Sibyl Hickson, her mother, knew that money had been sent to support Andrew Low's family in Scotland.

43. *Duchess of Jermyn Street,* p. 105.

44. Revisionist history is as commonplace in family lore as it is in academia; and after Evelyn Waugh wrote *Brideshead Revisited*, his best-known opus to modern-day audiences due to the ubiquity of television, author William Amos in *The Originals* unequivocally states that the main character of Sebastian Flyte is based on his "life-long friend Alistair Graham." In the manuscript he claims the name Alistair occasionally occurs instead of Sebastian. Even more coincidentally, perhaps, the character of Lady Circumference in *Vile Bodies* is reputed to be based on Jessie. Family wisdom has it that they all loathed Evelyn Waugh although that contention is not conceded by Waugh himself. In his published diaries, despite his claims that though Jessie Graham was rude to him, he also reports that she was frequently extremely kind to him, mothering him at Barford, and taking him to dinner and the theatre when in London.

Bibliography

I. Books

Adams, Ephraim Douglass. *Great Britain and the American Civil War.* New York: Russel & Russel, 1924.

Anderson, James. *Black Book of Kincardineshire—Lists of the Covenanters Confined in Dunnottar Castle with an Account of the Persecution of Episcopacy.* Stonehaven: William Johnston, 1843.

Andrews, William L., and Henry Louis Gates, Jr. *The Civitas Anthology of African American Slave Narratives.* Washington, D.C.: Civitas Counterpoint, 1999.

Arnold, R. Arthur. *The History of the Cotton Famine from the Fall of Fort Sumter to the Passing of the Public Works Act.* London: Saunders, Otley & Co., 1865.

Baines, Edward. *History of the Cotton Manufacturer in Great Britain.* London: H. Fisher, R. Fisher, & P. Johnson, ca. 1845.

Ball, Edward. *Slaves in the Family.* New York: Ballantine Books, 1998.

Banks, Sara H., and Catharine E. Varnedoe, *Tomo-chi-chi, Gentle Warrior.* Savannah: Talking Leaves Press, 1992.

Bell, Malcolm, Jr. *Major Butler's Legacy. Five Generations of a Slaveholding Family.* Athens: University of Georgia Press, 1987.

———. *Savannah, Ahoy.* Savannah: Pigeonhole Press, 1959.

Bird, Vivian. *Warwickshire.* Leamington: 1973.

Black, David D. *History of Brechin to 1864.* Brechin, Scotland: 1860's.

Blassingame, John W. *The Slave Community. Plantation Life in the Antebellum South.* London: Oxford University Press, 1972.

Bolton, Peter, and Rosalind Bolton. *A Wellesbourne Guide.* Leamington: 1989.

Bontemps, Alex. *The Punished Self-Surviving Slavery in the Colonial South.* Ithaca and London: Cornell University Press, 2001.

Bowden, Witt. *Industrial Society in England towards the End of the 18th Century.* New York: Macmillan Co., 1925.

Bryant, Pat. *Entry of Claims for Georgia Landholders, 1733–1755.* Atlanta, Ga.: Surveyor's General Dept, 1975.

Bulloch, James D. *The Secret Service of the Confederate States in Europe or How the Confederate Cruisers were Equipped.* New York: G. P. Putnam's Sons, 1884.

Bulloch, J. G. B. *A History and Genealogy of Habersham, Adams, Clay, Stiles, and Other Related Families.* Columbia, S.C.: R. L. Bryan, 1901.

Bumstead, J. M. *The People's Clearance, 1770–1815.*

Burton, Anthony. *The Rise and Fall of King Cotton.* London: André Deutsch, British Broadcasting Corporation, 1984.

Byrd, Vivian. *Warwickshire.* Leamington: Self-published, 1973.

Cameron, Archibald Cowie. *The History of Fettercairn—A Parish in the County of Kincardine.* Edinburgh: John Menzies & Co.; London: Houlston & Sons, 1899.

Cameron, David Kerr. *The Cornkister Days—A Portrait of a Land and its Rituals.* England: Penguin, 1986.

Cashin. Edward J. *Beloved Bethesda.* Macon: Mercer University Press, 2002.

Cave, Lyndon E. *Royal Leamington Spa.* Chichester, Sussex: Phillimore, 1988.

Chambers, Bradford. *Chronicles of Black Protest.* New York: New American Library, 1968.

Chandler, George. *The Merchant Venturers.* Liverpool: Rondo Publications, Ltd., 1973.

Churchill, Winston S. *The Age of Revolution—A History of the English Speaking Peoples.* New York: Dodd, Mead & Co., 1957.

Cohn, David. *The Life and Times of King Cotton—America's Cotton Story.* New York: Oxford University Press, 1956.

Cole, Hubert. *Christophe, King of Haiti.* London: Eyre & Spottiswoode, Ltd., 1967.

Coleman, Kenneth. *A History of Georgia, Second Edition.* Athens: University of Georgia Press, 1991.

Colley, Linda. *Britons—Forging the Nation, 1707–1837.* New Haven and London: Yale University Press, 1992.

Crane, Verner. *Southern Frontier, 1670–1732.* Durham, N.C.: Duke University Press, 1928.

Cunyus, Lucy Josephine. *History of Bartow County—Formerly Cass.* Greenville, S.C.: Southern Historical Press, 1933.

Devine, T. M. *The Scottish Nation—A History, 1700–2000.* New York: Viking, 1999.

Dickson, Tony. *Scottish Capitalism. Class, State and Nation from before the Union to the Present.* London: Lawrence & Wishart, 1980.

Dobson, David. *Scottish Maritime Records—A Guide for Family Historians.* Fife, Scotland: David Dobson, n.d.

Dodge, Bertha S. *Cotton: The Plant That Would Be King.* Austin: University of Texas Press, 1984.

Douglass, Frederick. *Narrative of the Life of Frederick Douglass, an American Slave.* Originally published in 1845 by the Anti-Slavery Office. New York: Penguin Books, 1982.

Edgar, Walter. *South Carolina: A History.* Columbia: University of South Carolina Press, 1998.

Edwards, D. H. *Pocket History and Guide to Brechin and District.* Brechin: Black Printers, 1880.

Edwards, Michael M. *The Growth of the British Cotton Trade, 1780–1815.* Manchester: Manchester University Press, 1967.

Ehle, John. *Trail of Tears: The Rise and Fall of the Cherokee Nation.* New York: Anchor Books, 1988.

Elliott, L. L. D. *Cotton Is King and Pro-Slavery Arguments—Writings of Hammond, Harper, Christy, Stringfellow, Hodge, Bledsoe, and Cartwright.* Augusta, Ga.: Pritchard, Abbott and Loomis, 1860.

Ellison, Mary. *Support for Secession, Lancashire and the American Civil War.* Chicago: University of Chicago Press, 1972.

Evans, R. J. *The Victorian Age, 1815–1914.* London: Edward Arnold, Ltd., 1950.

Fielding, Daphne. *The Duchess of Jermyn Street—The Life and Good Times of Rosa Lewis of the Cavendish Hotel.* London: Eyre & Spottiswoode, 1964.

Foner, Eric. *A Short History of Reconstruction, 1863–1877.* New York: Harper & Row, 1990.

Foot, Michael, and Isaac Kramnick, eds. *The Thomas Paine Reader.* London: Penguin Books, 1987.

Foote, Shelby. *The Civil War—A Narrative: Fredericksburg to Meridian.* New York: Vintage Books, 1963.

Franklin, John Hope, and Alfred A. Moss, Jr. *From Slavery to Freedom.* New York: Alfred A. Knopf, 1947.

Fraser, Walter J., Jr. *Savannah in the Old South.* Athens: University of Georgia Press, 2003.

Freeman, Ronald H. *Savannah Under Siege.* Savannah: Freeport Publishing, 2002.

Fyfe. Christopher. *History of Sierra Leone.* London: Longmans, Green & Co., Ltd., 1962.

Geneaological Committee. *Marriages of Chatham County, Georgia,* Vol. 1. Savannah: Georgia Historical Society (1993).

———. *Register of Deaths in Savannah, Georgia,* Vol. II. Savannah: Georgia Historical Society (1984).

Graham, H. Grey. *The Social Life of Scotland in the Eighteenth Century.* London: A. & C. Black, Ltd., 1937.

Granger, Mary, ed. *Savannah River Plantations.* Savannah Writers' Project. Savannah: Oglethorpe Press, 1997.

Guthrie, D. C., and The Hon. Mrs. Stuart Wortley. *The Guthrie Family.* (Private Circulation) England, 1906.

Guthrie, Jennifer Ryan, and Margaret A. Strom, eds. *Guthrie Stories, Book 1.* Bangor, Maine. (For Clan Guthrie,U.S.A., Inc.)

Hamilton, Elizabeth. *The Warwickshire Scandal.* Norwich: Michael Russell, 1999.

——. *Wellesbourne and Walton at Work.* Wellesbourne History Group, 1993.

Hamilton, Henry. *History of the Homeland—The Story of the British Background.* London: George Allen & Unwin, Ltd., 1947.

Hamilton, William, of Gilbertfield. *Blind Harry's Wallace, 1722.* Edinburgh: Luath Press, 1998.

Harris, J. R. *Liverpool & Merseyside. Essays in Economic and Social History of the Port and Its Hinterlands.* Liverpool: Frank Cass & Co., Ltd., 1969.

Hartridge, Walter Charlton, ed. *The Letters of Don Juan McQueen to His Family, 1791–1807.* Columbia, S.C.: Bostick & Thornley, 1943.

——. *The Letters of Robert Mackay to His Wife.* Athens: University of Georgia Press, 1949.

Hillcourt, William, with Olave Soames, Lady Baden-Powell. *Baden-Powell: The Two Lives of a Hero.* New York: Putnam, 1964.

Hollett, David. *The Alabama Affair: The British Shipyards Conspiracy in the American Civil War.* Liverpool: Avid Publications, 1993.

Hoole, Stanley W. *Four Years in the Confederate Navy: The Career of Captain John Low on the CSS Fingal, Florida, Alabama, Tuscaloosa and Ajax.* Athens: University of Georgia Press, 1964.

Hoole, Stanley W., ed. *Confederate Foreign Agent: The European Diary of Major Edward C. Anderson, 1861–1862.* Tuscaloosa: University of Alabama–Confederate Publishing Co., 1976.

——. *Afloat and Ashore: The Confederate Diary of Colonel Edward Clifford Anderson.* Self-published in 1970's.

——. *The Logs of the CSS Alabama and CSS Tuscaloosa, 1862–1863.* Tuscaloosa: University of Alabama–Confederate Publishing Company, 1972.

Hudson, Charles. *The Southeastern Indians.* Knoxville: University of Tennessee Press, 1976.

Hume, David. *A Treatise on Human Nature.* London: J. M. Dent & Sons, Ltd., 1911.

Hunter, James. *A Dance Called America—The Scottish Highlands, the United States and Canada.* Edinburgh: Mainstream Publishing Co., Ltd., 1994.

Index to English Crown Grants in Georgia, 1755–1775. Spartanburg: Reprint Co., 1989.

Inscoe, John C. *James Edward Oglethorpe—New Perspectives on His Life and Legacy.* Savannah: Georgia Historical Society, 1997.

Insh, George Pratt. *Scottish Colonial Schemes, 1620–1686.* Glasgow: Maclehose, Jackson & Co., 1922.

James, C. L. R. *A History of Negro Revolt.* London: Race Today Collective, 1985.

———. *The Black Jacobin—Touissant L'Ouverture and the San Domingo Revolution.* London: Allison & Busby, 1938.

Johnson, Charles, and Patricia Smith. *Africans in America—America's Journey through Slavery.* New York: Harcourt, Brace & Co., 1986.

Johnson, Charles J., Jr. *Mary Telfair—The Life and Legacy of a Nineteenth-Century Woman.* Savannah: Frederic C. Beil, 2002.

Johnson, Paul. *The Birth of the Modern World Society, 1815–1830.* Great Britain: George Weidenfeld & Nicholson, Ltd., 1991.

Johnson, Whittington B. *Black Savannah, 1788–1864.* Fayetteville: University of Arkansas Press, 1996.

Jones, C. C., Jr. *Historical Sketch of Tomochichi—Mico of the Yamacraws.* Savannah: Oglethorpe Press, 1998.

Keay, John. *The Honourable Company—A History of the English East India Company.* London: HarperCollins, 1991.

Kemble, Frances Anne. *Journal of a Residence on a Georgian Plantation in 1838–1839.* Athens: University of Georgia Press, 1984.

King, Stephen Bidwell, Jr. *Ebbtide—As Seen Through the Diary of Josephine Clay Habersham.* Athens: University of Georgia Press, 1958.

Kolchin, Peter. *American Slavery, 1619–1877.* New York: Hill & Wang, 1993.

Lane, Mills. *Savannah Revisited—History & Architecture.* Savannah: Beehive Press, 1994.

Lawrence, Alexander A. *A Present for Mr. Lincoln.* Savannah: Oglethorpe Press, 1997.

Lee, Christopher. *This Sceptred Isle: 55BC–1901.* London: British Broadcasting Corporation, 1997. Based on BBC Radio 4 series.

Lee, Robert E. *Recollections and Letters of General Robert E. Lee.* New York: Doubleday, Page & Co., 1904.

Leslie, Anita. *Edwardians in Love.* London: Arrow Books, 1974.

Locke, John. *An Essay Concerning Human Understanding.* United Kingdom: Constable & Co., Ltd., 1959.

———. *Some Thoughts Concerning Education.* Oxford: Clarendon Press, 1989.

———. *On Civil Government.* London: J. M. Dent & Sons, Ltd., 1924.

Long, Jenny, and Andrew Barber. *Graciously Pleased—Royal Leamington Spa—150 Years.* Leamington: Mayneset, Ltd., 1988.

Longmate, Norman. *The Hungry Mills: The Story of the Lancashire Cotton Famine, 1851–1865.* London: Maurice Temple Smith, 1978.

Lovell, Caroline Couper. *The Light of Other Days.* Macon: Mercer University Press, 1995.

———. *The Bend of the River.* Unpublished manuscript, ca. 1935.

Low, Jessie. *Jessie Low's Diary, November 29, 1880–December 26, 1881.* Collection of Katherine Hickson Macduff-Duncan.

McCullough, David. *Mornings on Horseback.* New York: Simon & Schuster, 1981.

McDuncan, A. *Roll and Legend of the Georgia Hussars.* Savannah: Morning News, 1906.

McMillen, Sally G. *Motherhood in the Old South—Pregnancy, Childbirth and Infant Rearing.* Baton Rouge: Louisiana State University Press, 1990.

Malone, Dumas. *Jefferson the President—Second Term.* Boston: Little, Brown & Co., 1974.

Marriner, Sheila. *Rathbone's of Liverpool, 1845–1873.* Liverpool: Liverpool University Press, 1961.

Martin, Ralph. G. *Jennie—The Life of Lady Randolph Churchill. The Romantic Years, 1854–1895.* New York: Signet Classics, 1970.

Mettger, Zak. *Reconstruction—America After the Civil War.* New York: Lodestar Press, 1994.

Middlemass, Keith. *The Life and Times of Edward VII.* London: Book Club Associates, n.d.

Mitchell, Alison. *Monumental Inscriptions of Kincardineshire, Pre-1855.* Aberdeen: Scottish Genealogical Society, 1999.

Mooney, James. *History, Myths, and Sacred Formulas of the Cherokees: From Original Myths of the Cherokees (1900) and the Sacred Formulas of the Cherokees (1891).* Asheville: Historical Images, 1992.

Morrison, Mary Lane. *John S. Norris—Architect in Savannah, 1846–1860.* Savannah: Beehive Press, 1980.

Mumford, Lewis. *The Condition of Man.* London: Martin Secker & Warburg, Ltd., 1944.

Myers, Robert Manson. *The Children of Pride: A True Story of Georgia and the Civil War.* New Haven: Yale University Press, 1972.

Newby, Eric. *A Book of Traveller's Tales.* London: Picador, 1985.

Nicol, W. E. *The Genealogy of the Nicol Family—Kincardineshire Branch.* South Kensington: Lamley & Co., 1909.

Nobbs, Douglas. *England and Scotland, 1560–1707.* London: Hutchinson House, 1952.

Olmsted, Frederick Law. *The Cotton Kingdom: A Traveller's Observations on Cotton and Slavery in the American Slave States.* New York: Mason Brothers, 1861.

Pace, Mildred Mastin. *Juliette Low.* New York: Charles Scribner's Sons, 1947.

Pachter, Marc. *Abroad In America: Visitors to the New Nation, 1776–1914.* Washington, D.C.: Addison-Wesley Publishing Co., 1976.

Packer, Boyd. *The Holy Temple.* Salt Lake City: Bookcraft, 1980.

Parker, Anthony W. *Scottish Highlanders in Colonial Georgia. The Recruitment, Emigration, and Settlement at Darien, 1735–1748.* Athens: University of Georgia Press, 1997.

Parkes, Henry Bamford. *The American People.* London: Eyre & Spottiswoode, 1949.

Paxman, Jeremy. *The English—A Portrait of a People.* London: Penguin Books, 1999.

———. *Friends in High Places—Who Runs Britain.* London: Penguin Books, 1991.

Pearce, Roy Harvey. *Colonial American Writing.* New York: Holt, Rinehart & Winston, 1961.

Penrose, Boies. *Travel and Discovery in the Renaissance, 1420–1620.* New York: Atheneum, 1962.

Perkins, Bradford. *The Causes of the War of 1812—National Honor or National Interest?* New York: Holt, Rinehart & Winston, 1962.

Pope-Hennessy, James. *Sins of the Fathers—The Atlantic Slave Trade, 1441–1807.* Great Britain: Weidenfeld & Nicholson, 1967.

Prebble, John. *Culloden.* England: Penguin, 1967.

———. *The Darien Disaster.* Edinburgh: Mainstream Publishing, 1968.

———. *The Highland Clearances.* England: Penguin, 1969.

———. *The Lion in the North—One Thousand Years of Scotland's History.* England: Penguin, 1973.

Price, Eugenia. *Stranger in Savannah.* New York: Doubleday & Co., 1983.

———. *Don Juan McQueen.* New York: J. B. Lippincott Co., 1974.

Priestley, J. B. *Victoria's Heyday.* Middlesex, England: Penguin Books, 1974.

Rawley, James. A. *Race and Politics: "Bleeding Kansas" and the Coming of the Civil War.* New York: J. B. Lippincott Co., 1969.

Reynolds, Edward. *Stand the Storm—A History of the Atlantic Slave Trade.* London: Allison & Busby, 1985.

Ritchie, Gordon. *Picturesque Stonehaven—A Descriptive Guide of 1899.* Stonehaven: Stonehaven Heritage Society, 1999.

Rose, Willie Lee. *A Documentary History of Slavery in North America.* London: Oxford University Press, 1976.

Rowland, Lawrence S., Alexander Moore, and George C. Rogers, Jr. *The History of Beaufort County, South Carolina, 1514–1861. Vol. 1.* Columbia: University of South Carolina Press, 1996.

Russell, Preston, and Barbara Hines. *Savannah: A History of Her People Since 1733.* Savannah: Frederic C. Beil, 1992.

Russell, William Howard. *My Diary North and South.* New York: McGraw-Hill, Inc., 1988.

Rutland, Robert. *Madison's Alternatives: The Jeffersonian Republicans and the Coming of War, 1805–1812.* New York: J. B. Lippincott. 1975.

St. Andrew's Society. *History of the St. Andrew's Society of the City of Savannah.* Savannah: Morning News Print, 1901.

Samhaber, Ernst. *Merchants Make History—How Trade Has Influenced the Course of History Throughout the World.* London: George G. Harrap & Co., Ltd., 1963.

Schultz, Gladys Denny, and Daisy Gordon Lawrence. *Lady From Savannah—The Life of Juliette Low.* New York: J. B. Lippincott, 1958.

Scott, P. H. *1707: The Union of Scotland and England.* Edinburgh: W. & R. Chambers, Ltd., 1979.

Sholes, A. E. *Chronological History of Savannah.* Savannah Morning News, 1900.

Simpson, Brooks D., and Jean V. Berlin, eds. *Sherman's Selected Correspondence of Civil War, 1860–1865.* Chapel Hill: University of North Carolina Press, 1999.

Sinclair, Cecil. *Tracing Scottish Local History—A Guide to Local History Research in the Scottish Record Office.* Edinburgh: Scottish Record Office, 1994.

———. *Tracing Your Scottish Ancestors: A Guide to Ancestry Research in the Scottish Record Office.* Rev. ed., 1990.

Sinclair-Stevenson, Christopher. *Inglorious Rebellion—The Jacobite Risings of 1708, 1715 and 1719.* London: Hamish Hamilton, 1971.

Skinner, Elliott P. *Drums & Shadows. Georgia Writer's Project. W.P.A.* New York: Anchor Books, 1972.

Smith, Abbot Emerson. *Colonists in Bondage—White Servitude and Convict Labour in America, 1607–1776.* New York: W. W. Norton & Co., 1947.

Smith, Anna Habersham Wright, ed. *A Savannah Family, 1830–1901.* (Papers from the Clermont Huger Lee Collection). Milledgeville, Ga.: Boyd Publishing. 1999.

Smith, Derek. *Civil War Savannah.* Savannah: Frederic C. Beil, 1997.

Smith, Gordon Burns. *History of the Georgia Militia, 1783–1861,* Vols. 1–4. Milledgeville, Ga.: Boyd Publishing, 2001.

Smith, Julia Floyd. *Slavery and Rice in Low Country Georgia, 1750–1860.* Knoxville: University of Tennessee Press, 1985.

Smout, T. C. *A History of the Scottish People, 1560–1830.* London: Collins, 1969.

Sorrel, G. Moxley. *Recollections of a Confederate Staff Officer.* Jackson, Tenn.: McCowat-Mercer Press, 1958.

Spalding, Phinizy. *Oglethorpe in America.* Athens: University of Georgia Press, 1984.

Spiegel, Marjorie. *The Dreaded Comparison—Human and Animal Slavery.* New York: Mirror Books, 1988.

Stiles, Henry Reed. *The Stiles Family in America.* Jersey City: Doan & Pilson, 1895.

Stiles, Robert. *Four Years Under Marse Robert.* New York and Washington: Neale Publishing Co., 1903.

Stokes, Thomas L. *The Savannah—Rivers of America.* New York: Rinehart & Co., 1951.

Sullivan, Buddy. *Early Days on the Georgia Tidewater—The Story of McIntosh County and Sapelo.* Darien: McIntosh County Board of Commissioners, 1997.

Taylor, Alan. *American Colonies.* New York: Viking, 2001.

Taylor, George Rogers. *The Great Tariff Debate, 1820–1830.* Boston: D. C. Heath, 1953.

———. *The War of 1812—Past Justifications and Present Interpretations.* Boston: D. C. Heath, 1963.

Terry, C. Sanford. *The Rising of 1745, With a Bibliography of Jacobite History, 1689–1788.* London: David Nutt, 1903

Thackeray, William Makepeace. *Vanity Fair.* London: Penguin Popular Classics, 1877.

Thistlethwaite, Frank. *The Great Experiment: An Introduction to the History of the American People.* London: Cambridge University, 1955.

Thomas, Hugh. *The Slave Trade—The History of the Atlantic Slave Trade, 1440–1870.* New York: Simon & Schuster, Inc., 1997.

Thomas, Peter D. G. *Revolution in America: Britain & the Colonies, 1736–1776.* Cardiff: University of Wales Press, 1992.

Tocqueville, Alexis de. *Democracy in America.* New York: Bantam Classics, 2000. Original text published 1835.

Wallace, David Duncan. *South Carolina: A Short History, 1520–1948.* Columbia: University of South Carolina Press, 1961.

Waring, Joseph F. *Cerveau's Savannah.* Savannah: Georgia Historical Society, 1973.

Warwick, Earl of. *Memories of Sixty Years.* London: 1917.

Watt, Archibald. *Highways and Byways Round Stonehaven.* Stonehaven: Stonehaven Heritage Society, 1992.

Waugh, Evelyn, and Michael Davie, eds. *The Diaries of Evelyn Waugh.* London: Weidenfeld & Nicolson, 1976.

West, Richard. *A History of Sierra Leone and Liberia.* New York: Holt, Rinehart & Winston, 1970.

Wilkinson, Henry C. *Bermuda From Sail to Steam*, 2 vols. London: Oxford University Press, 1973.

Williams, Eric. *From Columbus to Castro—The History of the Caribbean.* New York: Vintage Books, 1984.

Williams, K. J. *Ghost Ships of the Mersey—A Brief History of Confederate Cruisers with Mersey Connections.* Liverpool: Countyvise, Ltd., n.d.

Wilson, A. N. *The Victorians.* London: Arrow Books, 2002

Witherington, Donald J. *Statistical Accounts of Scotland: Accounts of Scottish Life from the 18th and 19th Centuries. 1790, by Sir John Sinclair of Ulbster.* Aberdeen: 1982. An on-line data base: http://edina.ac.uk/statacc

Wood, Michael. *Domesday: A Search for the Roots of England.* London: Book Club Associates, 1987.

Woodward, Grace Steele. *The Cherokees.* Norman: University of Oklahoma Press, 1963.

World Almanac and Book of Facts 2001. Mahwah, N.J.: World Almanac Books.

Zinn, Howard. *A People's History of the United States, 1492–Present.* New York: Harper Perennial, 1980.

———. *Declarations of Independence. Cross-Examining American Ideology.* New York: Harper Perennial, 1990.

II. ARTICLES, PUBLICATIONS, MAPS, AND CHARTS

Adams, Davy. "The Ancient Village of Crawton—Forgotten Villages of the Mearns." *The Leopard* (Jan. 1994).

American Civil War Round Table U.K., Articles, www.americancivilwar.org.uk/articles.htm

Anderson, Mrs. Clarence Gordon. "Eleanor Kinzie Gordon." *Georgia Historical Quarterly* 42, no. 2 (1958), 163–69.

Anderson, Edward C. "Confederate Foreign Agent: The European Diary of Major Edward C. Anderson." Original handwritten diary, MS 3602. Manuscripts Department, University of North Carolina Library, Chapel Hill, n.d.

Andrew Low Papers. "Transcript of the Trial and Hanging of Andrew Low in 1785." Angus Archives, Montrose Library, Scotland.

Annals of Fordoun, 1740. Aberdeen Family History Centre.

Barron, The Reverend Douglas Gordon. *The Court Book of the Barony of Urie in Kincardineshire, 1604–1747.* Edinburgh: Printed at University Press by T. and A. Constable for the Scottish History Society, 1892.

Bennet, John. "A Popular Place with Rebels—A Footnote in Confederate History." American Civil War Round Table, 2005. Article on Leamington's Spa's Rebel visitors.

Britt, Albert S., Jr, and Lilla M. Hawes. "The Mackenzie Papers, Part I." *Georgia Historical Quarterly* 56, no. 3 (Fall 1972), 535–82.

Brooke, Richard. "Liverpool As It Was, 1775–1800." Liverpool Record Office.

Buttars, Grant E. L. "Early American Colonies: Stuart's Town and East Jersey." University of Dundee, 1999.

Callander, A. *Land Ownership in Scotland—the 18th Century.* Aberdeen Family History Centre Library.

Cashin, Edward J. "Glimpses of Oglethorpe in Boswell's Life of Johnson." *Georgia Historical Quarterly* 83, no. 3 (Fall 2004).

Cohen, Fanny. "Journal of Sherman's Occupation of Savannah." *Georgia Historical Quarterly* 41 (1957).

Cooper, John M. "Map of the City of Savannah," 1856.

Cumming, Montgomery. "Table of the Descendants of Joseph Clay." 1897.

Daily, Alice. Friends of Andrew Low Newsletters. Series of quarterly newsletters containing historical articles on history, furniture, and artifacts deposited in the Andrew Low House & Museum.

Davidson, Jane Hickson. "Monograph on Willie Low, [1988]." Private collection of Hugh Stiles Golson, Savannah.

Delaney, Norman C. "When Can You Start? The Strange Occupation of James Bulloch." Maritime Museum, Liverpool.

Dixon, Max. "Building the Central Railroad of Georgia." *Georgia Historical Quarterly* 45, no. 1 (Mar. 1961), 1–21.

Dobson, David. *The Jacobites of Angus, 1689–1746.* Baltimore: Printed for Clearfield Co., by Genealogical Publishing Co., 1997.

———. *Scots in Georgia and the Deep South, 1735–1845.*

———. *Scottish American Heirs, 1683–1883."* Library of Aberdeen Family History Centre, Clearfield Co.

———. *Scottish American Wills, 1650–1900.* Library of Aberdeen Family History Centre, Clearfield Co.

———. *Directory of Scots Banished to American Plantations, 1650–1775.* Clearfield Co.

———. *Directory of Scots in the Carolinas, 1680–1830.* Baltimore: Genealogical Publishing Co.

———. *The Original Scots Colonists of Early America, 1612–1783.* Baltimore: Genealogical Publishing Co..

Duffie, April S. *Andrew Low House Research Project on Milledge Family.* Savannah: Spring 2005.

Dunlop. J. G. "William Dunlop's Mission to St. Augustine in 1688." Reprinted in the *South Carolina Historical and Genealogical Magazine* 35, no. 1 (Jan. 1933).

Durie, Alistair. J. "The Scottish Linen Industry in the Eighteenth Century." Stonehaven Town Library, Scotland.

Easterhold, John A. "Savannah: Lumber Center of the South Atlantic." *Georgia Historical Quarterly* 57, no. 4 (Winter 1973), 526–43.

Ellison, T. "The Cotton Trade of Great Britain." Liverpool: Cass Library of Industrial Classics, 1968.

Erskine of Carnock's Journal, 1683–1687. Edinburgh: Scottish Record Office.

Fraser, William Ruxton. "A History of the Parish and Burgh of Laurencekirk." Edinburgh and London: William Blackwood and Sons, 1880.

Ferguson, John P. S. *Scottish Family Histories.* Edinburgh: National Library of Scotland, 1986.

Fleming, Barry. "199 Years of Augusta's Library." *Georgia Historical Quarterly* 33, no. 2 (June 1949), 124–81.

Forfeited Estate Papers, 1715–1745 Jacobite Rebellion. Edinburgh: Scottish Record Office.

Foster, Kevin *The Diplomats Who Sank A Fleet. The Confederacy's Undelivered European Fleet and the Union Consular Service.* Washington, D.C.: U.S. National Archives and Records Administration, 2001.

Georgia Writers' Project, W.P.A., Savannah Unit. "The Plantation of the Royal Vale." *Georgia Historical Quarterly* 27, no. 1 (Mar. 1943), 88–110.

Gladstone. *Gladstone Family History.* Fasque Estate, Fettercairn.

Golson, Hugh Stiles. "The Privateer Riots of 1811." Paper prepared for Madeira Club, 2004.

Griffin, David, Jr. "Savannah's City Income Tax." *Georgia Historical Quarterly* 50, no. 2 (June 1966), 173–76.

Guthrie, Jennifer Ryan. *The Daisy Chain.* Los Angeles, 1979. Treatment for a television series based on the life of Juliette Gordon Low.

———. *Chronology—Timeline from 1619—Present.* Research files for Andrew Low Project.

Habersham, Josephine Clay. *Ebb Tide—As Seen Through the Diary of Josephine Clay Habersham, 1863.* Edited by Spencer Bidwell Long, Jr.

Habersham, Leila Elliott. *A Sketch of the Life of Frederic Augustus Habersham, 1831–1863.* Manuscript owned by Miss Clermont H. Lee, Savannah.

Hardee, Charles Seton Henry. *Reminiscences and Recollections of Old Savannah.* Savannah: Privately printed, 1928.

Harney, John, Dr. "A Farewell to Savannah." *Savannah Georgian* (Nov. 25, 1818).

Hartridge, Walter Charlton. "Andrew Low's House." Lecture given by W.C.H. at Georgia Historical Society, Jan. 5, 1966. Transcript at Archives of Andrew Low House and Museum.

———. "The Green-Meldrim House." In Historic Savannah Homes, Savannah Public Library.

Haunton, Richard M. "Law and Order in Savannah, 1850–1860." *Georgia Historical Quarterly* 56, no. 1 (Spring 1972), 1–24.

Hawes, Lilla. "The Memoirs of Charles H. Olmstead." *Georgia Historical Quarterly* 14 (1964).

Hay, Thomas Robson. "Gazaway Bugg Lamar, Confederate Banker and Business Man." *Georgia Historical Quarterly* 37, no. 2 (June 1953), 89–128.

Hemperly, Marion R. "Federal Naturalization Oaths, Savannah, Georgia, 1700–1860." *Georgia Historical Quarterly* 51, no. 4 (Dec. 1967), 454–87.

Hotze, Henry. *The Index—Civil War Journals. A Weekly Journal of Politics, Literature and News Devoted to the Exposition of the Mutual Interests, Political and Commercial of Great Britain and the Confederate States of America, 1862–1865.* London.

How, Henry K. "Slaveholding Not Sinful." New Brunswick, N.J.: Printed by *Fredonian and Daily New Brunswicker*, 1856.

Howe, George. "The Scotch Irish and Their First Settlements on the Tyger River in South Carolina—A Centennial Discourse Delivered Sept. 1861." Greenville: A. Press, 1981.

Insh, George Pratt. "Scottish Colonial Schemes, 1620–1686: East New Jersey," ch. 5, pp. 145–85; "Stuart's Town, South Carolina," ch. 6, pp. 186–211. Glasgow: Macklehose, Jackson & Co., 1922.

———. "Arrival of the Cardross Settlers, Led by Lord Cardross and William Dunlop." *Scottish Historical Review* 25 (Jan. 1928). Reprinted in *S.C. Historical and Genealogical Magazine* 30, no. 2 (Apr. 1929).

Kincardineshire. *Valuation Rolls, 1744–1806.* Edinburgh: National Archives of Scotland.

King, Spencer B., Jr. "Fanny Cohen's Journal of Sherman's Occupation of Savannah." *Georgia Historical Quarterly* 61, no. 4 (Dec. 1957), 407–16.

Kirk Sessions. *Record of Discipline in Dunnottar Parish Church Session Records. September 1744–November 1786.* Edinburgh: Scottish Record Office.

Lancashire & Cheshire History Society, 1849–1850 Cotton Trade in Liverpool. Liverpool: Council of Members.

Lawton, Alexander R. "An Address by Alexander R. Lawton: Transportation, Railroads and Canals in Steamship Savannah." *Georgia Historical Quarterly* 3, no. 1 (June 1919), 45–60.

Liverpool Customs Bills of Entry. 1840's. Liverpool Record Offices.

Low, Andrew. "Transcript of Last Will & Testament, Liverpool, 1841." Archives of Andrew Low House & Museum, Savannah.

Low, Andrew, Jr. "Transcript of Last Will and Testament of Andrew Low, 14th August, 1879." Archives of Andrew Low House & Museum, Savannah.

MacDonell, Alexander R. "The Settlement of the Scotch Highlanders at Darien." *Georgia Historical Quarterly* 20, no. 3 (Sept. 1936), 250–62.

MacDuncan, A. *Roll and Legend of the Georgia Hussars.* Savannah: Morning News, 1906.

MacLean, J. P. *An Historical Account of the Settlement of the Scotch Highlanders in America Prior to the Peace of 1783.* Baltimore: Genealogical Publishing Co., 1968.

Mays, Susan. "Interpretive Plan Proposal for the Andrew Low House." Savannah, 1995.

Millett, Stephen M. *The Scottish Settlers of America in the 17th and 18th Centuries.* Library of Aberdeen Family History Centre.

Murray, David. *The York Building Company—A Chapter in Scottish History. Read before the Institutes of Bankers and Chartered Accountants, Glasgow, 19th February, 1883.* Glasgow.

Murray-Best, David M. *Quakers In Brief or Quakerism Made Easy—An Overview of the Quaker Movement From 1650 to 1990.* Birkenhead Meeting, Merseyside, U.K., 1995.

Neblett, Thomas R. "Major Edward C. Anderson and the C.S.S. Fingal." *Georgia Historical Quarterly* 52, no. 2 (June 1965), 132–58.

Nicol, Norman D., and David Esson. *"Tenant Farmer in the Parish of Maryculter, Kincardineshire."* (Jan. 1977).

Olmstead, Charles H. "Savannah in the 40's." *Georgia Historical Quarterly* 1, no. 3, 243–52.

Passenger and Immigration Lists Index: 1982–85. Cumulation. Aberdeen, Scotland: Library of Aberdeen Family History Centre..

Pearson, Mowbray. *Fitting the Flakes: The Diary of J. Badenach, A Stonehaven Farmer. 1789–1797.* European Ethnological Research Centre.

Scott, Kenneth. *British Aliens in the United States During the War of 1812.* Aberdeen, Scotland: Library of Aberdeen Family History Centre.

Screven, Frank B. "The Georgia Bryans and Screvens, 1685–1861." *Georgia Historical Quarterly* 40, no. 1 (Mar. 1956), 325–48.

Slack, John. *Remarks on Cotton and Retrospective Occurrences. Private Publication by Liverpool Cotton Broker and Accountant.* Liverpool, 1817. Pamphlets from Sydney Jones Library, University of Liverpool.

Smith, Gordon B. "The Andrew Low Building, Lots 1 & 2, Frederick Tything, Derby Ward, Savannah." Savannah: Georgia Historical Society.

Spilman, Aminta E. V. *Letters and Family Documents Relating to Charles Green of Savannah, Georgia and Greenwhich, Virginia.* Privately printed and presented by General Offset Co., Inc., Chas. H. Bohn & Co., Henry Lindenmeyer & Sons, and DePamphilis Press, 1941.

Steven, Maisie. "Parish Life in Eighteenth-Century Scotland—A Review of the Old Statistical Accounts." Aberfeldy, Perthsire, Scotland.

Stiles, Eliza Mackay. "Letter to My Grandchildren—Diary of Eliza Mackay Stiles to Mary Low's Children Recounting Events Surrounding Arrest of their Father, 1861–62." Unpublished manuscript. Andrew Low House & Museum Archives, Savannah.

Stiles, The Reverend J. C. "National Rectitude the Only True Basis of National Prosperity—Appeal to the Confederate States." Petersburg: Evangelical Tract Society, 1863.

———. "Voices of Our Fathers." New York: Rudd and Carleton, 1861.

Summerell, Martha L. *Faithfully Yours, Charles Green: The Life and Times of a 19th Century Cotton Merchant.* Savannah: St. John's Parish House Acquisition Fund.

Timperly, Loretta. "A Directory of Landowners in Scotland, ca. 1770–1800, Kincardinshire." The National Archives of Scotland.

Tolley, B. H. *Liverpool & Merseyside. The Liverpool Campaign Against the Order In Council and the War of 1812.* Liverpool Record Offices.

War of the Rebellion: A Compilation of the Official Records of the Union and Confederate Armies: Series 11, Vol. 11. (Prisoners of War) The Cases of Andrew Low, Mrs. John Low and Charles Green. Washington D.C.: Government Printing Office, 1897.

Waring, William R. "Description of a febrile disease which lately prevailed epidemically among the Negroes of the Rice Plantations in the vicinity of the City of Savannah." *The North American Medical and Surgical Journal* (Jan. 1826).

Watt, Archibald. *A Goodly Heritage. David Barclay 1610–1688.* Stonehaven, Kincardineshire.

Watt, Crabb. *Mearns of Old: Ancient Kincardine Allegiances—Scotland and England Animosities.* Aberdeen: Family History Library.

Williams, D. M. "Liverpool Merchants and the Cotton Trade, 1820–1850." Essay in Dr. J. Harris' *Liverpool and the Merseyside.* Liverpool Records Office.

Yates, Bowling C. "Macon, Georgia Inland Trading Centre: 1826–1836." *Georgia Historical Quarterly* 55, no. 15 (Fall 1971), 365–77.

III. Archives and Collections

United Kingdom

Dundee University, Dundee

Liverpool Maritime Archives and Library and Merseyside Maritime Museum:

- Customs Bills of Entry for Britain & Ireland, 1820–1939.
- Liverpool and the American Civil War.
- Lloyd's Captains Registers, 1874–1887.
- Lloyd's Register of Shipping from 1764.
- Transatlantic Slavery. Permanent Exhibition.

Liverpool Records Office, William Brown Library:

- Annals of Liverpool, 1076–1876
- Civil War and Confederacy. Records of Fraser, Trenholm & Co. of Charleston and Liverpool, 1860–1866.
- Gore's General Advertiser. Directory for Liverpool and Its Environs.

Liverpool University:

- Cotton: A Bibliography of North West England, Cotton Ledger, 1799–1801.
- Liverpool Pamphlets, 1757–1857. Manuscript Collection #13.
- The Rathbone Papers.

Scottish Record Office: Archives and Libraries:

- Aberdeen and N.E. Scotland Family History Society.
- Aberdeen Public Library.
- Angus Archives, Montrose Library.
- Brechin Public Library.
- Fettercairn Public Library.
- Glasgow City Archives, Mitchell Library, Scotland.
- Laurencekirk Public Library.
- National Archives of Scotland, General Register House and West Register House.
- National Library of Scotland, Map Library.
- Scottish Genealogical Society, Edinburgh, Scotland.
- Stonehaven Public Library.

United States

Georgia

Emory University, Special Collections and Archives, Robert W. Woodruff Library, Decatur:

- Barnsley, Godfrey. Manuscript Collection #13.
- Harwell, Christopher Lee. William Henry Stiles: Georgia Gentleman Politician. (Ph.D. diss., Emory University, 1959.

Haunton, Richard. Savannah in the 1850's. (Ph.D. diss., Emory University, 1968).
Lamar, C. A L. Manuscript Collection #400.
Lumpkin, Wilson. Manuscript Collection #286.
Savannah, Great Britain Consulate, 1859–1866. Original of Keith Read Collection, Customs.
Stiles, William Henry Papers, 1749–1892. Manuscript Collection #229.
Georgia Genealogical Society, Atlanta.
Georgia Historical Society, Savannah, Georgia:
Anderson, Edward Anderson (1815–1883). Manuscript Collection #6.
Anderson, George Wayne. Manuscript Collection #7.
Anderson, Robert Houston. Manuscript Collection #8.
Barnsley, Godfrey, and Company. Manuscript Collection #50.
Berrien, John McPherson, 1781–1856. Manuscript Collection #67.
Bragg, Lillian Chaplin, 1856–1967. Manuscript Collection #83.
Bulloch, James Dunwoody, 1823–1901. Manuscript Collection #105.
Burroughs Papers, Manuscript Collection #112.
Census of the City of Savannah Together with Statistics Relating to the Trade, Commerce, Mechanical Arts and of Same. Edward Purse, Printer, 1848.
Colonial Dames of Georgia. Manuscript Collection #965.
Cosmos Club, Savannah. Manuscript Collection #974.
Cowper, Basil, and Cowper and Telfair Papers. Manuscript Collections #179 and #180.
Cunningham, Sarah Alexander (Lawton). Manuscript Collection #194.
Duncan, William. Letters. Manuscript Collection #227.
Galloway, David H. Directory of the City of Savannah for the Year 1849.
———. Directory of the City of Savannah for the Year 1850.
———. Directory of the City of Savannah for the Year 1858.
Gamble, Thomas. Scrapbooks. 1883–1945. Manuscript Collection #271.
Georgia Historical Quarterly: Index. Various articles on Andrew Low, Sr., Andrew Low, Jr., and Andrew Low Company.
Gordon Family Papers. Manuscript Collection #318.
Habersham, James. Papers, 1747–1775. Collection #337.
Hartridge, Walter C. Manuscript Collection #1349.
Hutchison-Dawson Papers. Manuscript Collection #2226.
Jones, Noble. Papers, 1723–1936. Manuscript Collection #440.
King-Wilder Papers, 1817–1946. Manuscript Collection #465.
Kollock, Lemuel. Papers, 1793–1822. Manuscript Collections #469 and #470.

Lewis, Bessie. Manuscript Collection #2138.
Mackay Family Papers. Manuscript Collections #530 and #531.
Meldrim Family Papers, 1809–1973. Manuscript Collection #1288.
Newspaper digests, and microfilm collection, 1767–1886.
Read, Keith. Manuscript Collection #648.
St. Andrew's Society of Savannah, 1762–1995. Manuscript Collection #993.
Savannah Historical Research Association. Manuscript Collection #994.
Scarbrough, William. Manuscript Collection #1400.
Tax Digests: various entries for Andrew Low, Sr., Andrew Low, Jr., and Andrew Low Company.
Georgia State Archives, Atlanta.

NORTH CAROLINA
Wilson Library, University of North Carolina, Chapel Hill, N.C. Southern Historical Collection:
Anderson, Edward Clifford, 1813–1882. Collection #3602. Including original transrcipt of diary of Edward Clifford Anderson.
Barnsley, George Scarborough, 1837–1918. Collection #1521.
Mackay and Stiles Family Papers, 1743–1975. Collection #470.
Page, William, Papers, 1783–1825. Collection #1254. Records of Ante-Bellum Southern Plantations From the Revolution through the Civil War. Series J., Part 4, Georgia and Florida.

SOUTH CAROLINA
South Carolina Historical Society, Beaufort.
South Carolina Historical Society, Charleston.

UTAH
Family History Library of Church of Latter Day Saints. Salt Lake City, Utah.

Index

This book was composed and prepared for press in Adobe Warnock Pro by the Nangle Type Shop in Meriden, Connecticut, and PerfecType in Nashville, Tennessee. Adobe's Warnock Pro was designed by Robert Slimbach as a pleasing all-purpose type and named in honor of John Warnock, cofounder of Adobe Systems, and also a developer of the Portable Document Format.